Lancashire and Cheshire, Past and Present

LANCASHIRE AND CHESHIRE,

PAST AND PRESENT.

Lancashire and Cheshire

PAST & PRESENT

BY

THOMAS BAINES.

MEMBER OF THE HISTORIC SOCIETY OF LANCASHIRE & CHESHIRE

AND

WILLIAM FAIRBAIRN LL.D. F.R.S.

SIDENT OF THE LITERARY AND PHILOSOPHICAL SOCIETY OF MANCHESTER

VOL. I.

LANCASHIRE AND CHESHIRE,

PAST AND PRESENT:

A HISTORY AND A DESCRIPTION OF THE

PALATINE COUNTIES OF LANCASTER AND CHESTER, FORMING THE NORTH-WESTERN DIVISION OF ENGLAND,

FROM THE EARLIEST AGES TO THE PRESENT TIME (1867)

BY THOMAS BAINES,

MEMBER OF THE HISTORIC SOCIETY OF LANCASHIRE AND CHESHIRE, AND AUTHOR OF "THE HISTORY OF LIVERPOOL

WITH AN ACCOUNT OF THE

RISE AND PROGRESS OF MANUFACTURES AND COMMERCE, AND CIVIL AND MECHANICAL ENGINEERING IN THESE DISTRICTS.

BY WILLIAM FAIRBAIRN, LL.D., F.R.S.

CORRESPONDING MEMBER OF THE INSTITUTE OF FRANCE, EX-PRESID. OF THE LITERARY AND PHILOSOPHICAL SOCIETY OF MANCHESTER, ETC., ETC.

WITH NUMEROUS ILLUSTRATIONS FROM ORIGINAL DRAWINGS BY H. WARREN, R.A., AND A SERIES OF PORTRAITS.

VOL. I.

WILLIAM MACKENZIE, 22 PATERNOSTER ROW, LONDON;
LIVERPOOL, 14 GREAT GEORGE STREET, MANCHESTER, 59 DALE STREET,
LEEDS, 27 PARK SQUARE; CARLISLE, 3 EARL STREET.

PRINTED BY WILLIAM MACKENZIE, 45 & 47 HOWARD STREET, GLASGOW

ADDRESS BY MR. THOMAS BAINES.

IT is now nearly forty years since the History of the County Palatine of Lancaster was written by my late father, Edward Baines, M P, and it is nearly fifty years since Dr George Ormerod's learned and elegant History of the County Palatine of Chester was published The Counties described in those two excellent works are closely connected with each other, both in their political and social history, and by their position and natural formation Together they include the whole of the great valley of the Mersey, which is the most populous and the richest portion of the United Kingdom, with the single exception of the Metropolitan district On account of their proximity to each other, and of the close connection of many of their most important interests, the Counties of Lancaster and Chester have been united with each other, during the whole of the present century, in the decennial census of the English people, under the title of the "North western Division" of England, a portion of the kingdom containing, in round numbers, a population of three million persons, and yielding from the products of its soil, its mines, its manufacturing industry, and its wide-reaching commerce, a yearly income of about £50,000,000 towards the resources of the nation. It is the object of this work to combine the history of the two counties thus forming the North western Division of England In doing this, the earlier parts of the History have been rewritten down to the periods at which Dr Ormerod and my father completed their labours, and the History of both the Counties has been carefully continued to the present time The historical portion has also been preceded by a much fuller description of the natural history and productions of this portion of the kingdom than has ever been before published.

In the interval of from forty to fifty years which has elapsed since the publication of the histories of Lancashire and Cheshire above referred to, the ancient history of the two counties has been illustrated in almost innumerable points by the publications of the Cheetham Society, and of other societies formed in those counties for the purpose of illustrating their earlier history The publications of the Cheetham Society alone—which were commenced in the year 1841—contain nearly seventy volumes of original matter illustrative of that history Those publications consist entirely of the contents of original manuscripts never before published *in extenso*, and many of them absolutely new The earliest of the papers thus brought to light by the Cheetham Society commence in the twelfth century, and the series extends to the beginning of the eighteenth century Together they form such a mass of original and interesting materials as was never before brought together to illustrate the early history of any one division of England In addition to the publications of the Cheetham Society, there have also been many other papers illustrative of the early history of the two counties published in the Transactions of the Historical Society of Lancashire and Cheshire, the Memoirs of the Manchester Philosophical and Literary Society, and in the Transactions of the Archæological Society of Chester I have also had access to the historical papers collected during many years' labour by the late Charles Okill, of Liverpool, for the purpose of writing the history of that populous part of the County of Lancaster known as the Hundred of West Derby

In preparing the introductory description of the Natural History of Lancashire and Cheshire, I have availed myself of the numerous papers published during the last forty years by the most eminent writers on the geology, the minerals, the agriculture, and the other branches of natural history connected with this part of England Within that period the whole history of the Lancashire Coal-field has been written by Mr. Edward W Binney, and other distinguished local geologists, with a clearness which has thrown new light, not only on the history of the formation and the deposit of coal in this district, but also in other parts of the kingdom and in other countries. In the same period there have appeared new and original accounts of the Salt field of Cheshire, the iron district of Furness, and of all the principal rocks, soils, and mineral products of the two Counties. Within the same period excellent accounts of the agriculture of Lancashire and Cheshire have been published in the Transactions of the Royal Society of Agriculture, as well as in local works. In preparing the description of the two Counties this information has been carefully condensed into a connected description of the natural history of the whole district.

It is also within the same period that the railway system has grown up in Lancashire, and has extended throughout the whole kingdom, and that ocean steam navigation has connected the ports of the two Counties with almost every part of the Globe. The rise of these two great systems of communication has in that period brought the industry and the personal communications of this populous district into close connection with those of all parts of the United Kingdom, and of the whole world, and has given an impulse, both to industry and intercourse, that was entirely unknown in former times.

Within the same period the cotton manufacture, the greatest of all branches of manufacturing industry, has increased at least threefold, so as now to require a yearly supply of more than one thousand millions of pounds of cotton for the employment of the mills and looms of the two Counties. In the latter part of this period the cotton manufacture has passed through a season of the severest trial, owing to the Civil War in America, and the sudden and violent breaking up of the system of slave labour in the cotton districts of that country. But it has survived the terrible trials of that period, it has succeeded in drawing supplies of its raw material from numerous and distant countries, and it is freed from its dangerous dependence on a single source of supply, and on a description of labour which is rapidly disappearing before the progress of freedom and of justice. This great branch of industry has thus escaped from the principal perils which have long threatened its existence. The progress of this great change and its influence, both at home and abroad, will be carefully traced in this work along with the history of the heroic patience with which the sufferings of the cotton district were borne, and of the noble generosity with which they were relieved.

I shall also endeavour to trace in this work that great migration of the people from all parts of the United Kingdom, by which the population of the manufacturing districts of Lancashire and Cheshire, as well as that of a few other districts of England, have been so rapidly increased during the last forty years, the general result of which is, that the population of the North-western District is now four times as great, in proportion to its area, as that of the United Kingdom in general.

Engraved by [illegible] from a Photograph by [illegible]

LANCASHIRE AND CHESHIRE:

PAST AND PRESENT.

CHAPTER I

HISTORY AND NATURAL RESOURCES—GENERAL INTRODUCTION.

The object of this Work is to trace the progress of Society, Industry, and Invention, in the populous counties of Lancaster and Chester, forming the north-western division of England, from the earliest and rudest ages to the present time In carrying out this undertaking, it will be necessary to give an account of the geographical position of the north-western district of England, with reference to the other parts of the United Kingdom and to Foreign countries, with both of which it is now so closely connected by the relations of trade and commerce It will also be requisite to describe the abundant and varied natural resources and means of production, which a bountiful Providence has placed at the disposal of its inhabitants, in a fertile soil, a mild climate, a coast indented with ports and harbours, numerous rivers and streams flowing from the lofty hills that bound it on the east, and abundant supplies of coal and other valuable minerals Having described the position and the resources of this district, we shall then trace the gradual development of those resources, by the industry and intelligence of its inhabitants, under the various races of men, and the different forms of society, that have successively existed in it. We shall thus be able to show what influence the position of the north-western district in the British islands, and on the shores of the Atlantic ocean—combined with its natural resources, the industry and intelligence of its inhabitants, and more general causes, connected with the progress of the whole kingdom and with the development of distant countries—has had in promoting its prosperity, and in bringing together, within the narrow limits of the two counties that compose it, a population of three millions of persons, endowed by the genius of Arkwright, Watt, and their successors in the race of mechanical and scientific discovery, with unlimited powers of industrial production, and in there establishing the greatest branch of manufacturing industry that exists in this kingdom, and a commerce with foreign nations extending to the whole world

Commencing with the dawn of society in this district, in times far different from our own, we shall have to pass in review before our readers the original inhabitants of this part of Britain, such as they were when Agricola led the armies of Rome into the north-western parts of Britain, in the campaign of A D 79. We shall find that the British tribes which then inhabited this district were a rude and uncultured people, sprung from the Celtic branch of the great Indo-European family of nations, long cut off from the only civilization then existing, namely, that of Greece and Rome, by their remote position at the extremity of the then known world, and by a stormy ocean, whose real dangers were magnified by ignorance and superstition; but who, nevertheless, possessed great natural intelligence and aptitude for acquiring the arts of civilized life.* We shall also find that, even at that time, they had sufficient skill to work mines of copper, tin, lead, and silver, and even to extract gold from some of the ores found in their mountains; that they understood the art of improving and increasing the produce of the soil, by dressings of marl of various kinds; that they tamed horses, built and armed chariots, and no doubt made roads for them to traverse, that although they themselves were ignorant of navigation, and possessed no larger vessels than mere canoes, built of laths and covered with skins, they had for many ages been willing to trade in the produce of their mines and fields, first with the merchants of Cadiz, Tyre, and Carthage, who visited these shores by way of the ocean; and afterwards with the Greek colonists of Massilia—the present Marseilles—and with the people of Italy, who found their way to Britain, by ascending the river Rhone from the Mediterranean, and then, descending the Loire, the Garonne, and the Seine, to the shores of the Atlantic.†

Under the influence of Roman cultivation, we shall next see order and civilization, though without freedom, slowly taking the place of a stormy independence throughout the more fertile and accessible

* C C Tacitus' Life of Julius Agricola.

† Prichard's Eastern Origin of the Celtic Nations C C Tacitus' Life of Julius Agricola, c. xxi. Strabo's Geography, Book III Pliny's Natural History, Book III

portions of Britain; the British youth drafted into the Roman armies, and shedding their blood in distant lands; Britain governed by three great Roman Legions, and by multitudes of auxiliary troops, the city of Devana, or Deva, the present Chester, occupied for nearly three hundred years as the head-quarters of the twentieth victorious Legion, and the north-western district of Britain ruled by that Legion, and by auxiliary bands of Gauls, Spaniards, Dalmatians, Noricans, Frieslanders, and Dacians, numerous cities and towns, most of which still exist and flourish, founded, and rising into note in all parts of the island, including the city of Deva or Chester, Mamucium or Mancunium (the present Manchester), Ribodunum or Ribchester, and Alauna or Lancaster, on the banks of the rivers Dee, Irwell, Ribble, and Lune. We shall further see military roads, which almost defy the ravages of time, laid out with the greatest engineering skill, and run along the valleys and over the hills of this district, and of the whole island, for the purpose of connecting them with that great system of military roads, extending through all the countries of Europe, Asia, and Africa, from the Euphrates and the Deserts of Libya to the borders of Caledonia, which the Romans formed as the means of governing the ancient world by their armies; great lines of fortification constructed from sea to sea, to restrain the inroads of the hardy mountain tribes whom the Romans were unable to conquer, agriculture so much improved, that the Roman garrisons along the Rhine were frequently fed with the harvests of Britain; the metals produced in so great abundance as to induce some of the Roman emperors to limit the production, in order to raise the price, the tribute paid by Britain so much increased as to be considered an important part of the Roman revenue, and the cruel rites of the Druids superseded, even in the most remote parts of Britain, first, by the milder, though not purer heathenism of Greece and Rome, and before the close of the Roman dominion in Britain, by the light and purity of Christain truth *

Passing forward to another race of the inhabitants of this district, from whom we claim to be descended, we shall see nearly all the fruits of this early development of British and Roman civilization swept away, after the withdrawal of the Romans from Britain, by the internal divisions of the Britons, and by the irruption of the Angles, Saxons, and other Germanic tribes, whose bold and independent manners and wild life, in their native forests and on their native shores, had been long before described in the eloquent pages of

* Pliny's Natural History Itinerary of Antoninus Augustus Tertullian's Works

Cæsar and Tacitus, and from whom we justly claim to derive the greater portion of our language, of our love of freedom, and the germs of our noblest political institutions. These races, which were then the boldest navigators and the most daring adventurers on the shores of the ocean, we shall be able to trace gradually, and after overcoming a most determined resistance on the part of the British people, continued for several hundred years, spreading themselves over the level parts of the north-western district to the Irish sea; conquering the islands between Britain and Ireland, forcing the Britons back into Cartmel and the Cumbrian mountains in one direction, and beyond the river Dee in another; and occupying the whole of the present counties of Lancaster and Chester, with their numerous septs or tribes, whose names can be still traced in the names of existing towns, villages, and families.*

Before the Angles and Saxons were firmly established in the western parts of Britain, or were collected as one nation, but when they had lost their original familiarity with the perils of the sea, and their love of naval adventure, and when they were beginning to settle themselves down to the cultivation of the soil, and other peaceful pursuits which they have since so successfully followed—we shall find that the coasts of the north-western district, in common with those of the greater part of England, were overrun and conquered by another daring race of sea rovers, known by the names of Danes and Northmen These Scandinavian tribes, who were in the ninth and tenth centuries what the Saxons and Angles had been in the fourth and fifth, after occupying all the smaller islands, from the Shetland and the Orkneys to the Isle of Man, and even to the Scilly Islands, poured into England, both from the east and from the west, conquering extensive districts, including the coasts of Lancashire and Cheshire, and drove the Angles and Saxons, previously inhabiting them, into the wilder and more inaccessible regions lying on the borders of the present counties of Lancashire and Yorkshire Once established in England, we shall find that the Danes and Northmen, continually reinforced from the north held their ground even against the great Saxon kings of the race of Alfred, and established themselves permanently along the coasts of England, creating or reviving that love of the ocean and that spirit of naval enterprise that have prevailed in England ever

* C. C Tacitus on the Site, Manners, and People of Germany C. J Cæsar on the Gallic War, Book VI J M Kemble's Saxons in England The Saxon Chronicle Bede's History of the English Church Life of St. Cuthbert.

since, both in peace and war. Whilst one race of the Scandinavian tribes crossed the Atlantic in their frail vessels, and colonized Iceland, Greenland, and the northern parts of America, others spread themselves along the coasts and islands of Europe, from Britain and France to Sicily and Naples. In the long and sanguinary conflicts between the Danes and Saxons in this country, we shall find that Chester, the capital of the north-west, was ruined by the Danes, was besieged by Alfred the Great, and was reconquered and partially restored by his son, Edward the Elder, and his daughter Ethelfleda, the Lady of the Mercians. We shall also find that Manchester was destroyed, but afterwards partially restored by the same Edward, that all the other towns and villages of the district were plundered or burnt, that the cultivation of the soil was abandoned, except in inaccessible districts; and that the whole land, wasted and plundered by invading hordes, was again in danger of becoming a refuge for wild beasts Yet amidst all this horror and desolation, we shall still find Christanity gaining its final triumph over the heathenism of the north, and in the days of Olaff the Holy, and Canute, the greatest of the Danish kings (whose names are probably preserved in Olaffs or Olive Mount near Liverpool, as well as in numerous churches dedicated to St. Olave, and in Knutsford, or the Ford of Canute, in the county of Chester), giving a short breathing time to the exhausted nation *

Passing onward to another dominant race, and another form of society, we shall find the confusion produced by more than five hundred years of foreign ravage and internal strife, succeeded by the stern rule of the Norman and Plantagenet kings, and the Scandinavian sea-kings subdued or swept from the surrounding seas and islands of Britain. Under the tyrannical but energetic administration of the Normans, we shall see the present counties of Lancaster and Chester ruled by great military chiefs, and secured against attack from abroad by a military organization, which rendered the whole people available for the purposes of national defence, both by sea and land † During this period some symptoms of returning prosperity will be discovered in the forming of municipal governments, either by royal or other charters, at Chester, Lancaster, Manchester, Liverpool, Wigan, Preston, and other of the more ancient boroughs of the two counties. We shall also find in this age the freeholders of the counties, and the burgesses of Lancaster, Liverpool, Wigan, and Preston, summoned

* Anglo-Saxon Chronicle Worsaae's Danes in England.

† Domesday Book Chronicle of the Kings of Man, in Camden's Britannia.

to send members to represent them in the early parliaments of England. In the first two hundred years of this period, we shall see the earls of Chester invested with sovereign power within their own territories, and on more than one occasion, waging open war with the Crown; whilst, in the next two hundred years, we shall find the earls and dukes of Lancaster frequently in open rebellion against the Crown, and at length successful in seizing, and even in retaining the throne, after a long and murderous conflict, in which all the male members of the royal house of Plantagenet, and the greater part of the ancient nobility, were destroyed.*

With the accession of the House of Tudor to the throne, we shall see the foundations laid of agriculture, manufactures, and industry, in this as well as in other parts of the kingdom, and shall find the middle class coming into existence. The land, instead of being held in a few hands, will be found to be divided amongst a greater number of proprietors, including a numerous class of yeomen, indebted for their lands to the confiscations of the previous civil wars, and partly to the alienation and sale of church lands at the time of the Reformation In this period the condition of serfdom or villeinage entirely disappears The towns become more populous, Manchester and Bolton being already flourishing manufacturing places, the coal mines of Wigan beginning now to be worked, Newton and Clitheroe being added to the number of parliamentary boroughs; the salt works of Cheshire being extensively wrought, and Liverpool and Chester having a considerable trade in the export of woollen goods, cutlery, salt, and coal, chiefly to Ireland, Scotland, France, and Spain, and in return, importing considerable quantities of linen and woollen yarn, and of wine and fruits, from the south of Europe Although there was in this age no direct trade from England to the newly discovered regions of America and India, yet we shall find that there was a considerable trade with the New World by way of Antwerp, Bruges, Cadiz, and Lisbon, all of which places then belonged either to Spain or Portugal, and purchased largely English manufactures for the use of the Spanish and Portuguese colonists in America and the East. During this period the daring navigators of England spread themselves over every sea, both of the New and of the Old World, and prepared the way by their discoveries for the planting of America and the trade with India.†

From the accession of the House of Stuart to the English throne,

* Baines' History of Lancashire Ormerod's History of Cheshire, and Hall's Chronicle

† Hakluyt's Voyages and Travels. Camden's History of the Reign of Queen Elizabeth. Leland's Itinerary.

we shall see the industry and population of the north-western district, as well as those of the whole kingdom, stimulated and extended by the forming of flourishing British colonies on the North American continent and in the West Indies It was during this period that cotton was introduced into Lancashire from the Levant by the manufacturers of Manchester, and that a considerable trade sprung up between Liverpool and the British colonies in America. In the midst of this period of improvement, we shall find that many of the fruits of peace and industry were rudely crushed, in a fierce and often renewed struggle for power, between the King and the Parliament This contest we shall see fought out with extraordinary obstinacy in the north-western district of England, where all the principal towns and cities, including Chester, Manchester, Liverpool, Nantwich, Bolton, Wigan, Preston, and Lancaster, were frequently besieged, and several of them taken by storm, and where several of the most desperate battles of the war were fought by Cromwell, James, the great earl of Derby, and other leaders on the side of the Parliament or of the King. Yet we shall see this storm gradually passing away, and at the time of the final downfall of the Stuarts, the north-western division of the kingdom already entering on that progress in commerce, arts, and industry, which it has since pursued with such wonderful success.*

With the accession of the House of Hanover, we shall witness the rapid development of an era of continually increasing freedom, intelligence, industry, enterprise, and wealth We shall see the descendants of the various races and classes that formerly contended for dominion, blended together into one people, possessed of well-ascertained rights and duties, personal, political, religious and commercial freedom secured by just and continually improving laws, industry, knowledge, and the paths to wealth and honour open to all men, and trod with distinguished success by many who had been the founders of their own fortunes, wonderful discoveries made in mechanics, machinery, chemistry, agriculture, and the means of transport and communication; every discovery, that can in any manner advance the arts of life, eagerly seized upon by the people of these two counties, and perseveringly applied to the purposes of manufacture, trade, and commerce, the immense mineral riches of the district

* Dr. George Ormerod's Civil War Tracts of Lancashire and Cheshire, being vol ii of the Chetham Society's Remains, Historical and Literary, connected with the Palatine Counties of Lancaster and Chester Bancroft's History of the Colonization of America.

fully developed, innumerable applications of the mechanical powers, kept in constant activity by the exhaustless power of steam; canals and railroads extending to almost every town, great or small, of the two counties, and connecting them with every part of the kingdom; lines of steamers, from the ports of the north-western district, covering the seas of Europe and the ocean, the varied and beautiful products of that district sought in all countries, the population of two small counties rapidly increasing to millions, chiefly by immigration from all other parts of the three kingdoms; and industry and skill rewarded with a yearly return, which may be safely estimated at fifty millions sterling, including at least twelve millions paid yearly, as the wages of labour, in the great manufacture of the district, namely, that of cotton.*

We shall first describe the position and the natural resources of the two counties of Lancaster and Chester; and shall then proceed to trace the manner in which those resources have been gradually developed, by the people resident in that division of the kingdom

Geographical Position of Lancashire and Cheshire—The counties of Lancaster and Chester, forming the north-western division of England, stretch along the shores of that great gulf or bay of the Atlantic Ocean, which is known by the name of the Irish Sea, from the river Duddon and the mountains of Cumberland on the north, to the river Dee and the mountains of Wales on the south The coasts of both these counties are level and free from rocks, and though lined by sandbanks, are easily approached, through numerous channels, into estuaries or arms of the sea, stretching far into the mainland In this respect the form and structure of the shores of Lancashire and Cheshire differ greatly from those of the other parts of the western coast of England, lying either to the south or to the north, which are in general rocky, and dangerous to vessels approaching the coast. The ports of Lancashire and Cheshire are the only ports accessible to the large vessels used in modern commerce, between Milford Haven, in South Wales, and the estuary of the Clyde—a coast line of about 300 miles in length The shores of Wales are lined throughout with lofty slate or limestone rocks, from Milford Haven to the entrance of the river Dee. These in many places rise to the height of several hundred feet, around deep bays, and threaten destruction to all vessels that enter, or are driven by winds and currents, within their wide

* Miscellaneous Statistics of the United Kingdom for the year 1859, laid before the two Houses of Parliament page 808. Returns of Property and Income Tax 1860–61

openings. There is a strong indraught towards this coast in westerly and southerly winds, which renders it doubly dangerous. These bays are then the terror of seamen, for they are open to all the prevailing winds; and the force of those winds, joined to powerful currents and strong tides, frequently drives vessels that may have the misfortune to be drawn within them on the rocks An almost equally wild and rocky coast stretches along the shores of Cumberland, from the mouth of the river Duddon northwards, and extends to the entrance of the Clyde Owing to these causes, as well as to the ease with which the coasts of Lancashire and Cheshire are approached from the interior of England, those two counties are, and ever have been, the principal seats of the commerce that is carried on from the northern and midland counties of England, in a westerly direction, either with ports in the Irish Sea, or with the more distant counties of the Atlantic. Lancashire and Cheshire are thus the outlets of the richest and most populous counties of England, and more especially of the districts in which there are the most abundant supplies of coal and water power, available for the purposes of manufacturing industry, and where an active, industrious, and constantly increasing population, of six or eight millions of persons, is collected From these coasts also there is the easiest, cheapest, and quickest communication with the western coasts of Scotland, and with every part of Ireland Owing to these causes, upwards of one-third of the whole foreign trade of the United Kingdom is now carried on from the ports of Lancashire and Cheshire There also assemble yearly, from all parts of the United Kingdom and of the Continent, the numerous passengers who are continually crossing between Europe and America, including the tens and hundreds of thousands of emigrants, who issue from the British islands and the continent of Europe, to spread themselves over the unoccupied regions of America, South Africa, and Australia. Of the five millions of emigrants who have sailed from the United Kingdom during the last forty years, at least four millions have taken their departure from Liverpool and Birkenhead, from which ports there is a continual communication across the Atlantic, and even to more distant regions, by means of innumerable sailing vessels, and the swiftest and most powerful lines of ocean steamers *

The Tides and Winds on the North-western Coast—The powerful tides of the Atlantic Ocean, in approaching the western coast of Ireland, divide into two great tidal waves, one of which enters the

* Emigration Returns, and Annual Trade and Navigation Returns, published by the Board of Trade

Irish Sea, and approaches the coasts of Lancashire and Cheshire from the south, whilst the other enters the same sea, and approaches the same coasts, from the north. These tides flow onward, until they meet each other, twice in twenty-four hours, off the coasts of Lancashire, between Liverpool and Morecambe Bays, and then return in the same direction by which they advanced from the ocean They thus give to the numerous vessels approaching to, or sailing from these coasts, the choice of approaching or leaving the ports of Lancashire and Cheshire, in either direction, and with different winds Vessels can thus either approach or leave by the southern or the northern channel This choice of course into and out of port is very convenient at all times, and formerly, when we were continually involved in wars with France, Spain, and Holland, the northern passage into Liverpool was found much more secure, for vessels sailing to or from the Lancashire ports, than the southern passage, which led them down St. George's Channel, and within a short distance of the continental coasts. Happily, this reason for using the northern instead of the southern channel has not existed for the last fifty years, and it is to be hoped that it will not exist again; but independent of that, there are many other causes which render the possession of a double line of approach to, and of departure from, this part of the coast of England, a great advantage to trade and shipping *

The tides of the Atlantic, in rushing along the shores of Cheshire and Lancashire, enter numerous large estuaries on the coasts of the two counties, raising the water rapidly, in those estuaries, to the height of upwards of thirty-three feet above dead low water of spring tides, or of sixteen to twenty feet above what is called the datum, or level, of the Old Dock sill at Liverpool, a point, at the entrance of the earliest dock formed at that port, from which the rise of the tides is usually calculated in the estuary of the Mersey These tides flow many miles inland, creating a moving force twice in twenty-four hours, up and down the streams, and furnishing a sufficient depth of water, and a motive power capable of conveying vessels at least twenty miles into the interior. Nearly all the more ancient ports of the two counties are situated at a distance of fifteen to twenty miles from the open sea. At that distance the small vessels used in former times could be anchored in the stream, or even laid up on the beach, without any great danger of being wrecked or beaten to pieces by the fury of the waves But in modern times, as vessels of a much larger class,

* Admiralty Chart of St George's Channel

some of them of the burden of 2000 and 3000 tons, or even of greater size and draught of water, have come into use, the principal ports of the two counties have been formed at the entrance of the estuaries, where the water is deepest. There the vessels frequenting those ports are secured against the fury of winds and waves, tides and currents, by the forming of artificial harbours or docks, in which they lie in perfect safety, even in the terrible storms that frequently sweep along those coasts.

The winds along the western coast of Great Britain blow from the Atlantic towards the land during the greater part of the year, yet with frequent changes in their direction It appears from a careful record of the direction of the winds on each day of the year, during a period of six years, made at the Liverpool Observatory, that the N.W. winds blew on the average for one hundred and twelve days in the year, with a force represented by a speed of fifteen miles an hour, that the S W winds blew seventy-seven days, with a force of nearly fourteen miles an hour, that the S E winds blew for one hundred and sixteen days, with a force of eleven miles an hour; and that the N.E. winds blew sixty days in the year, with an average force of eight miles an hour. A longer series of observations on the direction of the winds, made at Manchester, gives the following results —Between the years 1849 and 1861, the direction of the wind throughout the year, at eight o'clock in the morning, on an average of the whole period, was, W, 115 8 days, S, 105 8, E., 78 0, and N, 68 0. In some years the westerly and southerly winds are much more prevalent and powerful Thus in 1854 the wind blew from the N W, during one hundred and thirty-eight days, with the average velocity of more than seventeen miles an hour, and from the S W eighty-nine days, with an average velocity of nearly fifteen miles an hour On the whole, there is a considerable prevalence of southerly and westerly winds, but the northerly and easterly winds are sufficiently frequent to answer all purposes of navigation. Occasionally, in the spring months, the easterly winds blow so long as to be inconvenient to commerce and shipping, by keeping large fleets out at sea, but this is not a frequent occurrence From the greater strength and prevalence of the winds blowing from the W and S, the average time in which the best sailing vessels make the voyage from America to Europe—or rather, from New York to Liverpool—is about twenty-one days, whilst the average voyage from Liverpool to New York is about thirty-five days. The powerful steamers that now cross the Atlantic perform the voyage both ways, in from ten to twelve days, according to the direction of the winds at different seasons.

The above figures show the force and velocity of the winds that usually prevail on the coast of Lancashire and Cheshire; but in great gales from the N.W. and the S.W., they sometimes move at the rate of forty miles an hour, and in a great storm in 1852, the wind rushed over sea and land at the rate of seventy-one miles an hour—a speed surpassing that of the swiftest railway train.

The Ports, Harbours, and Estuaries of Lancashire and Cheshire.—Each of the estuaries on the coast of Lancashire and Cheshire receives one or more considerable rivers from the interior, and is the natural outlet of a great valley or district of country, extending from thirty to ninety miles into the interior. The navigation of some of these rivers has been much improved by art, and has been rendered available for the purposes of intercourse with the interior. In some cases the rivers and estuaries are the outlets and inlets of the trade and commerce, not only of large districts in the counties in which they are situated, but also of much larger portions of the kingdom. The river Mersey, especially, may be regarded as the gate through which nearly all the commerce, and all the personal intercourse of England and the northern countries of Europe with America, is now carried on.*

The first great opening on the coast of Lancashire, commencing from the north, is that formed by the deep and wide bay of Morecambe—a grand natural object, which still bears the name that it bore seventeen hundred years ago, when it was described in the Geography of Claudius Ptolemy of Alexandria. This beautiful bay receives the tides from the south, and is divided at the north into the estuaries of the Duddon, the Leven, and the Kent. It also contains the safe and commodious natural harbour of the Pile of Fouldry, long a place of refuge in stormy weather for vessels frequenting these seas.

The estuary of the Duddon, like the beautiful river of the same name, is the boundary between the counties of Lancaster and Cumberland. Borwick harbour lies near the entrance, on the Cumberland side of the stream, and the river is navigable for small vessels as high as Broughton in Furness. There are shipping places near Broughton, and also near Kirkby Ireleth, and at other places, for the copper and iron ore, the slates, the larch and fir timber, and the sheep and cattle of Higher Furness. The cotton and coal used at the

* Annual Trade and Navigation Returns, published by the Board of Trade.

Broughton mills, and the coal, as well as the colonial and foreign produce consumed in this district, were formerly brought into it entirely by sea. But this part, and indeed the whole of the Furness district, is now well supplied with railways, and has cheap railway carriage, as well as water carriage, to all parts both of Lancashire and of Cumberland The valley or watershed of the Duddon extends over an area of 117 square miles Nearly the whole district, through which the river flows, is covered with lofty mountains, and is very thinly peopled.*

The harbour of the Pile of Fouldry lies to the east of Duddon Sands. It forms part of a long, but not very wide arm of the sea, running between the mainland of Lower Furness and the island of Walney, which is about eight miles in length, and lies parallel to the coast It is a perfectly safe and land-locked harbour, of considerable extent, protected from the waves and the storms of the Irish Sea by Walney Island, which rises like a breakwater, sheltering it on the west and the south To the north and east, it is protected either by other small islands, or by the coast of Furness, which here rises into lofty banks, and also by the more distant range of mountains that extends across Higher Furness, from Black Combe in Cumberland to the Fells at the head of Windermere

There are two light-houses on Walney Island at the entrance of the harbour, which is approached through a deep narrow channel, between Walney Island and the shoals of Foulney Island The isle of Fouldry, with the ruined Pile or Peel—a castle of the fourteenth century, from which the harbour takes its name—is near the entrance. which it formerly commanded There are also several other small islands, the names of the principal ones being Walney, Foulney, Fouldry, Barrow, and Roe Islands. Within the last few years a steam-boat pier has been built on Roe Island, which is now connected with the mainland by the embankment of the Furness Railway, extending from Rampside to the island By means of this railway there is an easy communication inland, from the harbour of the Pile of Fouldry to the beautiful ruins of Furness Abbey, four or five miles distant, to the iron mines of Dalton and Lindale, and to many points in the Lake district, as well as to more distant parts.

But the principal commerce of this district is now at Barrow, a rising town, higher up the strait that divides the isle of Walney from

* Ordnance Survey, Lancashire, Report on Salmon Fisheries of England and Wales, with a Table of Rivers and their Watershed Parliamentary Returns

Furness. Barrow is the nearest point on the sea-coast to the rich hæmatite iron mines of Furness The greater part of the iron ore that is raised in this district is shipped at Barrow, whence it is forwarded to Liverpool, Runcorn, and Chester, to be sent into Staffordshire, there to be smelted with the poorer iron ores of that district Barrow is also becoming an important place for the smelting of iron and the making of steel, having great facilities for those purposes, owing to its vicinity to the iron mines of Furness and the coal mines of Cumberland There is a pier at Barrow for the shipping and landing of iron ore, coal, and other articles; and a branch of the Furness Railway gives every facility for land carriage, both to the Cumberland coalfields, and into South Lancashire.*

To the east of the harbour of Pile of Fouldry is the estuary of the Leven This is navigable for moderate-sized steamers and smaller vessels to Ulverstone, the chief port and town of Furness A wide and deep canal, about half a mile in length, has been formed from the sea to the town, with a convenient basin for the loading and discharging of vessels Ulverstone, like Barrow, has a large trade in iron ore, as well as in timber, slates, and other articles There are also cotton mills and iron furnaces in and around the town, and there is a very easy and cheap access to the Lake district by the steamers that ply between Liverpool and Ulverstone Higher up the Leven there are also manufactories of cotton and iron, and an extensive gunpowder manufactory The river Crake flows into the Leven above Ulverstone, and has a shipping pier at Greenodd The Furness Railway has recently been carried across the estuaries of the Kent, the Leven, and the Duddon, forming the head of Morecambe Bay, and it now gives the whole of this district, what it never possessed before, an easy and safe communication with the other parts of Lancashire

Proceeding to the east side of Morecambe Bay, we find Port Morecambe, formerly known as Poulton on the Sands, where a commodious pier has been erected, from which a steamboat communication is kept up with Belfast and the north of Ireland. This is now a terminus of the great railway system of the Midland Railway Company, which extends over nearly the whole of England, and, by a system of railway alliances, over great part of Scotland

Further south is the pleasantly situated village of Heysham, where a pier is in course of construction

The entrance to the Lune is at Glasson, where there is a convenient

* The new docks of the Furness Railway Company were opened September 19 1867

dock, and from that point vessels of considerable size proceed up to Lancaster. The Lune is the outlet of a beautiful and fertile valley, extending over an area of 434 square miles; but the river is not navigable for any distance above Lancaster, and there is neither coal, iron, nor any other mineral of much value, found in the neighbourhood The trade of Lancaster is therefore small, although there are a few cotton mills in and around the town Lancaster may be regarded as the principal terminus of the Midland Railway in this direction, it also stands on the great line of railway communication between Scotland and Lancashire

Further to the south is the estuary of the Wyre, with the port of Fleetwood The entrance of the harbour is from Lune Deeps, through a channel lying between extensive sand-banks After passing the town of Fleetwood the estuary widens, and forms one of the best harbours in Lancashire But there are no manufactures in the immediate neighbourhood, nor any minerals of value; and the principal occupation of the harbour of Fleetwood is in affording a quick and easy communication, by steamers, between the north of Ireland, the west of Scotland, and the manufacturing districts of Lancashire and Yorkshire New works, for the fuller development of the port, are in course of construction, with the support of the London and North-western and the Lancashire and Yorkshire Railway Companies. The valley or watershed of the Wyre extends over an area of 179 square miles.

From Rossall Point to the river Ribble the coast is generally bold, consisting of lofty earth-banks, without any bays or creeks. On one of the boldest parts of this coast, the watering place of Blackpool is rapidly increasing in population, and improving in beauty A very long and handsome pier has recently been constructed, which affords great convenience for boats and yachts, besides forming a pleasant promenade for visitors Blackpool is now connected with the interior by railway, and is likely to become one of the most favourite watering places on the north-western coast of England

The entrance to the river Ribble is wide, but shallow, through great sand-banks, which prevent the entrance of large vessels But there is a considerable steamboat communication with Ireland from the port of Preston. A new pier has recently been erected at Lytham, on the north bank of the Ribble The lights at the entrance of the river are visible at a distance of ten miles. The valley of the Ribble covers an area of 501 square miles, and upon it and its tributaries are situate the flourishing towns of Preston, Clitheroe, Colne, Burnley, Blackburn, Wigan, and Chorley. But the foreign trade of those places is chiefly carried on through the port of Liverpool.

To the south of the Ribble is Southport, the largest and most flourishing watering-place in Lancashire, and rapidly becoming one of the handsomest and best built towns in the county. Southport is so easily accessible from Manchester, Liverpool, and all parts of South Lancashire, as to have become the habitual residence of numerous families, connected with those places. The new streets are laid out with great taste, and many of the public buildings and houses are very handsome A long and commodious pier has recently been erected, which adds very much to the advantages of Southport as a pleasant place of resort. Further south is Waterloo, now almost a marine suburb of Liverpool.

The town and port of Liverpool, and the estuary of the Mersey, are approached from the sea, through Liverpool Bay, which extends from Formby Point to the north-western point of the peninsula of Wirral. This is now the greatest port in the world, in point of trade, having a larger commerce even than London, New York, or any other of the great seaports of modern times

The main entrance to the river Mersey is through the Victoria Channel, where there is a depth of fifteen to eighteen feet, and through the Queen's Channel, where there is a depth of ten or twelve feet, at dead low water of spring tides.* Once past the bar the river widens and deepens, and presents a magnificent estuary, with deep water for a distance of five or six miles from the mouth, and a width varying from one to three or four miles.

The estuary of the Mersey possesses all the advantages of a large natural harbour, well sheltered from the most dangerous winds, with an entrance deep and wide enough to admit the largest vessels, an area of several thousand acres of water space, and sufficient depth of water for vessels to ride at anchor, in every state of the tide

All the estuaries of Lancashire and Cheshire are more or less valuable for the purposes of navigation. There is sufficient depth in all for vessels engaged in the coasting trade, including under that name the trade with Scotland and Ireland. In three of them there is sufficient depth of water for large vessels, at all tides, namely, in the Wyre at Fleetwood, the Pile of Fouldry, and the river Mersey.

* Report on the present state of the Navigation of the River Mersey, 1865, by Admiral George Evans, Acting Conservator of the River

The Mersey forms one of the best natural harbours in England, in point of shelter, extent, and depth of water. It has also been improved by all the resources of art, at the cost of many millions.* In the Mersey there is sufficient depth of water to receive the largest merchant ships, and even the greatest line-of-battle ships, now in existence. Indeed, the largest vessel ever built, namely, the *Great Eastern*, of upwards of 16,000 tons, lay at anchor in the river Mersey for several months. In general, the largest ships engaged in the ocean trade sail from the river Mersey, and make it their ordinary place of resort.

We shall give an account of the docks of Liverpool and Birkenhead, forming the artificial harbour of the river Mersey, when we come to describe the numerous public works that have been constructed in the north-western district, for the purpose of facilitating internal and external communication. At present we may merely state, that they are the greatest works of the kind ever constructed for commercial purposes. The trade carried on through them is worthy of their extent. The number of vessels of all classes that enter the port of Liverpool every year is from 20,000 to 30,000, with a burden of 5,000,000 to 6,000,000 tons. The value of the cargoes of all kinds which they convey into or out of the port is about £150,000,000 sterling. One half of all the British manufactures exported to other countries are shipped at the port of Liverpool.†

The valley or watershed of the river Mersey extends over an area of 1706 square miles, including the greater part of the counties of Lancaster and Chester.‡ Nearly the whole of the coal-field of the two counties, as well as the salt-field of Cheshire, lies on the three great rivers, Irwell, Mersey, and Weaver, which, with numerous smaller streams, flow into the estuary of the Mersey. In this great valley or watershed stand the city of Manchester, the port of Liverpool, the towns of Bolton, Leigh, Haslingden, Bacup, Bury, Rochdale, Middleton, Oldham, Ashton-under-Lyne, Warrington, Stockport, Staleybridge, Hyde, Macclesfield, Congleton, Nantwich, Northwich, Runcorn, and Birkenhead—places containing, with the intervening districts, upwards of 2,000,000 of inhabitants, and furnishing a large portion of the exports of England.

* Annual Reports of Mersey Docks and Harbour Board, laid before Parliament.

† Returns of Vessels and Tonnage, &c., of Twelve principal Ports of the United Kingdom. Parliamentary Paper, 1865.

‡ List of Rivers and Watershed of Valleys in Report on Salmon Fisheries of England and Wales, laid before Parliament, Session of 1861.

The means of communication from Liverpool and Birkenhead to other parts of the kingdom are numerous and perfect From the Northern Docks of Liverpool the railway systems of the Lancashire and Yorkshire and the East Lancashire Companies extend, more or less directly, to all the great towns of Lancashire and Yorkshire, and from this point also extends into the interior the Leeds and Liverpool Canal, more than 140 miles in length, which forms a means of water carriage from the Irish Sea to the navigable rivers that flow into the German Ocean. From the Central and Northern Docks of Liverpool the great system of railways of the London and North Western Company now extends to the metropolis, and to a large portion of the kingdom, through a course of 1200 miles in length. From the Southern Docks the systems of the Manchester and Sheffield, the Great Northern, and the Midland Companies, extend over a large part of the northern, central, and eastern counties of England Most of these railways are now connected with each other, and with every part of the docks, by lines of railways encircling the town, or tunnels running through it From Birkenhead the railway systems of the Great Western, and the London and North Western Companies, extend over the greater part of the west-midland and western counties of England, and over the principality of Wales, whilst the Hoylake Railway, besides opening the peninsula of Wirral, will no doubt be carried by extensions, across the river Dee, into the coal district of Flintshire and Denbighshire, and along the Welsh border. Higher up the river, at Garston, which is rapidly becoming a place of trade, the St Helens Railway extends over one of the richest coal-fields of Lancashire, and the London and North Western Railway Company, to which that line now belongs, is exerting itself to develope the resources of that rising place. Still higher up the river, the new town of Widness, and the very ancient town of Runcorn, are rapidly increasing in population and wealth, partly from the advantages which their position gives them for carrying on manufactures in which salt and coal are extensively employed, and partly from their position on the great lines of inland water communication, which terminate at one or other of those places They are also about to be connected with each other, and to be brought on to the main line of railway between Liverpool and London, by means of the lofty and commanding railway bridge, across the Mersey, at Runcorn, which is nearly completed, and when finished, will so far shorten and improve the route between Liverpool and London, as to render it practicable for the express trains to make the journey between those places in four hours

Descending the Mersey on the Cheshire side, the river Weaver connects the port of Liverpool with the Cheshire salt-field, at Northwich and Winsford. Still lower down, at Ellesmere Port, there is a communication by inland water carriage with Chester, and with all the interior districts of Cheshire, Shropshire, Denbighshire, and Montgomeryshire The ferries, by means of which many millions of persons cross the Mersey every year, commence on the Cheshire side at Eastham, and extend along the west bank of the river, by New Ferry, Rock Ferry, Tranmere, Birkenhead, Woodside, Seacombe, Egremont, and New Brighton to the sea On the Lancashire side of the river, the ferries from St. George's Pier and Toxteth Park keep up an incessant communication (one of them, that to Woodside, worked by the commissioners of Birkenhead, throughout the night, as well as during the day) with the Cheshire shore In addition to these numerous ferries across the Mersey, plans have for some time been under discussion for uniting Liverpool and Birkenhead with each other, either by means of a high level railway bridge, or of a tunnel or tunnels under the bed of the river It is said that nothing is now impossible to the skill of engineers of the class of those whose names are connected with the proposed undertakings, and we may therefore venture to hope, that after full inquiry and consideration, a plan will be adopted which will carry out the object of thoroughly uniting the two halves of the great system of docks now under the management of the Mersey Docks and Harbour Board, the railway systems on both sides of the river, with each other and with the whole of the docks; of giving Birkenhead, and the whole Cheshire shore, a certain entrance into Liverpool under all circumstances of wind, tide, and atmosphere, and of affording to the crowded population of Liverpool the unspeakable advantage of spreading itself freely over the healthy hills and coasts of the peninsula of Wirral, one of the most beautiful and attractive districts of Cheshire The great works of the Birkenhead Docks, which we shall describe fully, along with all the other principal public works of Lancashire and Cheshire, in a subsequent part of this work, are now open to the commerce of the world, and with those of Liverpool form the largest and most perfect artificial harbour ever constructed by human skill

Before leaving the shores of the Mersey, it will be well to describe the grand operation of nature, by which this port is kept open by the action of the tides, notwithstanding the continually threatening encroachments of the sand-banks which surround its entrance On the greater part of this coast the sand-banks rise above the level of the sea, at low water, in some places and at particular tides, to the height of from thirty to thirty-three feet. At low water the approach to the port is by narrow channels, running through these sand-banks. All these channels become nearly dry when the tide is out, except the Queen's Channel and the Victoria Channel, the former of which, as already mentioned, has a depth of ten or twelve feet over the Queen's Channel bar, and the latter one of from fifteen to eighteen feet over the inner and outer bars of the Victoria Channel, at the lowest spring tides At low water of spring tides, the only approach for vessels entering the Mersey is through these narrow channels, which then appear to be nearly dry; but no sooner does the tide begin to rise than the channels fill, and are suddenly changed into large arms of the sea, through which the tide flows with great rapidity, and in a stream deep enough to enable the largest vessels to enter in safety

These sand-banks have all been raised from the bottom of the sea by the action of its waters, and the general effect of the movement of the sea is to raise them still higher, and either to close the ports altogether, or to render them incapable of receiving large vessels This has already occurred in the estuaries of the Ribble and the Dee, which would be amongst the finest harbours in England, if it were not for the continual encroachments of the sands Happily this is not the case either in the river Mersey, in the river Wyre, or in the narrow passage that leads into the harbour of the Pile of Fouldry. The entrances to these three harbours are all comparatively narrow, the water spreading out over a wide area after it has entered the harbours, and in its rapid passage in and out, clearing away the sand that would otherwise choke up their entrances, as it has done the wider entrances into the Ribble and the Dee

According to the calculations and observations of Admiral Denham, R N., who carefully surveyed the coasts of Lancashire and Cheshire, the quantity of tidal water that enters the estuary of the Mersey at spring tides, is 774,000,000 of cubic yards, and at neap tides, 299,000,000, making an average of 535,000,000 cubic yards of water The vertical rise of the tide, at the entrance of the Mersey, is from thirty to thirty-three and a half feet at the highest spring tides, and the tide flows through the narrowest part of the river, between Seacombe and Prince's Dock, at a rate varying from four and a half to five and a half miles per hour. At high tide the immense mass of water brought into the wide basin of the Mersey is received into a great natural reservoir, presenting the appearance of a lake, twenty miles in length, and from two to five miles in breadth. No sooner does the tide turn, than this vast mass of water begins to flow back towards the sea, carrying along with it the fresh water that has been brought down by rivers and streams from the interior. At first its motion is slow, but the momentum increases as the mass of water descends towards the sea, and it finally rushes through the narrowest part of the estuary, opposite to Seacombe and the town of Liverpool, at a rate of between five and six miles an hour Owing to the force of the tide there is scarcely any deposit of sand in this part of the river, where the rocks on the side of the stream are quite bare at low water of spring tides After flowing rapidly through this narrow channel, this great natural sluice, charged with hundreds of millions of cubic yards of water, not only scours out the harbour, but strikes upon the sand-banks, at the entrance of the river, with sufficient force to clear a passage into the sea, in which passage there is never less than ten or twelve feet of water, and generally sufficient to admit the largest ships. Such is the natural process by which the harbour of the Mersey and the channels leading into it have hitherto been kept open, and by which they may be kept open for ages to come, if nothing be done in the interior of the river to diminish the immense stream of water which the rising and falling tides force through the passage, four times in every twenty-four hours, or about fourteen hundred times in every year.

A survey was made of the river Mersey, from the entrance up to Runcorn, in the year 1857, for the purpose of ascertaining whether any changes had taken place since the time of a previous survey, made in the year 1822. Within that period great extensions have been made in the sea-walls of the Liverpool Docks, and an entirely new sea-wall of great extent has been constructed at Birkenhead. Several piers and other works had also been constructed, on the Cheshire side of the river, rendering it desirable to ascertain whether any effect, either beneficial or injurious, has been produced on the harbour or its entrances The general result of the survey of 1857 was to show, that the course of the great tidal wave, which flows four times every twenty-four hours through the port and harbour, at flood and ebb tide, had become much stronger and more direct than it was at the time of the survey of 1822 When the former of these surveys was made, the Queen's Channel and the Victoria Channel, which now form the main entrance into the Mersey, and run right through the middle of the sand-banks, either did not exist at all, or were so much shallower as to be useless for the purposes of navigation. It was found, at the survey of 1857, that the tidal current is now more concentrated in these channels, and that consequently their depth is much greater. Within the river a similar change was found to have taken place The tidal wave now flows in a much straighter line—a circumstance that gives greater force and speed to the current, at its entrance into the river, and up and down the stream While the main stream of the tide through the channel, harbour, and estuary of the Mersey has thus become straighter and more direct, the channels, harbour, and estuary have all become deeper Within the harbour soundings were made, commencing at a point, at the entrance of the river, one hundred and fifty yards north of the jetty at New Brighton, and extending up the river, for twenty miles, as far as Runcorn By means of these soundings the depth of the Mersey, from bank to bank, was ascertained at forty-one different points, and the result in all cases, except one or two, was to show that there had been a considerable increase of depth, between the time of the survey of 1822 and that of 1857 From the mouth of the river to Dingle Point, the increase of depth varied from seven to ten feet in and near the navigable channel. It was not so great above that point, but even there it was considerable. In addition to this increase of depth there was also an increase of six per cent, in the area of water surface, in the upper part of the river, extending from the narrowest part of the stream, between Prince's Dock and Seacombe, to Ince, a distance of ten miles up the estuary Whilst the quantity of tidal water that enters the river had increased, the rate at which it flows out with the receding tide had also become greater The observed inclination on the surface of the ebbing tide, above the narrows at Seacombe and Prince's Dock, is 1 in 13,000, below Seacombe it is 1 in 6000, showing that Seacombe acts as a dam, from its narrowness and the shallowness of the water. The depth of the river at Seacombe is only sixty-three feet, whilst opposite to New Brighton, two miles lower down the stream, it is ninety-three feet, and opposite to Woodside, one mile above Seacombe, eighty feet. Seacombe may therefore be considered as the throat or gorge of the Mersey, so far as the navigation is concerned, both as being the narrowest part of the river, and also as having a bottom or bed of rock, which the current, though powerful, cannot remove Experiments have shown that the velocity of the current, opposite to Seacombe, is five and a half miles per hour with high tides, and four and a half with ordinary spring tides, which is one mile more than was observed either above or below the Seacombe narrows At neap tides the acceleration of the current is about half a mile per hour opposite Seacombe, its speed at that time being two miles per hour According to Captain Lord's chart of 1849, the velocity of the stream at high tides, in the Seacombe narrows, was five and a quarter miles

The above increase in the depth and straightness of the tides that flow through the harbour of Liverpool, is attributed to the great increase that has taken place in the length of the sea-walls, on both sides of the river In 1822, the length of the sea-wall on the Liverpool side of the river was about 3000 yards, or less than two miles, whilst in 1857, the length of the wall was 9700 yards, or upwards of five miles Since 1857, the sea-wall on the Liverpool side has been still further extended, and now reaches down to Seaforth, which is outside the river. On the west or Cheshire side of the river, an entirely new sea-wall has been built between 1822 and 1857, for the protection of the Birkenhead Docks, and subsequently a sea-wall has been carried down, on the Cheshire side of the river, as far as Egremont. The result of these immense works has been to narrow the entrance of the river, and to give both additional strength and greater directness to the course of the tide. In 1857, the width of the river was 1800 yards at its mouth, opposite the Rock Fort, and about 980 yards at the narrows between Seacombe Ferry pier and the north end of Prince's Dock pier The width also of the reclaimed area taken from the river was much greater at the entrance than higher up the stream, being 900 yards wide at the Bootle or north end, near the entrance of the river, and not more than 330 yards at the Prince's Basin The northern inclosures or reclamations at the entrance of the river, in 1857, formed an area of 560 acres; whilst the southern inclosure or reclamation was only about eighty acres Since 1857, the works have been carried on to a great additional extent, and more especially, Bootle Bay, which formerly received the advancing and the receding tides, has been almost entirely inclosed, and covered with new works and docks The effect of this inclosure must have been, not only to give a straighter line to the currents that flow into and out of the river, but also greatly to strengthen their force, by narrowing the passage

Whilst the main channel that leads directly into the river Mersey has thus been deepened, the side channels have become shallower, and the banks have become higher Between 1822 and 1857, the width of the Rock Channel narrowed from 1300 feet to 400 feet in width In the same period, the main entrance to the Horse Channel, between the Dove's Spit and the North Spit, narrowed from 1200 yards to 700 yards The Hoylake Channel into the river Dee, where there used formerly to be sufficient depth of water for large vessels, and where a frigate lay during the French war, is almost filled up. There was formerly four feet at low water of spring tides; and in 1857 it dried sixteen feet at those tides, being a difference of twenty-two feet*

The estuary of the Dee is the last great arm of the sea of which we shall have to speak. For many ages the city of Chester, the chief place on its banks, was the seat of the principal trade then existing in the north-western division of England, and Chester has still a considerable trade, though small in comparison with that of Liverpool. This is in some degree owing to the shallowing of the river Dee from the irruption of immense sand-banks, which have filled the greater part of the ancient estuary, and reduced the passage into the port of Chester to a narrow and not very deep channel At high tides large vessels can still get up to Chester, but not when the tides are low

The form of the entrance of the river Dee is altogether different from that of the river Mersey. In the Mersey, a narrow passage leads into a wide, long, and deep basin. In the Dee, a wide entrance leads into a narrow channel From this difference of form, the sand enters more freely into the Dee than into the Mersey, and the returning tide of the Dee has not the power to force it back into the sea. In former times almost the whole trade between the north of England and Ireland was carried on, either by way of Chester, or of Parkgate, lower down the estuary of

* Report to the Corporation of Liverpool by J Walker and J B Hartley, Esqs, Civil Engineers, on the river Mersey 1857.

the Dee, to which place vessels had then easy access; but Parkgate has now only water for fishing vessels, and the trade of Ireland is carried on from Liverpool and Holyhead It is proposed, and powers have been obtained, to construct a pier at Talacre, at the south entrance of the river Dee—a position where there is deep water, and excellent railway communication with Chester, and which stands on the edge of a rich mineral district.

Such are the principal ports and harbours on the coasts of Lancashire and Cheshire. They vary greatly in the extent of their accommodation, and the amount of their trade. But all of them have a considerable coasting trade, three of them are well adapted for foreign commerce, the port of Liverpool has a larger and more valuable trade, not only than any port in England, but than any in the world, surpassing that of London, New York, or New Orleans in the combined value of its exports and imports, and doubling its trade, vast as it already is, in less than twenty years. It is, in fact, the great port of communication between the Old and the New World.*

Having thus described the ports and harbours, by means of which the counties of Lancashire and Cheshire communicate with foreign countries, we shall proceed to state what are the natural resources existing within the limits of the two counties, from which they derive the means of carrying on so vast a trade We shall commence with an account of their soil, climate, vegetable and animal products, we shall next give a more detailed account of the sources of their great mineral wealth, and these we shall accompany with an account of their rivers, and their facilities for carrying on manufactures. But before doing this, we shall say a few words on the subject of the sea-fisheries on the coasts of Lancashire and Cheshire

The Sea-fisheries of Lancashire and Cheshire—All the seas around the British islands abound in fish of various kinds, some of them being found in shoals of unknown millions in number. The British seas are in general of moderate depth. Between England and the continent of Europe the average depth of the German Ocean is not more than ninety feet, and one-fifth of it is occupied by banks, which are always being added to by the muddy deposits of the rivers on both sides. In extent these banks are equal to the area of Ireland, and to these banks the animals of the ocean chiefly resort. On the west side of England, St George's

* Official Declared Value of Imports and Exports, 1865

Channel and the Irish Sea present another immense basin, well sheltered from the storms of the ocean, of moderate depth, and full of the refuse brought by numerous rivers both from England and Ireland. The whole of the Irish Channel, from the coasts of Lancashire and Cheshire to those of Ireland, is full of fish, but the Irish Sea is divided into two tolerably equal parts by the Isle of Man. The Lancashire and Cheshire fishermen carry on their operations, either amongst the banks on the coast, or in the deep trawling grounds between the Lancashire coast and the Isle of Man, sometimes going southward into Carnarvon and Cardigan Bays The Manx fishermen carry on their operations chiefly around their own island; whilst the Dublin, Howth, and other Irish fishermen, fish in the seas between the Irish coast and the Isle of Man

It appears from a report recently laid before Parliament, that the fishing grounds around Great Britain are of great and rapidly increasing value We are told, in this report, that the most frequented fishing grounds are much more prolific of food than the same extent of the richest land. Once in a year an acre of good land, it is said, carefully tilled, produces a ton of corn, or two or three cwt of meat or cheese. The same area at the bottom of the sea, on the best fishing grounds, yields a greater weight of food, to the persevering fisherman, every week in the year Five vessels, it is stated, in a single night's fishing, brought in seventeen tons weight of fish, an amount of wholesome food equal in weight to that of fifty cattle or 300 sheep The ground which these vessels covered during the night's fishing could not have exceeded an area of fifty acres. It is stated, in the same report, that the great importance of fish, as an article of food, may be clearly shown by a comparison of the total supply of fish and beef to London in the course of a single year. It has been roughly estimated that London consumes 300,000 fat cattle annually, which at an average weight of six cwt. each, would amount to 90,000 tons of beef At this moment there are between 800 and 900 trawl vessels engaged in supplying the London market with fish, and assuming the average annual take for each vessel to be ninety tons, this would give a total of some 80,000 tons of trawled fish. This is irrespective of the vast quantities of herrings, sprats, shell-fish, and fish of other descriptions, which are supplied by different modes of fishing The weight of the beef and of the fish annually consumed in London is thus in no great disproportion; but the price is very different. The fisherman receives, on an average, little over

£7 a ton for his fish, prime and offal together. The farmer is readily paid for his beef not less than £60 a ton.*

Lancashire and Cheshire are supplied with fish partly from the eastern, and partly from the western, seas of England The city of Manchester derives the greater part of its supply from the eastern coast, by means of the Manchester, Sheffield, and Lincolnshire Railway, which conveys into the interior the greater part of the fish caught on the coasts of Lincolnshire, and part of that caught on the coast of Yorkshire In 1856 the quantity of fish carried by this line was not more than 947 tons, but from that time there has been an increase every year, and in 1864 the quantity conveyed by the line was 8494 tons. The principal kinds of fish sold in the Manchester market, with their prices per pound, were as follows, in the year 1865:—Turbot, per pound, 8*d.* to 1*s* ; soles, 6*d.* to 8*d* ; cod, 3*d.* to 4*d.*; sparlings, 1*s.* to 1*s.* 6*d.*; haddock, 3*d.* to 4*d.*; plaice, 1½*d.* to 2*d*, brill, 4*d.* to 5*d.*; ray, 3*d.*, and halibut, 6*d.* In addition to these there were also brought to Manchester large quantities of herrings, mackerel, and other sea-fish of less importance. From Lowestoft, and other places on the coast of Norfolk and Suffolk, vast quantities of fresh herrings, amounting sometimes to from 700 to 800 tons per day, are distributed among the manufacturing towns, during the period of the fishery, Birmingham and Manchester taking the largest share The introduction of railways, by affording the means of rapid transport from the sea-coast to the populous districts of the interior, has given a wonderful impulse to the British fisheries In 1856 the quantity of fish conveyed by four lines of railway, viz.—the North Eastern, the Manchester, Sheffield, and Lincolnshire, the Great Northern, and the South Devon, was 11,714 tons, whilst in 1864 the quantity conveyed by the same four lines was 40,337 tons, an increase of threefold in a period of nine years The quantity of fish forwarded by the twelve principal railways, from the sea-coast to the interior, amounted in the year 1862, to 99,724 tons, and in 1864, to 122,381 tons. This is independent of a large portion of the fish consumed in London, Liverpool, Hull, Edinburgh, Glasgow, Belfast, Dublin, and other cities, towns, and places on the sea-coast. It is also independent of the trade in salt herrings, of which no less than 3,372,000 barrels were cured in the year 1864.

The three principal fishing stations on the Lancashire coast are

* Report of the Commissioners appointed to inquire into the Sea-fisheries of the United Kingdom Presented to both Houses of Parliament, 1866

Liverpool, Fleetwood, and Morecambe Bay At Liverpool there are more than fifty large trawling vessels; at Fleetwood, more than twenty; and in Morecambe Bay there is an extensive fishery, chiefly of shell-fish From Liverpool the larger class of trawlers work occasionally in the bays on the north coast of Wales, and lately have tried the open bays of Carnarvon and Cardigan, but their main fishing ground lies in the open sea, between Liverpool and the Isle of Man. There is also a smaller class of trawlers, from New Brighton and the fishing villages at the entrance of the Mersey, who trawl for soles and flounders in the estuaries of the Mersey and the Dee, and on the banks in their neighbourhood, and take considerable numbers of small fish. From Fleetwood, the trawlers never work in bays or in shallow water This deep-water trawling is quite different from the shrimp trawling, which is carried on to a very great extent in the Mersey, the Dee, and along the banks of those estuaries, as well as in Morecambe Bay, and other places In Morecambe Bay 150 large boats are engaged in shrimping, and thirty quarts each tide is reckoned a good catch for a boat now, as it was in former years The number of boats in Morecambe Bay, engaged in the shrimp fishery, has increased during the last fifty years from eight or nine to 150

The principal Lancashire fishing is on the trawling grounds between the coasts of that county and the Isle of Man. The net used in the beam trawl, or deep-sea fishing, is generally about seventy feet long, and forty feet wide at the mouth, gradually diminishing to a narrow passage about ten feet in length, at the end of the net, into which the fish swim, and from which it is scarcely possible for them to escape when once they have entered it The mouth of the net is kept open by a beam about forty feet long, and the whole apparatus is so arranged that the net is towed slowly along, with the mouth and beam in front. The beam is raised about three feet from the ground by the trawl-irons, and never touches the bottom, unless the trawl should capsize before it arrives there. The trawl can only be used with advantage on smooth ground. A sandy bottom is preferred, not only from that being the usual resort of soles and other valuable kinds of ground fish, but from the less danger there is on such a surface of tearing the net to pieces. The vessels from which these deep-sea trawls are worked are from thirty-five to sixty tons burthen, or even more, the size of the trawl depending on that of the vessel The whole number of trawlers at present in existence, is nearly 1000. The value is, at least,

£1,000,000 sterling. The whole number of fishing boats of all sizes is 9300, worked by 37,416 men and 5530 boys. Trawlers are fine sea-going craft, smack-rigged, and capable of standing a great deal of rough work, as will be evident when it is remembered that the large fleet of trawlers, exposed to the uncertain weather of the North Sea, stay out, as a rule, for six weeks at a time, in all seasons of the year, their fish being collected daily, packed in ice, and conveyed to market by fast-sailing cutters of 100 tons burthen, constructed expressly for speed, and whose captains or owners are interested in getting all the fish delivered in marketable condition. Codfish, ling, and haddock, are taken by means of long lines. A complete set of long lines consists of about fifteen dozen lines, each of which is forty fathoms long, and has twenty-six hooks, on short lines, called snoods, passing to the main line at intervals of a fathom and a half, so as to prevent their fouling one another. These lines, about 180 in number, are united into one, and as the vessel sails on are shot across the tide, so that the snoods may all hang clear. In this manner the whole eight miles or more of line, and nearly 5000 hooks, are paid out, small anchors being placed at the extremities, and at intervals of forty fathoms along the line, to keep it in position at the bottom. As soon as the cod and haddock are taken off the hook, they are put into a well, formed by a part of the smack's hold, divided from the rest of the vessel by water-tight bulkheads. The well occupies the whole breadth of the vessel, and the sea-water has free access to it through auger holes bored in the sides and bottom of that part of the smack. The fish are thus kept alive and fresh, until it is convenient to send them to market. The bait most in favour with the North Sea cod fishermen, is the common large whelk, but on many parts of the coast herrings are by far the most attractive, and at certain seasons, the only killing bait, for cod. Mussels are perhaps more commonly used as bait than anything else, for general line fishing. The shrimp nets are worked with a wooden beam nine or ten feet long, weighted with lead, placed on the lower side of the mouth of the net. These shrimp nets are towed with the tide, and are hauled up at intervals, ranging from a quarter of an hour to an hour, according to the wind and the extent of ground gone over. About thirty quarts is an ordinary take in boats used in Morecambe Bay; but in the shrimp fishery near the mouth of the Thames, 100 gallons of shrimps have been taken by one vessel in a single day; and it is no uncommon occurrence for 2000 gallons to be sent to London market, as the joint produce of a day's fishing, by the southern shrimpers. The quantity of shell-fish caught in Morecambe Bay, and sent inland by the Midland Railway, amounted in 1864 to 1506 tons, independent of 272 tons forwarded from Lancaster The whole quantity of fish caught in Morecambe Bay, and sent inland by the Midland Railway, amounted in the year 1862, to 2482 tons; in 1863, to 2274 tons; and in 1864, to 2056 tons. The quantity forwarded from Fleetwood in 1862, by railway, was 670 tons; in 1863, 886 tons, and in 1864, 1003 tons Large quantities of fish are also taken at Blackpool, Lytham, Preston, and Southport, but are consumed by the numerous visitors and resident population. In the same manner the still larger quantities taken by the Liverpool trawlers, in the Irish Sea, and by the smaller class of trawlers and shrimpers of the Mersey and the Dee, are consumed at Liverpool and Chester. The Chester and Holyhead Railway also brings about 2000 tons of fish yearly, to be disposed of in Lancashire and Cheshire.

Having described the seas, with their products, and the winds, tides, and bays of the north-western district, we proceed to give an account of the soil and the vegetable and mineral products of the same district.

The Soil, Climate, Plants, and Animals of Lancashire and Cheshire.—At the time when the Ordnance survey of Lancashire was made, about fifteen years ago, the land within the county, amounting to 1,117,260 statute acres, was in this condition:—About 350,000 acres was in tillage; about 450,000 acres in pasture; and 317,260 in woodland, mountain, moor or peat moss, much of the latter being uninclosed, and some of it entirely waste. In Cheshire the quantity of uninclosed and waste land was very much less, both absolutely and in proportion, than in Lancashire, though we have not so accurate or recent an account of its extent. The area of the registration county of Chester is 680,836 statute acres At the time when Holland published his very excellent account of the agriculture of Cheshire, in the year 1808, he estimated the arable, meadow, and pasture land of that county at 620,000 acres, and the waste lands at only 56,000 acres, leaving but a small quantity unaccounted for. Since that time several thousand acres of waste land have been reclaimed in Cheshire, so that even supposing Holland's estimate to have been below the mark, the quantity still lying waste cannot be much more than from 30,000 to 40,000 acres. Taking the whole of the land of the north-western district at 2,000,227 acres, there may probably be about 1,700,000 acres of arable, grass, and woodland, and 300,000 acres of uninclosed mountain and waste land, most of it covered with heath.*

But the reclaiming of the waste lands of this district is still proceeding actively, and up to the year 1858, out of 26,125 acres of land inclosed in England under the authority of the Inclosure Commissioners, 4446 acres were inclosed in the county of Lancaster; in addition to 2887 acres previously inclosed in the same county, and also to 1719 acres inclosed in the county of Chester, under the provisions of the General Inclosure Act. Since that time a moderate quantity of land has been inclosed every year; and these reclamations are likely to continue, for land is the kind of property most eagerly sought for in England by capitalists, it is that which is most steadily increasing in value; and it is the only kind of property of which there is a limited supply in this country. An account of the principal reclamations of land effected during the last fifty years will be found in these pages.†

The waste lands of Lancashire and Cheshire are of various kinds The first consist of heath-covered mountains, and barren rocks, rising to the height of from 1000 to 2500 feet, the second of wild hills and uplands, rising from 500 to 1000 feet, the third of peat mosses, some of them of the extent of 5000 to 6000 acres, and the fourth of marshes on the banks of estuaries and rivers, also very extensive, but exposed to the waves of the sea, and to sudden floods from the rivers, after heavy rain on the mountains.

The soils of the different districts of the counties of Lancaster and Chester vary greatly in fertility, with the geological formation of the rocks on which they rest, the nature of the earthy deposits of which they are composed, and with the amount of their elevation above the sea.

A rich alluvial plain, extending forty miles in length from north to south, and five to ten miles in breadth from west to east, runs along the western coast of Lancashire, from the mouth of the Lune to the entrance of the Mersey, and reappears to the south of the Mersey, in the Leasowes of Cheshire.‡

Between the Lune and the Ribble, in the fertile district known

* Ordnance Survey, Lancashire, 1852 Holland's Report on the Agriculture of Cheshire

† Land Inclosure, England and Wales Miscellaneous Statistics of the United Kingdom, laid before Parliament.

‡ Geological Map of England and Wales, by Andrew C. Ramsay, F R.S. & G S, Local Director of Geological Survey of Great Britain, Professor of Geology in the Government School of Mines, London

as the Fylde, this alluvial soil is of great depth and almost inexhaustible fertility It is chiefly formed of beds of drift, consisting of earth, clay, sand, and till, and is everywhere full of boulders, or large rounded stones of great size, apparently torn in some remote age from the rocks amongst the Cumbrian mountains, and carried far from their original site, either by the currents of the ocean, by floating icebergs, or by other great natural forces. These granite and other boulders extend from the Cumberland mountains at the head of Wast Water Lake, throughout great part of the counties of Lancashire, Cheshire, and Staffordshire An almost uninterrupted stream of boulders can be traced on the west side of the mountainous lands of Derbyshire, Yorkshire, and Lancashire, from the point from which the stream seems to have commenced, viz., in the granites and slates of the Cumbrian mountains, near Ravenglass It is believed that the origin and direction of the floods or currents by which the boulders buried in the drift beds of Lancashire and Cheshire, and occasionally scattered over the ground, were borne southward, can be traced by the nature of those stones In the northern parts of Lancashire, near to the Cumbrian mountains, the boulders consist of remains of granite, transition, and slate rocks, such as are found in the neighbouring mountains of Cumberland and Westmoreland, in the proportion of eighty per cent, whilst further south the boulders consist of the remains of rocks of the coal formation, such as are found in the hills of South Lancashire, in the proportion of fifty per cent; the other fifty belonging to the rocks of the Cumbrian mountains. Along the coast of North Lancashire, in the neighbourhood of Blackpool, the soil in which these boulders are buried rises from the sea-shore, in lofty earth-banks sixty to eighty feet in height. These earth-banks belong to the class of deposits to which geologists formerly gave the name of diluvium, from the belief that they had been left by the waters of the Deluge But that opinion has lost ground, owing to the great thickness of the beds, which speaks rather of ages than of weeks or months of immersion, and also on account of the immense extent of land that is covered by them According to Mr. E. W. Binney, the till, mixed with this earth, is the principal soil in which plants grow and seeds ripen, and from which men and animals are sustained In many places it is thinly scattered over the poorer soils, which it fertilizes; but in North Lancashire and some other districts it is found in beds many feet in thickness This soil is now known as "drift," from the evidence that its form and contents present of its having been drifted from a distance; as "northern drift," from the fact of its having apparently been generally drifted from the north towards the south, and as "glacial drift," from a belief prevalent among geologists, that it was originally deposited in the waters of an icy sea, covered with icebergs bearing along with them fragments of the rocks from the mountains amongst which the icebergs were formed It is stated that few sea-shells are found in the drift of Lancashire and Cheshire, deposited inland to the east of a line running from Preston to Congleton, in Cheshire, but that many sea-shells are found near the sea-coast, west of a line running from Preston to Runcorn. Between Preston and Longridge Fells, shells of still existing or recent species have been found in the gravel, at a height of 350 feet. An eminent geologist, Mr. E W. Binney, who has very carefully examined the earth-beds of the drift formation, in all parts of Lancashire and Cheshire, after giving many interesting particulars respecting them, adds, that "the sand and gravel found in the drift are supposed to be sands and beaches of ancient seas; and the clay, till, or earth found in it in thick beds, to be the mud deposited ages ago at the bottom of the seas, on the waters of which floated icebergs, freighted with various rocks, which on being dissolved or toppled over, deposited their loads on the soft mud below" Nearly the whole district of the Fylde in North Lancashire, containing the most fertile soils and some of the best cultivation in that county, consists of earth-beds covered with or belonging to the drift formation. That soil is equally favourable to the production of grain, roots, and grasses *

South of the Ribble, a considerable part of the division of Ormskirk, containing an area of 111,968 statute acres, and extending to the mouth of the river Mersey at Bootle, is composed of the same rich alluvial deposits. They form excellent, easily-worked land, very suitable for the growth of grain and roots Much of this land lies low, especially along the banks of the rivers Douglas and Yarrow and the lake of Martin Mere, and from being frequently flooded, it has in many places a peaty soil The natural herbage is rich and abundant, and the demand for milk and dairy produce is so great in this district, that the pastures and meadows are

* Essay on the Geology of the Lake District, by John Phillips, M A, F R S, F G S, in Black's Picturesque Guide to the English Lakes. E W Binney, Esq Memoirs of the Manchester Literary and Philosophical Society, vol x., p 128. Fourth Report of British Association, on Marine Shells of Recent Species found near Preston by William Gilbertson

often allowed to lie in grass for many years The extensive water meadows along the streams are seldom if ever touched with the plough

The soil of this part of the Lancashire plain varies considerably in proceeding from the sea-shore towards the hills. Near the sea the soil consists chiefly of sand, rising along the shore in downs of the height of sixty to eighty feet, and continually maintained at that elevation, by the action of the westerly winds on the sand of the sea-shore In many places the sand from these downs, or hills, has been driven inland for several miles In one case at least, that of Raven Meols, a few miles north of Liverpool, the encroachments of the sand have compelled the inhabitants to abandon their ancient village and burial-place These sand-hills, by cutting off the natural drainage to the sea, have in some cases produced swamps, covering beds of turf, and producing dwarf wild roses and other sea-plants in great abundance. The remains of ancient forests are also found imbedded in the soil, and along with the trunks, branches, and fruit of oaks and other forest trees, are found the bones and the horns of the wild oxen and deer that once sheltered in the forests, and grazed on the neighbouring plains The trunks and roots of numerous forest trees are also found on the shore, between high water and low water mark, firmly fixed in the ground on which they originally grew. This must then have been above the reach of the sea, whose waves now beat over these trunks at every tide, showing a considerable change in the level of the land Swarms of rabbits contrive to subsist amongst these sand-downs, in the numerous rabbit warrens that line the shore; and innumerable flocks of sea-birds, whose nests are on the rocky coasts of North Wales and North Lancashire, find an abundant subsistence on the marine remains, left on the sands of the shore and the adjoining sand-banks, which line the coasts of Cheshire and Lancashire from the mouth of the Dee to that of the Lune Such is the rapidity of the flight of many of the more powerful both of the sea and the land birds, that they easily traverse a distance of thirty or forty miles from their breeding places, both morning and evening. Thousands of these birds may be seen on the banks or in the shallow waters at the entrance of the Lancashire and Cheshire rivers, when the tide is out, feeding on the small animals left by the receding tide

Between the Mersey and the Dee still loftier sand-hills line the sea-coasts, and in high winds disperse the sand from their summits over the level lands of the interior, when the sand is not held together by the planting of star grass or other marine plants.

Several small streams, of which the Douglas, the Alt, and the Birkett bear the name of rivers, make their way into the sea, or into the estuaries of the Ribble and the Mersey, through or along these sandy shores On their banks the land is very rich, and forms the moist pastures, named Leasowes, which are natural meadows, generally flooded in the winter months Herds of cattle and young stock graze in the leasowes. The water meadows along the banks of the Ribble, the Douglas, and the Alt, have been formed with great care and skill, being thoroughly irrigated in the winter and spring months, and well embanked to guard against summer floods, they produce large quantities of juicy hay, suited for milk cows. Many cows are kept in this district, and much milk and butter produced

In severe winters the Alt meadows, which are then always flooded, are frozen, and form a fine skating ground for the youth of Liverpool, numbers of whom resort to them for that favourite amusement When dry, these meadows are also used for the sport of coursing Hares are very plentiful in the Alt meadows, and there are no hedges to conceal their rapid movements, or those of the pursuing greyhounds. Behind the sand-hills, and above the level of the meadows, a range of alluvial lands runs into the interior for a distance of five or six miles This land is sandy and light when not marled, but constant cultivation and manuring has turned it into a very rich soil It yields large crops of potatoes, wheat, oats, clover, and garden produce The Southport and East Lancashire Railways, and the Leeds and Liverpool Canal, run through this district for many miles, and bring from Liverpool the means of renewing the soil at a small cost Much of the garden produce, consumed by the half million persons collected in and around Liverpool, is grown on this land, which is as easily worked with the spade as with the plough. On the Cheshire side of the Mersey the market gardens of Wallasey produce the earliest spring vegetables for the Liverpool market Those gardens are formed on the sunny slopes, with a south-western aspect, stretching from the new red sandstone rock on which Wallasey is built, to the rich mould of the alluvial formation. Market gardening is an extensive branch of industry in Lancashire and Cheshire, and furnishes support to several thousand families*

The valleys of all the principal rivers of Lancashire and Cheshire are also covered with a rich alluvial soil deposited by the streams On the banks of the river Dee, the alluvium commences a little below Bangor, and extends, by the meadows of Eaton Hall, down to Chester, where it widens out on one side into the Sealands—a district recovered from the estuary of the Dee in modern times, and on the other, into the rich levels that extend along the south side of the Dee, from Chester to the mouth of the river On the banks of the river Weaver, the alluvial deposits commence below Winsford Bridge, disappear where the stream runs through the narrow passage at Northwich, and then widen into beds of wonderful richness, which clothe the beautiful Vale Royal of Chester with perpetual green On the river Dane, the alluvial deposits commence almost immediately after the stream rushes from the hills, and enters the plain of Cheshire at Congleton, and continue to Northwich, where the Dane joins the Weaver In the Mersey, the alluvial soil commences near Irlam and Cadishead, where the Mersey and the Irwell join their waters, and continues down to Runcorn, the river cutting its way through the soft beds of earth with a hundred windings, and forming numerous "eeas" or river peninsulas, some of which have been cut through to improve the navigation of the stream. The Douglas, the Ribble, and the Wyre, all flow through the alluvial formation for many miles before they reach the sea The Lune enters a rich district of alluvial land after rushing through the rapids of the Crook of Lune There are immense tracts of alluvial land about the mouth of the Lune, and in Morecambe Bay, which will no doubt be reclaimed before many years have passed†

The alluvial meadows of Lancashire and Cheshire are very rich, consisting of a deep deposit, constantly freshened by fine earth brought down by heavy floods from the higher grounds. Without any manuring they yield large crops of the most fragrant hay every summer, and afford rich pasture for cattle during the winter months, when there is no grass on the uplands. Each of the numerous streams that descends from the hills of the two counties has its fringe of green meadow. Many of these streams are skilfully embanked, and furnished with floodgates and artificial water courses,

* Census of England and Wales, 1861 Occupations of the People.
† Geological Survey of Board of Ordnance

by means of which the waters can be brought on the land as the streams rise, and be let off as they fall. Some of the finest meadows are in the neighbourhood of Stretford and Ashton-on-Mersey, where a new water-course has been cut to carry off the floods of the river after heavy rains Most of the streams of Lancashire and Cheshire used to rise rapidly within six or seven hours after a heavy fall of rain on the hills, but during the last thirty years, many large reservoirs, including those for the supply of Liverpool, Manchester, Bolton, and other populous towns, have been formed amongst the hills, and retain many million gallons of water that was formerly discharged into the sea within twelve hours after it had fallen on the mountains

Many thousand acres of land have been added to the available extent of the two counties by reclaiming from the sea, and from the banks of the numerous estuaries which indent the coast, extensive districts of land, formerly overflowed at spring tides by the waves of the sea.

Near the mouth of the river Lune, a very valuable tract of land was reclaimed by the late Mr. Edward Dawson of Aldcliffe Hall, and has been so thoroughly improved as to increase its value from 2*s* 6*d* to 25*s*. per acre Mr W G Garnett also states, in his Report to the Royal Society of Agriculture on the Agriculture of Lancashire, that there are very extensive tracts of land in Morecambe Bay, now overflowed by spring tides, but which might be converted into valuable land if secured against the irruptions of the sea. The sands of Cockerham, Pilling, and Turnham, which cover upwards of 5000 acres, and are at present worth little or nothing, are capable of being made into good land, worth upwards of £5000 a year On this subject, Mr Garnett says —"Of late years science has been directed to the great scheme of internal communication by railway, which has absorbed the surplus funds of the country; but as those extensive works approach their completion, it is to be hoped that public attention will be turned to such undertakings as the inclosure of the bay of Morecambe, for which the coast of Lancashire seems distinguished by peculiar advantages, as it is estimated that more than 80,000 acres of land might be reclaimed to the north of the river Wyre"*

In the estuary of the Mersey upwards of 13,000 acres of land,

* Report on the Agriculture of Lancashire by William James Garnett Journal of the Royal Agricultural Society of England, vol x, p 45

formerly flooded at high tides, has been embanked and reclaimed at various times; and this would have been carried much further if the inclosing of the shores of this estuary had not been put an end to by the provisions of the Mersey Conservancy Act of 1842. That Act has forbidden the reclaiming of any additional land on the shores of the Mersey, from a fear that it might have the effect of diminishing the quantity of water which flows into and out of the river at every tide, and by doing so, of decreasing the force of the tidal wave, whose continual flux and reflux keeps open the narrow passage into the Mersey. By that Act the Conservators have the right of pulling down and removing anything that may be erected in the river, below the level of high water mark.*

In the river Dee, on the other hand, the reclaiming of the bed of the estuary has been carried on, under authority of an Act of Parliament, for upwards of one hundred years, and is in progress to the present day. What is called the Sealand of Chester is the land reclaimed from the estuary. It covers some thousands of acres, and forms a light soil, easily worked, and producing large crops of potatoes, grass, and corn. The salt marshes of the river Dee are still more extensive, and they will be inclosed when they are completely covered with grass. That will soon be the case with the salt marshes extending down to Burton Point, on the Cheshire side of the river. These marshes are already grazed in summer by flocks of sheep, though they are still flooded at high tides. In the winter months they form a feeding ground and place of resort for numerous flocks of wild fowl, including wild ducks, wild geese, and occasionally swans. This is one of the few spots in England in which a fowler is able to live by the produce of his gun. A very large quantity of land has also been inclosed on the banks of the river Ribble.

The power of the steam-engine, which has been applied successfully to the draining of many hundred thousand acres of land in the Fens of Lincolnshire, and of the Isle of Ely in Cambridgeshire, has also been applied with success in Lancashire in carrying off the waters of Martin Mere, the great natural reservoir which receives the drainage of the mosses and the floodings of the rivers from the Leyland hundred. In former times Martin Mere was a great lake or swamp, not less than eighteen miles in circumference, and covered an extensive district, great part of which

* Mersey Conservancy Act, 1842.

is now converted into fertile land. It was in the earlier attempts to drain this morass that some singular remains of antiquity were found, consisting of coracles or canoes of the kind used by the ancient Britons. Several of these were found in a bed of marl below the waters of the mere. A few years ago, an additional portion of this ancient mere was drained by Sir Thomas Hesketh, Bart., M.P., of Rufford Hall, by means of steam-power. For this purpose he caused a steam-engine of twenty horse-power to be constructed, which pumps up the waters of the mere to such a height as to cause them to flow into the sea. The process of pumping is as follows:—"To the engine is attached a large water-wheel thirty feet in diameter, with forty scoops or buckets ranged around its circumference. These buckets, when the wheel is revolving at its ordinary speed, raise and discharge into a sluice forty-five tons of water per minute, or upwards of seven million and a half of gallons in twelve hours. The water thus discharged into the sluice flows for a distance of four miles before it reaches the Cylinders of Crossens, where it passes into the river Ribble. It is calculated that the whole quantity of water which is lodged in Martin Mere yearly is 25,000,000,000 gallons, of which the land belonging to Sir Thomas Hesketh formerly received 250,000,000 gallons. This is carried off in the manner above described. To prevent the return of the water on to the land after it has been raised into the sluices, an embankment of four and a half feet in height, and upwards of three miles in length, has been raised along the margin of the sluice. This new draining apparatus was set to work, for the first time, on Tuesday the 9th of April, 1850, and on the Thursday following the water was reduced to four feet below the surface of the land, to which depth the pumps easily keep it. About 800 acres of land, a large portion of which formerly produced a scanty herbage of the poorest grasses, has thus been brought into cultivation, and now produces all kinds of crops." Some of the land is very fertile and suited to the growth of potatoes, turnips, and other vegetables, which are grown as well if not better on the light rich lands around Rufford, than in any other part of England.*

But the alluvial soil of Lancashire and Cheshire forms only a fringe along the sea-shore, and on the banks of the rivers. The soil that covers the greater part of the plain of Lancashire and Cheshire, extending over an area of a million of acres of land,

* Rothwell's Report on the Agriculture of Lancashire, p. 48.

employing the greater part of the cultivators of the district, and feeding a considerable portion of its inhabitants, is formed of beds of earth, sand, and marl, covering the new red sandstone rock. This formation, which is now divided by geologists into two parts, known as the permian and the trias formations, extends over a greater portion of the two counties than any other, but it is much more extensively developed in Cheshire than in Lancashire, and is almost everywhere a fertile soil, except where covered with beds of peat.

The hills of the new red sandstone formation seldom rise to a greater height than 500 to 600 feet, and are usually covered with grass to the summit. The greatest height to which the new red sandstone rock rises in Lancashire or Cheshire is between 500 and 600 feet Even that is only at two or three points, chiefly situated in Delamere Forest and the Peckforton hills, in Cheshire, two divisions of the sandstone chain of heights, which together extend across the county from the Mersey, at Runcorn, to the Dee, near Overton At Helsby Hill, where Delamere Forest terminates northward in a bold sandstone cliff, still covered with the remains or the outline of a British camp, this rock rises to a height of 500 feet above the waters of the Mersey, whose course it overlooks from Runcorn to the open sea. The same rock rises to the height of nearly 600 feet in the middle of Delamere Forest, at Eddisbury Hill, where the daughter of Alfred the Great—Ethelfleda, the lady or queen of the Mercians—built the Saxon fortress of Eddisbury, the foundations of which can still be traced, and which gives name to the surrounding hundred of Eddisbury The new red sandstone rock also rises quite as high in the rugged precipitous cliff on which Ranulf, the great earl of Chester, erected the famous and still magnificent castle of Beeston It rises nearly as high on the rugged fronts of Roehead and Bickerton Hill. This is almost the only part of the formation on which the natural herbage of the soil consists of heath, and not of grass. Until the year 1813, the heights of Delamere Forest, as well as the summits of the Peckforton hills, were covered with heath and entirely uncultivated, forming a mountain pasture for 20,000 or 30,000 sheep. Since that time the forest has been inclosed, and much of it cultivated by private proprietors, whilst the large range of land assigned to the crown has been planted with a forest of oak trees, which extends over a wide expanse of land, and presents a noble appearance from the mound of Ethelfleda's Fortress. The heath still remains in its original wildness, and in autumn in all its natural beauty, on the side of Roehead, and on the summit of Bickerton Hill, where it covers and has helped to preserve the ramparts of the great British fortress formed on the rugged brow of that lofty hill. The line of Alderley Edge, now covered with beautiful villas, is another fine specimen of the bold escarpment of the new red sandstone rock, and commands magnificent views of the plains of Cheshire and the distant hills on the borders of Derbyshire With these, and a few other exceptions, the land resting on this formation is of very moderate height, both in the counties of Lancashire and Cheshire, and possesses a soil and elevation well suited for culture.

In former times Delamere Forest was a forest of red deer, of very great extent, and was the favourite hunting ground of the earls of Chester Oakmere, the largest of the many meres which still exist in the forest, belonged to the abbots of Vale Royal, who had a fishery there. By an Act of 1812, certain commissioners were authorized to inclose all that remained of the forest. The waste lands at that time amounted to 7755 acres, two roods, and thirty-five poles. In the division of this land, one-half was given to the crown, the other half to the adjoining landed proprietors. The Lake of Oakmere was allotted to the Cholmondeleys of Vale Royal, together with the stone quarries on Eddisbury Hill, and the two lakes, named Fish Pool and Halchew Mere, were assigned to the Egertons of Oulton One moiety of the whole forest was allotted to the crown, to be kept under the direction of the surveyor-general of Woods and Forests, as a nursery for timber trees The land allotted to private proprietors has been inclosed and let in farms, that allotted to the crown has been planted with oak and larch timber In driving from Northwich to Chester, in crossing the forest from east to west, you pass through the plantations for a distance of two or three miles, but their full extent is only seen by those who cross the forest from north to south, from Frodsham to Tarporley As a whole they are well-grown and healthy, but they vary in luxuriance with the nature of the soil. This in some places is a drift of sand and gravel, in others a hard rock, and in others a deep red marl—the last being particularly suitable for the growth of oaks. Dr Ormerod, writing forty years ago, in his learned and valuable "History of Cheshire," of the ancient forest of Delamere, and of the woods and timber of Cheshire, observed:—"In most parts of

Cheshire the hedgerow timber, and the extensive plantations which adorn the principal seats, amply atone for the loss of these (ancient) forests. Among the latter may be particularly mentioned the noble oak woods of Dunham Massey, and a similar scene will be exhibited in the course of this century by the plantations of Vale Royal and other seats near Delamere Forest, and those made there, under the recent Inclosure Acts, on royal allotment. In many parts of the country, land abandoned to itself would be spontaneously covered with ash and alder."* Great care is taken to guard and watch the plantations, and to preserve them from injury. Even the squirrels, which are very numerous in these woods, are not altogether allowed—

"To bound from tree to tree,
And shell their nuts at liberty,"

but are kept down in numbers, lest in eating too many acorns they should destroy the germs of future forests.

The land at the foot of these new red sandstone hills is very fertile; and in Cheshire it usually presents the appearance of a wide grassy plain, grazed by numerous herds of cattle of almost every variety of colour. In Lancashire it is more undulating, and a larger portion of it is under the plough. The soil is generally composed of beds of earth, with much marl and clay, except where the rock rises near the surface of the ground There the soil is generally thin, and requires to be well marled, to render it capable of bearing grain, or even the better kinds of grasses, for any length of time. Many parts of the plain of Cheshire are dotted with meres, or small lakes These meres are formed in natural hollows in the deep clay of the trias formation. Into these hollows the waters of the adjoining districts flow in small streams, or springs of water rise from them and fill the basins, until the water finds an exit either at the surface, or by openings in the higher strata. Many of these meres contain several kinds of fish, and are frequented by wild fowl, as well as by great flocks of swallows and starlings, in the autumn months. About Budworth Mere we have seen flocks of starlings, in the month of September, that completely darkened the air when they rose from the reeds around the mere. These meres form drinking places for the numerous cattle of the adjoining pastures There are from thirty to forty meres of considerable size in the county of Chester, and a few in Staffordshire and Shropshire.

* Ormerod's History of Cheshire

They are beautiful objects in the landscape, as seen from the neighbouring hills, glittering on the grassy plains in the sunshine, like mirrors of polished silver.

The stiff soils of the trias branch of the new red sandstone formation, in Lancashire and Cheshire, are also spotted in many places with brown peat mosses, some of the largest of which extend over several thousand acres of land. These mosses are produced by the gradual accumulation and partial decay of heaths and moss, on wet clayey soils, which afford no sufficient outlet for the abundant moisture of a rainy climate, either downwards by openings into the more pervious soils, or laterally by a natural fall into streams or rivers. On the clayey soils of the Lancashire and Cheshire plains, these mosses, in a long course of ages, and when land was of little value, gradually spread over great extents of ground; and the mosses, and other bog-plants which compose them, accumulated, till they formed beds of peat, in some cases from twenty to thirty feet in thickness. These peat mosses hold water like immense sponges, never becoming thoroughly dry, even in the hottest summers Very large tracts of the Lancashire and Cheshire mosses have, however, been reclaimed during the last fifty years, and some of them turned into good arable land. When thoroughly drained to a great depth, and if possible to the bottom of the peat, and well worked, marled, and manured, they form good light land, well suited for the growth of oats, potatoes, turnips, and clover. They also make excellent garden ground, producing every kind of garden vegetable in abundance, and generally of very good quality.

In former times, when these mosses were altogether neglected, they sometimes became so full of water as to burst and spread a lava-like stream of peat mud over the adjoining lands, sending it down even into the brooks and rivers. Thus Chat Moss burst, with an eruption of peat mud, a little before the time when Camden visited Lancashire, during the reign of Queen Elizabeth, when, as he tells us, "the great peat moss or swamp of Chat Moss burst, and sent down a torrent of peat, earth, and water, into the river Irwell," through the pretty little valley of Glazebrook But nothing of this kind has now happened for many years, or is likely to happen again; for large portions of all the Lancashire mosses have been drained, and are now under cultivation; and the Liverpool and Manchester Railway has been carried across the softest and deepest part of Chat Moss, by the bold and enterprising genius of George Stephenson. Since this great moss was drained the soil has collapsed, so that the moss has lost many feet of its previous thickness By constant draining it is gradually changing from the condition of a bog, twenty-eight to thirty feet thick, to that of a bed of solid peat earth, only a few feet in thickness.*

The peat mosses of Great Britain and Ireland are a continuation of that region of heaths, which Humboldt, in his "Views of Nature," describes as extending on the Continent from the extremity of Jutland to the mouth of the river Scheldt.† In the British Islands, the regions covered with heath are chiefly found in the northern and western districts, where the vicinity of the ocean produces a yearly rainfall of from thirty-five to forty inches on the plains, and of fifty to sixty inches amongst the mountains Wherever peat and heath are found on the eastern side of England, it is in districts, like the Isle of Ely and the Fens of Lincolnshire, which have been flooded by rivers Those immense swamps were formed about the twelfth century or earlier, by the accumulation of alluvial silt, near the mouths of the rivers Welland, Ouse, and Nene, causing a great backwater, which overspread the lower portion of the Bedford level and the Fens of Lincolnshire, and produced extensive tracts of peat moss. But in districts that are at once cool and moist, like Lancashire and Cheshire, the constant rainfall produces peat mosses without any overflow of rivers. "Peat," says Sir Charles Lyell, "has seldom if ever been discovered within the tropics, and rarely occurs in the valleys even in the south of France and Spain It abounds more and more in proportion as we proceed from the equator, and becomes, not only more frequent, but more inflammable in northern latitudes" On the sides of hills and mountains peat seldom attains a greater thickness than three or four feet, but on the plains and in the valleys it swells to a thickness of forty or fifty feet ‡ In those cases, however, it owes fully one-half of its volume to the water that it contains, which is held up in the pores of the moss by capillary attraction, as it is held in the pores of a sponge

The production of peat is thus confined to moist situations, where the temperature is low, and where the vegetable substances from which it is formed are produced in abundance. It is formed by the decay of a great variety of plants, even of the grasses; but,

* Camden's Britannia, Lancashire. † Ansichten der Natur, Alexander von Humboldt, vol i., p 5
‡ Lyell's Principles of Geology, p 719

according to Forchamer, vegetation does not throw down peat at a higher mean temperature than 43° to 44° of Fahrenheit. Frost occasionally causes its precipitation in warmer climates; but in such climates the attraction of the carbon for the oxygen of the air mechanically mixed with the water, increases with the increasing temperature, and the dissolved vegetable matter, or humic acid, being converted into carbonic acid, rises and is absorbed into the atmosphere.* At a lower temperature, the matter of peat is deposited in abundance in moist climates, and when deposited it produces and sustains a vegetation of its own. The plant named Sphagnum constitutes the principal part of the mosses found in Northern Europe. It possesses the property of throwing up new shoots in its upper part whilst its lower extremities are decaying; and thus, by its rapid growth and partial decay, it is always adding something to the beds of peat in which it flourishes. The growth of this and other bog-plants, continued through a long course of ages, has produced the enormous beds of peat which exist in the northern parts of Europe.

Many of the larger mosses of Lancashire and Cheshire have been reclaimed with extreme difficulty, and portions of them still remain unreclaimed, owing to the lowness of the ground on which they are situated, compared with the level of the rivers and estuaries into which they have to be drained, and even with the sea itself. In some of them a deposit of peat seems to have taken place in deep hollows in the marl beds of the trias formation, which have become filled in the course of ages. In others, peat has been formed in hollows on upland plains, from which the half fluid moss has spread over the adjoining lands. Thus the highest point of the surface of Chat Moss is 100 feet above the level of the sea, whilst the bottom of the lowest of the peat beds of Chat Moss is stated by Mr G W. Ormerod, to be 100 feet below the sea level. On the peat mosses in the Fylde even the surface is so low as to give a fall of only a few inches per mile into the sea. In Martin Mere there is no natural fall into the sea, and there the water has to be pumped up by means of a steam-engine, into sluices embanked on both sides, which carry it down into the Ribble.

These extensive mosses still afford food and shelter to numbers of grouse, which, however, are very wild and difficult to shoot, although they allow the railway trains to rush and scream past

* Lyell's Principles of Geology, p 179

them without rising from their nests. The bittern was also formerly found among the deep pits around the larger mosses. Snipes are still pretty common, and wild ducks are occasionally found Before the winter sets in, these mosses are also visited by large flocks of wild geese, driven southward by the freezing of the northern marshes, and in the spring months they are revisited by the same flocks, in their flight back to the Highlands, and to the marshes of Scandinavia. The flocks of wild geese generally rest and recruit themselves on the Lancashire mosses for a few days. During that time their cries may be heard as they cruise above high in the air, sometimes flying in long lines, at other times in two sides of an acute-angled triangle, according to their usual mode of advancing on their great migrations The main body generally disappear in a few days, flying northward or southward, according to the season of the year, with that unerring instinct which Providence has given them for their preservation. The weaker birds sometimes stay a week or a fortnight, and occasionally a disabled bird remains during the winter, and disappears with the flocks of birds which fly northward in the spring In old times, when hawking was one of the favourite sports of our ancestors, footpaths, called hawk-paths, were formed into these mosses, whence the hawks could be seen darting on their prey They are still much frequented by wild hawks in pursuit of grouse and other birds The windhover hawk is often seen poising itself in the air by the beating of its wings, watching for its prey, and rushing, like a flash of lightning, through the air to seize it.

A few of the most extensive improvements that have been effected on the peat mosses of Lancashire and Cheshire, from the commencement of this century to the present time, may be noticed in passing

Fully one-half of the great swamp of Chat Moss, which formerly extended over between 6000 and 7000 acres of land, and was the largest as well as the most celebrated of all the mosses of Lancashire, has been reclaimed, from a state of utter barrenness and desolation, during the present century. Fifty years ago Chat Moss was an impassable wilderness, without a tree, a field, a house, or an inhabitant. About that time, and in a season when the whole country was suffering from scarcity and high prices of food, William Roscoe, of Liverpool—a man alike distinguished by his talents and his benevolence—first undertook the arduous task of reclaiming a large portion of that great waste, with a view of rendering it available for the support of man. For this purpose he obtained a lease of nearly 3000 acres of mossland, granted, under the authority of a private Act of Parliament, by the De Traffords of Trafford Park, who have been lords of the manor of Barton-on-Irwell, in which this part of Chat Moss is situated, for many ages With this permanent tenure, and at a rent of not more than one shilling an acre, Mr. Roscoe commenced his improvements. He built, drained, marled, planted, and reclaimed several hundred acres of land, forming wide and deep out-fall drains from the middle of the moss into the river Irwell, and whilst his affairs prospered, carried on cultivation with great spirit. About twenty years after Mr. Roscoe had commenced the cultivation of Chat Moss, the late Mr. Edward Baines, M P, of Leeds, took from Mr. Roscoe, for the remainder of his term, between 1100 and 1200 acres of the raw moss This he began to cultivate about the year 1822–23, and during the last thirty years of a most active life, chiefly spent in towns and cities, it was his favourite recreation to visit and watch the progress of the farms, plantations, orchards, and gardens, which he had formed on this great waste He had the pleasure of seeing a large tract of land, that he found a wilderness, transformed into fertile fields and flourishing plantations More than half the land held by Mr. Baines was sub-leased by him to Mr. Edward Evans, formerly of the Haigh Foundry, near Wigan, and was cultivated by him and his partners with very great spirit and skill. The farms that lie along the south side of the Liverpool and Manchester Railway, near the middle of the moss, were formed by Mr. Evans In these improvements light railways, both fixed and movable, and worked by horses, were first used for farming purposes, and steam-power was applied to every kind of indoor work in which it could be made available The land was abundantly marled, from the immense marl beds that lie under and around the moss.

During the last five and twenty years a considerable portion of Chat Moss, lying on the north side of the Liverpool and Manchester Railway, was reclaimed by the first earl of Ellesmere, and formed part of the numerous improvements made on the Worsley estate, and elsewhere, by a most amiable and accomplished nobleman, whose life was unfortunately too short to enable him to carry out the many plans of public usefulness which he steadily pursued from the commencement to the close of his useful and honourable career. Extensive improvements have also been made, on that part of Chat Moss that lies near to Astley, by Colonel Ross of Astley Hall, and on the parts adjoining Tildesley by Mr. G W. Ormerod, who has published a sketch of his improvements, together with many curious particulars as to the natural history of this great morass, along with other valuable papers, in the "Reports of the British Association for the Advancement of Science." On the south-west side of Chat Moss, that portion of it known as Cadishead Moss was reclaimed, inclosed, and divided amongst the owners of the adjoining lands about the years 1852–53. Much waste land has also been reclaimed on the central plain, which forms the highest part of the moss, by Mr. Makinson, and others, chiefly connected with Manchester. The general result of all these improvements is that some thousand acres of land, that had not produced a blade of useful grass or an ear of corn in the memory of man, are now converted into good land. In a few years the several plans of improvement commenced on all sides of Chat Moss will meet in the centre, and meadows, pastures, and cornfields will everywhere take the place of barren heath.

Very extensive mosses, covering an area of 20,000 acres, exist in that part of North Lancashire which is known as the Fylde. These mosses, which are named Pilling, Rowcliffe, and Nately, rest, like the mosses of South Lancashire and Cheshire, on thick beds of clay or marl, and are situate near the junction of the trias formation, with the millstone grit on one side, and the alluvial deposits of the Fylde on the other. That part of this extensive range of mosses, which is named Rowcliffe Moss, was cultivated with great spirit and success by the late Mr T R. Wilson Ffrance of Rowcliffe Hall. The principal difficulty in this case was in the lowness of the land, in comparison with the level of the adjoining sea, into which the water drained from these mosses had to be carried. Mr Wilson Ffrance, in commencing his improvements, found it necessary to open a great out-fall drain from the mosses into the sea, which had to be carried by a winding and circuitous route, for a distance of five or six miles, before a fall of even seven or eight inches to the mile could be obtained from the mosses into Lancaster Bay, into which they had to be drained. By means of this outfall an escape was formed for the waters of the district. Rowcliffe Moss has been drained into this outfall, and many hundred acres of that moss have been cleared from stagnant water and brought into a high state of cultivation.*

The late and the present earls of Derby have reclaimed a large portion of the extensive mosses of Rainford and Kirby, which are their property Mossbury Hall, the centre of these mosses, is surrounded by a large extent of land which has been reclaimed from the waste in a very superior manner. The land, besides being well drained and marled, is fenced with flourishing white-thorn hedges, provided with commodious farm buildings, and rendered accessible by a wide road formed through it, and leading from Knowsley Hall to Bickerstaff†

Whitley Reed, one of the wildest and deepest mosses in Cheshire, was reclaimed in the years 1850–51–52, under the superintendence of Mr. Henry White, of Warrington From being a mere swamp, in which it is said that snipes occasionally bred in the summer, and in which the members of the Cheshire Hunt were frequently in danger of being ingulfed in the hunting season, Whitley Reed has been converted into solid land, covered with pastures and meadows.

The new red sandstone formation extends from Morecambe Bay and Lower Furness, in the north of Lancashire, to the borders of Staffordshire and the south of Cheshire, and forms more than half the soil of the two counties To the east it is overlaid by the alluvial soils of which we have already spoken, to the west it overlies the coal, limestone, and millstone grit, forming the carboniferous system, of which we have still to speak It varies in breadth, from three or four miles, in the north of Lancashire, to forty or fifty miles, in the south of Cheshire

In the north the new red sandstone forms the rich arable land of Lower Furness, which is one of the most fertile and best cultivated districts of Lancashire

Passing southward, across Morecambe Bay, it appears near Cleveley in Lower Wyresdale, and runs in a narrow band from that point, through Garstang, to the neighbourhood of Preston on the Ribble. To the west it is bounded and covered by the alluvial beds of the Fylde, to the east it runs up into the valleys and openings in the millstone and limestone formations, presenting the appearance of

* Report on the Agriculture of Lancashire, by William James Garnett, Esq Journal of the Royal Agricultural Society of England, vol x, p 28

† Rothwell's Report on the Agriculture of the County of Lancaster, pp 34–41

the arms of a dried-up sea, whose waves seem once to have flowed amongst the hills It forms several very deep indentations both into the millstone grit and the mountain limestone formation The new red sandstone soil in this district is generally good land, and is kept chiefly in grass. The old vaccaries, or cow pastures of Wyresdale, which have existed from the most ancient times, and yielded a considerable income to the dukes of Lancaster, extended over parts of this formation, and up to the tops of the wilder hills. From the river Ribble to the Mersey the new red sandstone runs in a south-westerly direction, passing between Ormskirk and Scarisbrick, in a narrow band, and then widening, so as to fill up the whole district of country between Liverpool and Widness. It thence extends up the valley of the Mersey and the Irwell to Manchester and Stockport, running up the valley of the Irwell to Ringley above Manchester, and also up the valley of the Tame for a considerable distance above Stockport *

South of the Mersey the new red sandstone formation stretches over the length and breadth of Cheshire, covering the whole of that county, except in the mountainous range on the borders of Derbyshire, which belongs to the coal formation The quality of the land throughout Cheshire is in general very good. It is chiefly kept in grass, owing to the great demand for the cheese of that county. It is said, by a competent judge, that the produce of the grass lands of Cheshire has been, at least, doubled during the last thirty years †

To the east of the new red sandstone of Lancashire and Cheshire lie the soils which rest on the rocks of the carboniferous system, that is to say, the coal formation, the millstone grit, and the mountain limestone These soils cover only a small part of Cheshire, but they extend over more than the half of Lancashire ‡

The soil of the coal formation is in general stiff and wet, and not well suited for the growth either of roots or grain. In Lancashire it is generally kept in grass, and when well drained and manured, forms excellent pasture land, besides yielding large crops of hay During the last thirty years the grass land on the coal formation of Lancashire has been greatly improved by drainage and manuring. From the elevation and the nature of the soil this land does best in dry summers, such as those of 1864 and

* Geological Maps of Lancashire and Cheshire Ordnance Survey † Mr Henry White of Warrington
‡ Geological Maps of Lancashire and Cheshire Ordnance Survey

1865, in both of which the stiff soils of this district were covered with grass crops greatly superior to those of most parts of England *

The millstone grit, which also belongs to the carboniferous system, and sometimes contains thin beds of coal, is one of the most barren formations found in the kingdom. It almost defies cultivation Its natural herbage is heath and bent, without any mixture of the finer grasses. The rock is everywhere close to the surface. In general the millstone grit rises to a great elevation, with steep declivities, down which any good soil that may ever have covered them has been long since washed, by the heavy bursts of rain that fall on these hills. The millstone grit is very extensively spread over the county of Lancaster, both in the north and in the south It forms the great range of mountains, from 1200 to 1500 feet in height, that constitutes the eastern boundary of the two counties, running northward from the lofty height of Mowcop, where the Trent rises, on the borders of Staffordshire, to the northern bank of the river Lune.

South of the river Ribble, on the hills of the coal and millstone grit formation, in the neighbourhood of Accrington, the late Sir Robert Peel drained almost all his land, to the extent of 1000 acres, and improved the moorlands attached to his estate, in the township of Oswaldtwistle, situated at a height of 500 to 600 feet above the sea. Extensive improvements have also been made at a still greater elevation in the same neighbourhood, in the township of Haslingden, which rises 1000 feet and more above the level of the sea, by Mr John Hoyle of Haslingden, who is mentioned, in Mr. Rothwell's Report, as one of the most successful cultivators of waste or moorland, as well as by several other gentlemen who own property about Haslingden. The method of improvement generally adopted in this neighbourhood has been to inclose and drain, and then to spread lime on the surface, and, in some cases, both lime and marl. "In a few years that beautiful plant, in the summer and autumn, the red heath (*Erica vulgaris rubra*), and those sweet-smelling ones, the long myrtle, and the Lancashire asphodel, all die away, and better herbage springs up in their place" Improvements of the same kind have also been made on Horwich Moor and Turton Moor, at a still greater elevation. Cockey Moor, lying between Bolton and Bury, and belonging to the earl of Wilton, has also been reclaimed, trenched eighteen inches deep, and planted with

* MS Notes made by the Author

forest trees Bolton Moor and Dean Moor have been inclosed and improved, and so also has Siddal Moor, near Heywood Mr Rothwell mentions that part of Siddal Moor, purchased by Mr John Owen, of Prestwich, has been reclaimed in a very superior manner*

Nearly the whole of the long and lofty ridge of Longridge Fell, rising to the height of 1000 feet, has been planted, and partly with larch; there is also a good deal of planting in the wild cloughs and glens in the higher parts of Roeburndale, Wenningdale, Grizedale, and Wyresdale, to a height of 800 to 1000 feet.

On the high grounds rising above the valley of the Greta, in the neighbourhood of Wittington and Dalton, where the mountain shale and limestone, the millstone grit, the coal measures, and the red marls are strangely intermingled, considerable quantities of land have been reclaimed, on the line of road that crosses the hills from Burton to Kirkby Lonsdale. Mr. Rothwell states that the draining in these improvements is not sufficient, but adds that good fencing, and in some situations, planting, thorough draining, and a sufficient dressing of lime or bone dust would make a great portion of this land good pasture ground, whilst some of the flat, sheltered, or mossy parts would make excellent meadow, and might be irrigated at slight expense He says that in improving these high-lying moors, stone walls are the fences principally used for the inclosures, but recommends, as a better fence and shelter, that a cop should be raised eighteen inches above the surface of the ground, three feet thick at the top, with a quantity of lime, with guano or other manure mixed in on the top of the cop, and that on the soil thus prepared, hollies and gorse, or whins, should be planted These hardy bushes grow at great elevations, and if properly trained for a few years, not only serve as fences, but give that shelter against storms and winds which is so much needed on these lofty hills†

A few miles south of Lancaster considerable improvements have been made on Ellel Moor, where the millstone-grit formation approaches near to the sea The height of the ground is upwards of 300 feet, and the position of the land fully exposed to the western winds The soil is from two to five inches deep, producing in its natural state whins, or gorse, alder bushes, heather, and rushes. The subsoil is a yellow bastard clay, full of stones, frequently containing large quantities of iron, which makes the cutting of drains very difficult, the subsoil resting on the millstone-grit rock. This

* Rothwell's Report on the Agriculture of Lancashire, pp 22 and 21 † Ibid, p 23

wild land was greatly improved by Mr. Ford, of Ellel, and Mr. Richard Hinde, of Lancaster, and was made so friable and rich, as to enable the latter to gain the prize of the Lancaster Agricultural Society for Swedish turnips, and to produce the heaviest crops of mangold, rye-grass, oats, and beans. Thorough draining, the removing of upwards of a thousand one-horse cart loads of stones, and trenching on the deeper, stiffer soils, were the means of improvement adopted in this case.*

The mountain or carboniferous limestone is, on the contrary, a good soil, at almost all elevations. It is the prevailing formation in the valley of the Lune, and in the upper part of the valley of the Ribble. It contains much rich land on the lower grounds, and good sheep pasture on the hills. The meadows on the banks of the Lune and the Ribble are as fertile as they are beautiful, and the hills of this formation are covered with short sweet grass, even amongst the cliffs and scars. The mountain limestone is not found either in South Lancashire or in Cheshire, except in the township of Newbold Astbury, on the borders of Derbyshire and Staffordshire.

Nearly the whole of the limestone lands of Lancashire are in meadow or pasture, and yield the best herbage that is found in the country. Lunedale and Ribblesdale are amongst the richest districts in England.

The most ancient geological formation existing in Lancashire, but which is not found in Cheshire, is that of the Cumbrian shales and slates, closely connected with the Silurian formation. This is found in the district of Higher Furness, the extreme northern division of Lancashire, adjoining the mountains of Cumberland and Westmoreland. This district presents the aspect of lofty mountains, intersected by narrow valleys, with numerous streams and lakes. That portion of Furness which consists of limestone shale has a fertile, though shallow soil, and is covered with short sweet grass, grazed by sheep. At the extreme northern part of the county of Lancaster, near the springs of the river Duddon, the land rises into lofty mountains of slate, intersected here and there with dykes of porphyry, and other primitive rocks. Here vegetation nearly dies away, the mountains scarcely yielding sufficient herbage to support a few mountain sheep.†

On the limestone and limestone-shale hills of Cartmell and Furness many thousand acres of ground have been reclaimed, during the

* Mr. J. W. Gernett's Report on the Farming of Lancashire, in Journal of the Royal Agricultural Society, pp. 10–85.

† Ordnance Survey, Lancashire.

present generation, in the neighbourhood both of Broughton and Cartmell. The reclamations on Cartmell Fells have been very extensive, and much of the reclaimed land has been planted with larches and other kinds of trees. The rest is under the plough or in pasture. The method of reclamation adopted in this case was by inclosing, draining, and dressing the land with marl, clay, and sand No lime was used, the whole district lying on the limestone rock

In Higher Furness there are many thousand acres of thriving woods, consisting principally of the oak, the common and mountain ash, the elm, the hazel, and all such trees as shoot again quickly when cut down. These woods are cut every fifteen years, and the produce sells at from £5 to £25 per acre.* The woodlands of North Lancashire, as of most hilly districts, have been rendered much more valuable during the last fifty or sixty years, by the introduction of that hardy and useful tree, the larch, which has taken the place of the firs and pines that formerly darkened the hills. The larch being a native of the lower ranges of the Alps, where it grows in the chasms and gullies of the mountains, at an elevation of 5000 feet above the sea, and flourishing most in the coolness of a northern aspect, grows well in the highland districts of England and Scotland The decomposing rocks of the primary and transition formations, as granite, gneiss, mica, and clay slate, as Selby informs us in his valuable work on British Forest Trees, are its favourite ground Fixed in such a soil, on the steep and shelving sides of glens and narrow valleys, the roots of the larch are cooled and refreshed by the constant percolation of moisture, and receive the nourishment that is most favourable for the luxuriant growth and perfect development of the tree † The wood of the larch, according to Selby, is remarkable for its strength and durability, at every period of its growth, and it is pervaded by a resinous matter that gives it the power of resisting moisture As a mere stake it is of some value, at ten or twelve years' growth it becomes useful for railing; at fifteen or twenty years for posts, coal-mine props, and railway sleepers. At a later growth it forms a durable piling for the foundations of buildings, especially on the banks of rivers and in the beds of estuaries; and when fully grown it is available for nearly every purpose to which timber is applied. This most useful and hardy tree has given a greatly increased value to the woodlands of this and other mountain districts, and might be still more extensively planted with advantage, on nearly

* Rothwell's Report on the Agriculture of Lancashire

† Selby's History of British Forest Trees, p 483

all ground situated at an elevation of from 500 to 1500 feet above the level of the sea.

Lancashire and Cheshire are separated from the adjoining counties of Cumberland, Westmoreland, York, and Derby by lofty ranges of mountains, running southward from the Lake district of England, to the lofty height of Mowcop, on the borders of Staffordshire. The length of this range from north to south is nearly one hundred miles, its breadth is from ten to twenty miles, and the height of the mountains which compose it is from 1500 to 2500 feet It forms a large portion of what is called the Backbone of England, or more classically, the Pennine chain

In the district of Higher Furness, between the river Duddon and Windermere Lake, the highest point of this great chain rises steeply at the head of Coniston Water, in the mountain known as Coniston Old Man (the last word being a corruption of the ancient British word *maun*, a rock or stone), to the height of 2597 feet above the level of the sea. The Coniston mountain is surrounded by several other peaks, not more than 100 to 200 feet less lofty, some of which are in Lancashire and others in Westmoreland or Cumberland. The whole of Higher Furness is a region of mountains, lakes, and deep ravines, the sides of the latter overgrown with larches, firs, and pines. A hardy breed of sheep grazes the mountain pastures of Higher Furness and the adjoining counties, and furnishes the wool that in former times rendered the woollen manufactures of Kendal and Cartmell famous throughout England. A few years ago the black cock was very frequently found in the heather on these hills, and not many years before, the roe deer and even the red deer were sheltered in the woods of Higher Furness

Further south, between the Lune and the Ribble, the peaks and fells that separate Lancashire from Yorkshire rise almost as high as those of Furness The Colm or County stone, at the junction of Lancashire, Westmoreland, and Yorkshire, stands at a height of 2253 feet. The adjoining height of Greygarth Fell rises to 2057 feet The Wolfshole Crag is 1731, and the Wardstone, or Beacon, on Littledale Fell is 1836 feet above the sea. Further southward the Trough bank, above the mountain pass known as the Trough of Bowland, rises to the height of 1383 feet, being the highest point in the ancient red deer forest of Bowland The highest point of the Bleasdale Fells, where there was also another forest of red deer, in the time of Leland, rises to the height of 1750 feet, and the land around the springs of the Wyre, where there was a third forest of red deer in the same age, is of equal height. Even the long outline of Longridge Fell planted with larches and firs, rises to the height of more than 1000 feet. The Roman road from Ribchester to Overborow, on the higher part of the Lune, runs through the midst of these mountains, and can still be clearly traced at many points.*

South of the river Ribble, the country on the borders of Yorkshire and Lancashire is a mass of mountains. These mountains run westward almost across South Lancashire, and form a sort of amphitheatre of lofty heights, extending along the northern boundary of the Salford hundred and the southern boundary of the Blackburn hundred, sending almost innumerable streams both into the Mersey and the Ribble. Pendlehill is really the head of the dale, and towers over Ribblesdale to the height of 1830 feet. The Wolfstones in Trawden Forest rise to the height of 1400 feet, the Gorplestones to 1535 feet, Knoll-hill to 1375 feet; and Rivington Pike, almost in the centre of South Lancashire, and serving as a landmark to vessels in the Irish sea, to the height of 1545 feet. Most of the hills in the ancient deer forest of Rossendale are of the height of from 1200 to 1500 feet. Boulsworth-hill, which divides the watershed of the Yorkshire Calder from that of one of the Lancashire rivers of the same name, rises to the height of 1689 feet. These mountains contain numerous remains of antiquity, in the form of Druidical circles, hanging stones, tumuli, and camps erected by the Britons or the Romans. Three Roman roads run through these mountains from west to east, one a little to the south of Clitheroe, another to the south of Colne, and the third near Littleborough, and the great Roman road from Mamucium, or Mancunium (the present Manchester) to Ribchester, crosses it from south-east to north-west, passing close to the present town of Blackburn. To the south of Boulsworth-hill extends the long range of Blackstone-edge and Stanedge, the former of which is 1553 feet in height. Holme Moss, on the borders of Lancashire, Cheshire, and Yorkshire, rises to the height of 1859 feet.†

The land on the borders of Cheshire and Derbyshire, to the south of the Mersey and of its tributaries, the Etherow and the Goyt, though wild and mountainous, is not so barren as that of the district above described. The mountain chain is narrower, being bounded by the

* Memoirs of the Manchester Philosophical Society, second series, vol. vi. Papers on the Roman Roads in Lancashire, by John Just, Esq., Corresponding Member of the Society.

† All these heights are from the Ordnance Survey.

limestone district of Derbyshire on one side, and by the rich plains of Cheshire on the other. Cultivation is here carried higher up the sides of the hills The highest parts of Lyme Park, the ancient residence of the Leghs of Lyme, rise nearly 1000 feet above the Cheshire plain, and in these lofty pastures still roam in safety some specimens of the ancient breed of British cattle, that wandered at large on the hills of Lancashire and Cheshire as late as the reign of Henry VII In this district the Cwm rocks rise to the height of 1377 feet Chinley Churn rises to the height of 1403 feet, and the highest points of Macclesfield Forest to 1800 feet. In the reign of Edward I the wolves were so numerous and ferocious in Macclesfield Forest, that the king allowed a sum of money in the sheriffs' accounts, for the cost of wolf traps to destroy them. South of Macclesfield Forest, Axeridge, on the borders of Cheshire and Derbyshire, rises to the height of 1750 feet, whilst Mowcop, on the borders of Cheshire and Staffordshire, rises to about the same elevation. The range of mountains above described encircles the counties of Lancaster and Chester on the northern and eastern sides A range of hills rising more gradually to a height of 500 or 600 feet, runs along the southern border of Cheshire, separating that county from the greater part of Staffordshire and Shropshire, whilst the river Dee divides it from the loftier mountains of North Wales.

There are several Roman roads and other remains of antiquity on the mountains near, or to the south of, the river Mersey. Two of their lines of road pass up the valley of the river Tame above Staleybridge, one up that of the Mersey and the Etherow, near Mottram, whilst a fourth crosses the heights of Macclesfield Forest, near Rainow There are also three great camps, probably of British or of Roman origin, now known by the names of Buckton castle, Melandra castle, and Monslow castle, in these mountains. There are also numerous tumuli and circles of stone and hanging rocks, which are generally attributed to the age of the Druids.

On the northern and eastern sides of Lancashire and Cheshire the names of several of the mountains and hills have still a wild and desolate sound, the Wolf's Crags, the Wolfhole Rocks, Wolfenden, and Wild Boar's Clough, carry us back in imagination to the times when the ferocious animals, from which they took their names, were the terror of the surrounding districts We also meet with numerous places named after other wild animals, as the beaver, the badger, the otter, the fox, and the raven, all of which were formerly found in these mountains In our own happier times, the grouse share the produce of these heath-covered hills with the mountain sheep, and it is worthy of note amongst naturalists, that the earliest brood of young grouse known to have been seen in England, was found on the side of Pendlehill.* Hawks and falcons are still numerous on these hills, and in the old coaching days an eagle might occasionally be seen on the higher parts of the moors, sailing along over the heaths and rocks in search of its prey.

Having described the various soils that are found in the counties of Lancaster and Chester, we shall next proceed to give a brief account of the plants which they produce, and of the animals which those plants sustain, including as well those that may be considered indigenous to the soil as those that have been introduced within the historic period It will be necessary at the same time to add a few observations, as to the climate of this division of England, and its influence on the growth and production of plants and animals.

A most observant and discriminating writer of antiquity, in describing the soil and climate of Britain, says, that they are such as to produce all the ordinary cultivated plants, except the vine and the olive, the products of hot countries, that the soil is fertile and patient of crops, but that the plants produced in Britain grow more rapidly than they ripen, owing to the abundance of moisture in the earth and the air † This observation is not only applicable to Britain as a whole, and as compared with the drier countries of the continent of Europe, but it is also applicable to the western and north-western districts of England and Scotland, and to the whole of Ireland, as compared to the eastern and southern districts of England. In ordinary years wheat ripens and is generally harvested from a fortnight to three weeks earlier in Kent and Surrey than it is in Lancashire and Cheshire, and nearly a month earlier than it is in most parts of Ireland In the very early summer of 1864, for instance, wheat was cut and carried in the Isle of Thanet, which is considered the earliest spot in Kent, in the last week in July; in Lancashire and Cheshire a fortnight later; in the first week in September, in the neighbourhood both of Belfast and of Limerick. In early summers, like those of 1864 and 1865, this difference is of little consequence; but, when the time of ripening is late all over the three kingdoms, it becomes difficult to secure the grain crops in

* Yarell's British Birds—Grouse. † C C Tacitus' Life of Julius Agricola.

good condition, in the more westerly and backward districts bordering on the Irish Sea and the ocean. The difference of climate has always had the effect of inducing the cultivators of the soil to pay more attention to the production of grain in the southern and eastern counties, and to the production of grasses and roots, and the breeding and rearing of cattle, in the western and southern counties. In ancient times, when cultivation was very rude, this was so much the case that one of the Roman historians, in describing the people of Britain, says, that in the eastern and northern parts of the island they subsisted chiefly by the cultivation of the soil and the growth of grain, whilst in the interior and more remote parts they subsisted almost entirely on the produce of their cattle. This continued to be the case to a considerable extent until much more recent times. William of Malmesbury, writing five hundred years ago, spoke of Cheshire as a country poor in grain, but rich in cattle. Even in the reign of Henry VIII, when Leland visited the north-western counties, he notes very particularly the districts in which wheat and other kinds of grain were grown Thus, in travelling between Northwich and Manchester, he observes, "that the soil was sandy, and that little corn was grown, owing to the deer that strayed out of Delamere Forest and devoured the young corn." But in proceeding forward by way of Altringham to Manchester, he observes, in passing Dunham Massey ("Mr Booth's house," as he calls it), "that about that place, by good culture, there had been made very good corn ground." Continuing his journey northward from Manchester to the house of his friend Mr. Leland at Morley, in the parish of Leigh, he remarks, "that he passed by inclosed ground, partly pasture, and partly fruitful of corn." Further north, between Morley and Preston, he observes, "that the ground was inclosed for pasture and corn, except where the vast moors and mosses were" In travelling between Preston and Garstang, he remarks, "that wheat is not very commonly sown in those parts," but about Lancaster, he observes, "that the soil is very fair, plentiful of wood, meadow, pasture, and corn." A few years later, in the reign of Queen Elizabeth, Camden in his "Britannia," in describing the more level parts of Lancashire, states, "that it produced good crops of wheat and barley, and that the land nearer the hills yielded good crops of oats" But even to the present day both Lancashire and Cheshire are much more remarkable for their meadows, pastures, oats, root crops, and garden produce, than for their crops of wheat and barley. This is not because the art of growing grain is not perfectly well understood everywhere in those counties, and is not practised with great skill in some districts, such as Lower Furness, the Fylde, the Ormskirk district of South Lancashire, and the peninsula of Wirral, but because both the soil and climate are better suited for green crops than for white, and because it is more profitable to raise those descriptions of produce that cannot be brought from a distance *

The climate of Lancashire and Cheshire, on the average of years, is much milder than that of the corresponding districts on the eastern side of the island, which are more exposed to the land winds blowing over the northern parts of Europe and Asia. The lofty hills on the east of the two counties, and on the north of Lancashire, rise like a great natural wall more than 1000 feet high, and shelter them from these winds But they lie entirely open to the winds from the south and west, blowing over the Atlantic ocean, and rendered mild by the waters brought by the Gulf stream from the tropics The warmth of that great ocean river, we are told, tempers the severity of the climate even to Spitzbergen, and indeed, that but for its mild influence, the shores of the British islands would be ice-bound even in June, like those of Labrador † In general, therefore, the winters are mild, especially on the great estuaries that open towards the south, such as those of Morecambe Bay and the Lune. Thus in average winters the thermometer does not sink below 40° in the month of January at Liverpool, or in the middle of the Irish Sea, at the Isle of Man, whilst in London it sinks on the average in the same month to 37°, and on the coast of Yorkshire to 33° ‡ Even in very severe winters the cold is seldom so intense in Lancashire and Cheshire, as it is on the eastern side of the island Thus in the winter of 1819–20 which was an intensely cold winter all over England, the thermometer sank to 9° or 10° below zero in the neighbourhood of London, whilst it never sank quite to zero in the neighbourhood of Liverpool, where the temperature was very carefully marked at the Botanic Gardens. Still the winters are occasionally intensely severe even in this district, as, for instance, in 1829–30, when all the rivers and canals were frozen for several weeks, when the wild animals came around the houses and into the gardens, when the rooks had to seek their food on the sea-shore,

* C C Tacitus Life of Julius Agricola. Dion Cassius William of Malmesbury Leland's Itinerary, and Camden's Britannia

† Physical Geography, by Mrs. Somerville, p 234

‡ Keith Johnstone's Physical Atlas.

and when numerous wild birds were shot on the Lancashire estuaries, including wild swans as well as wild geese, and other more ordinary visitors. But winters of this kind are very unusual, and sometimes winter can scarcely be said to be felt Thus in the winter of 1840 there were flowers in the gardens during the whole of December and January, including monthly roses, snowdrops, and polyanthuses, whilst the gorse or furze was covered with blossoms The most remarkable characteristics of the climate of the north-west are its rapid changes, and the general abundance of moisture. It appears from a register of the time at which the different kinds of vegetables and early fruit are brought to market at Liverpool, that there is a difference of six weeks between the time at which potatoes, asparagus, and gooseberries are brought to market in early seasons, and that at which they are brought in backward seasons. The summer heat, on the contrary, is less on the Lancashire and Cheshire coast than it is in the south and east of England, the average summer heat in those two counties, in the month of July, being 61°, whilst in the south of England at London it is 64°, at York 63°, and even as far north as Elgin 61°* In very early seasons there have been summers in which the greater part of the hay crops were cut and carried in the first fortnight in June, but in later seasons they are often out till near the end of July In one year early rye, quite ripe, was cut in Lancashire in the second week in July, in another barley was cut near Ulverstone in the last week of July, and in the year 1844 wheat grown on the sandy lands near New Brighton in Cheshire, was shown in Liverpool Exchange in the first week in August. But on the average of years there is not much ripe grain, either in Lancashire or Cheshire, before the third or even the fourth week in August. Something, however, in this respect depends on the nature of the soil and on its cultivation. Those causes make a difference of ten days or a fortnight, independent of climate

Cheshire was described in one of the Agricultural Reports in the early part of the present century, as consisting of "665,600 acres of verdant surface," and the same description applies to a considerable portion of Lancashire They are amongst the most productive grass-land districts in the kingdom, the grass retaining its growth and verdure in a great degree during the whole year, owing to the moistness and mildness of the climate. The same report describes the natural meadows of Cheshire as numerous, rich, and fertile. They are

* Keith Johnstone's Physical Atlas.

many of them situated on rivers, which, from the frequency of heavy rains on the high grounds from which they descend, overflow and enrich the soil The extent of upland pasture is very considerable. That on tolerably stiff clay, with a good substratum of marl, is reckoned the best for the dairy. More milk may be had from the cows fed on a rich loamy soil, and such soils are sought for where the sale of fresh milk is the principal object, but on dairy farms, land of the kind described above is considered more useful. In Lancashire there is much less permanent grass than in Cheshire, but still the meadows on both sides of the Mersey are very fine, and nothing can surpass the grass land on the banks of the Ribble and the Lune. Nearly every kind of natural grass that grows in England is found in the meadows or on the uplands in the two counties, the nature and quality of the herbage varying chiefly with the different degrees of moistness and of richness in the soil. In the meadows the principal grasses are the fescue, foxtail, meadow grass, white clover, cow grass, or perennial red clover, with cat's-tail or timothy grass in the moister places. White clover and the more lasting variety of red clover grow very freely in most parts of the two counties. A wonderful effect has been produced on the pasture lands of Cheshire during the last fifty years, by the use of bone dust, which was first introduced, in that county, on the estates of the late Viscount Combermere. It is now very extensively applied in many parts of Cheshire, as well as in Lancashire, and on the poorest soils it produces a luxuriant herbage, consisting of red and white clover, trefoil, and other fine grasses, which the cattle devour eagerly Thistles and rushes soon disappear before this richer herbage, especially on land that is naturally dry or has been sufficiently drained. A great improvement has also been made during the last thirty years, in the manner of laying down grass lands. Formerly this was done chiefly with red clover and rye grass, which yield a large crop the first year, but then die away, leaving little in the land except weedy grass. This mode of laying down grass lands has in a great measure been abandoned, and in place of one or two exhausting annual grasses, a good selection of permanent grasses is sown, including such as come at different times of the year, and thus supply cattle and sheep with more or less food at all seasons.

The principal artificial grasses grown in Lancashire are red clover and rye-grass, which are both excellent grasses when not allowed to kill everything else, and to exhaust the land Italian rye grass was introduced about thirty years ago, in the neighbourhood of large towns, where it is grown in small plots, chiefly by cowkeepers, whom it furnishes with early green forage. The rapidity of its growth is extraordinary. Soon after Italian rye-grass was introduced, a crop of it was grown on the land of Mr. Harold Littledale, at Liscard in Cheshire, which was 33 inches in length in the first week of May. Lucerne, which does so well in the dry gravelly soils in the south of England, is not much cultivated either in Lancashire or Cheshire, though it grows very well on the sandy soils near the sea, from Seaforth to Southport. The variety of clover with the blood red flowers, the *trifolium incarnatum*, was tried some years ago in Lancashire, but was soon abandoned, though it is still occasionally grown on the chalk lands in Berkshire and Devonshire. It is a native of the south of France, where it generally grows in very dry soils. Vetches, and Belgian or St. John's Day rye, are pretty extensively cultivated as green forage, though not so extensively as Italian rye-grass.

Wheat, barley, and oats are grown very successfully in some districts, but not over a very wide range of country. Owing to the wetness of the climate, neither the colour nor quality is quite equal to those of the eastern counties. The best wheat lands are along the coast, especially in Lower Furness, the Fylde, the country from Rufford through Ormskirk to the neighbourhood of the river Mersey, and part of the peninsula of Wirral. Very fine barley is also grown in Lower Furness, and oats are grown extensively in many parts of Lancashire Formerly much oaten and barley bread was consumed, especially in the hilly districts, and oaten cakes are still eaten in the hilly country on the borders of Yorkshire; but it is because the people prefer them, and not that they are unable to buy wheaten bread The import of wheat is enormous, from all wheat-growing countries, as well as from other districts of the United Kingdom.

Beans and peas grow very luxuriantly, as well in the field as in gardens, especially on the stronger class of soils But both the soil and climate of the two counties are more especially suited for the growth of roots, of nearly every description produced in England.

Turnip husbandry is carried on with great success in Lower Furness and the Fylde, and considerable quantities of turnips are grown on the lighter lands of South Lancashire, within ten or twelve miles of the sea-coast, and also in the district of Wirral in Cheshire. Further inland the turnip is not extensively cultivated, except on the moss lands, where it grows very luxuriantly, and seldom fails, even in the driest summers, owing to the moisture remaining in the ground

Potato cultivation is carried on almost as extensively in South Lancashire, and in those parts of Cheshire that extend along the banks of the Mersey, as it is in Ireland. The soil and climate of the two counties are especially suited for the growth of the potato plant, which has been extensively cultivated in the open fields, as well as in the gardens of Lancashire and Cheshire, for more than two hundred years. "The history of the first introduction of the potato into Europe," says Humboldt in his "Views of Nature," "is involved in much obscurity; but the merit of the introduction is still very generally supposed to be due to Sir John Hawkins, who is said to have brought the plant from Santa Fe, in South America, in the year 1563 or 1565. But the fact which appears to be better authenticated is, that the first potatoes were those planted by Sir Walter Raleigh on his estate at Youghal, in Ireland, from whence they were conveyed into Lancashire." Both farmers and cottagers in Lancashire cultivate the potato, the former generally in drills worked with the horse-hoe, and the latter in beds or dibbled in rows, and hoed with the hand The earliest kinds of potatoes are cultivated in rich sheltered spots, and no sooner are they cleared off the land than some other crop takes their place The demand for the potato is almost unlimited, in a district which contains a population of 3,000,000 persons, or nearly 600,000 families, in each of which, from the highest to the lowest, the potato forms an article of daily food. The cultivation of this valuable root forms a considerable portion of the agriculture of South Lancashire It is there, however, grown on farms of all sizes, and the loss of the crop, when it does occur, is more a question of profit and loss, than one of the subsistence of the whole people, as it unhappily has been in Ireland. The varieties of the potato grown in Lancashire and Cheshire are very numerous, and as old varieties disappear, new ones spring up and take their place

In the years between 1846 and 1849, at the time of the potato famine in Ireland, the failures in the potato crop in the north-west of England were so frequent and so disastrous, as to create a general apprehension that the cultivation of the root would have to be abandoned. But these fears have not been realized, for the disease appeared to lose its intensity in a few years, and the cultivation is probably as extensive now as it ever was in this part of the kingdom.

Whatever may have been the cause of the potato disease, the disease itself both came and passed away very gradually. For five or six years before it became a matter of national importance the local failures were very frequent. So early as the years 1840 and 1841 there were considerable failures in the pink-eye, then considered the finest potato grown in Lancashire, and in many other varieties; and the disease spread until it became almost universal Even at that time, however, the peaty soils were found to be much less exposed to the ravages of the potato disease than the older and richer soils On many of the moss farms the disease was scarcely felt at all, whilst on the richer lands, at a distance of not more than a few hundred yards, the most luxuriant crops when in full bloom, and with every appearance of perfect health, were completely blighted in a single night.

Market gardening in all its departments is carried on very extensively around nearly all the large towns of Lancashire and Cheshire The whole valley of the Mersey and Irwell, from the neigbourhood of Manchester to that of Liverpool, as well as the banks of the Bridgewater and the Leeds and Liverpool canals, abound in market gardens, and much even of the farm cultivation of some districts of the two counties is a mixture of horticulture and agriculture. Through a considerable part of the two counties there are good gardens and orchards around most of the farm houses. All the varieties of garden fruit and produce are met with in the farm and cottage gardens, and still more abundantly in the large market gardens The common fruit trees, such as the apple, pear, cherry, and plum, are found everywhere. The damson plum is the most abundant, and is an article of profit to the cottagers, as well as to the small farmers. Wall fruit also grows well in the hotter summers The vegetables that come to the greatest perfection in Lancashire are celery and asparagus, both of which grow luxuriantly in the lighter soils, with a mixture of peat Dickson, in his "Report on the Agriculture of Lancashire," published some years ago, says, "There is a certain farm in Kirkby, about eight miles north-east of Liverpool, the soil of which is composed of loamy sand, which produces great quantities of early and strong asparagus, and another farm, a part of which is of the same nature, at Orrel, four miles north-east of Liverpool, both of which produce this plant, with less attention and less manure than is requisite in the rich vale of Kirkdale, about two miles from Liverpool, where the greatest quantity of land, in any place in that neighbourhood, is appropriated solely to horticulture" Since this was written the market gardens of Kirkdale have been turned into streets and docks, and covered with houses and warehouses; but all around Liverpool and Manchester, as well as Warrington, Frodsham, Altringham, and numerous other places, garden culture is carried on to a great extent, and with constantly increasing skill

When Dickson wrote the report above quoted, many of the mechanics of Lancashire had gardens, to which they paid great attention, and in which they raised many beautiful varieties of flowers. "A small patch of ground, appended to his cottage, furnishes the weaver, smith, or carpenter with health and pleasure, and contributes to his sobriety, intemperance frequently proceeding from want of recreation to fill up a vacant hour This small space is devoted to the cultivating of his young seedlings, trimming his more mature plants, contemplating new varieties, in expectation of honours through the medium of promised premiums. Thus starting, at intervals, from his more toilsome labours, the mechanic finds his stagnating fluids put in motion, and his lungs refreshed with the fragrant breeze, while he has been raising new flowers of the auricola, carnation, polyanthus, or pink of the most approved qualities, in their respective kinds, and which after being raised here have been dispersed over the whole kingdom. But not only flowers, but fruit, have been objects of their attention. The best gooseberries now in existence had their origin in the county of Lancaster; and to provoke this spirit meetings are annually appointed at different places, and premiums given for different kinds of fruit and flowers"

Since the above was writen, which is now nearly fifty years ago, the towns of Lancashire have increased two or threefold, and the hand-loom weaver has given place to the much better paid workman, who labours with, and not in rivalry with, machinery Multitudes of small gardens must have been swept away in the change, though cottage horticulture is still pursued wherever it is possible Happily the forming of people's parks in all the large towns, and the greater facility which now exists for getting into the country, do something to familiarize the labouring population with the beauties of nature

The extent of garden cultivation as a whole must have greatly increased during the last thirty years, in which period omnibuses, railways, and steamboats have given the middle classes the power of residing in the country, whilst actively engaged in the pursuits of trade Within that period thousands, if not tens of thousands of houses, each possessed of its plot of land and pleasant garden, have been built around the towns in the manufacturing districts, and multitudes of persons have now the pleasure of living in the country, who were formerly shut up from one end of the year to the other in the streets of large towns. Most of the villas now erected by our more successful merchants and manufacturers, are handsome and agreeable residences, and surrounded by gardens and pleasure grounds laid out and planted with excellent taste.

The parks of the more wealthy classes, scattered over the two counties, include some of the finest residences, the most tasteful gardens, and the most beautiful pleasure grounds in the kingdom In these also we find the greatest variety of beautiful plants, and the noblest specimens of timber. Speaking of the woods and plantations of Cheshire, a writer observes, "that few of them are of large extent, yet that much timber is scattered about in woods and hedgerows. In some parts of the country the number of trees in the hedgerows and coppices is so considerable, that from some points of view, the whole country has the appearance of an extensive forest." The most considerable ancient woods are in the park of the earl of Stamford and Warrington, at Dunham Massey Few spots could boast such an assemblage of stately oaks, elms, and beeches. During a storm of wind on the 21st January, 1802, several hundred trees were torn up by the roots in this park One of these, when barked, contained 403 cubic feet of timber, and was sold at 6*s* 6*d* per foot, to the extent of 373½ feet. An elm, blown down at the same time, measured 146 feet in height. A colony of herons had for ages fixed their residence on the summit of these trees, but when the oaks were blown down they settled on the neighbouring beeches There are still many noble trees at Dunham Massey, and in others of the great parks in the rich valleys of Cheshire. Lancashire is not so favourably situated for producing fine timber, the winds being very trying along the whole coast, and the soil in the interior being seldom suited for the growth of oak timber The beech, the elm, and the sycamore all grow to be fine trees, when they are well taken care of in the early years of their growth. The larches are also very fine on the hills of Higher Furness. Formerly this district was celebrated for its yew trees, which furnished the archers—for whom it was still more famous—with the great national weapon, the bow But these are now only found growing wild in the clefts of the rocks in the northern districts of the county, or in a few of the parks. Amongst the finest yew trees in England are those growing in Gresford churchyard, about ten miles south of

Chester, but across the Welsh border One of these yew trees is fifty feet in girth below the branches, and is supposed to be more than 1400 years old.* During the last fifty years numerous shrubs and trees, either ornamental or combining use with ornament, have been introduced into this in common with other districts The rhododendron and the azalea are now amongst the most beautiful ornaments of our gardens and shrubberies, and both grow with extraordinary luxuriance in the light peat soils, and under the mild climate of the north-western district. The pines of South America, and the cedars of the Himalaya mountains, also now adorn our shrubberies, and may possibly, like the larch, at a future time become timber trees on our hills

A district diversified with woods, meadows, corn-fields, and gardens, always contains abundance of birds, and most of the principal song-birds of England are found in the two counties. Early in January the missel-thrush, the earliest and largest of the song-birds of this country, is heard singing in the woods, even amidst the storms, from which it takes its local name of the storm-cock In February, the skylarks are heard singing as they rise, from their nests in the grass, into the skies. In the same month the loud cheerful note of the song-thrush begins to be heard, and increases in richness and in power as the season advances In the course of March and April, the mellow note of the blackbird is heard in gardens and orchards. In the month of April the swallow begins to fly around the streams and brooks, and its chirp or twitter is heard under the eaves of the houses. Early in May the cuckoo is heard, and occasionally seen, before the trees are fully covered with leaves "The voice of the turtle-dove is heard in the land" in the months of April and May; and towards the end of the latter month the sound of the land-rail, or corn-crake, resounds from the long grass The principal birds that come in the spring, and more especially the swallow, appear to arrive in Lancashire about three weeks later than the time of their arrival in the south of England. In the spring of the year 1774, the swallow was seen at Selborne, in Hampshire, on the 4th April, the swift on the 24th, and the bank-marten on the 12th April, and the house-marten on the 30th April, whilst in the same year at Blackburn, in Lancashire, the swallow was first seen on the 29th April, the swift on the 28th, and the house-marten on the 1st of May.†

There is some uncertainty as to the furthest point northward to

* Humboldt's Views of Nature, p. 278 † White's Natural History of Selborne, p. 174.

which the nightingale extends its migration It is generally allowed that it is heard on the eastern side of England, as far north as Doncaster, and it has been heard repeatedly on the western side, as far north as the valley of the Mersey and the Irwell, in the woody district between Stretford and Dunham Massey. Scarcely a year passes in which its beautiful song is not heard, in the stillness of the night, in that neighbourhood It has seldom, however, been found much further north, and that may be considered the extreme limit of its migration on the north-western side of the island.

In a country abounding in grass and herbage, and with a mild, moist climate, the presence of numerous tribes of birds is absolutely necessary to keep the ravages of insects and reptiles within the limits that are required for the protection of vegetable growth In mild winters, the wheat fields of this district are frequently laid waste by innumerable swarms of the shell-less snails, too well known to the farmer by the name of slugs The gardens, especially in mild seasons, abound with caterpillars. In the summer months, the turnip fly makes great ravages in the turnip fields. All these creatures no doubt have their use in the system of creation, but they all have a tendency to increase to such an extent as to be injurious to cultivation. They are infinitely too numerous and too minute to be destroyed by the efforts of man; but they are kept within safe limits by the incessant attacks of the feathered tribes, to which they afford the larger part of their subsistence.

Bees find an abundant supply of honey in the heath-flowers on the Lancashire mosses, and the vegetation of the newly reclaimed lands around their edges, consisting chiefly of red and white clover, beans and peas, and other plants, producing rich and fragrant flowers In those situations the yield of honey is large, and the swarms increase very rapidly.

Much the larger portion of the produce of the soil of the two counties consists of grasses, hay, and roots; and much the larger part is consumed in the feeding of cattle, horses, sheep, and swine. The whole number of domestic animals existing in the two counties, in ordinary times, appears to be from 900,000 to 1,000,000—a large number, but not more than is required to supply the various wants, and to answer the different purposes, of a population of 3,000,000 of persons. This is independent of fat cattle, sheep, and swine imported from Ireland, Scotland, Wales, and other parts of England, and immediately consumed within the district. These also are very numerous, the cattle imported into Liverpool alone being about 150,000 a year, the sheep about 400,000, and the swine about 200,000, in round numbers The quantity of cattle usually kept in the counties of Lancaster and Chester appears, from a return recently laid before Parliament, to be rather less than 300,000, of which number nearly 200,000 are milk cows. The number of horses kept in the two counties cannot be ascertained with equal certainty, but probably amounts to upwards of 100,000. The number of sheep is rather more than 300,000, and the number of swine upwards of 100,000.

The native breed of long-horned cattle that formerly covered the plains, as well as the hills of Lancashire, is now nearly extinct, having been supplanted, except in a few remote and hilly districts, by a finer and larger breed. In former times, before turnip husbandry was invented and artificial grasses or oil cake were introduced, and when little provision was made for feeding cattle in the winter months, the hardy, active, long-horned breed of Lancashire cattle, with thick hides and long shaggy hair, were the only race of cattle that could live, and keep up their strength, during the winter months, and guard themselves in the vaccaries, in the hollows of the mountains, against the wolves that then infested the wilder parts of the district. The Lancashire cattle are spoken of, by the old English writers, as the finest breed then existing in the country; especially Camden, in his "Britannia," says that the fertility and healthiness of the region of Lancashire may be judged of from the appearance of the people, who are remarkably handsome, and from the fineness of the cattle, which, with their long horns and well-formed bodies, possess all the good points that the ancient writers on agriculture, namely, Mago the Carthaginian, and Columella in his work on rural affairs, state that cattle should possess. This eulogium was no doubt well deserved; but during the last hundred years the breeding of cattle has been greatly improved, and a new breed created, by carefully cultivating the best points in several existing ones The result is the short-horned breed, which has now spread over the whole of England, and seems likely to supersede all the others The Lancashire breed of long-horned cattle, as described by Culley, the great improver of the breed of cattle, are said to have been distinguished from others by the length of their horns, the thickness and firm texture of their hides, the length and closeness of their hair, the large size of their hoofs, and their coarse, leathery, thick necks He states that they are deeper in their fore quarters, and lighter in their hind quarters, than most other breeds, narrower in their shape; less in weight than the short horns, though better weighers in proportion to their size; and though they give considerably less milk, it is said to afford more cream in proportion to its quantity The Lancashire cattle, he says, are more varied in their colours than any other breed; but whatever the colour may be, they have in general a white streak along the back, which the breeders term finched, and mostly a white spot on the inside of the hough. The short-horned, or Yorkshire, Durham, or Northumberland breed, as they are called in different places, have in a great measure superseded the Lancashire cattle. According to the same writer, the bone, head, and neck, of the short-horned cattle are fine, and the hide is very thin; the chine is full, the loin broad, the carcass throughout large and well-proportioned, and the flesh, or fattening quality, equal or perhaps superior to that of any other large breed The short-horns give a greater quantity of milk than any other cattle; a cow yielding usually twenty-four quarts a day, and making three firkins of butter during the grass season The colours of the short-horned breed are much varied, but they are generally red and white mixed, or what breeders call flecked. The cattle on the cheese farms in Cheshire are of various breeds, including a large number of short-horns, but also many other breeds, the quantity of caseine matter in the milk being of more consequence than the quantity of milk, or the amount of butter, that it contains

The number of horses kept in the two counties is also very great, and probably bears a close proportion to the number of persons resident in the district, and the amount of goods, merchandise, minerals, and building materials transported within it The number of horses employed in the cultivation of the ground may be somewhat less than in other counties, owing to the large quantity of land that remains in permanent grass, yet it is not so much less as might be supposed, owing to the large quantities of farm produce that are carted into the towns, and the large quantity of manure that is carted from the towns into the country Lancashire and Cheshire farmers have a very good useful breed of horses, both for the farm and the road, though neither of these counties can rank with Yorkshire, Lincolnshire, and some others, in the breeding of horses. When railways were invented, and mail coaches, stage coaches, post chaises, and waggons, were driven from the road, it appeared as if the demand for horses would almost cease. But this is very far from having been the case, and there are probably a greater number of horses, of all kinds, employed in the two counties, than there were in those days when Bartholomew Bretherton kept 1200 coach horses in his stables at Rainhill, near Prescot, and when his partner, Mr Lacy, had nearly as many at the other end of the Liverpool and Manchester road, near Irlam, and when those roads resounded, from early morning till late at night, with the tramp of horses and the rattle of coaches. Since stage coaches and post chaises disappeared, omnibuses, cabs, and hansoms have come in, and probably occupy as many horses as were formerly employed in travelling on the high roads. There are also a greater number of private carriages kept now than were ever kept at any previous time, and also a greater number of saddle horses Some of the Lancashire landowners have paid great attention to the breeding of the finest class of horses, especially Lieutenant-colonel Towneley, of Towneley Park, near Burnley, whose racers have been amongst the finest and most successful ever produced in England Many of the hunters that turn out with the Cheshire foxhounds, are also amongst the finest animals in the kingdom.

But, in addition to the number of horses kept for pleasure or for drawing light vehicles, there is an immense demand in Liverpool and Manchester, and all the other towns of the two counties, for draught horses, both for carts and waggons. The quantity of merchandise moved for greater or smaller distances, by means of horse-power, amounts to several million tons yearly, and the quantity of coal and of building materials is still greater These articles are now moved for long distances by steam, but they are almost all either originally collected at the railway stations, or removed from those stations, or from docks to warehouses, by means of horse-power. Thousands of teams, of the most powerful draught horses, are continually in use in Liverpool, Manchester, and all the other towns of the two counties, assisting in the removal of goods, coal, and building materials. For horses of this kind, as well as of a lighter breed, the horse fairs of Yorkshire, Lincolnshire, Cumberland, Shropshire, and Denbighshire, as well as those of Lancashire and Cheshire, are constantly visited by the horse dealers of Manchester and Liverpool, and a large quantity of the hay, forage, oats, and beans, grown in the two counties, is used in feeding these powerful and most useful animals.

The native breeds of sheep, like those of cattle, have almost disappeared on the plains of Lancashire and Cheshire, though they are still found on the hills. The Haslingden breed, found on the moors extending from Haslingden, the highest town in Lancashire, to the borders of Yorkshire, are probably remains of the ancient Lancashire breed. In the hilly district of South Lancashire, of which Haslingden and the ancient forest of Rossendale are the centre, the farmers of the highlands have a hardy breed of sheep of a fair size, generally known as the Haslingden breed. These sheep are horned, and have gray faces; their wool is said to be quite as good as that of the Cheviot sheep, and with as heavy a fleece. They make excellent mutton when fat, weighing from 18 to 20 lbs. per quarter, and being by many preferred even to the mutton of the highland blackfaced sheep They are probably remains of the original breed of Lancashire sheep * Another native breed of sheep, known as the Herdwick, is found in Higher Furness, which is a continuation of the Cumberland and Westmoreland range of mountains. The Herdwick sheep are natives of that rocky mountainous district, at the head of the river Duddon and the river Esk They are without horns, have speckled faces and legs, and short wool, weighing from 2 lbs to 2½ lbs per sheep The wool, though coarser than that of any other short-woolled breed, is yet much finer than the wool of the heath sheep In the plains of Lancashire and Cheshire the native breeds of sheep have given way to finer breeds, introduced from other districts The white-faced Cheviots are very prevalent in the north of Lancashire, and the Shropshire sheep have been extensively introduced in Cheshire. In South Lancashire there are very few sheep, except on the hills; but some landowners have introduced small numbers, both of the Leicester and the South Down sheep, the two great breeds of the midland and the southern counties These do well with great care and attention, but neither the soil nor the climate of Lancashire and Cheshire is well suited to either of the breeds The principal supply of sheep for immediate use is obtained from Ireland and Scotland.

Ireland also supplies the greater part of the pigs consumed in Lancashire, though some of the native breeders, in the large towns, have taken great pains to improve the breed. Until the potato failure Irish pigs had continued to improve very rapidly, and from being amongst the worst in the United Kingdom, they had become amongst the best. The number of pigs in Lancashire and Cheshire amounts to about 100,000, but this is independent of the supplies that are continually arriving from Ireland.

* Rothwell's Report on the Agriculture of Lancashire

The quantity of poultry and of game produced in these counties is very considerable. The Bolton grays are the best known poultry of the Lancashire breed, but the greatest pains have been taken during the last twenty years to introduce all the newest and best breeds of poultry existing in England. Poultry shows now take place every year in different parts of the two counties, and some of the very finest birds are presented as competitors for the prizes.

Game of all kinds is abundant, but hard to keep, poachers generally getting the lion's share Hares are numerous, and increase very rapidly A few years ago, upwards of 700 hares were killed, in about five weeks, on the Bold Hall estate, the then owner of which had issued an order or given permission for their destruction. Pheasants are found in tolerable abundance in some of the larger parks and deeper covers, but are difficult to preserve. Partridges find abundant food, and breed quickly, wherever the land is farmed in turnip husbandry. The red grouse are still pretty plentiful on some of the larger mosses and wilder ranges of heath, but they are generally wild and difficult to shoot Snipes are found in most of the large mosses. The black grouse was formerly pretty frequently met with on the Lancashire hills, but has been exterminated or driven northward by the increase of cultivation and of people Several of the larger parks are well-stocked with fallow deer, and a few of them contain specimens of the ancient red deer, which once wandered over the hills of Lancashire and Cheshire, and which are still found at large on the moors in the west of England and in the Highlands of Scotland

Ravages of the Cattle Plague or Rinderpest in Cheshire—We cannot pass from the subject of the animals of Lancashire and Cheshire, without referring to the terrible ravages made amongst the cattle in the county of Chester, in the years 1865 and 1866, by the cattle plague or Rinderpest, as it is called in some of the countries through which it passed on its way to this country This disease has prevailed more or less severely in all parts of England, but in no part of the kingdom with anything like the severity with which it has raged in the county of Chester. In the adjoining county of Lancaster the cattle disease destroyed, from the time when it broke out in June, 1865, to the 21st of April, 1866, 3841 head of cattle, in a stock of 205,130 But this is nothing in comparison with the destruction that took place in the same period in the county of Chester, where the number of cattle destroyed, either by the disease itself, or for the purpose of arresting its progress, amounted to 42,922 head of cattle in a stock of 125,092. Up to that date the average decrease in the stock of cattle, from the ravages of this disease, in the whole of England was 4·14 per cent, whilst in Cheshire it was no less than 34·28 per cent. This is a difference so enormous, as to be almost unaccountable, but the causes of which require to be investigated with the utmost care. In England generally, the malady was little more than a slight aggravation of existing maladies, whilst in Cheshire it amounted to a destroying plague.

According to the reports and the information collected by the commissioners appointed by the Crown, at the request of Parliament, to inquire into the origin and nature of the cattle plague, the original seat of this fatal disease was in the steppes, or vast grassy plains, of Russia and Central Asia. The primary cause of the disease is supposed to have been the great droughts to which those plains are subject in dry summers, and the deprivation of proper supplies of green pasturage or other fresh vegetable aliments suited for cattle.* It is worthy of note, in passing, that the summers of 1864 and 1865 were two of the driest summers ever known in England, and were seasons in which cattle, sheep, and all other animals suffered greatly from want of water. In Russia the belief is that this disease has broken out at intervals during a long course of ages, but has died out in a few years, on each occasion, after making greater or smaller ravages. According to the researches of the Imperial Agricultural Society of Southern Russia, the disease appeared in Europe in the years, 809, 820, and 850, commencing on the shores of the Black Sea, and spreading over the whole of Europe as far as Germany, France, and Spain. According to the same researches, the disease again appeared in 1240, first showing itself in Hungary, and thence spreading throughout nearly the whole of Europe. In the year 1514 it appeared in Spain. In 1625 it reappeared in Hungary, passing thence into Italy. In 1709 the disease ravaged the whole of Tartary, passing thence into Russia, Podolia, Bessarabia, Poland, Moravia, Dalmatia, Croatia, and destroying immense numbers of cattle, so that between the years 1711 and 1713, 2,000,000 head of horned cattle are known to have died in Europe from this plague. From 1740 to 1756, cattle plague

* Third Report of Commissioners appointed to inquire into the Origin and Nature &c., of the Cattle Plague, with an appendix, presented to both Houses of Parliament, by command of her Majesty, May, 1866. Report of Consul Paton to Earl Russell, dated Ragusa, October 18, 1865.

ravaged nearly every country in Europe. In the year 1765 it was brought from Turkey into Illyria, Moldavia, and Hungary, whence it again spread throughout Europe, and only ceased in the year 1770, after destroying 300,000 head of horned cattle in Holland alone In 1795 it appeared during the wars in the south of Europe. In 1801 it again appeared in Illyria, Switzerland, France, Saxony, Prussia, Poland, and Russia, ravaging all those countries constantly, during the wars of Napoleon. In 1827, during the war between Russia and Turkey, the disease appeared in Russia, Poland, Podolia, Hungary, Bessarabia, Moldavia, and Austria, lasting three years. In 1844 it appeared in Poland, Hungary, and Wallachia. In 1857 it again appeared throughout New Russia, and the countries bordering on the Lower Danube. In 1861 it appeared again in Southern Russia, Moldavia, Poland, Podolia, Hungary, and Bessarabia, lasting till the year 1863. According to the statistics collected by Dr Faust, Europe has lost 200,000,000 head of horned cattle, by the cattle plague, since its first appearance.*

The researches of the commissioners, appointed by the Crown to inquire into the origin and nature of the cattle disease in this country, induced them to believe that it made its appearance in England in the month of June, 1865 They state that the first known cases were all in animals collected from different parts of England and Holland, brought to the metropolitan market on one particular day, viz, the 19th of June. These cattle were purchased by different dairymen, and were taken to five sheds in different parts of London, viz, to Islington, Hackney, Lambeth, and Paddington. As there was no cattle plague in the parts of England whence those cattle came on their way to market, and none in the sheds to which they were taken, the commissioners believe that the cattle must have caught the disease whilst standing for sale in the metropolitan market This market the commissioners consider to be the most likely place in England for cattle plague to be brought to from abroad, and an unlikely place for it to spring up in by spontaneous origination. It ought, in the opinion of the commissioners, to be a matter of no surprise that we have been unable to indicate the precise channel by which the poison came into the market, for from the universal ignorance of the signs of the disease at that time, and the probable slaughter of the affected animal soon after, evidence

* Report of Commissioners Letter of Consul-general Murray to the Earl of Clarendon, dated Odessa, March 23, 1866.

which might have led to the detection of it at the time would pass unnoticed, and would soon be lost altogether But as we have since traced several introductions of the disease from the Continent, there can be little doubt that it was introduced in the same way, in the first instance, and was overlooked. Moreover, in most places in England where the disease has broken out, its introduction can be traced. It follows the lines of cattle traffic, and does not arise spontaneously. In confirmation of this, we find the Austrian and Prussian veterinary surgeons declare, that whatever may be the origin of the disease in other countries, it is always brought by diseased cattle to them The way in which the disease broke out and was destroyed in the Jardin d'Acclimatation in Paris, and over and over again in Aberdeenshire; its comparative absence from Ireland, the manner in which it spread in England and Scotland during the summer, autumn, and winter—all these facts are conclusive against the assumption of an occult atmospheric condition, and in favour of its spread by contagion, in the bodies of living animals

The progress and symptoms of this fatal disease are stated by the commissioners to be as follows:—It results from the inquiries set on foot in this country, first by Professor Gamgee, and then by Dr. Sanderson, that a rise of temperature in the body of the animal affected, precedes any other symptom of the disease Within a period ranging from thirty-six to forty-eight hours after an animal has taken the cattle plague by inoculation, the natural temperature of its body rises from 102° Fahr, or a little above, to 104°, or even to 105½°. This occurs at a time when the animal appears to be in no way ill, and by means of this premonitory symptom the disease can be detected at least two days earlier than had been previously supposed. Two days after the perceptible rise of temperature has begun, the next sign occurs, viz., an eruption on the lining membrane of the animal's mouth. Dr. Sanderson found this symptom in every case (eighty in all), seen by him, and in every instance he was able to recognize the disease from this sign alone On the day following the appearance of the eruption, or about seventy-two hours after the first elevation of temperature, the animal may be observed to be a little ill, to have less appetite than usual, and to ruminate irregularly. Even at this time, however, the pulse may be unaltered. On the following day, the fourth from the first rise of the temperature, the animal for the first time shows marked symptoms of illness, and this period, which may be 110 hours after the real commencement, is usually considered by superficial observers to be the beginning of the disease. After the fourth day is over the constitution of the animal is thoroughly invaded. Then ensue the urgent symptoms, the drooping head, the hanging ears, the distressed look, the failing pulse, the oppressed breathing, the discharge from the eyes, nose, and mouth, the eruption from the skin, the fetid breath, and other well known signs of the disease During the sixth day there occurs a great diminution of the contractile force of the heart and voluntary muscles, the pulse becomes very feeble and thready, the respiratory movements are modified, and the animal sometimes shows such weakness in the limbs, that it has even been thought that some special paralytic affection of the spinal nerves must exist. The temperature now rapidly falls, and signs of a great diminution in the normal chemical changes in the body appear. Death usually occurs on the following or seventh day, from the first perceptible elevation of temperature Although this is given as the typical course of this disease, there are great deviations from it; as some animals live a longer, many a much shorter time, and the severity and sequence of the symptoms vary considerably.*

Coincident with the first elevation of temperature, and long before there is the least appearance of ill health, the blood of an animal that has taken the cattle plague contains an agent which can produce the plague in another animal; in other words, the blood contains the poison of the disease. But no examination of the blood textures, although tried by a microscope that magnifies 2800 diameters, shows any substance which can be supposed to be the agent that poisons the blood, though it would be perceived if it was of the magnitude of the one-millionth part of an inch.†

The conditions which the commissioners mention as apparently affecting the origin, progress, and results of the disease, appear to them to be as follows:—1 The disease seems to be most prevalent on low lands and in the plains, not a single outbreak of cattle disease being recorded at an elevation of 1000 feet. In several counties—Norfolk, Cheshire, Staffordshire, and Buckinghamshire—the disease has been observed to be more severe, if not more prevalent, in marshy and low-lying districts. 2. The commissioners state that there can be no doubt that overcrowding, or what is the same thing, deficient ventilation, and the custom of retaining the manure

* Third Report of the Commissioners appointed to inquire into the Origin and Nature, &c., of the Cattle Plague

† Report of Commissioners

within or close to cattle sheds, cause the plague to spread faster, and to be more fatal. 3. They consider that the use of impure water appears to increase the fatality of the disease. 4. They believe that the true mode of preventing the spread of the cattle plague is to treat it as an entirely contagious disease, and to prevent all contact between animals affected and those that are free from disease 5 The commissioners believe the best disinfectants to be chloride, ozone, sulphur, and the tar acids (carbolic and cresylic). They produce some evidence to show that, by judicious feeding, with soft mashes of easily digestible food, the proportion of recoveries has been considerably, and in some places very largely increased. They add that it does not appear that any advantage is to be obtained by giving large quantities of stimulants, and state that there can be no question that powerful drugs of all kinds greatly heighten the mortality of the cattle plague 6 They conclude that perfect cleanliness, ample ventilation, constant disinfection of the air by tar acids, and the most careful feeding, with soft mashes of the most digestible food, such, and such only, are the measures which our present experience sanctions for the treatment of the disease 7 With regard to the method of stopping the disease by slaughtering the animals attacked with it, the commissioners state, that the very principle of stoppage by slaughter is to make the killing follow immediately on the attack If there be any delay—if treatment be resorted to, and killing be delayed till hope of recovery is lost—the object of slaughter is frustrated.

The districts in which the mortality by the cattle disease has been greatest are the following.—In the county of Huntingdon, which is a very level country, and close to the marshes of the Isle of Ely, the mortality, from the commencement of the disease to the 21st April, 1866, was 11 30 per cent In the metropolitan police district, where the cattle are almost entirely kept in lairs or shippens, it amounted to 15·80 per cent. In the county of Cambridge, a very level, and in some parts a very marshy district, the mortality was 17 90 per cent But in the county of Chester, a very level and fertile country, indifferently drained in some parts, and where the cattle were kept in large herds in the fields in summer, and in barns and shippens during the winter months, and are chiefly fed with dry food at that season, the mortality amounted to 34 28 per cent. The average mortality of the whole of England was 4 14 per cent, and that of Lancashire was only 1·87 per cent. It is impossible to account for these extraordinary differences in the rate of mortality; but we have brought the above facts and opinions together, from the reports of the commissioners, who have inquired into the history and progress of this fatal disease, in the hope that they may be of some use in checking its future progress, if it should still continue to rage amongst the cattle, on the beautiful farms of Cheshire and the adjoining districts. The loss of property by the cattle disease in Cheshire and Lancashire cannot be less than a million sterling, and renders the question one of painful interest to all who are concerned in the agricultural prosperity of the two counties

The Rivers, Streams, and Water-power of Lancashire and Cheshire—The amount of water-power furnished by the numerous rivers and streams of Lancashire and Cheshire is much greater than that of most districts of England of equal extent, owing to their proximity to the ocean, to the heaviness of the rain-fall on the mountains that bound the two counties on the east and north, and to the height and steepness of the mountains from which the streams, fed by that rain-fall, flow down into the level country, and ultimately into the sea. "The invisible vapour which rises from both the land and water, but more especially from the latter, ascends into the air until it is condensed by the coldness of the atmosphere into clouds, that restore it again to the earth in the form of rain, hail, and snow." * The greater portion of this aerial moisture falls in hilly or mountainous regions, from which much of it flows immediately down by streams and rivers into the sea; but a considerable portion of it is retained for a time by impermeable strata in the mountains, which prevent its rapid escape from the ground into which it sinks, and thus a system of natural reservoirs is formed in the mountains, from which streams and rivers receive a continual supply †

It has been computed that the quantity of moisture that is raised from the sea and the earth by evaporation, in the course of a single year, amounts to not less than 186,280 cubic miles of water. This is carried by the winds in all directions, over sea and land, to water the earth and feed the rivers and streams. In a few spots on the coast of South America, and one or two other places on the coast of Africa and Arabia, there is no rain-fall whatever, and those regions seem to be condemned to perpetual

* Physical Geography, by Mrs. Somerville † Ibid., page 254

barrenness, although they furnish the supplies of guano that fertilize other lands But these are rare exceptions, for rain descends in greater or less amount in almost every part of the globe, and is everywhere the great means of producing fertility, and of forming the rivers and streams, which are amongst the greatest means of advancing industry, communication, transport, and all the arts of civilized life.

The North Atlantic ocean, which washes the shores of the north-western division of England, furnishes the whole of Europe with greater or smaller supplies of moisture and of rain The amount of evaporation in different parts of the ocean depends in a great measure on the temperature of the water and the air, being much the greatest within the tropics. The Gulf Stream pours a continual supply of water, warmed by the equatorial currents and the tropical heat, into the North Atlantic, and thus produces a continual evaporation, which spreads large masses of clouds and moisture over all the countries of western Europe, and more especially over the British islands.

The amount of rain-fall varies greatly in different countries and districts, depending chiefly on their proximity to the sea, and on the elevation and position of their mountains In the loftiest mountains of the world, as for instance the Himalayas, the rain-fall at the heads of mountain valleys, so placed as to catch the greatest masses of clouds and vapour borne by the prevailing winds from the ocean, amounts to not less than 600 inches per annum This is the source from which the Ganges and other great rivers of India are fed, and by means of which the plains of Bengal are watered and fertilized. Even amongst the Alps, at a great distance from the ocean, the rain-fall at particular points amounts to 100 inches in the year, and supplies the streams which spread beauty and fertility over the Italian plains. On the sea-coasts, especially in tropical regions, the amount of rain-fall is also very great, amounting on the Gold Coast of Africa to 187 inches per annum, and at some spots to from 500 to 600 inches There is also a heavy rain-fall along the western shores of Europe, especially at those points where ranges of mountains approach the sea-coast, and catch the clouds in their progress into the interior. Thus amongst the mountains of Portugal, between Cintra and Coimbra, there is a rain-fall of 118 inches, although the amount of rain in the neighbourhood of Madrid is not much more than 10 inches in the year There is also an enormous rain-fall in the south of Ireland, amongst the mountains which surround the lakes of Killarney, where a vegetation prevails as rich as that of Italy. On the west coast of England and Ireland the average rain-fall is about 35 inches yearly; but amongst the mountains which surround the Westmoreland lakes, where the clouds are caught by lofty ranges 3000 feet in height, as they are carried by the winds inland from the Atlantic, the average rain-fall is not less than 89·93 inches. At some of the highest points amongst these mountains, it is much greater. Thus at Wastdalehead it is said to amount to 101·4 inches; at Stonethwaite to 111·4 inches; at Gatesgarth to 114·7 inches; and at Seathwaite, amongst the lofty mountains rising above the higher part of the valley of the Duddon, to 140·5 inches.* In North Wales the rain-fall amongst mountains nearly 3000 feet in height, is between 65 and 70 inches per annum.† Proceeding inland from the Atlantic, the amount of rain-fall diminishes rapidly. Thus about London the average is 25 inches, at Paris it is 20 inches; at St. Petersburg it is 19 inches, and in central Russia it is about 12 inches; whilst in the centre of Spain it is not more than 10 inches.‡

Lancashire and Cheshire have both of them a much greater rain-fall than the average of English counties. This they owe partly to the circumstance of their being situated on the western shores of the Atlantic, and partly to the fact of their being bounded on the east and north by a lofty range of hills and mountains, from 1500 to 2000 feet high, which arrest the progress of the clouds in their flight inland. Owing to these causes the rain-fall of Lancashire and Cheshire is nearly, and in some years twice, as great as that of the eastern counties; though not equal to that of the lake district, which is twenty miles nearer to the sea, and where the mountains are about a thousand feet higher than they are in the Pennine chain, that bounds Lancashire and Cheshire on the east. The amount of rain-fall about London is not more than 25 inches, whilst the driest season that has been known in Lancashire for many years, viz., that of 1865, gave a rain-fall of 34·80 inches, on the sides of the Lancashire hills. During the seventeen years from 1849 to 1866, the average yearly rain-fall on the Lancashire hills in the neighbourhood of Riving-

* Table showing the average Rain-fall in the Lake District, by the late Dr Miller, F R S, from 1844 to 1858.

† See Table from Observations of Captain Mathew, of Wern, near Portmadoc, quoted in appendix to Pamphlet, on the Supply of Water to London from the sources of the River Severn, by John Frederic Bateman, C.E., F R.S, F G S, 1865

‡ Keith Johnstone's Atlas of Physical Geography

ton was 45 70 inches, and in the season of 1861, which was the wettest in that period, the rain-fall amounted to 61·70 inches.* Amongst the hills at the head of the Mottram valley, from which the city of Manchester obtains its supply of water, the average rain-fall of the district is 45 786 inches, and at the Woodhead reservoir, at an elevation of 680 feet above sea-level, the rain-fall is 48 104 inches At the Holme reservoirs, and at Dinford bridge, on the eastern slopes of the summit ridge dividing this district from that of the Manchester water-works, the mean rain-fall of the district is 49 69 inches per annum The average rain-fall on the range of hills that bounds the hundred of Salford on the north and east sides may therefore be taken at from 45 to 46 inches, amounting in wet seasons to 55 to 60 inches, and in dry ones to 35 to 36 inches. The yearly rain-fall of the whole of Lancashire and Cheshire, which cover 2,000,000 acres of ground, supposing that it could all be collected in a lake or reservoir covering an area of 50,000 acres, would fill it to the depth of from 50 to 100 feet, according to the nature of the seasons. How vast a quantity of water this is may be judged from the fact, that the immense reservoirs formed for the supply of Liverpool and Manchester, which places together contain a million of inhabitants, do not together cover an area of much more than from 1000 to 1200 acres of land, with the same depth of water.

But it is not merely this immense supply of rain, discharged from the clouds on the Lancashire and Cheshire hills, that is the cause of the great water-power of the district, that is also due to the great elevation at which it falls, and the number of the streams by which it flows down from the mountains The force of every cubic foot of this mass of water, falling at a rate of twelve feet per second, is computed to be equal to one horse-power, and as the greatest rain-fall in these counties is at elevations of from 500 to 1500 feet, some notion may be formed of the momentum of such a mass of water, flowing from so great a height, and rushing from the mountain chain which we have described, through a hundred streams. It is one of the grandest powers of nature, and one of the principal sources of the wealth and population of this crowded district. Hundreds of years before the steam-engine was invented, this was the great moving power of the industry of Lancashire; and it is said that even James Watt, when he invented the steam-engine, doubted

* Report to the Corporation of Liverpool, by Thomas Duncan, Esq, C E., on the Rivington Water-works

whether it could contend successfully against the great natural water-power of the northern counties.* It was nearly twenty years after the steam-engine had been perfected by the genius of Watt, and had been applied to the pumping of mines in Cornwall, and to other purposes in the midland counties, before it began to take the place of the rivers and streams of Lancashire From the time when the first fulling mill was erected at Manchester, in the reign of Edward I or Edward II, to the year 1790, the only power used in the manufactories of that city was the one supplied by the three streams that run through the city, namely, the rivers Irwell, Irk, and Medlock Bolton, whose manufacturing prosperity dates at least from the time of the early Tudor kings, also owed much of its early success to the numerous and abundant streams of water that flow from the mountains on the north of that town, and pass through or near it, in their course to the river Irwell All the other Lancashire and Cheshire manufacturing towns, including Bury, Rochdale, Ashton, Stockport, Macclesfield, Congleton, Haslingden, Bacup, and Darwen, began their career with no other power than that of falling water, though they have continued and extended it with the still greater power of steam. There are at least a hundred streams, small and great, flowing from the hills of the two counties, and there is not one of them, from the Duddon on the north, to the Dane and the Dee on the south, that has not done much to promote the prosperity of the district through which it flows. They are still amongst the great sources of the manufacturing, as well as of the pastoral and agricultural wealth of the two counties, and we therefore proceed to give a sketch of their rise amongst the mountains, and their course back to the ocean, from which their waters originally came. An eminent writer observes, that there is probably not a drop of water on the earth's surface, that has not been borne on the wings of the wind; and we may add, that there is not a drop that has not rendered service to man.†

The beautiful river Duddon, rendered a classic stream by the genius of Wordsworth, rises in a mountainous region, at Three Shire Stones, on the borders of Lancashire, Cumberland, and Westmoreland, gushing from an abundant spring, at an elevation of upwards of 1200 feet above the level of the sea; and flows down into Morecambe Bay, after a rapid course of 27¼ miles, through a valley or water-shed of 117 square miles The Duddon rises

* Samuel Smiles, Esq Boulton and Watt † Mrs. Somerville's Physical Geography

amongst the Cumbrian beds of the Silurian rocks, and in its course to the sea receives the streams that flow eastward, from Black-combe, 1919 feet high, Stoneside Fell, Coney Fell, Hest Fell, Birker Fell, and Harter Fell; and on the east side, the streams that flow westward from the Old Man of Coniston, 2577 feet high, and from the western side of Furness Fells. The land about Wry-nose Fell, where the Duddon rises, is wild and barren, and scarcely affords subsistence to a few mountain sheep. The river descends rapidly through wild sheep pastures, and past Cockley Beck copper mine to Dalehead, where cultivation commences, in the narrow valley through which it flows. At that point it is still 650 feet above the level of the sea. From Dalehead, the Duddon flows southward through a fringe of meadow land—past Donner-dale, or the vale of thunder, Stainton slate mines, in a hollow of the mountains; and Ulpha, the river of the elves—to Duddon bridge, and the wooden fishguard across the river. Thence it flows to the neighbourhood of Broughton in Furness, where there is a tarn in the hills, an extensive park, and Broughton Tower, once the seat of the ancient family of the Broughtons, famous adherents of the house of York in the wars of York and Lancaster, there it becomes navigable at Mine Stage, for vessels of twenty tons

The Duddon, in its descent from the mountains to the sea, receives several abundant streams, all of which rise in the moun-tains of Higher Furness, or of Cumberland Amongst these is Tarn Beck, which flows from Seathwaite Tarn, at the top of the Furness Fells, where the rain-fall is said to be not less than 140 inches per year In flowing through the village of Seathwaite, this stream formerly turned a carding mill. Before the invention of the steam-engine such sites were eagerly sought, for their abundant water-power The river Leckle, which also flows from the Furness hills, turns extensive cotton machinery at Broughton mills, and formerly turned a walk or fulling mill at the same place, at an elevation of about 150 feet above the level of the sea.

In the same region of Higher Furness, the river Brathay also rises near the Three Shire Stones, on the borders of Cumberland, Westmoreland, and Lancashire, at an elevation of 1200 feet above the level of the sea, and flows down into Windermere Lake, after a course of 16½ miles; there it is joined by the Rothay, Trout-beck, and several smaller streams, all of which discharge their waters into the same beautiful lake. After passing through

Windermere they flow out of the lake by the stream of the Leven, 23 miles in length, into Morecambe Bay. The whole area of the watershed or valley of the Leven is 172 square miles, including Windermere Lake, Brathay, Rothay valleys, and the main valley of the Leven. The Brathay, in its course from the mountains to the lake, rushes through wild mountain passes, with frequent falls and rapids, flowing through Langdale Tarn, down Little Langdale, to Colwick Force, where it is still 250 feet above the level of the sea; thence it flows on through Elter Water, amongst woods and scars, to Skelwith Force, where it springs down the rocks from a height of twenty feet. From that point the Brathay flows through a beautiful grassy valley to Brathay bridge, and enters the head of Windermere near Gale Nase Crag

The river Brathay is the favourite breeding place of the char, which is caught in Windermere Lake. According to Yarrell, in his "History of British Fishes," the char remains in the lakes, except at the time of breeding, and then retires to streams in which the water is clear and the bottom hard. Windermere has two principal feeders, the Rothay and the Brathay. These streams unite just before entering the lake; but in the breeding season, which is in November and December, the char enters the river Brathay and deposits its ova in the rocky channel, while the trout at the same season prefers the Rothay. A few char also spawn in the lake, and it is observed that they frequent the hard rocky parts only, which resemble the bottom of the Brathay. The char is from nine to twelve inches in length; and the best season for catching it is from July to October, when it is in the greatest perfection.

Windermere Lake is 10½ miles in length, 1 mile in width, and 116 feet above the level of the sea. It fills a deep and winding hollow in the mountains, its waters moving slowly from north to south like a majestic river, with wooded banks, presenting every form of natural beauty. Near the middle of the lake there are a number of beautiful islands, of which Belle Isle is the largest and most beautiful, and also numerous woody promontories Below this point the stream from Esthwaite Water, a beautiful little lake a little higher in the hills, enters Windermere, and with several other streams swells the lake which extends down to Landing, near Newby bridge. Thus passing through the lake of Windermere, which divides Lancashire from Westmoreland, the collected waters take the name of the river Leven, and flow out of the lake at Newby bridge In its descent to the sea, the Leven turns a corn mill near Newby bridge, and lower down it supplies the power for working cotton mills, iron foundries, and the Low-wood gunpowder works.

The Leven in its course to the sea receives the river Crake. This stream takes its rise from Red Dell Beck, Lever's Water Beck, Yewdale Beck, and other large brooks on the side of the Coniston mountain, and, in flowing down to the lake of the same name, turns the wheels and machinery of the Coniston copper mines. These and several other smaller streams unite to form Coniston Water, at the head of which the Coniston mountain rises suddenly, over-towering all the other mountains of Higher Furness. Coniston Water is a beautiful river-like stream, though with only one island, and with banks less varied than those of Windermere. Its waters flow to the sea through Thurston vale, by the river Crake. This river, before it joins the Leven, turns a bobbin mill at Lower Nibthwaite, a cotton mill at Lowick bridge, and a cotton mill and foundry at Spark bridge. At Greenod it passes the pier at which the produce of the district is shipped on the Leven. At Ulverstone the Leven receives two or three large brooks that rise in the hills and flow through that town, turning several cotton mills, a paper mill, and the machinery of an iron foundry, and feeding the canal which connects the town of Ulverstone with the Leven The stream known by the name of the river Winster, 11½ miles in length, rises in Helston Tarn in Westmoreland, and flows down by Broughton East, so named to distinguish it from Broughton in Furness, and enters the sea near Castlehead, at the top of Morecambe Bay, at a point where the Romans are supposed to have had a military station, and where great numbers of Roman and British coins have been found

The river Kent, which also flows into Morecambe Bay, and divides Lonsdale beyond the Sands from Lonsdale on this side the Sands, rises in the mountains of Westmoreland, and flows through the valley of Kentmere, and by way of Kendal, to the sea. The rain-fall on the mountains of Hill Bell, 2436 feet high, on High Street, 2700 feet, and on Harter Fell, is enormous, and the river Kent rushes down after heavy rains like a mountain torrent, but in the summer months sinks into a comparatively narrow stream To secure a more regular supply of water and of water-power in the mills and manufactories about Kendal, a great reservoir or artificial lake has been formed in the higher part of Kentmere In this reservoir the rain-fall is collected in the wintry and wet months, and is there stored up to be discharged in the dry months in such quantities as will keep a steady flow of water in the river at all times. This has also been done in numerous rivers in the county of Lancaster, as well as in other districts; and the effect of thus collecting the floods of water that fall in wet weather and reserving them for periods of drought is, to render the rain-fall much more available for purposes of consumption, and much more valuable as a motive power, by giving a regular flow of water at all seasons, instead of a succession of floods and droughts

The river Keer enters the county of Lancaster from the east, at an elevation of 360 feet above the level of the sea, and flows into the estuary of the Kent.

Proceeding southward we come to the river Lune, which rises at Lune Head, near Orton, in the same mountainous region of Cumberland and Westmoreland in which the river Eden and one of the branches of the Tyne also rise. The Lune flows down to Lancaster Bay, with a course 53½ miles in length, and through a valley or water-shed extending over an area of 434 square miles. The Lune rises amongst lofty slate mountains, but in its course through Westmoreland flows through ranges of mountain limestone, down a grassy upland valley It enters the county of Lancaster in Tunstall parish, at an elevation of 150 feet above the level of the sea, and winds rapidly down to Barrow, or Over Barrow, the supposed site of the Roman station of Bremetonicæ, which stands in the angle of land where the Leck brook flows into the river Lune. From Barrow the Lune descends through the rich pastures known as the Priory Holmes, by the ruins of Hornby priory From this point it rushes with rapid windings and beautiful meanders through what is called the Crook of Lune. In flowing down to Lancaster, the stream turns cotton mills at Force Bank and Halton. The river Lune abounds with salmon, and a valuable salmon fishery exists in the river a few miles above Lancaster The Lune, after flowing under the railway and the county bridges, winds round the green hill on which the ancient town and castle of Lancaster stand, and passes down by Aldcliff and Ashton Hall to the sea.

The Lune, in its progress to the sea, receives numerous smaller streams. Amongst these is the river Wenning This stream rises in the Yorkshire hills, and enters Lancashire at an elevation of 200 feet above the level of the sea. It flows through meadows down to Wennington, where it turns a corn mill, and then passes below Tatham bridge, near which place it receives the streams of the Hindburn and the Roeburn. The Wenning enters the Lune about a mile south-west of the village of Hornby, after winding round the ancient and beautiful castle of Hornby, the seat of the Harringtons, and, after their downfall, in the wars of York and Lancaster, of the Stanleys, barons of Monteagle. The Hindburn river rises amongst the barren mountains of the millstone-grit formation, that separate Lancashire from Yorkshire, at an elevation of 1200 to 1500 feet above the level of the sea. It flows northward through wild sheep pastures, receiving numerous mountain streams, amongst which are Botton Mill Brook and Croasdale Brook, and entering a more fertile country, joins the Wenning, near Tatham bridge. The Roeburn river rises in the same range of hills as the Hindburn, and at an elevation of 1300 feet. It flows through moors and sheep pastures to the village of Wray, where its waters turn a silk mill It soon after falls into the Hindburn, and joins the Wenning and the Lune The river Greta also rises in Yorkshire, and enters Lancashire, at an elevation of 150 feet. It passes by Greta bridge, and the ruins of the ancient castle of Thurland, the seat of the Tunstalls, famed in border wars A little lower down the Greta turns a corn mill, and then flows into the river Lune. Artle Brook rises in the moors to the east of Lancaster, and flows into the Lune at Caton ; near which place its stream turns very extensive cotton mills. In Artle Brook there was discovered, a few years ago, a Roman milliarium, or mile-stone, marked with the name of the Emperor Hadrian, which had probably been washed down by heavy floods, from the Roman road that passes over the hills in which the stream rises. A very copious stream named the river Conder, eleven miles in length, also rises on the moors to the east of Lancaster, and flows into the Lune by Ellel, where it turns two silk mills, entering the Lune a little to the south of Ashton Hall. Further south a stream, named the river Cocker, flows into the sea through Cockerham sands, and another, named the Broadfleet, drains the mosses of the Fylde

The river Wyre rises in the mountain range of millstone grit that divides Lancashire from Yorkshire, at Tarn Brook Fell, at an elevation of about 1500 feet above the level of the sea. Its course is thirty-five and a half miles from Tarn Brook Fell to the sea at

Fleetwood, and the valley or water-shed, through which it flows, extends over an area of 179 square miles There are two streams flowing down from different points in the mountains, one named the Tarn Brook Wyre, and the other the Marshaw Wyre. These two streams meet near Abbeystead, and flow on to Dolphinholme, where the waters of the Wyre turn the machinery of a large manufactory. The river then flows by Cleveley mills to Garstang, the principal place of the district, where it turns other mills From this point the Wyre runs on to St. Michael's-on-Wyre, and passes by Carsford bridge into the estuary of the Wyre. The river Wyre receives numerous other streams in its course to the sea. Amongst these is the Grizedale river, a mountain stream that rises at Grizedale Head, at an elevation of 1400 feet, and descends rapidly into the valley of the Wyre, joining that river near Lower Lee. Another of the tributaries of the Wyre is the river Calder, one of three rivers of the same name found in Lancashire. This stream rises in the higher parts of the Bleasdale moors, and flows down by Calverdale mill and Pyrmont cotton works, joining the Wyre near Garstang church A third stream is the river Brock. This mountain stream rises at an elevation of nearly 1500 feet, and after a rapid course of seventeen miles, in which it turns the machinery of several mills, flows into the Wyre, a little above the village of St Michael's-on-Wyre

After heavy rains the grass lands in the valley are subject to great floods, and to guard against these the earl of Derby and other landowners have formed a very extensive water-course, for the purpose of carrying off the water This water-course is four miles in length, at its outfall at St. Michael's-on-Wyre, it is eight feet deep, twelve feet wide at the bottom, with sides sloped at an angle of thirty degrees, and embanked on both sides to a height of about three feet *

The river Ribble rises at Ribble Head, above Settle in Yorkshire, and flows down with a course of sixty-one miles, through a valley or water-shed of 501 square miles, watering the grassy limestone district of Craven in Yorkshire, until it reaches the borders of Lancashire, which it enters a few miles north of the town of Clitheroe. There it turns cotton mills, and receives several smaller streams which furnish water for the extensive print and bleaching works in the neighbourhood of Clitheroe. At Clitheroe it flows past the ruins of the ancient castle built by the De Laceys, earls of Lincoln and

* Report on the Agriculture of the County of Lancaster, by William Rothwell, p. 107

constables of Chester, and descends through a beautiful grassy valley, to the ancient Roman station at Ribchester, which stands on its north bank From Ribchester the Ribble flows to Preston, where it becomes a large and wide estuary, capable of receiving vessels of considerable size. Below Preston, the Ribble widens into a broad but shallow stream. There is an extensive salmon fishery on the Ribble, which also contains many other kinds of fish, and amongst them very large pike.

The river Ribble receives numerous smaller streams, both from the north and south Amongst those from the north is the river Hodder, which flows through the limestone district of Bowland Forest, receiving the river Langden from Bleasdale Fell, and the river Loud from Longridge Fell. The Hodder is one of the favourite breeding places of the salmon, which ascend its stream from the Ribble into the cool waters amongst the hills. The hills to the east of Preston abound in springs and brooks, and there extensive reservoirs have been formed to supply the town of Preston with water There are two sets of reservoirs—one near Alston, and the other near Longridge. In the same district is an extensive reservoir for the supply of Stoneyhurst college. From the south, the Ribble receives the river Calder, the second stream of that name which we have had occasion to mention. In addition to the river Calder previously described, two streams, both named the Calder, rise from one hill, at an elevation of 754 feet. One of them, known as the Yorkshire Calder, flows down to Todmorden, and reaches the river Aire, after a course of forty-seven miles, ultimately flowing into the Ouse and the Humber The other, commonly known as the Lancashire Calder, flows westward, and after a course of nineteen miles, joins the river Ribble This stream flows through Towneley Park to Burnley, where it is joined by the river Brun These two streams supply the principal part of the water-power of Burnley. From that place the Calder flows on to the flourishing town of Padiham, and thence passes by the ruins of the beautiful abbey of Whalley, founded by the De Laceys, to the Ribble, which it joins a few miles lower down the stream The Lancashire Calder, in its course to the Ribble, receives numerous streams from Pendlehill and the hills of the Padiham range. Amongst these are Pendlehill Brook, Roughlee Water, White-hough Water, Lanshaw River, the river Don, Colne Water, Sabden Brook, and Branden Brook. The whole of this lofty region abounds in streams. Here also, at Foulridge, are the three principal reservoirs of the Leeds and Liverpool canal, constructed above the tunnel which carries the canal through the mountains. There are numerous mills and manufactories along the banks of all the principal streams of this district, which flow from the northern edge of the Lancashire coal-field. The river Darwen, celebrated by Milton, in his lines on Cromwell, as

"Darwen's stream with blood of Scots embrued,"

which was the scene of a desperate battle in the great civil war between Cromwell and the duke of Hamilton, rises at a height of more than 1000 feet on the lofty hills between Darwen Moor and Crowberry Moss. It flows down through the towns of Over and Lower Darwen, turning numerous cotton mills In its course it approaches near to the still larger and more flourishing town of Blackburn, one of the principal seats of the cotton manufacture, and there receives the waters of the river Blackwater, which flows through that town, with those of Harwood Brook, Kudzen Brook, and several smaller streams There is another large reservoir, for supplying the Leeds and Liverpool canal with water, at Rishton in this neighbourhood, and the town of Blackburn is supplied from extensive reservoirs situated on the hills to the north of the town. Near Fennischoles bridge, the Darwen receives the waters of the river Roddlesworth. The Roddlesworth supplies one or two of the reservoirs of the Liverpool water-works, though the larger portion of them derive their supply from the rivers Douglas and Yarrow. Very recently the Corporation of Liverpool has obtained permission to take a still larger supply of water from the river Roddlesworth After being joined by that stream, the Darwen flows past Houghton Tower, and Salmesbury mill to Walton-le-dale, where it enters the river Ribble All along the stream of the Darwen there are mills, manufactories, and printworks, in which the cotton manufacture is most extensively carried on in all its branches. This county abounds with coal, as well as with water-power.

The river Douglas, which also reaches the Ribble, though very much lower down and by a most circuitous course, rises at a height of more than 1000 feet in the same range of hills, and flows for several miles in a south-westerly direction, until it reaches the large mining and manufacturing town of Wigan The Douglas flows into the Rivington water-works, and draws from them a daily supply of 4,000,000 gallons of water, both in summer and winter The Douglas, in its course down to Wigan, turns numerous mills, and, previous to the introduction of the steam-engine, was employed in pumping the water from several coal mines At Wigan, the Douglas, which has hitherto flowed in a south-westerly direction, is turned in its course by the hills of the coal formation, and from that point flows in a north-westerly direction, finally reaching the sea at the entrance of the Ribble, through Hoole Marsh. The river Douglas was the first Lancashire river that was rendered navigable; the line of navigation, made in the reign of George I. and George II, extending from the coal-field of Wigan to the sea. This was greatly improved when the Douglas navigation was transferred to the Leeds and Liverpool Canal Company, in the early part of the reign of George III.

The river Yarrow rises in the same range of hills from which the Douglas flows The first use made of the waters of the Yarrow, is to supply the reservoirs of the Liverpool water-works These reservoirs, with the connecting goit, are from twenty-four to thirty-five miles distant from Liverpool, being nine miles from end to end. They were constructed under the powers of an Act of Parliament passed in the year 1847, and derive their supplies of water from the Douglas, the Yarrow, the Roddlesworth, and a number of smaller streams. The mean daily yield of water in the Rivington district, on an average of five years, from 1861 to 1865, amounted to 20,772,692 gallons, but only about half that quantity was available for use in Liverpool, namely, 10,542,800 gallons. The reservoirs of the Liverpool water-works are six in number, cover an area of 549 acres, and when full contain 3,268,000,000 gallons of water. They are, together, three and a half miles in length, and from fifty to seventy feet in depth The names and capacities of the reservoirs are as follows:—1. The Roddlesworth upper reservoir, with an area of thirty-eight acres, and a depth of sixty-four feet, capable of containing, when full, 180,000,000 gallons of water. 2. The Roddlesworth lower reservoir, covering $16\frac{4}{10}$ acres, of the depth of seventy-eight feet, containing 99,700,000 gallons. 3. The Rake reservoir covering $13\frac{3}{10}$ acres, of the depth of seventy-eight feet, containing 79,600,000 gallons. These three reservoirs are connected with the others by means of a goit or canal three and a half miles in length. The other reservoirs are—

4. The Anglezark reservoir, covering $191\frac{6}{10}$ acres, of the depth of thirty-five feet, and containing when full 1,019,400,000 gallons of water. 5. The Chorley reservoir, covering $10\frac{1}{10}$ acres, of the depth of thirty-nine feet, and containing 48,3000,000 gallons. 6. The Rivington reservoir, covering 275 acres, with a greatest depth of forty feet, and capable of containing 1,841,000,000 gallons of water The filter beds cover $4\frac{1}{10}$ acres, and in ordinary work, and with a sufficient supply of water, will filter 14,000,000 gallons of water daily. In consequence of the deficiency of the supply, the Corporation of Liverpool have obtained powers from Parliament to take an additional quantity of about 2,000,000 gallons a day from the river Roddlesworth, instead of sending it down the stream as compensation water, and to construct an additional reservoir, to store up water in wet seasons, and retain it for use in dry In this manner they hope to obtain a further daily supply of 3,000,000 gallons, in addition to the 2,000,000 per day which they will obtain from the river Roddlesworth

The Rivington water-works, at their highest point, that is to say, at the Upper Roddlesworth reservoir, are 619·8 feet above the level of the Old Dock sill at Liverpool. At the lowest point of the works, that is, at the filter beds below the Rivington reservoir, they are 382 feet above the Old Dock sill. The extreme distance from the Upper Roddlesworth reservoir to Liverpool is thirty-four and a half miles. From the foot of the filter beds to Liverpool the water is conveyed through iron pipes, for a distance of about twenty-four miles On the line of the pipes there is a reservoir for storing a quantity of water for immediate use, at Eccleston near Prescot, and there are also smaller reservoirs around the town of Liverpool.

The river Yarrow, after contributing its share to supply the reservoirs of the Liverpool water-works, flows down into the Lancashire plain through rich meadows, supplies several mills and print-works, and joins the river Douglas near Rufford, its waters being carried, along with those of the Douglas, into the estuary of the Ribble

But by far the greatest source of water-supply and water-power in Lancashire and Cheshire is the river Mersey, with its great tributaries the Irwell and the Weaver. The length of the Mersey, from the junction of the Etherow and the Goyt, at Water Meeting, near Crumpstall, to the mouth of the river at the Black Rock, below Liverpool, is 68 miles. The length of the river Irwell is $45\frac{3}{4}$ miles;

and the length of the Weaver is 57¾ miles. The area of the valley or basin, through which these rivers flow, is 1706 square miles, being one of the largest in England, and only inferior to the Thames, the Severn, the Trent, the Humber in Yorkshire, and the Great Ouse in Northamptonshire. We shall describe the Mersey, the Irwell, and the Weaver separately, beginning with the main stream of the Mersey, which is the longest, though not the largest, according to the quantity of water that it brings down from the mountains to the sea.

The river Mersey is formed by the union of the streams of the Etherow and the Goyt, the former of which rises among the mountains on the borders of Yorkshire, and the latter on the borders of Cheshire and Derbyshire.

The river Etherow rises at an elevation of nearly 2000 feet above the level of the sea. It flows down from the moors, in which it rises, at the western end of the summit tunnel of the Manchester and Sheffield railway, passing down by Woodhead, into the valley of Longdendale, with a south-westerly course. The Etherow, when not swollen by floods, caused by heavy rain among the mountains, sends down from fifteen to thirty cubic feet of water per second, but after the heavy falls of rain, which frequently take place in that mountain district, it has been known to discharge 1500 cubic feet of water per second for twenty-four hours, and when at its highest, between 3600 and 4000 cubic feet per second.

The first great public use to which the waters of the river Etherow are applied, is that of feeding the reservoirs constructed by the Corporation of Manchester, for the supply of that city. These reservoirs are formed in the valley through which the river flows They are three in number, and fill the valley for a distance of nearly five miles in length. They cover about 344 statute acres of land, and contain, when full, rather more than 515,000,000 of cubic feet, or 3,218,500,000 gallons of water 1 The Woodhead reservoir, which first receives the waters of the Etherow, covers an area of 134 acres, and contains when full very nearly 198,000,000 cubic feet of water, or 1,237,000,000 gallons The embankment of the reservoir is ninety feet high at its greatest elevation. It is about a mile and two-thirds in length, and receives the water of an area of about 7500 acres of high mountain land 2. The Torside reservoir covers an area of 160 acres, and is capable of containing nearly 237,000,000 cubic feet, or 1,731,000,000 gallons of water.

The embankment of this reservoir is 100 feet high at its greatest elevation The Torside reservoir is nearly two miles in length. 3. The Rhodes Wood reservoir covers an area of fifty-four acres, and is capable of holding upwards of 80,000,000 cubic feet, or 1,481,000,000 gallons of water. Its embankment is eighty feet high at the highest point, and its length is about one mile. The whole collecting ground for the three reservoirs is 15,400 acres

The elevation of the Manchester water-works at the Woodhead reservoir, is 680 feet above the level of the sea. The height of the Rhodes Wood reservoir, which is the lowest of the Manchester reservoirs, is 520 feet above the sea

The river Etherow, after supplying the Manchester water-works, flows down the valley of Longdendale to the flourishing manufacturing town of Mottram in Longdendale At Mottram the river turns to the south, and winding round by an old Roman station, passes by Bankwood Mill, Broadbottom and Hopwood Tor, down to Crumpstall Near that point it is joined by the river Goyt, at Water Meetings, where the two streams become one, and take the name of the river Mersey

The river Goyt also rises at an elevation of nearly 2000 feet, in the highest part of the hills of Macclesfield Forest, and runs almost due north across Goyt's Moor. It flows past How Moor and Taxall, through a wild and thinly peopled district; but at Whaleybridge enters a much more populous country From Whaleybridge the Goyt flows by the populous village of Newmills, turning the machinery of many manufactories, and supplying water for print-works At Newmills it is joined by the waters of the Settbrook, flowing down the Hayfield valley Below Newmills the Goyt flows through the populous and industrious township of Marple. At Marple bridge it receives the streams that descend from the extensive and populous township of Mellor. Thence the Goyt flows almost due north, until it joins the Etherow at Water Meetings near Crumpstall, where it loses its name, and becomes a part of the river Mersey.

The river Mersey, thus formed by the union of the Etherow and the Goyt, is the boundary of the counties of Lancaster and Chester, from the junction of those two streams to the sea. In ancient times it was the boundary between the Anglo-Saxon kingdoms of Northumberland and Mercia, and probably took its name from the latter kingdom. At present it flows between the boundaries of Lancashire and Cheshire, from the junction of the Etherow and Goyt, with a W S.W. course towards Chadkirk, near which place it is crossed by the aqueduct of the Peak of Derbyshire canal. It then flows by Atterspool bridge and the print-works in that neighbourhood, and turns northward towards Stockport, passing by Waterside and Woodbank, in the township of Bredbury. There it furnishes water to the reservoirs of the Stockport water-works, from which the Portwood reservoir, in the town of Stockport, is supplied.

The river Mersey flows through the town of Stockport, turning numerous cotton mills, and supplying water for condensing purposes, and for dyeworks, foundries, and other branches of industry At Stockport the river Tame enters the Mersey from the north The Mersey, winding round the reservoir of the Stockport water-works, flows through the town. At Heaton Mersey it supplies bleachworks and mills, and passing under Cheadle bridge, turns the corn mills at Didsbury. At this point the Mersey is still 100 feet above the level of the sea At Didsbury the "eeas," or river peninsulas, formed by the windings of the Mersey, commence, which continue all the way down to Warrington. After passing the woods of Redbank and Barlow Hall, the Mersey flows under Jackson's bridge, and receives the Chorlton Brook from the north-east At Barfoot bridge the river is still seventy-five feet above the sea From this point the Mersey enters a rural country, adorned with villas belonging chiefly to the merchants and manufacturers of Manchester, and flows down to Stretford, which is now almost within the limits of the city of Manchester There it passes under Stretford bridge, near the point where the old Roman road—the stratum or street, from Chester to Manchester—crossed the river Mersey.

The district south-west of Manchester is one of the richest and best cultivated in England. This district comprises the townships of Stretford, Flixton, and Urmston, lying between the Mersey and the Irwell, or along the banks of these rivers Some years ago, a new cut, or overflow river, was made through the townships of Stretford and Urmston, for the purpose of relieving the Mersey in time of high floods. This has been of very great advantage to the occupiers of land adjoining the river. A canal was made at the joint expense of the trustees of the Bridgewater estate, of the late Sir Thomas de Trafford, of Trafford Park, and of Lord Egerton, of Tatton; they being the principal landowners in the neighbourhood It is twenty yards wide at the bottom, and the sides are well sloped, so as to be convenient to mow and to pasture. The embankments on each side are from four to eight feet high above the surface of the meadow, varying with the undulations of the land The overflow river commences above the village of Stretford, where there is a very substantial weir or overflow, and no water runs down the new river until the water in the Mersey rises to the height of the overflow, thus, in dry seasons, there is a considerable produce of hay and pasture in the bed of the new river It enters the Mersey again in Urmston, its length being three miles and a quarter.*

From Stretford the Mersey winds round the Stretford "eeas" or meadows to Urmston, through meadows and willow plantations down to Flixton, which is also one of the most fertile districts in South Lancashire, chiefly laid out and cultivated in market gardens and orchards Below Flixton the Mersey continues to flow westward to Higher Irlam, where it is joined by the much larger stream of the river Irwell. But the united stream of the Mersey and the Irwell retains the name of the Mersey for the remainder of its course. Here the river is navigable, having been rendered so from Manchester to Warrington in the reign of George I, and from Warrington to Runcorn in the reign of William III But the natural course of the Mersey is excessively winding, and it has been necessary to form short cuts, at several points, to shorten and straighten the navigation Near Cadishead the river receives the stream of Glazebrook, which flows down from the north, bringing the drainage of Chat Moss, and that of the hills lying to the north of Bury Lane. The country is very moist about Glazebrook bridge, and large quantities of willows are grown in osieries, near the junction of the two streams

Below Glazebrook the Mersey flows westward past Hollins ferry, which is an ancient ferry between the two counties Near that point it receives the river Bollin, which enters it from the south-east, flowing down from the heights of Macclesfield Forest. The Mersey then passes by Martin's Croft, and at Woolston weir reaches the tide-water of the sea. Thence it flows on to Warrington, through meadows that are flooded at high tides, passing Thelwall, where also there is an ancient ferry, and where there was a fortified borough in the time of the Anglo-Saxons. Below Warrington the Mersey flows, chiefly through salt marshes, to Widness and Runcorn, where there has been long a very ancient ferry, and where a magnificent

* Rothwell's Report on the Agriculture of Lancashire, p 50

railway bridge is now being built by the London and North-western Railway Company, to shorten the journey from Liverpool to London. Below this point is the estuary of the Mersey, which has been already described.

The river Mersey, flowing from east to west, receives all the streams of South Lancashire that flow from north to south, and the greater part of the streams of Cheshire, flowing from south to north and north-west.

The first river that the Mersey receives on the north, or Lancashire side, is the Tame. This river rises in Yorkshire, among the hills generally known as Stenage, over which the old road from Manchester to Huddersfield formerly passed The Tame flows through the manufacturing district of Saddleworth, in Yorkshire, in the first part of its course, turning the machinery of numerous woollen mills. It enters Lancashire at the manufacturing village of Mossley, where it is still 500 feet above the level of the sea Thence it flows nearly due south to Staleybridge and Dukinfield, turning numerous cotton mills in its course, and supplying water for all manufacturing purposes. From Staleybridge the Tame runs westward to Ashton-under-Lyne, where it contributes greatly to the manufacturing prosperity of that flourishing town, being extensively employed in the working of mills, dye-works, and foundries. From Ashton-under-Lyne the Tame flows south-west to the Guide Bridge railway station; and from that point nearly due south to the flourishing town of Hyde. Thence it flows southward by Haughton, and through Haughton-dale to Reddish mills. There the Tame turns westward, and flowing through the town of Stockport, discharges its waters into the river Mersey

The river Irwell, which also flows into the Mersey, is the largest of all the streams that join that river. The Irwell rises in the mountains of Rossendale Forest, at a height of 1427 feet above the level of the sea, and in its course of forty-seven miles through Bury and Manchester to the river Mersey, collects and brings down with it the waters of nearly all the streams of South Lancashire There is no other river in England that has been rendered so useful for manufacturing purposes, and it was on the banks of the Irwell, and its numerous tributaries, that the manufacturing industry of Lancashire was founded, at least three hundred years previous to the discovery of the steam-engine.

The river Irwell rises at Irwell Spring, on Deerplay Hill, one of the highest points in that range of hills which forms the northern boundary of the Salford hundred, and separates the streams flowing southward into the Mersey, from those flowing northward into the Ribble. The stream of the Irwell rushes rapidly down from the hills into a narrow valley, passing by the print-works and the cotton mill of Irwell Spring to Broadclough, where it is still 924 feet above the level of the sea. In flowing down the higher part of Rossendale it turns numerous mills, and supplies many reservoirs before it reaches the flourishing town of Bacup, at an elevation of 847 feet above the sea. Here the Irwell works the machinery of numerous manufactories. From Bacup it flows southward to Waterfoot, where it receives Whitwell Brook. Thence it runs to Rawtenstall, and to the rising manufacturing town of Newchurch, in Rossendale, where it receives Limy Water. Thence it flows on to Holme mill, near Ewood bridge, where it is still 500 feet above the level of the sea, and to Ramsbottom, 418 feet above the sea. At Summerseat the Irwell has still an elevation of 350 feet above the sea. Near that point it receives the waters of the river Croal, from Bolton, and those of the river Tonge, which flow within a short distance of that busy town. Thence it descends by Barlow's Croft to the flourishing town of Bury, where its elevation is still 270 feet above the sea.

Leaving Bury the river Irwell flows down to Radcliff bridge, where it receives the river Roch, from Rochdale, at an elevation of 250 feet. At Prestolee the Irwell is still 200 feet above the level of the sea, at Ringley 165 feet, at Kersley Hall 157 feet; and at Agecroft 100 feet. From Agecroft the Irwell flows down through a rich well-wooded valley to Manchester and Salford, where it turns or supplies water for innumerable mills, dyeworks, foundries, and every kind of industrial establishment in which water is used. At Manchester it receives the rivers Irk and Medlock, and several smaller streams. Passing through Manchester with a most winding course, the river Irwell flows between Trafford Park and Eccles down to Barton-on-Irwell, and thence through meadows and orchards by Flixton and Lower Irlam to Higher Irlam, where it joins its waters to those of the river Mersey, swelling them to at least twice their original volume.

From the west the river Irwell receives numerous streams, descending from the hilly district around Bolton. The river Tonge rises on the cloughs of the hills to the north-west of Bolton, and flows past Dean mill, approaching very near to the town of Bolton. After passing through the populous manufacturing townships of Great and Little Lever, Farnworth, and Kersley, the Tonge flows into the river Irwell. The river Croal rises in the hills to the west of Bolton, flows through that town, and joins the river Tonge The river Eagle, or Eagle Brook, rises in the millstone hills above Eagley Bank, where the clearness of the waters has caused several bleachworks and printworks to be established The Eagle flows down to Astle Bank, where it joins the river Tonge The Bradshaw Brook, a very abundant stream, rises in the same hills, and flows through Bradshaw into the Tonge below Bolton, carrying with it other small streams that descend from the hills above Harwood and Ainsworth.

From the east the Irwell receives numerous streams. Amongst these is the river Roch, which rises in the wild ravines of Blackstone Edge. Thence it flows down to Littleborough, and winds through Wuerdale and Wardleworth to Rochdale. After leaving Rochdale the Roch flows north of Heywood and Heap, and south of Chadwick and Birtle to Heap bridge, Redvales, and Blackford bridge, and so on to Redcliffe, where it joins the Irwell.

At Manchester the Irwell receives the waters of the rivers Irk and Medlock. The Irk rises, near Royston, at a height of 500 feet above the sea. It flows to Middleton, which is a flourishing manufacturing town, and then by way of Heaton Park, Blackley, and Lower Crumpsall, through Harpurhey to Manchester, where it joins the river Irwell. The river Medlock, rises at a height of upwards of 1000 feet above the level of the sea, in the millstone-grit hills that there separate Lancashire from Yorkshire. At the height of 800 feet above the sea the Medlock fills the reservoirs of the Oldham water-works, and thence flows southward to Waterhead mill, leaving the town of Oldham to the west. Descending through Strine Dale, the Medlock flows southward to Lees, turning the cotton mills at Springside. At Holt's mill the Medlock receives another large brook from the east, and flows on to Park bridge. Here it is still 425 feet above the level of the sea. Thence it flows towards Bardsley, and so down Medlock vale, and by the Medlock and Clayton-bridge print-works to the city of Manchester, where it joins the river Irwell.

Such is this great manufacturing stream, with its numerous tributaries. The immense and incalculable amount of water-power, and of water available for every manufacturing purpose, furnished by these streams, may be considered as the first natural cause of the development of manufacturing industry in South Lancashire. At the time when the last great Ordnance Survey of Lancashire was made, the persons employed in the survey marked more than a thousand manufacturing establishments of various kinds, including cotton and woollen mills, print-works, dye-works, iron foundries, and workshops of various kinds upon its banks. This survey was completed about the year 1852, and between that time and the present the manufacturing establishments of Lancashire have increased from 30 to 40 per cent in number and importance.

In addition to the streams that flow into the Mersey from Lancashire, and enter it on the north, it also receives numerous important streams from the south, or Cheshire side of the river

First is the river Bollin, which rises in Macclesfield Forest, at an elevation of nearly 1800 feet, and flows down into the plain of Cheshire by the town of Macclesfield. The Bollin receives numerous small streams in the neighbourhood of that town, which gave a great impulse to its manufactures more than 100 years ago, and powerfully assisted in fixing the silk manufacture, as well as a portion of the cotton trade, in that place. In the same manner the river Dane was the primary cause of the manufacturing prosperity of the town of Congleton, the most southerly manufacturing town of the two counties The river Dane rises on the summit of the lofty hills that divide Cheshire from Derbyshire, and rushes down from the mountains by the town of Congleton, cutting itself a deep channel through the red marls of the Cheshire plain After turning the mills of Congleton and the neighbouring villages, where the silk and cotton manufactures are both carried on, the Dane flows across the plain of Cheshire, through a deep alluvial bed, to Middlewich, where it turns northward and soon after discharges its waters into the river Weaver at Northwich. The numerous springs in the hills from which the Bollin and the Dane descend, fill the reservoirs, by which the Grand Trunk canal and its branches are supplied with water.

The above are the principal rivers connected with the manufacturing system of the two counties. We shall now have to speak of the river Weaver, and some small streams that flow through the salt-field of Cheshire, and the river Dee, which separates the north-western division of England from the Principality of Wales

The river Weaver springs in the slopes of the hills of the new red sandstone formation, which rise to the south of Cheshire and separate that county from Staffordshire and Shropshire. These hills are of no great height, but the rise of the land is sufficient to divide the streams that flow from their northern slope, from those that flow from their southern The waters that flow down the southern front of these hills run into the river Trent, and after a long and winding course reach the Humber and the German Ocean. Those which flow towards the north run across the salt-field of Cheshire, and pass by way of Northwich and Frodsham bridge into the Mersey and the Irish Sea. The Weaver soon after its rise flows across the permian branch of the new red sandstone formation, down to Audlem and on to Nantwich This was formerly the chief place in the salt district of Cheshire, but ceased to be so when the firewood on the neighbouring hills was exhausted, and when it became necessary to bring coal from the Lancashire coal-field to seethe the brine, from which the salt is obtained by evaporation From Nantwich to Winsford bridge the Weaver flows through a country rich in salt and brine, but it is only when it reaches Winsford bridge that the manufacture of salt commences. The river Weaver has been rendered navigable to that point, so that there is no difficulty either in bringing up coal from the banks of the Mersey, or in conveying the salt down the river to Liverpool The Weaver was rendered navigable in the reigns of George I. and George II, and now supplies the means of conveying three-fourths of the salt that is made in England. Northwich is the principal town engaged in the salt manufacture, and at that point, as already mentioned, the Weaver is joined by the river Dane and by other smaller streams From Northwich to the Mersey the river Weaver flows through a deep, rich, alluvial valley, cut out by the stream of the river to a great depth in the red marls, which form the principal strata of the district

The beautiful and classic Dee, the last river of which we shall have to speak, rises in the eastern slopes of the lofty granite mountains of Merionethshire, and flows through the lake of Bala, down to Corwen, bringing with it the waters of the Treweryn and many other copious streams Near Corwen the Dee receives another set of beautiful streams flowing down from the east side of Snowdon. At Llandisillio the waters of the Dee are collected and raised by means of a wear, and a portion of them turned into an artificial channel, which supplies the Chester and Ellesmere canal with water. The river Dee then flows down the valley to Llangollen, and so on to Ruabon and Wynnstay Park, round which it winds amongst the most lovely river scenery After passing Wynnstay the river Dee descends into the plain of Cheshire, flowing by Overton bridge and Bangor, the ancient seat of learning and religion in the time of the early British Christians. From Bangor the Dee flows, with innumerable windings, down to Holt bridge. This ancient bridge was in former times one of the principal means of connection between England and Wales, and was guarded by the castle of Holt, supposed to have been built on the site of an old Roman fortress. From Holt bridge the river Dee flows down to the ancient city of Deva, Devana, or Chester, where its waters mingle with those of the sea.

A bold and original plan was brought forward several years ago by Mr. Rawlinson, C.B, C.E., for furnishing the town and neighbourhood of Liverpool, which now contain a rapidly increasing population of 600,000 persons, with a supply of water from the Dee. The proposal to have recourse to the Dee as a source of supply has recently been revived by Mr. Duncan, C.E, the engineer of the Liverpool water-works. He proposes to construct works at Bala Lake, through which the Dee flows, and to draw his supply of water from the lake The water of the Upper Dee is known to be pure and soft in quality, and Mr. Duncan calculates that a supply of 60,000,000 gallons per day might be brought from Bala Lake to Liverpool, a distance of seventy-eight miles. Bold as is this scheme, it must yield in boldness to a plan recently brought forward by Mr. Bateman, C.E., the constructor of the Manchester and Glasgow water-works, who proposes to supply London and the metropolitan district, containing upwards of 3,000,000 inhabitants, with a daily supply of 100,000,000 gallons, capable of being increased to 200,000,000 gallons of water, from the streams that flow down from the Welsh mountains into the river Severn The distance which it is proposed to carry the water in this case is 180 miles.*

The length of the course of the river Dee is ninety-three miles, and the area of the valley or watershed over which it flows is

* Borough of Liverpool Report of the Water-works Engineer (Thomas Duncan, Esq, C E) on Extension of Water-supply and New Works, 1866 Metropolis Water-supply on the Supply of Water to London from the Sources of the River Severn, by John Frederick Bateman, C.E, F R.S., F G S., &c. 1865.

850 square miles. It is not navigable above Bangor. At this point it loses the character of a wild romantic mountain stream, and acquires that of a beautiful English river

Such are the principal streams of the counties of Lancaster and Chester, and it is not too much to say of them that they have had the most powerful influence in the development of the prosperity of the counties through which they flow. Nearly all the more ancient towns of the two counties stand on one or other of these rivers, and none of these towns could have attained their present position of population and wealth, without the advantage which they have derived from their proximity to the streams that flow by or through them.

The quality of all rain-water when it falls from the clouds must be much the same, but, after it has reached the earth, it varies with the contents of the rocks and soils over which it flows, or through which it percolates. Thus the waters of mountainous countries, composed of the more ancient strata, are generally soft. "All the highland rivers," says Dr Ramsay, "as a rule, are soft, the mountains being composed of granitic rocks, gneiss, mica, schist, and the like—a very small portion of limestone being intermixed therewith, and the other rocks being comparatively free from lime Again, the waters which flow from the Pennine chain, that extends from the southern borders of Scotland into Derbyshire, are all hard, because they drain areas composed chiefly of carboniferous limestone, and all the rivers that run east from this range, and all those that flow in areas as far south as the British Channel, over the new red sandstone and lias, and the oolitic and the cretaceous rocks, are of necessity charged with those substances in solution that make water hard The water from the Welsh mountains is in great part soft, the country being composed of silurian rocks, here and there slightly calcareous, from the presence of fossils, mixed with the hardened sandy or slaty sediment that forms the larger part of that country From this cause, so sweet and pleasant are the waters of Bala Lake, compared with the inferior mixtures that we drink in London, that it has been more than once proposed to lead it all the way for the supply of water for the capital"*

A large portion of the water supplied by the rainfall on mountains and hills runs at once into streams and rivers, and discharges itself

* Physical Geography and Geology of Great Britain, by A C Ramsay, F R.S., Local Director of the Geological Survey of Great Britain, 1864

into the sea, through these channels, along the surface of the ground. But even in hilly districts it is seldom found to be possible to collect more than eighty per cent. in wet seasons, and more than from sixty to seventy per cent in dry seasons, of the total rainfall of the district, into reservoirs formed for the purpose of containing it The remainder is either lost, for a time, by evaporation, or sinks into cracks and crevices of the earth, to levels below that of the reservoirs. Thence it either finds its way into the streams and rivers at still lower levels, or it sinks into the earth, spreading itself, with much of the water that falls on the plains, through the different strata under the ground. In some of these strata, especially in the mountain limestone, the water forms subterranean rivers, like those that run through the caves of Adelsburg, of Derbyshire, and of Craven in Yorkshire, and that which gushes out of the earth with the force of a mill stream at Holywell in Flintshire, sending forth more than twenty tons of water per minute. In other formations, as in the chalk under the London clay, the water collects in great natural reservoirs in the chalk, and rushes to the surface, when deep Artesian wells are driven through the thick beds of clay, into the chalk which contains the water. In some of the brine pits in Cheshire, the brine is found at great depths under thick beds of plaster of Paris, but rushes up nearly to the surface when those beds are pierced by the miner's auger. In general, however, the water is very widely diffused, and is found almost everywhere In the new red sandstone the water is most abundant in what are called the waterstone rocks, which form one of the divisions of what is now known to geologists as the trias formation. The rocks of the waterstone run through the whole of Cheshire, from Malpas and Overton to the river Mersey at Frodsham and Helsby; thence they extend through the peninsula of Wirral to the sea at New Brighton. They are also found in Lancashire in and around Liverpool, where the public wells yield a supply of between 7,000,000 and 8,000,000 gallons of water daily *

The Mineral Resources of Lancashire and Cheshire. The Coal-field of the Two Counties.—But fire, water, and steam (the product of both united) are the great instruments by which the irresistible and inexhaustible powers of nature are brought to the aid of the feeble strength of man, in his efforts to adapt and fashion the most useful products of the animal, vegetable, and mineral kingdoms to the

* See Ordnance Maps of Geological Survey, where the line of the Waterstone is marked both in Lancashire and Cheshire.

purpose of supplying human wants, and developing human industry. The force of steam applied in the working of the steam-engine is incomparably the greatest and most useful of these powers. But fire and water are also used for numerous purposes connected with industry, besides that of generating steam Fire especially is an instrument of immense power in changing the forms of substances, both internally and externally, and is so applied in all districts in which coal is found in abundance. Previous to the great improvement in the steam-engine made by James Watt, the force of running water, as already stated, was the chief power of inanimate nature used in propelling machinery; and the hilly districts of Lancashire, Cheshire, and Yorkshire, abounding in streams of water, were already the principal seats of the manufacturing industry of England. But the power of steam has to a great extent superseded, and to a still greater extent has been united to water-power, as the chief instrument of manufacturing industry. Coal is now the only means of producing steam found in sufficient abundance in thickly peopled and highly cultivated countries, in which the primeval forests have been consumed or cleared away for the purposes of cultivation. Hence the comparative power of this and other countries, and of the several districts of this country, depends chiefly on the greater or smaller quantities of coal which they possess Without an abundant supply of this kind of fuel, manufacturing wealth and greatness are now scarcely attainable in many of the most important branches of industry. With an abundant supply of coal there is no practical limit to the capacity of generating motive power, or of producing the articles to which it can be applied The manufacturing superiority of Great Britain arises chiefly from the circumstance, that this country possesses much more abundant supplies of coal than any other country of Europe. In the same manner, the superior wealth and more abundant population of several districts of the United Kingdom depend chiefly on the comparative abundance of their supplies of coal, and on the manner in which the coal produced in each district is applied to the purposes of industry.

The coal-field of Lancashire and Cheshire is one of the richest and most productive in Great Britain. It extends with an irregular area about forty-six miles in length from north to south, commencing northward near Colne in Lancashire, at a short distance from the river Ribble, and running southward to the neighbourhood of Congleton in Cheshire, within a few miles of the sources of the river

Trent. At its broadest point it is about forty miles in breadth, extending from Todmorden, on the borders of Yorkshire on the east, to Whiston and Croxteth on the west, which latter places are within three or four miles of the estuary of the Mersey, and of the Irish Sea. But the outline of this great coal-field is too irregular, to render these data of much value in computing the area covered by the whole field. In round numbers, however, it may be stated that it covers an area of about 400,000 statute acres of land, or about the fifth part of the area of the counties of Lancaster and Chester.

In the number and the richness of its beds of coal, as well as the amount of its produce, the Lancashire coal-field is one of the most valuable of the coal-fields of England. The aggregate thickness of the coal measures of this coal-field is about 6200 feet, the measures forming a mass of strata which, heaped on each other, would rise to twice the height of the highest mountain in England. But these strata are now scattered about in all positions, some of the beds being nearly horizontal, and not more than about 150 feet above the level of the sea, whilst others rise rapidly to the height of 1500, and in a few cases, of 1800 feet, above the level of the sea. The number of beds of coal existing in the coal measures of Lancashire and Cheshire is about 120, and of these upwards of thirty are of sufficient thickness to be worked with advantage. The amount of coal raised yearly from this coal-field is about 12,000,000 tons, with a continual tendency to increase.

The numerous seams of coal found in the two counties exhibit all the fosilized plants that are usually found in the coal formation. "All these plants," says Professor Sedgwick, speaking of the carboniferous plants in general, "are of extinct species, many of them are of extinct genera, and they are of forms which indicate a high tropical temperature. Amongst them are coniferous trees, like those found in some of the South Sea Islands; gigantic reeds, tree ferns, enormous creeping plants, with sharp pinnated leaves, trees with fluted stems; and many other strange but beautiful forms of vegetable life, forced to rankness and luxuriance by great heat and moisture." Upwards of 500 varieties of fossil plants are enumerated by Adolphe Brongniart, as belonging to the carboniferous system. These, according to Sir Charles Lyell, must be regarded as mere fragments of the ancient flora, since in Europe alone there are now 11,000 living species of plants.*

* Lyell's Principles of Geology, p. 138

The plants found in the greatest abundance in the Lancashire coal-field, are the fluted stems of *Sigillaria*, so named, from the seal-like impressions with which they are covered The *Stigmaria*, covered with innumerable marks, like punctures, are almost equally abundant. These were formerly supposed to be the remains of different plants, but it is now clearly ascertained that the *Stigmaria* are the roots of the *Sigillaria*. This was discovered several years ago, by Mr. William Edward Binney, president of the Manchester Geological Society, whose researches have thrown so much light on the natural history, both of the Lancashire and Cheshire coal-field, and of coal-fields in general. In addition to the above-named plants there are also found, in the coal of this field, the remains of the plants known as *Lepidodendra*, covered with scale-like leaf-marks, together with numerous ferns. All the above are found buried in masses of carbonaceous matter, something like charcoal, being probably the compressed remains of smaller plants, all of which show a woody structure under the microscope

The stems of the trees or plants known as *Sigillaria*, and the roots of the same, known as *Stigmaria*, have been discovered by Mr Binney in about 100 of the seams of coal, in the coal-fields of Lancashire and Cheshire. Rootlets of the *Stigmaria* have also been found in the thin partings of the fine silt and fire-clay of this formation. Large specimens of the *Sigillaria* have been found in some of the coal seams of this field Several fossil trees, most of which exhibit the undoubted characteristics of *Sigillaria*, have been traced into the strata, to a height of twenty-five feet, and one of them has been traced by Mr. Ray, the engineer of the Duchess of Lancaster colliery at Patricroft, to a height of fifty or sixty feet. A portion of the stem of this tree, converted into coal, is now in the Museum of the Manchester Geological Society. A magnificent specimen of *Sigillaria* was also discovered a few years ago in the Victoria mine, Dukinfield, a few miles from Manchester, at the depth of 1100 feet from the surface. Mr. Binney observes that the stem of this tree exhibits the respective characters of the species *Pachyderma reniformis* and *organon* The stem was about two feet high, and true *Stigmaria*, eighteen or twenty feet in length, were traced as its roots. Four main roots appear to have proceeded from the base of the trunk, one of which has been preserved entire, and has been deposited in the Museum of the Manchester Geological Society. This root, after running some distance, divides into two branch roots, and each of these into two more. They run in a horizontal direction, as *Stigmaria,* at a depth of two feet under the coal. But their extremities have not been reached, although they were traced for upwards of twenty feet. Four fossil trees, all *Sigillaria,* have been found at St. Helen's in the coal-field. "Sufficient evidence" says Mr. Binney, "has not been adduced to prove that the various other plants found in the coal measures were grown on the places where they are now found; for we have not been able to detect their roots *in situ.* This remains to be done." With respect to the *Sigillaria* there can scarcely be a doubt that it grew in water, on the deposits where it is now discovered, and that it is the plant which in a great measure contributed to form our valuable beds of coal. On this subject Sir Charles Lyell observes, "The progress of modern discovery has led to the very general admission of the doctrine, that beds of coal have for the most part been formed of the remains of trees and plants that grew on the spot where the coal now exists; the land having been successively submerged, so that a covering of mud and sand was deposited upon accumulations of vegetable matter. That such has been the origin of some coal seams is proved by the upright position of fossil trees, both in Europe and America, in which the roots terminate downwards in beds of coal" On the same subject Sir Roderick Murchison makes the following observations in the last edition of his "Siluria" —"An opinion has been gradually gaining ground amongst geologists and naturalists, that by far the greater part of the coal is the result of littoral growths in sea-water, or swamps, of succulent vegetables suited to those conditions; and that the occurrence of marine spoils among and over the beds of coal has been the normal condition of many basins It is certainly more likely that there should have been a gradual subsidence, with periodical pauses, in a mass of coal strata 12,000 feet thick, as in South Wales, than that there should have been repeated oscillations of the land, descending to receive marine productions, and raised again to sustain the growth of terrestrial plants. We are perhaps warranted in believing, that a theory of the formation of coal which should embrace, as its chief element, a widely extended series of shallow and partially inclosed seas, fringed with swampy forests of water-loving plants, subject to frequent subsidence, is most in harmony with observed phenomena."

It is stated by Mr. Steinhauer in the American "Philosophical Transactions," that the *Sigillaria,* which, with the *Stigmaria* appears to be the chief constituent of several of the American coal-fields, as well as of those of England, was a cylindrical stem or plant, growing in a direction very nearly horizontal, in the soft mud in the hollows of lakes and seas, without branches, but sending out fibres on every side Lindley and Hutton state that it was a prostrate land plant, the branches of which extended from a common centre. This opinion was founded on the inspection of very perfect species found in the Jarrow colliery. Mr. Binney is of opinion that *Sigillaria* grew in rich mud, like the mangrove at the mouth of the river Niger, and other great rivers in the tropical regions, where intense heat, an abundant supply of moisture, and a soil continually refreshed by the mud washed down by the rivers, produces a richness and rankness of vegetation that is not to be found in any other part of the world The physical condition of the earth must have been very different from what it is at present, either from internal or external heat, when the immense masses of plants which now form the coal-fields of Europe and America were produced in the seas adjoining, or which then covered what are now the British Islands, British America, and the United States. Professor Dawson, of Montreal, states in a paper read before the Geological Society of London in January, 1866, that *Stigmaria* are found under every bed of coal in Nova Scotia and New Brunswick, and placed in such a manner as to prove that the coal was accumulated by the growth of those plants *in situ*, and that the intervening strata show abundant deposits of mud and sand by water, as in the deltas of rivers. Cannel coal, in his opinion, was formed of the fine vegetable mud that accumulates in ponds and in the hollows of swamps.*

A careful examination of the animal remains discovered in the coal-fields of Lancashire and Cheshire, has convinced the ablest of our local geologists that the coal of this district is the product of submarine, and not of terrestrial forests. The presence of specimens of bivalve shells, and of fossil fishes in cannel coal, is believed to prove that it was formed under water, though different opinions have been held as to whether the waters that prevailed during the deposition of the carboniferous series were fresh or salt. Mr. Binney states that upwards of 150 varieties of fossil fishes have been discovered in the coal measures generally, and though comparatively few fishes or shells have been discovered in the coal seams of the Lancashire

* Athenæum, January 6, 1866

and Cheshire coal-field, yet the black bass roofs in the upper coal field are many of them entire masses of cyprides, microconchi, shells, fishbones, and teeth, mixed with decomposed vegetable and animal matter. The shells of the genus *Unio* are found in the middle coal-field, and the *Pecten, Goniatites,* and other marine shells in the lower coal-fields. "Different opinions," says Mr. Binney, "have been held as to whether the waters which formerly prevailed during deposition of the higher strata of the carboniferous series were fresh or salt. The authors who take the former view adduce, in support of their hypothesis, the remains of *Cypris,* (a bivalve shell inhabiting the waters of lakes, marshes, and estuaries), and a questionable species or two of *Unio*; while those of the latter adduce shells of the genera *Goniatites, Nautilus, Posidonia, Pecten, Modiola,* and *Nucula,* and great sauroid, and squaloid fishes, as well as those of the *Platysomus, Scalacanthus, Palæoniscus* genera, common to the carboniferous and the magnesian limestone formation. Wherever the strata contain the remains of fishes, *Pecten, Goniatites,* or *Unio,* the remains of such plants as *Sigillaria* and its *Stigmaria* roots are equally present, which would not be expected to be the case if sudden changes of the waters from fresh to salt had taken place; for a flora is quite as sensitive of such a change as a fauna. The balance of evidence, therefore, is much in favour of the water having been of one kind, and on the whole probably salt, and not fresh.*

Though coal is found over extensive regions of Europe, America, Asia, and Australia, there are few portions of the earth's surface that have benefited mankind by their mineral products to the extent to which it has been benefited by the coal-fields of Lancashire and Cheshire. There may be coal-fields of larger area in England, but for richness and position, and taking into consideration the number and thickness of the beds of coal, as well as the extent of the area covered, it is probably inferior to none.

The coal-field of Lancashire and Cheshire is usually divided into three parts, differing from each other in the number and richness of the beds of coal that they contain, and in the nature of the strata in which those beds of coal are included. These three divisions are:—1. The upper or Manchester coal-field. 2. The middle or principal coal-field, extending completely across Lancashire from Oldham, Ashton, Dukinfield, and Poynton in Cheshire, to St. Helen's and Wigan. 3. The lower coal-field, so called from

* E. W Binney, Esq, on the Origin of Coal Memoirs of the Manchester Philosophical Society, vol. x. p, 158

having been originally deposited at the lowest depths of the sea, but which has now been forced up to the greatest heights by internal convulsions, and extends over great part of the hilly and mountainous region of South Lancashire and Cheshire.

The upper or Manchester coal-field is small in extent, and not very rich in its deposits of coal. The strata forming this division of the coal-field commence with the Ardwick limestones, close to Manchester, and extend from the Ardwick limestones to the coal measures under Smedley old hall, near to the same city.

The middle or principal coal-field is of great extent, and of extraordinary richness The strata of which it is composed commence with the Bardsley-bridge rock, and end with the Lower Woodley coal measures. The intervening strata include the thick coals of Poynton, near Stockport, Bench Lane, Ashton-under-Lyne, Oldham, Middleton, Heywood, Bury, Redcliffe, Clifton, Worsley, Atherton, St Helen's, and Wigan

The third or lower coal-field comprises the coal measures from the stratum of the Lower Woodley mine, which is known as the last thick bed of coal, to the thin strata of coal in the upper millstone grit, and to the edge of the lower millstone grit, where coal ceases to be found. The coal of the Lower Woodley mine is identical with the Riley mine, Oldham, the Dogshaw mine, at Bury; and the Arley mine, at Wigan. Below it are the coals of Whaleybridge, Newmills, Mellor, Ludworth, Stalcybridge, Rochdale, Todmorden, Bacup, Birtle, Cheesden bridge, Newchurch, Quarlton, Burnley, Colne, Blackburn, Rivington, and Chorley

Taking the coal measures for Lancashire and Cheshire as a whole, they comprise the strata extending from the freshwater limestones of Ardwick near Manchester, and of Whiston near Prescott, to the quartz or rough rock that crops up in many places, rising to a great height on the wild hills of Parbold on the north-west, Werneth Low on the south-east, and along the line of barren heights which divides Lancashire and Cheshire from Yorkshire and Derbyshire. The quartz rock is called the old mother rock at Werneth There are some small seams of coal in the upper millstone grit at Cheesden bridge, in Shuttleworth near Rochdale, and in other places, but they are seldom of much value. It was formerly supposed that the upper boundary of the Lancashire coal-field was the new red sandstone; but coal is now extensively worked under that formation at Pendleton, Patricroft, and other places. Mr.

E. W. Binney states in a paper, vol. ii., 3rd series, of the "Memoirs of the Manchester Literary and Philosophical Society," published in 1865, that the coal measures have also been found in Medlock Vale near Manchester, at the Park-bridge print-works, where Mr. Wood has succeeded on a second attempt, after having failed in the first, in penetrating through both the trias and permian formations of the new red sandstone, and in finding the coal measures at a depth of 250 yards Mr. Binney also mentions that the coal measures have been met with about a mile south-west of All Saints church, Manchester, at a depth of 400 feet. "This," he adds, "is of great importance, and proves that coal measures are met with at places under trias and permian deposits, much nearer to the surface than was previously expected, and where the upper rock gives no evidence of their existence" He suggests that borings should be made at Heaton Norris, to ascertain the thickness of the permian beds at that point, and whether an extensive coal-field does not lie under Heaton Norris and Stockport, and extend all the way to Manchester.

Some very interesting natural sections of the Lancashire and Cheshire coal-field, are obtained along the banks of the streams that flow through the coal measures at various points. The river Goyt, which rises in the higher ranges of the coal measures, in Macclesfield Forest, and flows northward to swell the river Mersey, shows a fine section of the inferior and lower coal-field, from Fog-brook in Offerton to Mellor The river Etherow, which flows to join the river Goyt, from the higher hills near the summit tunnel, on the Manchester and Sheffield railway, also affords a view of the lower coal beds at Crumstall bridge and Ludworth, of the rocks and shales of Broadbottom; and of the millstone grits and limestone shales of Tintwistle and Hollinsbrook The valley of the river Tame, in the course of the stream from the high hills on the eastern side of the two counties to the neighbourhood of Stockport, shows a good section of the whole coal-field from Reddish mills by Arden, Dukinfield, Ashton, and Staleybridge to Saddleworth A portion of the middle coal-field is well shown in the valley of Norbury brook, to the south of Stockport. The valley of the Irk, near Manchester, displays the best section of the lower members of the new red sandstone, overlying the coal formation, that is to be found in the north-west division of England The valley of the river Medlock shows the freshwater limestones of Ardwick, and the upper portion of the coal measures of the Manchester coal-field.

But by far the best view of the coal-field of Lancashire is obtained on the sides and in the valley of the river Irwell, the great manufacturing river of Lancashire, in the course of that stream from the lofty hills above Bacup, where it rises in the most ancient of the coal measures and millstone grits, to near Ringley, above five miles above Manchester, where it begins to flow over the new red sandstone formation The river in this part of its course crosses the main coal-field of Lancashire, and runs over between thirty and forty beds of coal, including nearly the whole of the richest coal seams of Lancashire. Mr. E. W Binney has traced the superposition of the coal strata along the banks of the Irwell, from the edge of the new red sandstone at Ringley, near Manchester, to the upper millstone grit at Brooksbottom, in the higher part of the hills The following is a summary of the information which he has obtained, and recorded in a tabular form :—

Commencing at the northern point of that great indentation of the new red sandstone, which in ancient times probably formed a bay of the sea, running up into a hollow in the coal formation at Ringley, the coal is met with under a bed of shale six yards thick This first bed of coal is two feet in thickness Immediately below the first bed are shales or clay hardened into thin laminæ, and binds thirty feet in thickness Beneath these is a second bed of coal five feet thick This is what is called the Ellams mine coal A bed of white rock twenty yards thick, with layers of shale, and a black stone roof, covers the third bed of coal. This seam of is only nine inches thick, at the point where it is here seen; but Mr Binney states that it is supposed by some persons to be identical with the Pendleton and Worsley four-foot coal, and if so, with the coal of the same name found at Bradford, near Manchester A bed of shale, four yards thick, interposes between the third and fourth bed of coal. This fourth bed is one foot thick, and is of the quality named "bassy." Beds of blue shale, eight yards in thickness, and forty-five yards of solid red rock, cover the fifth bed of coal, which is only nine inches in thickness A gray folding rock more than fifteen yards thick, and a blue metal ten yards thick, separate the sixth from the fifth bed of coal. This rock, Mr. Binney says, cannot be identified with the Bardsley-bridge rock. The coal of the sixth bed is one foot four inches in thickness.

A stony shale, twenty yards in thickness, covers the seventh bed of coal, which is one foot thick. Beds of shale fifteen yards thick; shale two yards thick, with ironstone nodules, and shale and white earth sixteen yards thick—cover the eighth bed of coal, which is three feet thick A bed of light-coloured dirt, one yard thick, covers the ninth bed of coal, known as Garbutt's mine This ninth bed of coal is three feet thick A bed of shale two yards thick, one of brown rock two yards thick, twelve yards of gray slate, with limestone bands, and six yards of black shale—cover the tenth bed. This tenth bed is four feet ten inches in thickness; of which twenty inches is good coal, fourteen inches bad, and twenty-four inches middling

Between the tenth and the eleventh bed of coal are three yards of fine white rock, and thirty yards of strong metal, with layers of ironstone The eleventh bed of coal is two feet three inches in thickness, and is divided into three folds. Above the twelfth bed of coal is shale with ironstone nodules, six yards, and red rock with layers of blue shale The twelfth bed of coal is that known as the Five-quarters mine. This coal is six feet thick, or rather one foot coal, one foot dirt, and four feet coal Below the Five-quarters mine is reddish rock with layers of slate, twenty yards in thickness. The thirteenth bed of coal is three feet thick Below this is strong gray slate, fifteen yards thick. The fourteenth bed of coal is what is called the old Doe mine, containing coal nine feet thick, in three folds Blue shale sixteen yards thick, and whitish rock twelve yards thick, overlie the fifteenth bed, consisting of six feet of good solid coal, known as the Trencherbone coal The sixteenth bed of coal is covered with forty yards of white rock, "ladyshore" The coal of the sixteenth bed is three feet thick. The next metal is not well-known The seventeenth bed of coal is two feet three inches thick The eighteenth bed is covered with ten yards of red rock; fifteen of white rock, and fifteen of light-coloured shale. The eighteenth bed of coal is two feet thick, the next bed is covered with forty yards of light-coloured strong metals The nineteenth bed, known as Hind's coal, is ten feet thick, but only five feet is good coal This is succeeded by sixteen yards of white and brown earth, below which is the twentieth bed of coal, one foot three inches in thickness

The twenty-first bed of coal, known as the Gingham mine, is four feet thick Above it are twenty yards of light-coloured metals, and below it a floor two yards thick. At Bury bridge is red rock, with shale thirty-five yards thick, and six yards of black shale These cover the twenty-second bed of coal, one foot three inches in thickness The twenty-third seam of coal, one foot thick, is covered by nine yards of strong gray metals, with ironstone nodules, and six yards of light shale with bands of ironstone Light-coloured rock six yards thick covers the twenty-fourth bed of coal, which is nine inches thick The twenty-fifth vein of coal, five feet thick, and known as the Lees or Dogshaw coal, is covered with thick beds of shale, white soapy earth and black shale, altogether more than sixty yards in thickness.

Mr Binney observes on this rich vein of coal:—"This coal is the last thick seam of coal, and identical with the Lower Woodley mine of Dukinfield, the Riley mine of Oldham, and the Arley mine of Wigan At Harwood it is very thin"

Below this bed of coal is a bed of black heavy stone of a crystalline structure, one yard in thickness, six yards of blue shale, twenty-one yards of light-coloured rock, which has a red tinge at Harwood, sixty yards of white earthy shale; thirty yards very black shale; two feet of a stone resembling impure gannister coal, ten yards light shale, six yards flaggy rock, Old Lawrence, with thirty yards of black stone shale Mr Binney remarks on the above gray flaggy rock, "It sometimes exceeds twenty yards in thickness, but is always parted by layers of shale three or four feet thick It is worked at Kerridge near Bollington in Cheshire, at Holyfold in Romilly, at Catlow near Colne, at Harwood, at Doffcocker near Bolton, and at Enfield near Accrington" Beneath these beds of slate are black iridescent shale, containing shells of the genera *Pecten*, *Goniatites*, &c, six yards in thickness. Below this is the twenty-sixth bed of coal, one foot thick, which, however, is eighteen inches thick in the neighbourhood of Bacup. The twenty-seventh bed of coal, which is only eight inches thick, is covered with gray lumpy shale, three yards thick; brown dirty rock, full of black streaks; hard sharp sandstone four yards thick, well seen at Ending near Whitworth, and dark gray shale forty yards thick White flaggy rock, marked with red streaks, and a dark shale containing the shells mentioned above, cover the twenty-eighth bed of coal. This is gannister coal, excellent for smithy purposes, and often called the Rabbit or Mountain mine, from the circumstance of its being generally worked by means of levels made like rabbit holes, in the hill sides Mr. Binney observes on the above coal:—"The principal mine of Staleybridge, Rochdale, Bacup, Burnley, Blackburn, Halliwell, Darwen, and Chorley It varies in thickness from five feet eight inches in Dulesgate, Todmorden, to about two inches at Aftside and Harwood near Bolton." Next is a hard heavy stone full of *Stigmaria ficoides.* This rock is excellent material for roads Beneath is light-coloured stone four yards thick, gray metals five yards thick, and two yards black shale. These cover the twenty-ninth seam of coal, which is the principal mine of Quarlton and Aftside, where it is four feet thick. Beds of black shale cover the thirtieth bed of coal (bassy) This coal is never worked in the neighbourhood of Bury, but it is the chief mine in Newmills, Mellor, Crumpsall, and Ludworth

The thirty-first bed of coal is covered by six yards gray and brown shale, three yards close-bedded rock, which divides into cubes; seven yards of excellent light-coloured building stone (Woodhead-hill, Lomax-wood rock, sometimes much thicker), six yards of stony gray shale; and fourteen yards of very black shale, containing *Pecten, Goniatites,* &c The thirty-first bed of coal is only nine inches thick, and rests on a shale floor one yard thick The thirty-second or Featheredge coal is covered by eight yards of coarse-grained rock, and by dark shale full of the *Pecten, Posidonia, Goniatites,* mixed with ferns and *Lepidodendra.* The Featheredge coal is the principal mine of Walmesley, Lomax-wood, Fecit, and Birtle-dean, and is the lowest mine worth working in the vicinity of Bury Below the Featheredge coal is rough or quartz rock, full of large rounded quartz pebbles Mr Binney observes, "This rock is often taken for one of the millstone grits. It is exposed at Wibbersley, Werneth Low, Blackstone Edge, Birtle Moor, Pilsworth, Turton Tower, Horwich Moor, Holcombe, and Parbold"

Next is found gray stony shale often approaching to flags, twenty-five yards thick; rough flaggy rock provincially termed "ragg," four yards, fine smooth flags, two yards, strong brown stone parted with shale, containing thin beds of flags, fifty yards, found on Rowley Moor, Summit, and near Whitworth, fine-grained rock of a bluish-colour, two yards, gray shale, eight yards and black shales containing *Pecten.* These cover a bed of coal six inches thick This rests on two yards of black shale, below which is another bed of coal eight inches thick Under these is eight yards of bluish shale and six yards of black shale, with layers of stone Below them is the last bed of coal, which is one foot three inches in thickness. Underneath this bed is four yards of dark shale After that comes the upper millstone grit of unknown depth, found at Brooksbottom, Cheesden bridge, Sunnyside, Holcombe-hill, and the Summit tunnel.

Such are the principal beds of coal, thirty-five in number, over which the river Irwell flows in its course from the mountainous district in which it rises, to the plain at Ringley, near Manchester They are by no means the whole of the beds of coal existing in Lancashire, for there are no less than 120 seams of coal of greater or less thickness, but many of them are amongst the most valuable beds of coal in the two counties, and they may be regarded as the principal cause of the crowded population and the great wealth of the north-western district

To obtain an adequate view of the mineral wealth of particular districts of South Lancashire, it is necessary to trace the beds of coal through their different workings, in several parts of the county The richest points in the coal-field are in the neighbourhood of Manchester, in the neighbourhood of Oldham, Ashton-under-Lyne and Dukinfield, about St. Helen's, and in the neighbourhood of Wigan At all those points the beds both of coal and of ironstone, as well as those of building stone, are of the greatest value, and have largely contributed to, indeed have chiefly produced, the prosperity of the districts in which they are found This information is given in the general sections of the Lancashire and Cheshire coal measures, which accompanied the Annual Report of Joseph Dickinson, Esq, F G S, Inspector of Mines, dated Manchester, 27th February, 1858 These sections show very clearly the succession of the strata, and the number and thickness of the seams of coal found in the whole of the 6600 feet of coal measures, which constitute the coal-field of Lancashire and Cheshire. These sections were compiled from memoirs furnished by Mr. Edward William Binney, aided by valuable contributions from John Hall, Esq, of Nangreaves, William Peace, Esq, F G S, Andrew Knowles, Thomas Knowles, of Ince, Andrew Ray, George Peace, James Oliver, John Evans, Josiah Evans, John Daglish, James Darlington, John Mercer, George Gilroy, Robert Daglish, senr, Ralph Fletcher, Esq, and others, who possessed, or still possess, the fullest knowledge of the coal-fields of Lancashire and Cheshire

The first section is that of the upper or Manchester coal-field, the most recent part of that great coal-field This division of the coal-field is only found in the neighbourhood of Manchester, and is best traced in sections commencing at Ardwick, on the east side of that city, and extending through strata of the thickness of about 1800 feet This part of the coal-field lies immediately below the permian beds of the new red sandstone, and was deposited at the time when the luxuriant vegetation that produced the richer beds of the coal formation was beginning to lose its richness

In the upper part of this formation the beds of clay now hardened into shale, and of sand now hardened into sandstone, are of great thickness, whilst the seams of coal are few in number, and only of the thickness of a few inches But as we descend, the thickness of the seams of coal increases, and before we reach the middle coal-field, which lies immediately under the upper, the beds of coal become large and valuable, and everything indicates the existence of a luxuriant growth of the coal plants, at the time when they were here deposited.

The first 100 yards of the strata of the upper or Manchester coal-field, does not contain any coal, but is chiefly composed of the sands and shales belonging to the coal measures, with a few beds of limestone varying from one to three feet in thickness The second 100 yards of this coal-field contains two thin seams of coal, the upper six inches, and the lower three inches in thickness It also contains a bed of blackband ironstone four inches in thickness; and a bed of limestone five to seven feet in thickness The coal in the upper of these two beds is very sulphurous The upper bed of coal and the blackband ironstone, which latter contains a large quantity of coal mixed with the iron, rest on a bed of warren earth and shale, in which the plants that form the coal originally grew The rest of this portion of the coal measures consists of shale and of sandstone Amongst the sandstones is one of a reddish colour, called the Holt-town sandstone. In the third 100 yards there is no coal The strata consist entirely of shale and sandstone, amongst the latter is the Openshaw sandstone. The fourth 100 yards contains two beds of coal. The first is one foot one inch thick, the second, called the Openshaw coal, is two feet in thickness There are thick beds of warren earth and shale, which is hardened clay, under both these seams of coal The fifth 100 yards contains two beds of coal. The first of these, named the Charlotte coal, is two feet two inches in thickness; the second, named the Three-quarters coal, is one foot eight inches The rest of this portion of the strata consists of warren earth and shale.

In the sixth 100 yards the coal becomes very rich, and the beds are much more numerous. In this part of the strata there are seven beds of coal, namely, the Four-feet or Big coal, in two bands—the upper one foot, the lower two feet nine inches in thickness, separated by four inches of bass Below this is a seam of coal nine inches thick, succeeded by what is called the Yard coal, two feet ten inches in thickness. That is succeeded by the New coal, one foot four inches thick; the Smut coal, one foot one inch thick, and the Coarse coal, twelve inches thick. These beds of coal are separated from each other by beds of warren earth and shale The seventh and lowest 100 yards of the upper or Manchester coal-field, contains five seams of coal. The first, named the Doctor coal, is one foot eight inches in thickness; the second, named the Two-feet coal, consists of two beds of coal each ten inches thick, separated by four inches of earth The next consists of coarse coal, one foot six inches in thickness; and the lowest is a seam of coal one foot thick. The rest of this part of the strata consists of warren earth and shale.

The whole number of seams of coal in the upper or Manchester coal-field is fifteen, and the aggregate thickness of all the seams of coal of which they are composed is thirty feet.

SEAMS OF COAL IN THE UPPER OR MANCHESTER COAL-FIELD AT ARDWICK, NEAR MANCHESTER.

	Yds	Ft.	Ins		Yds	Ft.	Ins
In First 100 yards—				Yard coal, . . .	1	—	—
Coal,	—	—	—	In Sixth 100 yards—			
In Second 100 yards—				Coarse coal, .	—	—	8
Coal, .	—	—	6	Coal, .	—	2	8
Coal, ...	—	—	3	New coal, .	—	2	10
In Third 100 yards—				Smut coal, .	—	1	4
Coal, . .	—	1	1	Coal, .	—	1	1
Openshaw coal, . .	—	2	—	Coarse coal, .	—	1	—
In Fourth 100 yards—				In Seventh 100 yards—			
Charlotte coal,	—	2	2	Doctor coal,	—	1	8
Three-quarters coal, . .	—	1	8	Two feet coal, .	—	1	8
In Fifth 100 yards—				Coarse coal, ...	—	1	6
Four-feet or Big coal,	1	—	9	Coal, ...	—	—	—
Coal, ...	—	—	9	Coal, ...	—	1	—

The general sections of the Lancashire and Cheshire coal measures drawn up by Mr. Dickinson, contain plans of the middle coal-field at four different places The first is in the great manufacturing district lying between the city of Manchester and the large manufacturing towns of Bolton and Bury, and includes the rich mines of Pendleton, Patricroft, Worsley, Atherton, and Hulton. The second is in the neighbourhood of, and extends to, the great manufacturing towns of Oldham, Ashton, Staleybridge, and Stockport, and includes the mines of Dukinfield, Ashton, Oldham, and Poynton The third is the coal-field of St. Helen's, the principal seat of the glass and chemical manufactures of South Lancashire The fourth and last is the great coal-field of Wigan, one of the richest coal-fields of England, and the source from which Liverpool draws its large supplies of coal for industrial and domestic purposes, as well as for the purposes of export. These subdivisions all belong to the middle coal-field, and from them much the greater part and the best varieties of coal produced in Lancashire and Cheshire are derived

The first division of the middle coal-field of Lancashire of which we shall speak is that of Pendleton, Patricroft, Atherton, Worsley, and Hulton, extending to Manchester, Bolton, and Bury, and from which those great seats of manufacturing industry derive their principal supplies of fuel. In some of the mines of this district, the coal measures have to be sought by sinking through thick beds of drift, and then by boring, first through the trias or upper new red sandstone, and then through the permian or lower division of the new red sandstone, which immediately overlies the coal measures The first 100 yards only contains a thin seam of coal two inches thick, and a bed of bass and coal one foot thick but it contains a bed of ironstone two feet thick, and a great number of beds of limestone and of red shale, together with a bed of hard sandstone The ironstone rests on a bed of warren earth The second 100 yards contains no less than eight beds of coal, and numerous beds of black bass. The first of these beds of coal is one foot ten inches in thickness, the second is also one foot ten inches, the third is only two inches, the fourth is three inches, the fifth is one foot one inch, the sixth is four inches, the seventh is one foot three inches, and there is a bed of coarse coal, bass, &c., five feet in thickness. Nearly all these seams of coal rest on thick beds of earth, forming the floors of the mine, and known among the miners by the name of warren earth In the whole of this series the roots of the *Sigillaria*, known to geologists by the name of *Stigmaria*, have been found, generally imbedded in the warren earth. There are also ironstone bands in one of the strata, and large quantities of gray shale and white sandstone, the former being hardened clay, the latter hardened sand The third 100 yards contains three seams of coal The first of these is nine inches thick, the second is eleven inches, and the third is three inches. These seams of coal rest on beds of earth There are also several beds of black bass, some of which also rest on beds of earth The remainder of this portion of the strata is composed of brown and white sandstone, or of a blue shale The fourth 100 yards contains six beds of coal. The first of these, which is coarse coal mixed with earth, is four inches thick, the second is coal of a better quality, nine inches thick, the third is a seam two feet thick, the fourth is three inches, the fifth nine inches, and the sixth also nine inches. All these lie on beds of warren earth. There are also several beds of black bass, which contain some of the constituents of coal, mixed with earth and shale The rest consist chiefly of beds of blue and gray shale, with a very thick bed of white sandstone The fifth 100 yards contains immense quantities of coal, divided into eleven seams The first seam is seven inches thick, the second one foot two inches The third is the celebrated Worsley four-feet coal, which is four feet three inches in thickness, and rests on a bed of warren earth Below the Worsley four-feet coal is another bed, one foot seven inches in thickness, which is succeeded by a bed eleven inches thick, another bed composed of coarse coal eight inches thick, another one foot six inches thick, a fourth ten inches thick, and two others, one only four inches thick, but the other two feet six inches There are thick beds of earth under all these seams of coal, and there are also numerous thick beds of black bass Ironstone is also found in a bed two inches thick, mixed with blue shale in a bed five feet thick, and mixed with cannel coal in a bed four feet six inches thick, and with blue shale in a bed four feet thick. There are also beds of blue shale and several beds of sandstone, but neither the shale nor the sandstone beds are as thick as in the higher strata. In the sixth 100 yards there are nine beds of coal, the first one foot thick, the second ten inches, the third one foot; the fourth subdivided into three beds, containing altogether about four feet of coal, and the remaining three containing from seven inches to one foot of coal. The earth beds are very clearly seen in all this part of the coal measures Iron is found in hard black stone, containing spar and ironstone, in light shale with ironstone, and in dark shale, also with ironstone. There is a considerable quantity of gray, blue, and dark shale in this part of the coal measures, together with some beds of gray and red sandstone. The seventh 100 yards contains no less than fifteen beds of coal; the first seven inches thick, with black bass of coal one foot five inches, and six inches of cannel coal lying under it. This is succeeded by a bed of coal one foot five inches thick. Then come in quick succession six beds of coal, varying from one foot nine inches and one foot ten inches to half an inch. These are succeeded by four beds of coal from one foot two inches to four inches. There are numerous beds of earth in this part of the strata. Iron is also found in the form of mussel-shell ironstone, brown ironstone, and shale with ironstone. There are also beds of shale and a few beds of hard sandstone The eighth 100 yards contains a very large quantity of coal in twelve beds The first is two feet three inches The second, called Bin coal, consists of two beds of coal—one two feet nine inches in thickness, the other ten inches, and separated by a thin bed of earth This is succeeded by a bed of coal one foot four inches thick, and a bed of cannel coal six inches thick The seam known as the Shuttle or Albert coal comes next, containing two feet nine inches of thick coal, and six inches of coarse coal. The Crumbouke four-feet coal, four feet thick, but with one foot of bass and coal above it, and two feet of bass and coal below it, comes next. Then are seams of coal six inches thick and eight inches thick Ironstone is found, in this part of the coal measures, in the form of mussel-shell ironstone. The beds of earth are very numerous and thick, and there are also several beds of shale and sandstone The ninth 100 yards is very rich in coal. It commences with the Rams or Seven-feet coal, which, however, is not more than five feet five inches in thickness Next comes the Kays coal, two feet thick, and the Windmill coal, one foot one inch thick, and a number of other thick beds of coal These are succeeded by two beds of coal each three feet thick, named the White coal and the Black coal, separated from each other by seven yards of warren earth, containing three large beds of bass and coal mixed with the earth. There are also thick beds of shale and sandstone in this part of the coal measures.

The tenth 100 yards includes a portion of the great mass of coal last mentioned and also several thinner seams, including a seam six inches thick, another two inches thick, and a third nine inches thick. There is much warren earth and several beds of sandstone and shale in this part of the coal measures, including seven yards of red sandstone. In the eleventh 100 yards coal is very abundant There is first the Old Doe coal, in three beds of the total thickness of eight feet There is next the Five-quarter coal, in two beds of two feet ten inches Then comes the Hill-hole coal, two feet thick; and this is succeeded by another seam of coal one foot in thickness The above seams of coal are separated by thick beds of sandstone and shale. The twelfth 100 yards is also very rich, containing altogether sixteen beds of coal. The first of these is only three inches thick, the second, known as the California coal, is one foot six inches, and the third, the Trencherbone coal, is three feet six inches. The Dyehouse coal is one foot six inches, and below it is a bed of coal nine inches thick This is succeeded by the cannel coal, in three beds, six inches, two feet nine inches, and one foot ten inches in thickness; and these are immediately followed by coal in two beds ten inches thick Next comes the Tapling coal consisting of a bed one foot two inches, and of coarse coal two feet ten inches These are succeeded by coal two inches thick. Then comes what is called the Plodder coal in six seams—respectively, one foot two inches, seven inches, two feet, three feet two inches, one foot two inches, and one foot five inches thick This is succeeded by the Yard coal, three feet two inches thick; the Half-yard coal, one foot six inches, and the Three-quarters coal in two seams, one two feet three inches, and the other one foot two inches The last seam of coal in the middle coal-field in this neighbourhood is the Daub-hill Arley mine, in three seams; namely, the top coal two feet, the coarse coal nine inches, and the bottom coal nine inches, with a fourth seam immediately below, one foot thick.

The whole thickness of the coal measures in this division of the coal-field is nearly 1200 yards. The number of seams of coal is 100; the aggregate thickness of the coal in all these seams is upwards of 140 feet. To this is to be added about twenty-four feet in thickness of coal found in the upper or Manchester coal-field. Together, these constitute that immense mass of mineral that is found in the neighbourhood of Manchester, which has had so great an influence in producing the manufacturing prosperity of that city. Bolton and Bury also stand within easy reach of two great coal-fields; namely, the middle coal-field, part of which has been just described, and the lower coal-field, which remains to be described. The following is the succession of the seams of coal in the middle coal-field, in the mines of Pendleton, Patricroft, Worsley, Atherton, Hulton, and other places, lying to the north-west of Manchester.

SEAMS OF COAL AT PENDLETON, PATRICROFT, ATHERTON, AND HULTON, IN THE MIDDLE COAL-FIELD, ON THE WEST SIDE OF MANCHESTER.

	Yds	Ft	Ins
In First 100 yards—			
Coal,	—	—	2
In Second 100 yards—			
Coal,	—	1	10
Coal,	—	1	10
Coal,	—	—	3
Coal,	—	1	1
Coal,	—	1	3
Coarse coal,	1	2	0
Coal,	—	—	7
In Third 100 yards—			
Coal,	—	—	9
Coal,	—	—	11
In Fourth 100 yards—			
Coarse coal and earth,	—	—	4
Coal,	—	—	9
Coal,	—	2	—
Coal,	—	—	3
Coal,	—	—	9
In Fifth 100 yards—			
Coal,	—	—	9
Coal,	—	—	7
Coal,	—	1	2
Worsley Four foot coal,	1	1	3
Coal,	—	1	7
Coal,	—	—	6
Coarse coal,	—	—	8
Black bass,	—	1	6
Coal,	—	—	10
Coal,	—	1	6
Coal,	—	2	6
In Sixth 100 yards—			
Coal,	—	1	—
Coal,	—	1	—
Coal,	—	1	9
Coal,	—	1	3
Coarse coal,	—	1	4
Coal,	—	—	7
Coal,	—	—	6

	Yds.	Ft	Ins
In Seventh 100 yards—			
Coal,	—	—	6
Coal,	—	—	7
Cannel coal	—	—	6
Coal,	—	1	5
Coal,	—	1	9
Coal,	—	—	3
Coal	—	1	10
Coal,	—	—	½
Coal,	—	—	3
Coal,	—	—	6
Coal,	—	1	2
Coal,	—	—	2
Coal,	—	—	8
Coal,	—	—	4
In Eighth 100 yards—			
Coal,	—	2	3
Coal,	—	—	10
Coal,	—	2	9
Coal,	—	1	4
Shuttle or Albert coal,	—	2	9
Coarse coal,	—	—	6
Bass and coal,	—	1	—
Crumbouke,	1	1	—
Coal,	—	—	6
Coal,	—	—	8
In Ninth 100 yards—			
Kay's coal,	—	2	—
Windmill coal,	—	1	1
White coal,	1	—	—
In Tenth 100 yards—			
Warren earth, bass, and coal,	7	—	—
Black coal,	1	—	—
Coal,	—	—	6
Coal,	—	—	2
Coal,	—	1	—
Coal,	—	—	9
In Eleventh 100 yards—			
Old Doe coal,	2	2	—

	Yds	Ft.	Ins.
In Eleventh 100 yards—			
Five-quarter coal,	—	2	10
Hill-hole coal,	—	2	—
Coal,	—	1	—
In Twelfth 100 yards—			
Coal,	—	—	3
California coal,	—	1	6
Trencher bone coal,	—	3	6
Coal,	—	—	9
Bassy cannel coal,	—	—	6
Coal,	—	2	9
Coal,	—	1	10
Tapling coal,	—	1	2
Coarse coal,	—	2	10
Coal,	—	—	2
Plodder coal,	—	1	2
Coal,	—	—	7
Coarse coal,	—	2	—
Coal,	—	3	2
In Twelfth 100 yards—			
Coarse coal,	—	1	2
Gray earth and coal,	—	—	7
Coal,	—	1	5
Coal,	—	—	6
Coal,	—	—	9
Yard coal,	1	—	2
Bone coal,	—	—	3
Coal,	—	—	6
Half-yard coal,	—	1	6
Coal,	—	—	5
Three-quarters coal,	—	2	3
Coal,	—	1	2
Daubhill Arley mine top coal,	—	2	—
Coarse coal,	—	—	9
Bottom coal,	—	—	9
Coal,	—	1	—

The middle coal-field is also very extensively developed in the neighbourhood of the flourishing manufacturing towns of Oldham, Ashton-under-Lyne, Staleybridge, Dukinfield, and in the neighbourhood of Stockport, it forms the main source of the manufacturing prosperity of those places In this part of the middle coal-field there are also numerous beds of ironstone, as well as very large quantities of fine and durable building stone The following particulars as to the number and thickness of the beds of coal found in this neighbourhood will go far to account for the industrial prosperity of these great and flourishing towns, and of the numerous villages by which they are surrounded

In this district, described as the Dukinfield, Ashton-under-Lyne, and Oldham coal-field, the coal measures are met with after penetrating through the thick beds of drift that everywhere cover the harder strata In the first 100 yards there are several beds of valuable coal One of these is one foot thick, the second two feet three inches, a third five inches, and in a fourth bass and coal are found mixed together, in a seam of the thickness of one foot five inches. There are also beds of warren earth under all the seams of coal Ironstone is found in the form of ironstone balls, spread through a great mass of soft dark shale more than thirty feet thick There are also several thick beds of black bass, with numerous beds of sandstone and shale The second 100 yards also contains several thick beds of coal One of these is one foot ten inches in thickness, another one foot four In what is called the Sod mine there are two beds of coal, the top one two feet three inches in thickness, the lower four feet. These rest on beds of warren earth Ironstone bands are also found in a thick bed of gray shale There are also thick beds of red sandstone and numerous beds of shale—blue, black, brown, and gray. In the third 100 yards both coal and ironstone are extremely abundant. First is the Blenfire coal, the top bed of which is five inches thick; then there is coal one foot four inches, and another bed of the same thickness, together with large quantities of coal mixed with shale The Great mine coal, six feet thick, comes next, then is a bed of coal two feet thick, succeeded by the Roger mine coal four feet thick, and a seam of inferior coal seven inches thick. Black shale mixed with coal is next found, four feet eight inches thick The beds of warren earth are all strongly marked A bed of iron pyrites is found in this part of the coal measures, with strong gray sandstone and ironstone of great thickness, ironstone in bands mixed with warren earth and mixed with shale There are also beds of hard gray sandstone, and numerous beds of blue, gray, and black shale The fourth 100 yards is also very rich in coal. It contains the Furnace-hill mine coal, one yard three inches in thickness, the coal under the Furnace-hill mine, one foot eight inches, and another seam of coal of good quality, two feet two and a half inches thick. The earth beds are very clearly marked under all the seams of coal. There is a thick bed of blue shale with ironstone bands, and also a thick bed of dark shale with balls of peroxide of iron. There is also a thick bed of very hard gray sandstone, and numerous beds of shale of various colours. The fifth 100 yards is also very rich in coal There is the Colonel mine, the top bed of which is ten and a half inches thick, and the bottom bed three feet three inches. There is also coal of good quality in a vein one foot three inches thick, and in what is called the Hard mine there are two thick beds of coal, the first eight inches thick, the second two feet seven inches. The coal of Cooks Folly mine is one foot six inches thick. There are three beds of ironstone in this part of the coal measures. There is also much sandstone, brown and red (Huncliffe), with some thick beds of purple, motley, gray, and red shale.

The sixth 100 yards is also very rich in coal. It contains the Mary's mine coal, (Foxholes) two feet seven inches thick, and another bed of coal two feet two inches thick. These are succeeded by the Town-lane mine in three seams. The first of these, or top coal, is one foot thick, the middle coal is three feet seven inches; and the bottom coal one foot three inches. Next is the top Shuttle mine coal, two feet thick, and the bottom Shuttle mine coal, two feet eleven inches thick. The warren earth beds are very fully developed in this part of the coal measures Ironstone is also found in very great abundance in this part of the coal measures. There is, first, strong gray shale with ironstone, hard gray shale with ironstone, shale with ironstone and sandstone, three beds of dark shale with ironstone bands, then dark shale and cakes of ironstone. These are succeeded by what is called the Danes Ironstone mine. There are also several beds of hard gray sandstone, and hard gray shale in this part of the coal measures The seventh 100 yards also contains large quantities of coal There is first the Osey Coes coal in two beds, the upper five inches thick, the lower one foot one inch thick. There are then three beds of what is called inferior coal, one three inches thick, another one foot two inches thick, and a third one foot four inches thick After this comes black bass with seams of coal five feet four inches thick; then the Old Man's or Fog's mine, with three beds of coal, first one foot thick, second four inches, the third one foot five inches. In this portion of the coal measures there are other large beds of ironstone. There are thick beds of red hardstone, and there is also a bed of gray shale with fossil plants The eighth 100 yards is also very rich. The first is the Rusty mine, with two beds of coal—one nine inches, the other one foot four inches There are then three beds of coal, the first one foot five inches thick, the second four inches, the third ten inches There are then beds of black bass and dark shale, with coal mixed up with it Then comes what is called the Saltpetre mine, in three beds of coal, six inches, two feet two inches, and two feet five inches thick This is succeeded by the Little Smithy mine coal, two feet four inches in thickness. The warren earth is found under these several seams of coal. There is little ironstone in this part of the strata, but a great quantity of very hard red and gray sandstone The ninth 100 yards also contains much valuable coal. There is first the Black mine coal, four feet eight inches thick. This is succeeded by a seam of coal one foot five inches thick, and by inferior coal three inches thick Next is the Stone mine coal three feet thick, succeeded by the Upper Bent mine coal, two feet thick. The warren earth is found through this part of the coal-field There is little ironstone, but very hard sandstone bands.

The tenth 100 yards commences with the Lower Bent or Peacock mine coal, two feet eleven inches in thickness. This is succeeded by the Nealy mine in two veins, the upper one foot six inches, the lower eight inches in thickness. The Davis mine coal, one foot five inches thick, comes next. Then is the Seddons mine coal, one foot thick, the Water mine coal, one foot eight inches, and the Jonah Lees mine coal, one foot two inches thick. The Hurst old mine comes next in three seams, the first one foot eight inches, the second one foot, and the third ten inches. These are succeeded by the New mine coal, three feet six inches thick. The earth beds are very perfect. There are thick sandstone beds, including the Bradshaw rock The eleventh 100 yards also contains several valuable beds of coal The first is one foot thick, the second, third, and fourth are each of them six inches. The rest of the strata consists chiefly of sandstone and shale, with some ironstone. In the twelfth 100 yards is the Royley mine coal, three feet thick, which is the lowest of the beds of the middle coal-field, and the last bed of thick coal

The number of beds of coal in this part of the middle coal-field, from which Oldham, Ashton, and Dukinfield draw their supplies, is ninety-two The aggregate thickness of the seams of coal, from which the industry of this neighbourhood draws its supplies, is 126 feet

The following is the succession of the seams of coal in this great and productive coal-field —

SEAMS OF COAL AT DUKINFIELD, ASHTON-UNDER-LYNE AND OLDHAM

	Yds.	Ft	Ins
In First 100 yards—			
Coal, . .	—	1	—
Coal, .	—	—	5
Coal, .	—	2	3
In 200 yards—			
Coal,	—	1	10
Coal,	—	1	4
Sod mine,	—		
In 300 yards—			
Coal, top bed, .	—	2	3
Bolt coal, .	1	1	—
Blenfire coal, top bed, .	—	—	5
Shale with coal, .	—	2	2
Coal of good quality, .	—	1	4
Great mine coal,	2	—	—
Coal,	—	—	1
Coal,	—	2	3
Roger mine coal, . . .	1	1	—
In 300 yards—			
Inferior coal,	—	—	7
In 400 yards—			
Furnace-hill mine coal, .	1	—	3
Coal under Furnace hill mine, .	—	1	6
Coal of good quality,	—	2	2½
In 500 yards,			
Colonel mine, top bed coal,	—	—	10½
Colonel mine, bottom bed coal, . .	1	—	3
Coal,	—	—	2
Coa',	—	—	4
Coal, .	—	—	7
Coal of good quality, .	—	1	3
Hard mine, ...	—		
Coal, top bed,	—	—	8½
Coal, bottom bed, ...	—	2	7

	Yds	Ft.	Ins
In 500 yards—			
Coal,	—	—	4
Coal,	—	—	4
Coal,	—	—	4
Cook's Folly mine coal,	—	1	6
In 600 yards—			
Mary's mine coal (Foxholes),	—	2	7
Coal,	—	2	2
Town Lane mine,	—	—	—
Top coal,	—	1	—
Middle coal,	1	—	7
Bottom coal,	—	1	3
Top Shuttle mine coal,	—	2	—
Bottom Shuttle mine coal,	—	2	11
In 700 yards—			
Osey Coes coal,	—	—	—
Coal, top bed,	—	—	5
Coal, bottom bed,	—	1	1
Inferior coal, top bed,	—	—	10
Inferior coal, middle bed,	—	1	2
Ditto, bottom bed,	—	1	4
Old Man's or Fog's mine,	—	—	—
Top bed coal,	—	1	—
Middle bed coal,	—	—	4
Dark earth seams of coal,	—	1	5
Bottom bed coal,	—	1	3
In 800 yards—			
Rusty mine,	—	—	—
Top coal,	—	—	6
Bottom coal,	—	1	4
Coal good quality,	—	1	5
Coal,	—	—	3
Coal,	—	—	10
Saltpetre mine,	—	—	—
Top bed coal,	—	—	6
Middle bed coal,	—	2	2
Bottom bed coal,	—	2	5

	Yds	Ft.	Ins.
In 800 yards—			
Little Smithy mine coal,	—	2	4
Coal,	—	1	3
In 900 yards—			
Black mine coal,	1	1	8
Coal,	—	—	3
Coal,	—	1	4
Inferior coal,	—	—	3
Stone mine coal,	1	—	—
Upper Bent, or Two feet mine coal,	—	2	—
In 1000 yards—			
Lower Bent, or Peacock mine coal,	—	2	11
Coal,	—	—	5
Coal,	—	1	2
Nealy mine,	—	—	—
Top coal,	—	1	6
Bottom coal,	—	—	8
Davis mine coal,	—	1	5
Seddons mine coal,	—	1	—
Coal,	—	—	3
Water mine coal,	—	1	8
Jonah Lees mine coal,	—	1	2
Hurst Old mine,	—	—	—
Top coal,	—	2	1
Middle coal,	—	1	—
Bottom coal,	—	—	10
New mine coal,	1	—	6
In 1100 yards—			
Coal,	—	1	—
Coal,	—	—	6
Coal,	—	—	6
Coal,	—	—	6
Coal,	—	—	5
In 1200 yards—			
Royley mine coal,	1	—	—

In the western parts of South Lancashire, in the hundred of West Derby, as well as the eastern and the central parts, the middle coal-field is very extensively developed. The richest portions of the middle coal-field, in the western division of the county, are those of St. Helen's and Wigan; and both those places are the seats of flourishing branches of industry, and of rapidly increasing trade. Both the St. Helen's and the Wigan coal-fields also supply large quantities of coal for export as well as for steam navigation. There is also a large export of steam coal from Atherton at another point in the middle coal-field

In the St. Helen's coal-field the coal is met with at a very short distance from the surface, and at some points it rises to the surface. In the first 100 yards of the St Helen's coal-field there are six beds of coal, of very considerable thickness. The first is the coal of Loons delf, or mine, two feet eight inches in thickness; the second is that of the London delf, two feet six inches thick, the third is a seam of coal ten inches thick, the fourth is a seam nine inches thick; and the fifth and sixth is the coal of what is called the Potato delf, in two seams, one of them four feet thick, and the other nine inches. The other portions of the coal measures in the first 100 yards, consist of beds of warren earth, bass, shale, and sandstone

In the second 100 yards there are six beds of coal. The coal of the Earthy delf is in three seams—the first one foot four inches, the second one foot six inches, and the third one foot eight inches in thickness What is called the Little coal, which is the next seam, is two feet in thickness There are then three seams almost close together, and respectively ten inches, seven inches, and one foot two inches in thickness. These are succeeded by a bed one foot eight inches in thickness. The coal measures consist of very thick beds of warren earth and shale, with a bed of silicious sandstone. The third 100 yards is also very rich in coal. There is first the St. Helen's main delf, or mine, containing five seams of coal The first of these is one foot seven inches, the second eight inches, the third eight inches, the fourth four feet six inches, and the cannel coal below it two feet three inches in thickness. Next is the Four-feet delf coal, as it is called, three feet two inches in thickness; then the Pigeon-house delf coal in two seams, the higher one foot six inches, the lower two feet. Below this is a thin seam of coal three inches thick, and a little lower a thicker bed one foot seven inches in thickness In this part of the coal-field there are beds of warren earth, thick beds of shale with ironstone bands, large quantities of shale, and some beds of sandstone. The fourth 100 yards is extremely rich in coal. There is first the Ravenhead main delf, or mine, with two thick beds of coal—one three feet ten inches in thickness, the other seven feet. Below this is the San Sebastian delf, with a bed of coal four feet three inches in thickness. Next comes the Roger delf with four seams of coal, six inches, three inches, two feet, one foot nine inches, and six inches in thickness There are also a bed of ironstone and numerous beds of shale in this part of the coal measures The fifth 100 yards is also rich in coal. The coal mine known as the Sir John delf is three feet four inches thick, and below it there is another seam ten inches thick. Below that is a bed of coal ten inches thick, and two masses of bassy cannel coal—one one foot thick, the other eleven inches. This is succeeded by the coal of the Flaggy delf, in two beds, each of them two feet thick. Next comes the coal of the Sir Roger delf, in three seams, two feet, nine inches, and one foot in thickness There is some iron ore in this part of the strata, but they are chiefly composed of warren earth, shale, and sandstone. The sixth 100 yards contains one very rich and valuable bed of coal, known as the Rushey Park delf This is in two seams, the higher one ten inches thick, the lower one three feet six inches thick There is also another small seam of coal six inches thick. The Rushey Park coal rests on a very thick bed of the warren earth The rest of the strata consists chiefly of sandy shale and sandstone. The seventh and last 100 yards contains the coal of the Little delf, three feet in thickness The rest of the strata is composed of beds of blue shale and white sandstone.

The number of beds of coal in the St Helen's coal-field is forty-four, and the aggregate thickness of the coal is seventy-four feet The following is the succession of the seams of coal in the St Helen's coal-field.

ST HELEN'S, LANCASHIRE.

	Yds	Ft	Ins.
In First 100 yards—			
Coal Loons delf,	—	2	8
Coal London delf,	—	2	6
Coal, ...	—	—	10
Coal, .	—	1	9
Potato delf, .	—	—	—
Coal, .	—	2	—
Coal,	—	—	11
In 200 yards—			
Earthy delf coal,	—	1	4
Coal, . . .	—	1	6
Coal, . .	—	1	8
Coal, Little coal,	—	2	—
Coal, . . .	—	—	10
Coal, .	—	—	7
Coal, . .	—	1	6
Coal, ...	—	1	8
In 300 yards—			
St. Helen's main delf, .	—	—	—
Coal, ...	—	1	7
In 300 yards—			
Coal, . . .	—	—	8
Coal,	—	—	8
Coal,	1	1	4
Cannel coal and coal delf,	—	2	3
Coal, Four-feet delf, . .	1	—	2
Coal, Higher Pigeon house delf, .	—	1	6
Coal, Lower Pigeon-house delf, . . .	—	2	—
Coal, . . .	—	—	3
Coal, . . .	—	1	7
In 400 yards—			
Ravenhead main delf, . .	1	—	10
Coal, .	3	1	—
Coal, St. Sebastian delf, .	1	1	3
Coal, ...	—	—	6
Coal,	—	—	3
In 500 yards—			
Coal, ...	—	2	—

	Yds.	Ft.	Ins.		Yds.	Ft.	Ins.
In 500 yards—				In 600 yards—			
Sir John delf,	—	—	—	Rushey Park delf,	—	—	—
Coal, .	—	1	9	Coal, . .	—	—	10
Coal,	—	—	6	Coal,	1	—	6
Sir Roger delf,	—	—	—	Coal, . .	—	—	6
Coal, . . .	—	2	—	In 700 yards—			
Coal,	—	—	9	Coal, Little delf, .	1	—	—
Coal, .	—	1	—				
Coal and bass,	1	—	—				

The Wigan coal-field, which also belongs to the middle coal-field, is one of the richest in Lancashire, both on account of the number and thickness of the beds of coal that it contains, and on account of the varieties of coal found within it. This coal-field has now been worked for upwards of 300 years, and is still very productive in all the most valuable descriptions of coal.

In the Wigan coal-field thick beds of coal are found close to the surface A bed of coal two feet eight inches thick crops out of the ground at the beginning of the series. This is followed by the coal of the Burgy delf, in two seams, the upper nine inches thick, the lower two feet two inches The large bed of coal known as the Big mine coal comes next, and is five feet two inches in thickness. This is succeeded by the Little mine coal, two feet five inches in thickness. The beds of warren earth mixed with shale form nearly the whole of the strata in the upper part of the Wigan coal measures The second 100 yards contains five large beds of coal. The first is two feet eight inches thick, the second two feet three inches, the third two feet eight inches. The fourth, consisting of Bone coal with bass, is three feet four inches thick, and the fifth seam is two feet seven inches The other strata are chiefly composed of warren earth and shale The third 100 yards contains seven beds of coal. The highest of these is two feet thick. Then comes the Ince four-feet coal in two seams, the higher one foot six inches in thickness, the lower four feet

The Ince seven-feet coal succeeds This is also in two seams, the higher one foot two inches in thickness, the lower four feet six inches. The Gidlows or Furnace coal comes next, and is five feet two inches in thickness, though with a slight parting in the middle. The beds of warren earth and shale are of great thickness, and one of the thickest beds of shale contains ironstone. The fourth 100 yards is also extremely rich in coal The first seam is that named the Little coal, two feet two inches in thickness. Next is the rich bed called the Pemberton five-feet coal, which is as nearly as possible five feet in thickness; then is the Two-feet coal, exactly that thickness; and next the Pemberton four-feet coal, which is four feet six inches in thickness. All these veins of coal rest on thick beds of warren earth, and are divided either by beds of shale or of sandstone. The fifth 100 yards is not so rich There is a bed of coal one inch thick; another six inches thick; and a bed of bass with coal partings six feet five inches thick. There is also a mass of black stone mixed with coal There is also a large quantity of sandstone and shale containing ironstone. The sixth 100 yards is much richer It contains, first, the Wigan five-feet coal in five seams This is succeeded by cannel coal, five inches; slaty coal, four inches, the Wigan four-feet coal, and two thinner beds of coal, one three inches thick, and the other one foot nine inches thick These are again succeeded by the Wigan nine-feet coal in three beds, together nearly nine feet in thickness. There is much ironstone, chiefly in the form of ironstone balls, in this part of the strata In the seventh 100 yards there are several rich beds of coal The first of very considerable thickness is a seam two feet two inches in thickness. Then comes the Cannel King coals in four beds, the highest consisting of two feet two inches and a half of cannel coal, the second of eight inches, the third of two feet, and the fourth of one foot five inches Dark shale with coal, and the Ravin or Rubbishy mine coal with bass, come next, and are altogether of the thickness of seventeen feet, of which the greater part is coal of various qualities. There is much warren earth and shale in this part of the coal measures. In the eighth 100 yards is a thick bed of coal, known by the name of the Yard coal, which is, however, four feet ten inches in thickness. There is also a thin bed of coal of eight inches, and the Bone coal in two seams, each of eight inches. In the ninth 100 yards are two veins of coal of great value. The first of these is the Orrel five-feet coal, or Smith coal, in two seams, the upper one one foot ten inches in thickness, the lower three feet one inch. This is succeeded by the Arley mine coal or Orrel four-feet coal, the lowest seam of the middle coal-field, of the thickness of three feet nine inches These seams rest on thick beds of warren earth and shale of various kinds.

The number of beds of coal in the Wigan coal-field is fifty-eight to sixty. The aggregate thickness of the coal is sixty-two feet.

The following is the succession of seams in the Wigan coal-field.—

SEAMS IN THE WIGAN COAL-FIELD, LANCASHIRE.

	Yds.	Ft.	Ins.
In First 100 yards—			
Coal,	—	2	8
Burgy delf,	—	—	—
Coal,	—	—	9
Coal,	—	2	2
Big mine coal,	1	2	2
Little mine coal,	—	2	5
In 200 yards—			
Coal,	—	2	8
Coal,	—	2	3
Coal,	—	2	8
Bone coal with bass,	1	—	4
Coal,	—	2	7
In 300 yards—			
Coal,	—	2	—
Coal, good,	—	1	6
Ince Four-feet coal,	1	1	—
Ince Seven-feet coal,	1	2	8
Coal,	1	—	6
Coal,	—	1	2
Gidlows or Furnace,	1	2	2
In 400 yards—			
Little coal,	—	2	2
Pemberton Five-feet coal,	1	2	—
Do Two-feet coal,	—	2	—
Do Four-feet coal,	1	1	6
In 500 yards—			
Coal,	—	—	1
Coal,	—	—	6
In 600 yards—			
Wigan Five feet coal,	—	—	—
Coal,	—	1	10
Coal,	—	1	1
Coal,	—	—	7
Coal,	—	—	9

	Yds.	Ft.	Ins.
In 600 yards—			
Coal,	—	1	9½
Cannel coal,	—	—	5
Slaty coal,	—	—	4
Wigan Four-feet coal,	1	1	4
Coal,	—	—	3
Coal,	—	1	9
Wigan Nine-feet coal,	3	—	—
Coal,	—	—	7
Coal,	1	1	3
Coal,	1	1	3
Coal,	—	—	1½
In 700 yards—			
Coal,	—	—	8
Coal,	—	—	6
Coal,	—	2	2½
Cannel King coal,	—	—	—
Cannel coal, good,	—	2	2½
Coal,	—	—	8
Coal,	—	2	—
Coal,	—	1	5½
Dark slate with coal,	5	1	—
Ravin or Rubbishy mine coal,	—	1	11½
In 800 yards—			
Yard coal,	1	1	10
Coal,	—	—	8
Bone coal,	—	—	8
Coal,	—	—	8
In 900 yards—			
Orrel Five-feet coal,	—	—	—
Coal,	—	1	10
Bottom coal,	1	—	1
Arley mine coal, or Orrel Four-feet,	1	—	9

The four portions of the middle coal-field above described are the four richest divisions of the coal-field of Lancashire and Cheshire. They all belong to the middle coal-field, and appear to have been produced in the ages in which the carboniferous vegetation was most luxuriant. The plants of which they are the fossilized remains seem to have grown on beds of earth, of clay, and sand, in tranquil waters, and to have sunk gradually and without any violence to greater depths in those waters, where they were covered by beds of sand, which sealed them up and preserved them for the use of man, in ages thousands of years subsequent to those in which they were thus engulphed. The mineral wealth of Lancashire and Cheshire is chiefly derived from these immense beds of fossil vegetation, and industry has been most abundantly developed in the districts in which the deposits of coal are most abundant. Manchester, Oldham, St. Helen's, and Wigan, may be regarded as the centres of the districts at which the deposit of coal was greatest, and each of those places is the centre of a district abounding in population, industry, and wealth. We have traced the history of the coal formation in the middle coal-field of Lancashire somewhat fully, that being the chief natural cause of the manufacturing prosperity of the north-western division of England

Ascending into the hills which extend to the north-east and west of the middle coal-field, we come to what was originally the lowest, but what is now the highest part, of the coal-field of Lancashire and Cheshire In this part of the field the deposits of coal are much thinner than they are in the middle coal-field, and the coal measures in which they are embedded consist chiefly of hard strong-grained rocks, or of very coarse shales The coal of the lower coal-field consists of three seams, each of them three inches in thickness, of one seam two inches thick, of what is called the Forty-yard coal, one foot six inches in thickness; of the Upper-foot coal, one foot in thickness, and containing iron balls; of the gannister coal, excellent for furnaces, two feet thick, of the Lower-foot coal, one foot six inches in thickness; of a bassy coal, three feet two inches thick, of another seam nine inches in thickness, of the Sand Rock or Featheredge coal, one foot six inches, and of two other veins of coal, one six inches, the other one foot eight inches in thickness The last of these lies on the strata which rest on the main bed of the millstone grit, where the coal ceases to be found. The lower coal-field is of great extent, running through the whole of the more hilly district of Lancashire and Cheshire, where in some places coal is mined for at elevations of 1000, 1500, and even of 1800 feet above the level of the sea. The thickness of the coal measures of the lower coal-field is nearly 1800 feet. The seams of coal in the lower coal-field are fifteen in number, and of the thickness of ten feet They are as follows —

SEAMS OF COAL IN THE LOWER DIVISION OF THE LANCASHIRE AND CHESHIRE COAL FIELD, COMMENCING AT THE BOTTOM OF THE ROYLEY MINE COAL.

	Yds.	Ft	Ins.		Yds	Ft.	Ins
Coal, ...	—	—	3	Coal, ...	—		6
Coal, .	—	—	3	Forty-yards coal,	—	1	6
Coal,	—	—	2	Upper foot coal with balls,	—	1	—
Coal, . . .	—	—	3	Gannister coal,	—	2	—

	Yds	Ft.	Ins.		Yds	Ft.	Ins.
Lower foot coal,	—	1	6	Coal,	—	—	6
Bassey coal,	1	—	2	Coal,	—	1	8
Coal,	—	—	9	Resting on main strata of millstone grit,	—	—	—
Sand Rock or Featheredge coal,	—	1	6				

The nature and composition of the various beds of sandstone, shale, and earth known as the coal measures, are the main characteristics that enable us to judge of the circumstances under which the coal was deposited. The thicker beds of the coal measures may be conveniently divided into sandy, or arenaceous, and clayey or argillaceous beds The circumstances favourable to the production of coal appear to have varied very greatly at the periods when different parts of the coal measures were deposited The lower seams of coal seem to have been deposited in stormy seas, in which coarse gritty sand and clay existed, and were in frequent motion. The seams of coal in that part of the field are few in number and of no great thickness In the middle coal-field fine-grained white sands and light-coloured clays appear to have been quietly deposited, and there the most numerous and valuable seams of coal are found In the upper coal-field, so long as the rock deposits resemble those of the middle field, the seams of coal are pretty much the same; but as soon as they become red in colour and are mixed with beds of limestone, the seams of coal become thin and of little value The changes in different parts of the coal-field are supposed to have arisen from the more or less favourable condition of the waters in which the coal plants grew to sustain vegetation. They were also more or less influenced by the force of the currents that prevailed while they were being deposited The strong currents which must have existed when the coarse grit-stones of the lower coal-field were deposited, were not favourable to the growth of plants, and were therefore unfavourable to the formation of thick and numerous beds of coal. The tranquil and quiet waters in which the fine sands found in the strata of the middle coal-field were deposited, were, on the other hand, most favourable to vegetation. It was whilst these conditions prevailed that those immense and numerous masses of vegetation were produced, which in their fossilized state constitute the wealth and sustain the industry of this district of England When the upper coal-field was formed the waters were charged with peroxide of iron and carbonate of lime, and were not favourable to the production either of thick or of numerous beds of coal. Hence the seams of coal found in the higher part of the coal-field of Lancashire are few in number and of no great thickness, being separated from each other by thick beds of shale and sandstone But although the different parts of the coal-field vary in richness, there is no part of it in which the coal is not sufficiently abundant to give support to numerous and flourishing branches of industry The quantity of coal raised yearly from the mines of these two counties, amounted in the year 1865 to 12,812,000, five-sixths of it being raised in Lancashire. The total quantity of coal used in the United Kingdom in the same year was 98,150,587 tons. The Lancashire and Cheshire coal-field thus yielded about the seventh part of the quantity of coal produced in the United Kingdom

The coal found in different parts of Lancashire and Cheshire, and at different levels in the same part, presents numerous differences of quality, according to the earthy impurities mingled with the vegetable mass, the nature of the plants themselves, and the degree of decomposition they may have undergone before they were finally engulphed and mineralized. Coal is generally divided, for purposes of industry, into steam-coal, gas-coal, furnace-coal, and house-coal. Coals suited for all these purposes are found in Lancashire and Cheshire; but the especial excellence of Lancashire coal is in its power of generating steam, and of forming gas The gannister coal, found in the mountainous or hilly district, is good for furnaces, and the Orrel, Ince, and various other kinds of coal, are chiefly valuable for household purposes

The Salt-field and Brine-pits of Cheshire—In the stratified rocks and gypseous marls of the new red sandstone, we also find, in the north-western district, other mineral deposits of the greatest value for the purposes of commerce and manufactures. Amongst these is the rock-salt of Cheshire, with the brine, holding salt in solution, and formed by the washing of subterranean waters against the rocks of salt, or by the percolation of water through soils charged with saline particles Deposits of salt are not found in the beds of the new red sandstone formation in any part of Europe except in the English counties of Chester and Worcester, and in the county of Down in the north of Ireland, where they also exist to a smaller extent. The great deposits of the continent of Europe are in entirely different geological formations Thus the salt deposit of

Saltzburg in Austria, is in the oolite; that of Spain, in the chalky green-sand, and those of Poland and Sicily, in the tertiary marls. It is stated by De la Beche, that salt in its mineral state is not found in the older stratified rocks, but that it appears in all the recent formations.

The new red sandstone, as already mentioned, is one of the most extensive of the formations of England. It stretches across the kingdom in a strongly-marked diagonal band, from the mouth of the river Tees to the mouth of the river Severn, forming what Professor Sedgwick calls the great red plain of England. South of the Severn it is continued, though in a somewhat broken line, to the coast of the British Channel It is also found, to a slight extent, in the north of Ireland and in the west of Scotland On the Continent it covers immense regions, forming in the Russian empire two-thirds of an enormous natural basin, extending over an area of 4000 square miles In South America, as appears from the recent researches of Agassiz, it extends across the continent from the foot of the Andes to the mouth of the Amazons river, forming the soil of the almost boundless pampas of South America In the north-western district of England it is very fully developed, extending over at least five-sixths of the county of Chester, and over one-third, if not more, of the county of Lancaster

The new red sandstone has been divided, within the last thirty years, into the two subdivisions of the trias or upper new red sandstone system, and the permian or lower new red sandstone system. Both these systems exist in Lancashire and Cheshire, and both of them yield valuable products to industry; but their development and the value of their products vary greatly in the north-western district. The trias, or upper new red sandstone, extends from the banks of the Dee very nearly to the banks of the Lune, and is found to the north of Morecambe Bay in the district of Furness. It thus stretches sixty or eighty miles from north to south, and in some places, from thirty to forty miles from east to west. The permian or lower new red sandstone formation, on the other hand, is much less fully developed, being only found in a thin line along the edge of the coal formation, where, however, it yields a quantity of magnesian limestone for purposes of industry

"The upper new red sandstone or trias formation," says Mr. Binney, "occupies a considerable part of England, overlies the true coal formation, and contains the valuable mines of salt and gypsum for which Cheshire is famous" It is more perfectly developed in the county of Chester than in any other part of England, though even there it is wanting in those thick beds of shell limestone, that form one of the three divisions from which it derives its name of the trias or triple formation. This shell limestone, known in Germany as the "Muschel-Kalk," scarcely exists in England, and the rich copper slates which abound in this formation in Germany are also very slightly developed in this country The trias, as found in England, consists of variegated marls, red, with blue, green, and white laminated clays or marls containing gypsum or rock-salt. Interstratified with these marls are certain gray and whitish sandstones, known as waterstones, and also sandstones of variegated colours, red, white, and yellow, the lower strata being in some districts full of pebbles, and forming breccias and conglomerates.

The new red sandstone formation of Lancashire and Cheshire, as drawn and coloured in the Geological Maps which are now in course of publication by the Board of Ordnance, is divided into five sections. Beginning from the lowest layers and ascending to the highest, the first, second, and third consist of the pebble beds and soft red sandstone, and yield building stone, though of somewhat inferior quality The fourth consists of the waterstones, generally white in colour, and furnishing good building stone The fifth consists of thick beds of red marl, containing the rock-salt and brine springs of Cheshire. It will be more in accordance with our plan to describe these strata, and the products which they yield, in the descending order, beginning with the new red marls, and going down afterwards to the pebbly conglomerates of the upper new sandstone, taking the permian formation or lower new red sandstone afterwards.

The upper new red sandstone or trias formation, as already stated, is more fully developed in the county of Chester than in any other part of England The depth of that formation is stated to be upwards of 2000 feet The thickness of the respective beds is stated by Mr Edward W. Binney to be as follows —

	Feet
Red and variegated marls,	800
Waterstones, .	440
Variegated stones, (Bunter)	900
Total, . . .	2140 *

* On the Permian Beds in the North-west of England, by E W Binney, Esq, F G S Memoirs of the Literary and Philosophical Society of Manchester, vol xii, p. 209

Mr G. Waring Ormerod, who has described the salt formation of Cheshire much more completely than it was ever described before, in his "Outlines of the Principal Geological Features of the Salt Field of Cheshire and the adjoining Districts," published in the fourth volume of the Journal of the Geological Society, states that the thickness of the trias formation in the county of Chester is considerably more than 1700 feet, and there is no doubt as much more as is shown by the above calculations and observations of Mr Binney Of the whole thickness, Mr G W. Ormerod states that the upper group, including the salt and gypseous marls, occupies from 700 to 800 feet. This he has ascertained by examining the borings made through the salt-field at Northwich and at Middlewich. The middle group, containing the laminated sandstone found in the centre of Cheshire, Mr. Ormerod estimates at upwards of 400 feet in thickness; and the subjacent sandstones, mostly red, and partially conglomerate, and believed to correspond with the "Bunter sandstein" of Germany, at considerably more than 600 feet. This Mr. Binney's observations induce him to extend to 900 feet

The valley of the Weaver, forming the south-eastern district of Cheshire, is the richest salt-field in England The river Weaver rises on the gently sloping hills of North Staffordshire, near the point at which the waters that flow into the Mersey separate from those that flow into the Trent The Weaver flows with a quiet course, and in a north-westerly direction, towards the estuary of the Mersey. The valley through which it flows consists of deep red marls, in which are found both the springs of brine and the masses of rock-salt from which the springs are derived The salt-field of Cheshire extends in length about thirty miles, and in breadth from ten to fifteen miles, but its greatest riches are collected near the centre of the valley, in the neighbourhood of Northwich and Winsford The red marls which constitute this valley of salt, are bounded on the east by the lofty hills belonging to the coal and mountain-grit formation that divide Cheshire from Derbyshire; on the south by the permian, lias, and Bunter sandstein of North Staffordshire, which rise with a gentle acclivity to a height of 300 feet, and separate the waters flowing northward by the river Weaver into the estuary of the Mersey, from those that flow southward into the river Trent, and ultimately into the estuary of the Humber, on the west by the lofty range of the Peckforton and Delamere hills, formed by the white sandstone or waterstone rocks, and on the north by the range of new red sandstone hills that runs along the southern bank of the river Mersey, from Altringham and Bowden, through Lymm, Walton, and Daresbury, until they join the hills of Delamere forest. Mr G. W. Ormerod describes this region as resembling a great natural trough, which is very much its form. It was probably in very remote times an arm or lagoon of the sea, the drying up of whose waters produced the immense deposit of salt that is found within it This may perhaps have been only one of a series of lagoons of the same kind, for there are other beds of salt found to the south of the Cheshire salt-field, in the neighbourhood of Stafford, and there are others still further south in the same formation, in the county of Worcester. The salt beds of Staffordshire are situated at Ingestre, about five miles from Stafford The brine alone is worked there, and yields about two pounds two ounces to the gallon. The beds from which the salt is derived at Ingestre consist of red marl and gypsum, to a depth of 324 feet; of similar beds with particles of salt to the thickness of fifteen feet, succeeded by red marl and gypsum of the depth of sixty-nine feet—in all 408 feet, of which 378 feet have been sunk and thirty bored This Staffordshire deposit of salt is separated from the Cheshire salt-field by the coal-field, by the permian bed, the variogated sandstones, and the lias of North Staffordshire and Shropshire The salt deposits of Worcester are much more extensive than those of Staffordshire, though much less extensive than those of Cheshire.*

The southern part of the broad valley which extends across the eastern part of the county of Cheshire, from Malpas to Congleton, sweeping in a crescent from the coal formation and millstone grit of Mowcop to the high grounds of the Peckforton hills, appears to be occupied by the saliferous and gypseous beds of the salt formation. The only point in the higher part of this southern range of hills in which the rock-salt is found, is at Lawton near Congleton, where thick beds of rock-salt have been met with at an elevation of 290 feet above the level of the sea. Although rock-salt has not been found in the higher part of the valley of the Weaver, there must be considerable deposits of mineral salt in those hills, as the waters that spring from them, and rise above the level of the ground, are charged with salt.

Proceeding from south to north, brine has been met with at Dirtwich or Foulwich, situated on the boundary of Cheshire, about

* Ormerod's Salt-fields of Cheshire, Journal of the Geological Society, vol IV, p 263

two miles south of Malpas. In a pit at Foulwich, sunk to a depth of 450 feet below the level of the sea, the brine comes into the shaft, at the depth of sixty feet, in a small stream about the thickness of a finger. At Combermere Abbey, the brine burst into the Mere in the reign of Henry VIII., about the year 1533, in such abundance as to induce the last abbot of Combermere to establish a salt manufactory. But the brine has long disappeared from the lake at Combermere. At Bickley, about three miles to the east of Malpas, a great subsidence of the ground and a sudden irruption of brine took place in the year 1659, at a spot called Barrell Fell, that is now dry land and overgrown with brushwood Still further to the south, at a place named Kent Rough, near Adderley, brine was found about two miles to the south of Audlem, at a depth of 300 feet, whilst boring for coal through the edge of the lias formation. Between Audlem and Nantwich, a distance of seven miles, the brine is found on both banks of the river Weaver, in some places under the soil, in others rising through the surface of the ground, and flowing into the river from both sides of the stream.

The town of Nantwich was formerly the principal seat of the salt manufacture; but not having, until recent times, any means of water communication with the coal-field of Lancashire or that of Staffordshire, it lost the trade when the neighbouring hills ceased to supply fuel, in the form of wood, for the heating of the pans in which the brine is evaporated. Brine has, however, been found in the neighbourhood of Nantwich at Acton, a mile from Nantwich on the Chester road, at Hatherton, about three miles to the north-east of Audlem; at Austerton and at Baddington, on the western side of Audlem, and at Baddiley, five miles to the north-west of Audlem

The brine is not again met with in the valley of the Weaver until within a little distance to the north of Church Coppenhall. Proceeding northward down the river Weaver, brine and rock-salt are found in great abundance at Winsford The rock-salt is met with there at a depth of from 150 to 180 feet below the sea level. The level at which the brine is found at Winsford is above that of the sea. At Winsford the salt-works commence, and continue by the side of the river to Newbridge or Moulton. The works at Winsford are mostly of brine, and when the brine is pumped its level is lowered many feet.

From Winsford towards Northwich the land sinks along the whole course of the valley, from the working of the salt mines and brine pits, both above and below, and the river spreads over its banks into large pools, named "the Flashes"

The rock-salt has been found from Winsford to below Newbridge In most cases, however, the brine has made its way into the shafts, and the mines are now converted into brine pits The strata that overlie the salt consist of red and blue marl with gypsum There, as elsewhere, the brine lies on the surface of the rock-salt. From Newbridge or Moulton to Northwich there are no salt-works, and no rock-salt has been found between those two places. The brine at Northwich is found at a lower level than at Winsford. Instead of being met with at the level of the sea, it is found about fifty-five feet below that level, and when the pits are at work, it is still further lowered to the extent of thirty to forty feet The rock-salt is found in great abundance at Northwich, and is extensively worked at that place, which is now the capital of the Cheshire salt district

It is a remarkable circumstance that the existence of the rock-salt deposits of Cheshire was not known until after the brine pits had been worked for many centuries The rock-salt was first discovered accidentally at Marbury, near Northwich, in the year 1670, in a vain search for coal.

Next to the brine springs and rock-salt of the main valley of the Weaver, those on the banks of the small stream known as the river Wheelock are the most abundant and most valuable. The Wheelock rises at the foot of the lofty hills that divide Cheshire from Derbyshire, and falls into the river Dane at Middlewich The Dane joins the Weaver at Northwich, at which point all the waters of the salt district unite.

The saliferous beds abut on the coal, millstone grit, and mountain limestone, near Mowcop and Cloud Edge, and at Lawton, near this lofty range of hills, deep beds of rock-salt were found in the year 1779. This rock-salt is said to be equal in quality to that of Northwich, but from want of water-carriage, to bring up supplies of coal and to take down the manufactured salt to the shipping ports, it was soon abandoned. Since the introduction of railways this is no longer a serious obstacle to the working of the salt mines at Lawton, or either of mines or brine pits in any part of Cheshire, if it should become desirable.

Following the course of the river Wheelock, the brine has been worked in the neighbourhood of Church Lawton, on both sides of the stream The depth of the brine springs at this point was 225 feet in the year 1848, and the level at which the brine stood was 210 feet from the surface, or about 200 feet above the sea level The spring from which the brine rises is abundant, and the brine strong. Lower down the Wheelock, at Malkin's Bank, on the north-east side of the stream, there is an abundant supply of brine, and it is believed that the rock-salt also exists there at a depth of 183 feet "At this point," says Mr. G W Ormerod, "a shaft six feet in diameter was sunk to the depth of 173 feet, and a boring of five inches diameter was then made When the boring instrument had penetrated the saturated plaster or gypsum beds to the brine spring, it suddenly dropped eighteen inches, and seemed to rest on a solid substance Immediately on the spring being tapped, it rushed in with such rapidity as to carry one of the men to the height of ninety feet before he could be rescued" Brine pits continue to be worked at Wheelock.

Following the course of the Wheelock to the point where it joins the river Dane, we come to Middlewich, where brine pits have been worked for many ages, probably from the time when Middlewich, under the old British name of Condate, was the point of meeting of all the old Roman roads in the north-western district of England, as Crewe, only a few miles south of Middlewich, is now the point of junction of all the railways in the same district

The rock-salt has not been found at Middlewich, although the strata have been penetrated to a depth of 214 feet below the sea level; and in seven of the brine pits there the brine oozes out of a layer of black gravel nine inches in thickness, between two horizontal beds of indurated clay or rock At the remaining pit the brine rises so near to the surface as to be within reach of the hand Brine has been found about one mile north-west of Middlewich, at Flint mill, but has not been worked

No brine or rock-salt has been found in the valley of the river Dane, from the point where it receives the Wheelock to that where it falls into the Weaver at Leftwich, opposite to Northwich. The whole valley of the Dane, although it flows through the middle of the salt-field of Cheshire, is almost destitute of brine, and entirely so of rock-salt, either from causes connected with the original formation of the deposit, or from the effect of faults in the rock, on the subterranean course of the waters impregnated with brine

The Witton brook, which enters the Weaver a mile or two below Northwich, flows through a rich salt-field as it approaches Northwich, at Anderton.

The whole of the rivers and brooks rising in or flowing over the salt-field of Cheshire discharge their waters by the main stream of the river Weaver, a little below Northwich, through a narrow pass that forms the only means of communication between the upper and lower part of the salt valley of Cheshire. Below the line of high ground that stretches eastward from Delamere forest to Winnington and Castle Northwich, and beyond the valley of the Weaver by Witton brook, Barnton, and Bellmont, in the direction of Ashley Park and High Leigh, the deposits of salt, from being excessively rich above, suddenly become quite insignificant. A great fault in the strata is supposed to be the cause. The boundary of the salt-field below Northwich seems to be the line of the valley that runs between Pickmere and Budworthmere. Here are the most northerly traces of the great salt-field, and that it exists to that line may be inferred from the gradual sinking of the ground that is there taking place. Near Budworthmere the water from the Lake has gradually increased on the fields, and a farm-house situated near that point has been shaken by the same cause. There it is probably cut off by a fault in the strata, and runs northward towards the Lancashire coal-field below the western mere.

On the surface of the salt-field frequent subsidence takes place in the land. From this cause the locks and banks of the Weaver have frequently been raised. The land on which a factory stood near Northwich bridge has sunk so low as to form a wharf. A few years since the subsidence near the junction of Witton brook and the Weaver was at the rate of three inches per week, at this point a lake is now rapidly forming. The salt pans at the works of the Weaver have been frequently raised, and many are now abandoned. The bed of Witton brook, which in 1811 was six feet deep, is now from ten to thirty feet.*

There are no salt-works of any importance below this line, though brine has been found in small quantities down the valley of the Weaver as far as Frodsham, the point where that river enters the Mersey. There a weak brine was discovered at a depth of 250 feet below the level of the sea. Brine has also been found at other

* Sixteenth Report of the British Association for the Advancement of Science, Transactions of Sections, p. 63. By Mr. G. W. Ormerod.

places. There was a salt-work at Weaverham, in the valley of the Weaver, in the seventeenth century; and it is stated by Holland that a bed of rock-salt was found at Whitley, in boring for coal, about the year 1803 Brine is also said to have been found at Dunham Massey, on the borders of the county of Chester, and in the valley of the Mersey brine has been met with at Woolston, near Warrington, at a depth of 104 feet, or about ninety feet below the sea level. Also at Woolden, on the south-west edge of Chat moss, a brine spring has been found whilst sinking in the variegated sandstone of that district.* Very recently the water of a deep well sunk at Hulme, near Manchester, was found to be too salt to be used for the purpose of dyeing.

The following table will show the points and the levels at which salt and brine have been sought for successfully and unsuccessfully —

LEVELS AT WHICH ROCK-SALT AND BRINE HAVE BEEN SOUGHT FOR IN CHESHIRE.

	Feet		
At Lawton, the rock salt found	290	above	sea level
Near the same place brine found	185	"	"
Near the same place brine stands at	200	"	"
Hassall Green, brine not found at	84	"	"
Malkin's Bank, brine found at	70	"	"
Malkin's Bank, brine stands	171	"	"
Wheelock Salt works, brine found	3	below	"
Wheelock Salt-works, brine stands	93	above	"
At Sandbatch, brine not found at	143	"	"
Near Elton, a spring rises to surface	130	"	"
Near Warmington, brine not found at	22	below	"
At Sproston, near Middlewich, brine not found at a little above sea level			
At Middlewich, brine rises to surface .	120	above	"
At Middlewich, rock salt not found	7	"	"
At Middlewich, rock-salt not found	214	below	"
At Winslow, no workable salt or brine found at	200	"	"
At Winsford, rock-salt and brine stood at	90	"	"
At Winsford, brine stands at about sea level.			
At Hartford, neither rock salt nor brine found at .	138	"	"
At Northwich, rock-salt and brine found at	55 to 59	"	"
At Northwich, the level at which brine stands	34 to 46	"	"
At Marston, Mr Nieuman's pit rock-salt found	27	"	"
At Marston, when at pit's head .	5	above	"
At Marston, level of brine standing	33	"	"
At Barnton, brine found .	130	below	"
At Barnton, brine rises to the surface	50	above	"
At Acton, brine not found at	230	below	"
At Frodsham Bridge, rock salt not found at	450	"	"
At Frodsham Bridge, weak brine found at .	250	"	"

* Ormerod's Salt-field of Cheshire, Journal of the Geological Society, vol iv, p 258

It will be seen from the above table that the rock-salt has been found and worked in three neighbourhoods, namely, at Lawton, Winsford, and Northwich. It has also been found, though not worked, at Wheelock, and perhaps at Whitley, though that is not quite certain

The first place at which the rock-salt was discovered, as already stated, was at Marbury, near Northwich, and subsequent discoveries have shown that the salt-rock underlies the town of Northwich, and is extensively found at Marston in the same neighbourhood. Beds of rock-salt, at least sixty yards thick, are marked in the Geological Maps of the Board of Ordnance, as extending from Winsford to Marston, below Northwich, a distance of eight miles These have not been proved for the whole of that distance, but the resemblance of the strata at Winsford to those of Northwich and Marston, shows that they are nearly identical

The rock-salt, as already mentioned, has been proved from Winsford down the valley of the Weaver as far as New Bridge The upper stratum of the rock-salt at Winsford is 120 feet in thickness, but it is full of earthy impurities, and is not worked. It is separated from the second bed of rock-salt by a stratum of indurated clay or stone This clay is from thirty-three to thirty-six feet in thickness, and is traversed by veins of salt, called leaders, reaching from the upper to the second stratum of salt. The higher portion of this bed of rock-salt at Winsford is also full of earthy impurities for a depth of sixty or seventy feet, then a bed of pure and almost transparent rock-salt, about fifteen feet in thickness, is come to This is the part of the salt-rock from which the supplies of rock-salt used for the purposes of trade are obtained After sinking through this part of the rock for a distance of fifteen feet, the salt again becomes discoloured and impure. The second bed of rock-salt at Winsford has been penetrated to the depth of 120 feet, but has not been sunk through.

The rock-salt at Northwich, at Marston, and at other places in the immediate neighbourhood of Northwich, also presents two beds. The upper bed at Northwich is eighty-four to ninety feet thick, and, like that at Winsford, of little value, in consequence of its earthy impurities A bed of indurated clay thirty feet thick, separates it from the lower bed of rock-salt. The upper part of the second bed is impure at Northwich, as at Winsford, for a depth of sixty to seventy-five feet, and is not worked Then comes a stratum of pure and beautiful salt from twelve to fifteen feet in thickness. From that point the second bed again becomes impure. Till within the last few years, the second bed of the Northwich salt-field had not been penetrated, but in a pit at Marston, to the north of the town of Northwich, belonging to Mr. Nieuman, a shaft has now been sunk through the second bed, proving it to be ninety-six feet in thickness at that point. At other places the rock-salt has been penetrated to a depth of 117 feet without being sunk through.

Beds of rock-salt of a totally different stratification have been found at Lawton, on the south-eastern edge of the Cheshire salt-field. In the Lawton salt-field the succession of the strata is as follows:— Soil and gypseous marls, 126 feet; salt, four feet; indurated clay, thirty feet; salt, twelve feet; indurated clay, forty-five feet; salt, penetrated to the depth of seventy-two feet: total, 289 feet.

Taking the rock salt-field of Cheshire as a whole, the succession of the strata is as follows:—

	Ft	Ins
Two upper salt marls, about	87	0
Upper salt	60 to 90	0
Hard clay,	30	0
Second salt, from	90 to 170	0
Stone,	5	8
Salt and clay,	6	7
Pale red salt,	3	4
Stone, with thin laminæ of salt,	13	9
Pale red salt,	6	0
Stone, with veins of salt,	7	6
Lowest bed of salt reached,	11	6
Stone,	77	0
Stone, with detached crystals of salt,	7	0
Stone, with salt laminæ,	11	0

'The brine-springs of Cheshire,' as Sir Charles Lyell observes, "are the richest in this country: those of Northwich are almost saturated." The brine of Northwich and Winsford is of the best quality. It is charged with saline matter to the amount of twenty-five per cent of its own weight. The brine found at Nantwich was examined by Daubeney, and was not found to differ to any considerable extent from the Northwich brine. Comparing this with the saltness of the sea, we find, from the experiments of Schweitzer, that the sea-water of the British Channel contains rather less than three per cent of chloride of sodium, or seventy-seven parts in 1000. According to Forchhammer, the greatest quantity of saline matter in the waters of the Atlantic Ocean is found in the tropics, far from land. In such places the sea-water contains more than three and a half per cent of saline matter, or more precisely, 3 56 per cent.

Some difference of opinion exists amongst eminent geologists as to the origin of the immense masses of rock-salt which are found in Cheshire, and the other salt-fields of this and other countries. Two of the most distinguished authorities on this subject, Professor Phillips and Sir Charles Lyell, thus express themselves. Professor Phillips observes, "The salt and gypsum usually associated in this remarkable system present their difficulties Not that it is hard to suppose the waters of the ancient sea to have been so evaporated, as to permit first the crystallization of the sulphate of lime, and finally of muriate of soda. But in this case we should expect to find almost over the whole area regular strata of gypsum below, and regular layers of salt above, while, in fact, we more commonly find salt in great broad masses rather than beds below, and gypsum in scattered masses above. A general drying of the waters in which the saliferous system was deposited is plainly inconsistent with probability, and we must have recourse to local causes, something analogous, perhaps, to those which influenced the deposit of the primary limestone, namely, the development of subterranean heat, which directly by change of temperature, or by intermediate chemical agencies, rendered the calcareous matter insoluble over limited areas. It may be conceived that the solubility of muriate of soda in water is capable of diminution through the admixture of other substances in the liquid, or through the effect of great pressure, or of pressure and heat combined It may be maintained that the limited deposits of salt happened in separate lagoons of the sea, exposed to local desiccation, as perhaps in Cheshire" On this subject Sir Charles Lyell observes, "The gypsum and saline matter, occasionally interstratified with red clays and sandstone of various ages, primary, secondary, and tertiary, have been thought by some geologists to be of volcanic origin Submarine and sub-aerial exhalations often occur in the regions of earthquakes and volcanoes, far from the point of actual eruption, and charged with sulphur, sulphuric salts, and with common salt or muriate of soda. In a word, such 'salfateras' are vents, by which all the products which issue in a state of sublimation from the craters of active volcanoes obtain a passage from the interior of the earth to the surface. That such gaseous emanations and mineral springs, impregnated with the ingredients before enumerated, and often intensely heated, continue to flow out, unaltered in composition and temperature for ages, is well known But before we can decide on their real instrumentality in producing, in the course of ages, gypsum, rock-salt, and dolomite, we require to know more respecting the chemical changes actually in progress in seas where volcanic agency is at work" Again, Sir C Lyell observes, "The brine-springs rise up through strata of sandstone and red marl, which contain large beds of rock-salt. The origin of the brine may therefore be from the salt, but as muriate of soda is one of the products of volcanic emanations and of springs in volcanic regions, the original source of salt may be as deeply seated as that of lava. In Auvergne (a region of extinct volcanoes), a hot spring rising through granite at St Nectaire may be mentioned as one of many which contains a large portion of muriate of soda, together with magnesia and other ingredients."* At the village of Sproston in Cheshire, there is also a curious mineral spring containing salt.

But whatever may have been the origin of salt in Cheshire, and of salt generally, there can be no doubt that it has long been, and is, a great source of national wealth and individual prosperity. The salt-field of Cheshire, being beyond comparison the largest and richest in the United Kingdom, and the most available for commercial and manufacturing purposes in the whole world, has been one of the principal sources of the prosperity of the county of Chester, certainly from the time of the Domesday survey, and probably from the time when the Romans ran their great roads through the midst of it Its importance has increased greatly in modern times, especially during the last thirty years, in which period the great practical chemists of the age have succeeded in decomposing muriate of soda or common salt, and in extracting from a few hundred thousand tons of salt chemical products of the value of several millions sterling

The manufactories of salt in the United Kingdom are about eighty in number Of these upwards of sixty are situated in Cheshire, two in Staffordshire, thirteen in Worcestershire, two in Durham, one in Lancashire, and one or two in the county of Down, Ireland According to the mineral statistics for 1864, the quantity of salt sent down the river Weaver yearly from the salt-works of Cheshire amounted to from 750,000 to 800,000 tons, on an average of several years; and to this must be added 300,000

* Sir Charles Lyell's Principles of Geology, p 247

to 400,000 tons of Cheshire salt otherwise disposed of, making the total yield of Cheshire upwards of 1,200,000 tons. The Worcester salt-field produced 167,000 tons, and the county Down salt-field 15,662 tons. The total quantity is thus about 1,500,000 tons per annum. The total exports of salt, on the average of the last three years, was thus upwards of 600,000 tons per annum.

The works in which this enormous supply of salt is produced, chiefly from brine, are formed of the following apparatus.—First, of a reservoir into which the brine is pumped from the spring, second, of the pans into which the brine is conveyed by means of pipes from the reservoir, third, of the furnaces which heat the brine, fourth, of hothouses for stoving the salt, and fifth of storehouses for storing the salt. The ordinary size of a salt-pan is forty-feet long, twenty-four feet wide, and fifteen inches deep A salt-work of average extent will produce about 250 tons of salt per week At Northwich there are from 1500 to 1600 men employed in the salt-works, of whom three-fourths work through the day, and one-fourth at night

It is an interesting sight to see the salt forming in crystals in the brine It commences in small cubes, which gradually increase until their density carries them to the bottom of the pan. It may be remarked that the salt is always found in cubes, even its most minute particles As the salt forms and falls, it is raked to the side of the pans, and piled on the barrows, as they are called, at the side, where it is allowed to drain, the drainage being carried back into the pans. It sometimes happens in seething the brine, that the crystals will not form In that case a little oil is thrown into the pan, which soon spreads over it, and causes a scum to rise from the brine. When this scum is taken off, the crystals commence forming After the salt has sufficiently drained, it is removed to the stove-house and stoved according to quality and texture There are three or four kinds of salt made. Bay salt is very large-grained, this is made by very slow evaporation at a temperature of 110° Common salt, which is coarse-grained, is produced at a heat of 175°, stoved, or fine table salt, at 220° The last description of salt is put into boxes from the pans, whence it is transferred to stoves, and there consolidated and dried in the course of five or six days *

* Transactions of the Historic Society of Lancashire and Cheshire The Salt Trade of Cheshire by John Stonehouse, vol v

The quantity of coal used in the manufacture of salt may be taken in these proportions—two tons of coal are required to produce three tons of fine or table salt, and one ton of coal to produce two tons of common salt Probably 1,000,000 tons of coal are consumed annually in the manufacture of salt in Cheshire

In mining for rock-salt, the second bed of salt, as already stated, is the only one used, the other being impure from a mixture of earth. The depth of the shaft is about 330 feet The old way of boring the mine was by puddling the sides and casing them with wood as the men went down, but iron cylinders are now used, the water is pumped up from the first or top brine spring, to prevent its flooding the mine below. There are two or more shafts to each mine. On looking down the yawning mouth of a rock-salt pit it certainly does require some nerve, in any one unused to such a style of locomotion, to descend 330 feet in a bucket The entrance to the mine is roofed over, and from a lofty pulley there is suspended a ponderous chain, to the end of which the bucket or tube used to bring the rock up to the surface is appended. Each bucket will hold about two tons of rock-salt There is a sliding platform over the mouth of the pit, which is withdrawn when the bucket is in motion On being drawn to the surface, the bucket rests upon the platform, and is then wheeled away to the barge or flat waiting to be loaded The miners find their way about very easily The mine is dry at the bottom, and the work is not of an unhealthy nature, nor so liable to danger as in coal mines A mine fully lit up is an extraordinary sight, the gigantic pillars supporting the roof having some resemblance to sugar-candy The "cavity" says Holland, "presents a striking appearance, and when illuminated with candles fixed in the rock, the effect is highly brilliant In some of the pits the roof is supported by pillars eight or ten yards square, which are in general regularly disposed, others are worked out in aisles" There are railways running from the workings to the mouth of the pit. The rock-salt is detached by blasting The temperature of the mine is about 53°. There are upwards of twenty-three mines in Cheshire, and the quantity of rock-salt brought to the surface averages about 100,000 tons annually The cost of the machinery in these mines may be estimated at £500,000

Examining a section of the rock-salt bed taken horizontally, the surface presents various figures, differing in form, size, and colour. Some of them appear to be circular, others approaching to an oval shape, whilst in others an irregular pentagon may be traced Some of these figures are two or three feet in diameter, others as much as ten or twelve feet The lines which form the boundaries of these figures are white, and from two to five or six inches wide On examination, these appearances are found to be owing to the rock-salt in the white lines forming the division of the figures being perfectly pure and free from earthy matter The general effect is that of mosaic work. The whole stratum of rock-salt may be compared to a mass of basaltic columns, the lines of separation in each pillar being marked by the pure and transparent rock-salt *

The Iron and Copper Ores of Lancashire and Cheshire.—Next in importance to the coal and salt of the north-western district are its rich beds of iron ore, of which those found in the district of Lower Furness, at the northern extremity of Lancashire, are the richest and most abundant But much iron ore also exists in the southern parts of the county

It has been customary to assume that the coal-field in the southern part of Lancashire has no beds of ironstone worth working In ancient times, however, considerable quantities of iron ore were manufactured from its argillaceous ores, especially those in the middle and lower coal-fields near Burnley, which occupy the same position as the beds of Low Moor in Yorkshire, from which that justly celebrated iron is made In modern times, it is true, there have only been in operation the furnaces of Messrs Swire & Co, of Dukinfield These were supplied with argillaceous ore procured from the middle coal-field, but were soon discontinued Whether this arose from the poor quality of the ore, or the unfavourable position of the measures, which there dip at an angle of 30°, and render the minerals expensive to work, is uncertain, but it was most probably owing to the latter cause, which would tell seriously both on the price of coal and iron

In the lower division of the Lancashire coal-field, there are, as Mr. Binney informs us, numerous beds of argillaceous ore, of such thickness as would cause them to be worked in many iron-making districts

In the middle coal-field of Lancashire, also, are many argillaceous

* Holland's Cheshire, p 87

and blackband ores, fully as rich as those wrought in other places, and so situated that they could be calcined together with great advantage. Among the former are those of Clifton and St. Helen's, and doubtless many other places in the same position, and amongst the latter are the blackband above the Cannel mine at Wigan, and impure cannels and blackbands in that neighbourhood and about Dukinfield Below the four-feet coal at Pendleton, near Manchester, a carbonaceous blackband was found, in sinking Mr Fitzgerald's new pit, about four feet in thickness. A fair average specimen of this was analyzed by Mr John Leigh, F.C.S., and was found to contain in 200 grains, 57 grains of peroxide of iron, with 98 grains of bituminous matter and of carbon. This gives 49 per cent of combustible matter, and 28.5 per cent. of peroxide of iron, equivalent to 19.95 per cent of metallic iron This is certainly not a rich ore, but if mixed with the argillaceous stones of Clifton, and calcined together, it is capable of yielding a fair description of iron In Lancashire many beds of cannel sink into blackbands, in a similar manner to what often takes place in Scotland

But the upper or Manchester coal-field is that which yields the most valuable iron ores found in South Lancashire Above the Four-feet mine at Patricroft, and extending under Chat Moss, is a bed of the carbonate of protoxide of iron about two feet six inches in thickness This was found on sinking the shafts at the colliery of Messrs Lancaster & Co, at Patricroft, not far from the Liverpool and Manchester railway On analysis this ore yielded about 72 per cent of carbonate of iron, and the gentleman—a medical man—who analyzed it, informed Mr Binney that it was pure enough to be used for medicinal purposes

There are beds of blackband of twelve and six inches thick, respectively, above the Three-quarter mine at Bradford, near Manchester, and over the main limestone at Ardwick, the representatives beyond, all doubt, of the redstone of the Pottery coal-field, as their geological position and the fossils they contain are exactly the same.

"Some of the above beds,' says Mr. E W Binney, writing in the year 1853, "only want thoroughly investigating to make them worthy of attention Coal is no doubt much in demand for manufacturing purposes throughout the district, but for the last five years the average price has not been greater, if so much, as that paid by the ironmasters in South Staffordshire Limestone is not very favourably placed, for the Derbyshire, North Lancashire, and Cheshire deposits are all at considerable distances The two last, however, are now accessible by rail"

The thick bed of carbonate at Patricroft, before mentioned, is free from the remains of fossil shells and fish, which will cause it to be in a great measure destitute of the compounds of phosphorus and sulphur, so detrimental to many of the argillaceous and blackband ores found in the carboniferous strata, and which are known to make so much cold short iron.*

But by far the most valuable of the iron ores of Lancashire are found in the northern division of the county, in the district of Lower Furness, in the strata of carboniferous or mountain limestone The southern boundary of this limestone is generally given in the geological maps on a line running from a little north of Aldingham, on the Leven, to the village of Stank, where magnesian limestone has been found Its north-west range, by Marston and Dalton to the Duddon at Kirkby-Ireleth, is pretty well known

The most valuable as well as interesting points in this deposit are the mines of red oxide of iron which are contained in it These have been worked for many ages, and so far from being exhausted, are at the present time yielding five times as much ore as they formerly yielded The Furness or limestone ore is now used in most of the iron-works of England and Scotland, for the purpose of mixing with the poorer ores of the coal measures

The Furness iron ore appears to lie in fissures in the limestone, which in general run from south-east to north-west, but these main lines are sometimes united by cross fissures. The iron mines occur in the limestone, near the junction of that deposit with the upper new red sandstone. The depth of the vein has not yet been found In some mines it has been proved to a depth of seventy yards, without ascertaining its lowest limit

One of the richest deposits of iron is situated on Lindal Moor, on the estates of the duke of Buccleuch and Lord Muncaster. It is partly an open work The fissure or valley in the limestone, where the iron occurs, must be from forty to fifty yards in width, and runs from north-west to south-east On the north wall of the vein the limestone is coated with kidney iron ore, but the bulk of the deposit is a red paste called "raddle", consisting of nearly pure

* Mr E W Binney, on the Origin of Ironstones, p 38.

hydrate of the peroxide of iron, in which are mingled numerous crystals of smoke-coloured quartz and pieces of kidney ore. The limestone composing the walls of the vein is so much saturated with silica, that it will scarcely effervesce when treated with hydrochloric acid.*

"The beds of iron," says Mr Binney, in his "Glance at the Geology of Low Furness," "appear to have been formed after the deposition of the carboniferous limestone, and before the deposition of the upper new red sandstone. The limestone rock, in some instances, seems to have been only fissured, but in others eroded or water-worn, before the introduction of the iron. During the formation of the old red, as well as of the new red sandstone, a vast amount of the pure oxide of iron appears to have been mingled with the waters of the ancient ocean. But still, the quantity in the iron mines of Low Furness is such as to indicate a proximity to the source from which it originated. It appears to have been thrown up by volcanic action, and then carried by some means into the valleys and fissures where it is now found. But whether the iron was injected into the places where it is now met with through the fissures immediately below, or was first mingled with the waters of the sea, which then flowed through the fissures and crevices of the limestone, and gradually filled them up with the metallic matter, held partly in solution, as Professor Sedgwick thinks, is difficult to determine. The neighbouring district, towards the mouth of the Duddon and Black Combe, shows abundance of proofs of having been formerly much disturbed by volcanic agency."

The quantity of ore produced from the hæmatite iron mines of Furness amounted to 691,421 tons, at the time when the Memoirs of the Geological Survey of Great Britain were published, in the year 1865, and it is constantly increasing as several improvements have been made in the process of mining in this district during the last half dozen years. In the year 1864, 224,729 tons of ores were shipped at Barrow; 223,431 were shipped via Ulverstone; 239,523 tons were forwarded to Hurdpool furnaces, and 430 to Duddon furnaces. At that time the number of hæmatite iron mines in the neighbourhood of Barrow and Ulverstone was twenty-two, and they were situated at the following places — Adgarley, Adlingham, Bolton Heads, Carr Kettle, Crossgates, Eure

* A Glance at the Geology of Low Furness, Lancashire, by E. W. Binney, Esq., F.G.S. Memoirs of the Literary and Philosophical Society of Manchester, vol. viii., p. 442.

Pits (two mines), Elliscales, Gillrow, Lindal Cote, Lindal Moor (two mines), Newton Heads, Mousell, Old-hills, Park, Roanhead, Rickethills, Stainton, and Whitcriggs (two mines). The ore of these mines is exported to the Staffordshire mining districts, South Wales, and the West of Scotland, by Barrow, Pile of Fouldry, Morecambe, and Fleetwood, the latter chiefly for Yorkshire; and a small quantity to France. The yield of iron ore in the Furness district in the year 1864 was 691,421 tons.*

Though neither copper nor lead can be said to be abundant in Lancashire, yet they are both found to a moderate extent. The Coniston copper mines are extensive and valuable, yielding, according to the "Memoirs of the Geological Survey of Great Britain," 1896 tons of copper ore yearly, of the value, at the prices of 1864, of £13,808. There are also a number of smaller mines in the district of Higher Furness. They are found, as Professor Sedgwick informs us, in the middle division of the Cumbrian slates, chiefly on the line where different strata join each other, bearing out the opinion, that the prevalence and richness of mineral veins are intimately connected with the proximity or junction of dissimilar rocks, where the electric, molecular, and electro-chemical actions are most energetic. The Coniston mines are found on the line at which the lower and upper Silurian rocks unite. Valuable deposits of copper have also been found at Alderley Edge, and at Mottram in Cheshire. The former yields 14,696 tons, the latter is estimated to yield 1000 tons.

Several small mines of lead ore are found in the mountain limestone, in the northern district of Lancashire.

Sand, Clay, and Stone.—In addition to the coal, salt, and iron, which form the most important part of the mineral wealth of the two counties, there are several other mineral products which also add considerably to it.

Commencing a few feet below the surface of the ground, in those beds of sand and clay to which geologists give the name of the post-tertiary formation, and which contain the remains of animals closely resembling some of those of the existing species, we find a pure silicious sand, admirably suited for the glass furnace. This, when melted, affords the best material for the making of plate and other descriptions of glass, which are amongst the most beautiful as

* Memoirs of the Geological Survey of Great Britain, &c., by Robert Hunt, F.R.S., Keeper of Mining Records, p. 56. Mineral Statistics for 1865, by Robert Hunt, Esq., F.R.S.

well as the most useful products of British industry The sand owes its value as a material for making glass to the purity of its silex or flinty base, and to its freedom from oxide of iron and other metallic oxides, which render ordinary sands unsuitable for that purpose The sand used for glass-making in Lancashire is found in beds of two or three feet in thickness, chiefly on the edges of the peat mosses, which have been spoken of as occupying so extensive an area in that county. It is met with in great abundance, and of the finest quality, in the neighbourhood of St Helen's, which is now the principal seat of the glass manufacture of Lancashire. This sand appears to have been deposited at a comparatively recent period, in hollows in the marl beds of the upper new red sandstone or trias formations. These hollows seem to have resembled originally those in which the meres, or small lakes, of Cheshire and Lancashire are held, though they are now filled with beds of peat From the extreme fineness of this sand, it would appear to have been deposited by slowly moving streams, or perhaps to have been produced by the friction of the waters of small lakes on the rocky beds in which they were contained. The slower and gentler the action of water, the finer is the sand that it produces The boulders, or masses of stone originally borne along by ocean currents, are all large, and any gravel produced by such action is of the coarsest kind The sand of rapid rivers is also coarse, in proportion to their rapidity. It is only in streams flowing along gently, or on the edges of small and sheltered lakes, where the water vibrates in its bed at the rate of a few inches per second, that the finest kind of sand is formed At the present day a fringe of sand, beautifully fine and white, is formed around the edges of the Cheshire meres, by the movement of the water in their beds, and the action of the rills that flow into or issue from them. A still finer kind of silicious sand or powder has occasionally been found under peat mosses. Under one of these mosses near Gainsborough, Lincolnshire, Mr Binney found a stratum of sand four to six inches in thickness, supposed to consist of the silicious skeletons of small fossil plants, in the form of a white impalpable powder. These plants appear to be pure silica, in a state of extremely minute subdivision On submitting this powder to the highest power of the compound microscope, it was found to consist of a mass of transparent squares and parallelograms of different relative proportions, whose edges were perfectly smooth and sharp, and their areas traced with very delicate lines. On comparing them with some existing conferveæ, the resemblance was found to be so strong as to prove the close alliance, if not perfect identity, of the two. They were therefore supposed to be the counterparts of the fossil infusoria of Ehrenberg, and to occupy the same place in the vegetable kingdom which those do in the animal * The extremely fine sand found in the neighbourhood of St Helen's, joined to the abundance of coal found in that neighbourhood, and the large production of soda, has fixed the glass manufacture in that district. The sea-sand found at no great distance in the estuary of the Mersey, has also been useful in the rubbing and polishing of glass This sand is produced by the action of the waves of the sea on the soft sandstone rocks which exist on the shores or form the beds of those estuaries. This sand is met with in abundance in the bed of the river Mersey, near Widness and Runcorn As much as twenty or thirty tons of this sand is used daily in some of the glass-houses, in rubbing off the irregularities of the rough plates of glass as they come from the furnace, which is the first step towards smoothing the plates. They are afterwards rubbed with seven or eight coats of emery, from Naxos in the Greek Archipelago, and thus prepared to receive the final polish, which gives to the glass the transparency and brilliancy that enable it to transmit light and to reflect the images of objects Moulding sand is also found in the permian beds in the neighbourhood of Manchester, and is extensively used in the iron foundries of that city and the neighbouring towns.

The materials for the building of mills, workshops, warehouses, and houses, exist in great abundance in most parts of the two counties, and have already been employed in erecting nearly half a million of buildings, public and private, of the yearly value of seven or eight millions sterling.

The thick beds of clay-marl and clay found in the alluvium, on the new red sandstone, and in the coal measures of Lancashire and Cheshire, supply the material, when burnt into bricks, with which nine-tenths of the buildings of the two counties are constructed. It is only in the neighbourhood of the limestone and Cumbrian hills, where stone is abundant, or in the case of large public buildings constructed with a view to durability and architectural effect, that stone is used as a material for building. The numerous and immense mills and workshops of the manufacturing district, the not less large and numerous warehouses of

* Ninth Report of the British Association for the Advancement of Science Transactions of Sections, p 72

the sea-ports, and all public works not requiring extraordinary strength or beauty, are built of brick, or of brick faced and ornamented with stone During the last thirty years the same kind of clay from which bricks are made has been very extensively used in the manufacture of draining tiles, of which many millions are now made every year, and used in draining the stiffer soils of the two counties. Tileries have been established on many of the larger estates The clay of the north-western district has been used for the purpose of forming bricks and tiles from the time of the Roman occupation of Britain Many bricks and tiles made by the Romans, and remarkable for their hardness and durability, have been dug up in the foundations of the four great Roman stations of Chester, Manchester, Ribchester, and Lancaster, and in the smaller Roman stations Most of these remains of ancient times are marked with the initials of the Twentieth Victorious Legion, L.V.V. (*Legio Vicesima Victrix*) The Twentieth Roman Legion had its head-quarters at Chester for a period of nearly 300 years and the engineers of the legion planned, and the soldiers formed, the great roads, walls, and buildings, whose remains still exist in this part of England after a lapse of 1500 to 1600 years. Many of the bricks and tiles dug up in the Roman stations in the north-western district are also stamped with the emblem of the Twentieth Legion, which was a wild boar rushing to battle

But the solid rock on which this part of England rests also furnishes an abundant supply of building materials

The upper new red sandstone, or trias formation, besides containing the deposits of rock-salt and the springs of brine above described, furnishes inexhaustible supplies of building stone, easily worked and of considerable durability. A sandstone generally red in colour, though also showing other colours, and soft in grain, is found throughout the two counties, from the point where the river Dee enters Chester on the south, as far north as Walney Island in Furness, and from the river Tame, near Stockport, to the sea. The formation in which it is found includes the beds known as the upper soft red sandstone, the pebble beds, and the lower soft red sandstone These rocks are many hundred feet thick, and consist of a soft red stone, very easily worked, but soon destroyed by the action of the elements

Portions of the walls of the cathedral of Chester are formed of this stone, and wherever that is the case the stonework soon becomes weather-worn and requires frequent repair. Amongst the most celebrated buildings constructed with this stone was the ancient castle of Holt, on the river Dee, once a place of great military importance, as commanding one of the principal bridges across that river into Wales. A large portion of the stone used in constructing Holt castle seems to have been got out of the ditches which surround the walls. The ditches are deep and wide, and are cut regularly into the solid rock. The castle is gone, the stonework having either crumbled to pieces or been pulled down to erect other buildings, but the excavations of the ditches are nearly perfect

But the white sandstone of the trias, often known as waterstone, from the abundance of water found in its fissures, is a very superior building stone The white sandstone rocks of the upper new red sandstone are supposed to have been the bold shores of the seas which formerly covered the more recent beds of this formation. Their surfaces are marked with ripples, which are thought to have resulted from the action of the wind on the shallow water with which they were occasionally covered Other ripples traced on the surface are supposed to mark the course of rills which formerly traversed a muddy shore. Tracks of footmarks, supposed to have been produced by the wanderings of marine animals over the mud and soft sand, are still found at numerous places on the waterstone rocks of Cheshire In fact, all the conditions that are observed on the shores of existing seas at the present day may be traced on the triassic rocks of the new red sandstone.*

The waterstone rocks rise abruptly above the plain of Cheshire, to the height of 300 and 400 feet, at Overton Scar, near Malpas, on the southern border of Cheshire, and run through the county northward to Helsby Hill, on the banks of the Mersey. They also send out a branch in a westerly direction, which runs through the peninsula of Wirral to the sea The hills rise to a still greater height, with a rocky outline, at Bickerton Hill, and along the range of hills to Peckforton, Beeston, and Eddisbury There are extensive stone quarries in these hills at several points, which have in different ages supplied the material used in building many noble piles Amongst these we may mention Beeston castle, built about the year 1229 by Ranulf de Blundeville, earl of Chester, and still a very fine specimen of a Norman castle, Eddisbury and Runcorn castles, built by

* On the Records of a Triassic Shore, by Professor Harkness, F R S Twenty-seventh Report of the British Association for the Advancement of Science, p. 68

Ethelfleda, the daughter of Alfred the Great, 300 years earlier, and of which nothing now remains except the outline of the foundations, the harder parts of Chester cathedral, including the modern repairs; Halton castle, still a stately pile, though built soon after the Norman conquest, and, it is believed, the foundations of the walls of Chester, built by the Romans from 1600 to 1700 years ago. It is supposed that the stone employed by the Romans in building these walls was obtained from some of the quarries in these hills. A small portion of the Roman stonework is believed still to exist in the north part of the walls of Chester, near the Northgate. This stone is cut into much larger blocks than those used in the Saxon, Norman, and mediæval times in repairing and rebuilding the walls, and is much harder than any stone found in the neighbourhood of Chester. "In the walls of Chester, where any of the Roman walls or foundations exist, they appear as imperishable as when first built, but the mediæval structure erected upon them is crumbling to decay. On closer inspection every Roman stone will be found to have its peculiar silver-gray lichens (*Urceolaria scruposa*), whilst those of the middle ages have a different species. The older portion of the wall is supposed to have been brought from Helsby Hill, or some other part of Delamere Forest." Large masses of building stone, of the kind above described, are found in the hills which extend from Chester to Birkenhead and New Brighton. Amongst the largest and best quarries in this formation are those on Storeton Hill, about five miles south of Birkenhead. These have supplied immense quantities of building stone for the docks, on both sides of the Mersey. Stone of the same kind exists at many places around Liverpool. The fine columns in the interior of the old Exchange news-room, and those in front of the chapel in Great George Street, Liverpool, are both from this formation.

In the quarries sunk in rocks of this formation, are found the footmarks of an animal which is supposed to have been one of the earliest, if not the earliest, of created animals capable of breathing the open air, and living on land as well as in water. Near Tarporley, in Cheshire, there were found, deeply imbedded in the sandstone, the footmarks of this gigantic animal, to which geologists have given the name of the Cheirotherium, or "handed" animal, from the extraordinary resemblance of the shape of its feet to that of the human hand. The footmarks found in the sandstone rock at Tarporley are preserved in specimens of that rock in the collection of Sir Philip

Egerton, Bart., M.P., who has described them in a paper read before the Geological Society of Great Britain. They are of gigantic size, being fifteen inches in length and ten inches in breadth; and Sir Philip Egerton, in compliance with the old adage, "*Ex pede Herculem*," proposed to name the animal by which they were made, *Cheirotherium Herculis.* Similar footmarks were discovered in the quarries at Weston and Higher Runcorn, and in them, says Mr. E. W. Binney, "we have the earliest positive evidence of the existence of dry land. At Weston, about thirty feet from the surface, and in the higher part of the deposit, there is a thin bed of red clay about half or three-quarters of an inch in thickness. This clay affords impressions of the footmarks of the cheirotherium, the rhyncosaurus, several other reptiles, and numerous worm-marks, besides lines of desiccation similar to what a bed of clay would undergo under a hot sun at the present day." Mr. Hawkshaw, C.E., states in a paper in the Twelfth Report of the British Association, that footmarks of this description have been discovered in the quarries at Lymm, also in Cheshire. "The length of the footmark," he says, "in the largest specimen was nine and a half inches. The impressions are left on a thin specimen of the finest clay, which was so well prepared to receive the mould as to leave a cast so delicate as to give us the texture of the skin that covered the sole of the foot. This appears to have been covered with small papillæ—about 100 to the square inch on the larger specimen, and about 220 to the square inch on the smaller, showing that the sole of the foot was furnished with a rough skin such as might have been expected in a creature that walked on a sandy shore." Similar marks were discovered in the Stourton quarries, near Liverpool, and were very clearly described by Mr John Cunningham, of Liverpool. There the casts discovered were situated in the upper surface of three beds of sandstone, each about two feet thick. It appeared as if each of the thin seams of clay on which the sandstone casts were moulded had formed successively a dry surface, over which the cheirotherium and other animals walked, leaving impressions of their footsteps. The lowest seam of clay was so thin that the marks penetrated into the subjacent sand, which sand afterwards hardened into sandstone. The extreme length of the foot was nine inches, its extreme breadth six inches. One hind-foot measured twelve inches in its greatest length. From the appearance of the casts, the sole of the foot must have been amply supplied with muscles, the casts of the ball of the thumb and the phalanges of the fingers being prominent. The toes are thick and strong, and the terminations are stout conical nails or claws The casts of the cheirotherium, although the most remarkable, are not the most numerous Many long slabs are crowded with casts in relievo, some of which are supposed to have been derived from the feet of saurian reptiles, and others from those of tortoises*

A bed of limestone known as magnesian limestone, and belonging to the permian system, is found at Ardwick, near Manchester Of this limestone the great chemist, Dalton, says —"A bed of limestone is found at a considerable depth underground, to the east of Manchester It has the property of forming a good cement under water Geologists call it a magnesian limestone, but it has very little resemblance to the true magnesian limestone from Yorkshire When analyzed, it appears to be pure carbonate of lime united or mixed with two per cent of clay, and a considerable trace of iron, perhaps half a grain per cent. It is probably to the two last ingredients that its peculiar qualities are ascribed It contains no more magnesia than chalk or mountain limestone in general does, which is a slight trace; whereas in the true magnesian limestone found in some parts of Yorkshire the lime is to the magnesia as twenty-four to seventeen Their specific gravity is generally below that of mountain limestone" Magnesian limestone is also found and extensively worked in the townships of Ashley, Bedford, and Atherton, in the parish of Leigh, in Lancashire, and furnishes a very valuable kind of cement, used in building bridges and piers. At Bedford, near Leigh, there is a depth of ten feet of magnesian limestone, arranged in twelve beds The limestone of Bedford, which has been analyzed by Mr. Watson, chemist, of Bolton, was found to contain in 100 parts 56 5 parts carbonate of lime, 38·5 parts of aluminous and silicious earths, 2 5 parts oxides of iron, and 2·5 parts of water. In the north of Lancashire, in the district of Furness, magnesian limestone, really containing a considerable quantity of magnesia, has been met with at a place named Stank This has been analyzed by Mr James Gibb, and has been found to yield the following products, in 100 parts carbonic acid, 38 40, silica, 11 65; magnesia, 9 95, oxide of iron, 9·45; lime, 29 75, water, 1·75 †

The permian or lower new red sandstone, as found in the neigh-

* Proceedings of the Geological Society, vol iii p 15. Twenty-seventh Report of the British Association for the Advancement of Science, p 68

† Memoirs of Literary and Philosophical Society of Manchester, vol v p. 8 (Second Series.)

bourhood of Manchester, is chiefly composed of a dark red sand, variegated by patches of yellowish-drab colour The upper part of it is much used in foundries for the purpose of iron moulding; but the lower part is not so well suited for that purpose, owing to the nodules of iron found in the stone The thin ribbon beds of limestone, containing much clay and iron, lying in the lower parts of the red marls in the neighbourhood of Manchester, become thick, and more like the Yorkshire and Durham limestone in grain, colour, and composition, in proceeding northward to Stank and Barrow Mouth in Furness "The sandy conglomerate beds, containing rolled pebbles, of Hug Bridge, Norbury, Cheetham Weir-hole, and other places in South Lancashire, appear to pass gradually at first into the arenaceous conglomerate of Barrow Mouth, and then into the calcareous conglomerates of Rougham Point, Kirkby-Stephen, Brough, and West-house When the deposit is near a coal-field, it is generally arenaceous in character, and when in a limestone district calcareous, thus showing that most of the materials composing it were derived from or near the neighbourhood in which it is now found, and not brought from a distance But certainly the cement in many places has a real resemblance to volcanic ash." Mr. Binney adds to the above, in a note, "I am convinced that some of the mottled clays and shales of the upper coal-field, as well as many of the permian beds, have a great deal of volcanic ash in their composition"*

The finest building stone in Lancashire is that of which Furness Abbey is constructed. It is a fine-grained stone, obtained from quarries in the neighbourhood of the abbey. At the end of 600 years it is still almost perfect.

The coal measures of Lancashire and Cheshire furnish numerous varieties of building stone, and contain several thick beds of flags. Most of these are mentioned, with their names and positions, in the account of the coal strata already given in this chapter Building stones of great value are found in the coal measures in the neighbourhood of Manchester, Dukinfield, Oldham, Rochdale, Littleborough, Bolton, Haslingden, and Blackburn Longridge Fell, composed of the millstone grit, is a mass of building stone

Mountain limestone, suited both for purposes of building and cement, exists in large quantities on the banks of the Ribble, the

* Memoirs of the Literary and Philosophical Society of Manchester · vol viii, p 431, vol xii, p 266. (Second Series)

Hodder, and the Lune, and around Morecambe Bay. The limestone also shows itself, though in small quantities, at Chipping in North Lancashire, and at Newbold-Astbury in Cheshire, but South Lancashire and Cheshire are chiefly supplied with lime from the Derbyshire quarries near Buxton, and from the coasts of Furness and North Wales, where limestone is very abundant

Roofing slate is also found in abundance in the Silurian beds of Higher Furness. Amongst the most productive and valuable beds of that district are those worked at Kirkby-Ireleth, on the estate of the duke of Devonshire. The greater part of Coniston mountain also consists of beds of roofing slate.

A small quantity of granite is also found on the sides of the Old Man of Coniston, but it does not appear in any quantity on the Lancashire side of the river Duddon. Veins of porphyry are found on the banks of that wild and beautiful stream

The various rocks existing in Lancashire and Cheshire have been examined by Mr William Fairbairn, of Manchester, for the purpose of ascertaining their comparative powers of resisting pressure Mr. Fairbairn found, in the course of these experiments, that a cubic inch of the new red Runcorn sandstone would bear a pressure of 2185 lbs weight before it crumbled into sand He found that the much stronger sandstone of the coal formation would bear a pressure of 6127 lbs. before it crumbled into sand, and that there were sandstones of this formation in the quarries of Littleborough, on the borders of Lancashire and Yorkshire, which did not give way until exposed to a pressure of 10,000 lbs. Limestone was found, in the same experiments, to bear a pressure of 8528 lbs to the square inch before it gave way Granite bore a pressure of 11,528 lbs before it crumbled into sand. The grauwacke of the slate or Silurian rocks resisted a pressure of 16,893 lbs ; and it required the enormous pressure of 40,416 lbs to crush a cubic inch of porphyry into sand *

These ancient rocks may be regarded as the solid framework or foundation of the earth, into which man has not yet succeeded in penetrating to a greater depth than 2000 to 3000 feet With this sketch of the more penetrable strata of the earth, and of such of their contents as have been rendered available for the service of man, we conclude our general sketch of the natural history of the north-western district of England.

* Memoirs of the Literary and Philosophical Society of Manchester, vol III, p 15

Natural Products of the different Districts of Lancashire and Cheshire, and their Influence on the Population, Industry, and Wealth of those Districts.—The natural products of Lancashire and Cheshire, like those of England in general, and indeed those of all countries, are very unequally distributed in different districts, and this is the principal cause of the various degrees of population and wealth that we find existing in different places In some portions, even of these crowded and wealthy counties, the people are still a race of shepherds, herdsmen, and woodmen, in other districts they add agriculture to pasturage, in others they seek wealth by mining in the recesses of the earth and rock, or by tilling its surface, in others they use the produce of their mines, as well as the power of their streams, in working machinery and producing articles of universal use; whilst in others they avail themselves of their position on the sea-coast in opening a vast commerce in raw materials of industry, food, and in the products of manufacturing skill In each of these pursuits great skill is shown, and industry and capital are freely expended But a nation engaged in pastoral pursuits, as in Australia, can only increase rapidly when it has the pastures of a continent at its disposal. An agricultural people only increases rapidly when it has the soil of vast and fertile regions at its disposal, as in the United States and in Canada Space is of less importance in a country rich in minerals, or in facilities for manufactures, trade, and commerce. Thus in Lancashire and Cheshire there are 3,000,000 persons, possessed of an aggregate yearly income of about £50,000,000 sterling, crowded together on an area of 2,000,000 acres of land, or, in other words, there are the tenth part of the people of the United Kingdom collected on about the fortieth part of its surface But within these two counties we have almost as great differences in population and wealth in the several districts, and those differences may be chiefly traced to the difference in the natural resources available for industry in those districts In England, taken as a whole, the population doubled its number in the first fifty-one years of the present century; whilst in the north-western division, formed of the counties of Lancaster and Chester, it increased nearly fourfold But there are districts of Lancashire and Cheshire in which the increase of the first fifty years of the present century is less than the average increase of England, others in which it is about equal; and others in which it is vastly greater. This will be clearly seen from the following rapid sketch of the natural resources, wealth, and rate of increase of population during the present century, in each of the divisions into which Lancashire and Cheshire are divided in taking the census of the numbers of the people —

The County of Lancaster.—The county of Lancaster, according to ancient arrangement, is divided into the six hundreds of Lonsdale, Amounderness, Blackburn, Leyland, Salford, and West Derby. In taking the census these six hundreds are subdivided into the districts of Ulverstone, Lancaster, Garstang, Fylde, Preston, Clitheroe, Burnley, Blackburn, Haslingden, Chorley, Bolton, Bury, Rochdale, Oldham, Ashton-under-Lyne, Chorlton, Manchester, Salford, Barton-on-Irwell, Leigh, Warrington, Wigan, St. Helen's, Ormskirk, West Derby, and Liverpool.

The County of Chester—The county of Chester, according to its ancient arrangement, is divided into the seven hundreds of Macclesfield, Nantwich, Northwich, Bucklow, Eddisbury, Broxton, and Wirral In taking the census these are divided into the census districts of Stockport, Macclesfield, Congleton, Nantwich, Northwich, Altringham, Runcorn, Boughton or Chester, Wirral, and Birkenhead

The Hundred of Lonsdale—The Hundred of Lonsdale, forming the most northerly hundred of Lancashire, and bordering on Cumberland and Westmoreland, is divided into two districts One of these is named Lonsdale beyond the Sands, and corresponds pretty nearly with the census division of Ulverstone, the other is named Lonsdale south of the Sands, and corresponds nearly with the census division of Lancaster

The District of Ulverstone and Higher and Lower Furness—The Ulverstone district, corresponding in extent with the division of Lonsdale beyond the Sands, includes Higher and Lower Furness, as well as Cartmel It is one of the most extensive census districts in Lancashire, extending over an area of 135,043 acres of land and water. Three-fourths of the district, including the whole of Higher Furness, is mountainous, the wilder parts of the hills being grazed by sheep, or planted with woods of larch, Scotch fir, and other mountain trees, and thinly peopled by a scattered population of small farmers, shepherds, and woodmen. In former times the rich copper and iron ores of Furness were smelted with charcoal made from the woods that then covered the whole of the hills, and one or two smelting-houses still exist in which charcoal is used The slate is the prevailing formation in Higher Furness, and at a few points, on the side of Coniston Old Man, the granite has forced its way through the slate, whilst boulders of syenite and other varieties of granite are scattered over the hills. The Coniston limestone commences west and north of Broughton in Furness, passing north of Coniston Lake above Waterhead, and running in a north-easterly direction by the line of Low Wood, Troutbeck, and Long Sleddale to Shapfells The mountain of Coniston Old Man is composed chiefly of fine roofing slate, but several veins of copper are found in the lower part of the mountain, which are extensively worked There are also extensive quarries of slate and limestone at Coniston, Kirkby-Ireleth, and several other places But the chief mineral wealth of the district consists in the rich hæmatite iron ores found in the neighbourhood of Dalton and Lindale, the greater part of which are exported to South Wales and Staffordshire, whilst a portion are smelted at Barrow. The soil of Lower Furness consists principally of the new red sandstone, with mountain limestone in close proximity The land in this district is extremely fertile, especially in the neighbourhood of Furness Abbey, and it is cultivated in large farms, and on a better system than prevails in almost any other part of Lancashire The crops consist of wheat, barley, oats, turnips, and grasses, and large quantities both of sheep and cattle are reared The lakes and rivers contain trout, char, pike, and most freshwater fish, and the bays are visited at the season by large shoals of herrings. The climate of Lower Furness is moist, but unusually mild, owing to the high ranges of mountains that shelter it on the north and east.

The wildest and most thinly peopled portions of the Ulverstone district, are those in the mountainous country about Hawkeshead, and on the banks of the river Duddon, above West Broughton In the Hawkeshead district, lying along the upper part of the Windermere Lake, the population is very thin, not amounting to much more than one person to every ten acres, which is about the fifth part the average density of the population of England. In the West Broughton district, where the river Duddon issues from the Cumberland mountains, the population is equally small. In the central and lower districts, where there is a greater quantity of arable land, the population is in the proportion of about one person to every five acres In the Dalton district, in which the great iron mines of Lower Furness are situated, there is one inhabitant to every three acres; and in the subdivision of Ulverstone, in which the town of Ulverstone is situated, there is more than one inhabitant to every acre.

At the beginning of the present century, the whole number of inhabitants living on the area of 135,043 acres comprised in the division of Ulverstone or Lonsdale beyond the Sands, was 17,881. This number increased during the first fifty years to 30,550, a rate of increase somewhat less than the average rate of increase in the population of England and Wales, which doubled itself in the first fifty-two years of the present century Between the census of 1851 and that of 1861, there was a further increase of 5178 persons, raising the population of the Ulverstone district, at the census of 1861, to 35,728 persons

At the valuation for the property and income tax, made in the year ending the 5th of April, 1860, the property and income of the Ulverstone district, or North Lonsdale, were returned at the yearly sum of £451,414 This was derived from different sources, in the following amounts —The land of the district produced a rent of £108,184, the profits of farming were assumed at the same sum, the messuages or buildings were valued at £45,343, the fines for manorial rights, which are more than usually valuable on account of the seigniorage paid to the owners of mines and quarries, were valued at £27,762, the quarries produced a direct revenue of £8676, the mines yield an income of £45,060, the iron-works, exclusive of the mines were valued at £272, the fisheries in the rivers and lakes were valued at £84, the canal that unites the town of Ulverstone with the sea was taken at £536, the railways, which have greatly increased during the last few years, were valued at £33,870, the gas-works were taken at £327, other property of the same kind was returned at £1316, and the profits of trade of the whole district were returned at £71,800 The value of the property of the town of Ulverstone, the chief place of the district, was returned at £59,840

The District of Lancaster, or Lonsdale South of the Sands— The census district of Lancaster, or Lonsdale south of the Sands, is still more extensive than that of Ulverstone, stretching over an area of 138,746 acres This includes the whole of that part of the fertile and beautiful valley of the Lune that lies in the county of Lancaster, and narrow slips of good pasture and meadow land on the banks of the smaller rivers, but it also includes an extensive range of barren hills, resting on the millstone grit formation. There are no mines of any value in the Lancaster district, and whatever manufactures exist are dependent either on water-power, which is very abundant, or on coal brought from a distance of more than twenty miles But since the Furness railway has been carried across the head of Morecambe Bay, extensive iron-works have been erected at Carnforth, where that railway joins the line from Lancaster to Carlisle

In the mountain districts of Arkholme, Tunstall, and Wray, in which the population is chiefly employed in pasturage, there is not more than one person to every ten acres of land. The soil is better and the population somewhat more numerous in the districts of Wharton, Heaton, and Ellel, where there is a considerable quantity of good land, and also down the valley of the Lune.

At the commencement of the present century the population of the census district of Lancaster, or Lonsdale south of the Sands, was 24,942 persons During the first fifty years of the present century the population increased to 34,660, which is about one-half the average rate of increase of the whole kingdom. But during the ten years between the census of 1851 and that of 1861, the increase was very slow, only 639 persons having been added to the population of the district. At the census of 1861 the population of the Lancaster, or South Lonsdale district, amounted to 35,299 persons

The value of the property of the Lancaster district as returned to the property and income tax, in the year ending April 5th, 1860, was £678,837 This was derived from various sources The yearly rent of the land of the district was £130,552, the tenants' profits were estimated at the same sum, messuages and buildings were valued at £63,407, fisheries at £140, railways at £232,691, gas-works at £1376, and profits of trade at £198,191 The property and income of the borough of Lancaster were returned at £380,726.

The whole hundred of Lonsdale North and South included property and income of the value of £1,130,251 per annum, in the year 1860 This was derived from the following sources —Rent of land £238,736; farming profits the same; messuages and buildings £108,750, quarries £9015, mines £45,100, fisheries £224; railways £266,561; gas-works £1703; other works £2793, profits of trade £170,091

The Borough of Lancaster —This ancient borough contained 9030

inhabitants at the commencement of the present century, and nearly doubled its numbers during the first fifty years of the century, having increased to 16,168 persons in that period In the ten years between 1851 and 1861 there was scarcely any change in the population of Lancaster, but the figures of the census of 1861 show a slight decrease, the numbers at the time having been 15,996 persons

The Hundred of Amounderness.—The ancient hundred of Amounderness is divided pretty nearly into the three census districts of Garstang, Fylde, and Preston, of each of which we shall give a separate account

The District of Garstang in Amounderness.—The Garstang census district extends over an area of 62,617 acres of land The eastern part of this district is one of the wildest and most mountainous regions of Lancashire, the land rising to an elevation of 1500 to 1800 feet. There is much good grass land in the lower part of the district, in the neighbourhood of Garstang, and along the banks of the Wyre. The formation of the higher part of the hills is chiefly millstone grit, whilst that of the lower ground is new red sandstone There is much water-power in the Garstang district, but no coal, and scarcely a single spot where limestone is to be found. The general character of the soil is that of a wild moorland or grassy district, with extensive plantations in the higher cloughs of the mountains. Cattle and sheep, milk and butter, are the principal products There are a few mills at the most commanding points on the streams, and those mills obtain their supplies of coal from South Lancashire, by railway and canal.

The population of the Garstang district is small, and its progress in numbers has been very slow At the beginning of the present century this district contained 9647 inhabitants. In fifty years the population had increased to 12,695, which is about equal to one-half the average rate of increase of England and Wales Between 1851 and 1861 there was a slight decrease of 271 persons in the population of the Garstang district, the numbers at the census of 1861 amounting to 12,424 persons

The Fylde District in Amounderness—The Fylde district, which is the lower part of the valley of the Wyre, is in general a level country, and contains, in addition to rich meadows and fine pastures, much good arable land, in many places cultivated with great spirit and skill. The Fylde district is bounded by the sea on the west, and a considerable population is collecting along the sea-coasts. This is the case at Blackpool, which is now a handsomely built, well situated, and much frequented watering-place. It is also the case in some degree at Fleetwood, at the mouth of the river Wyre. There are considerable manufactures at Kirkham, which derive their supplies of coal by canal and railway from South Lancashire; but there is no coal, nor are there any minerals, in the Fylde district.

At the beginning of the present century the Fylde district contained a population of 11,327 persons. This number nearly doubled itself in the first fifty years of the present century, having increased in 1851 to 22,002, showing a rate of increase as nearly as possible equal to the average rate of increase of England and Wales. Between 1851 and 1861 the rate has been fully maintained, the increase having been 3679 persons in ten years, making the population of the Fylde district, in the year 1861, 25,681 persons

The Preston District.—The Preston district is the most northern district of Lancashire, in which we obtain evidence of that wonderful increase of population and wealth, that has taken place in all the manufacturing districts of this county during the present century. The district itself, with the exception of the town of Preston and its immediate neighbourhood, is purely agricultural, and contains land of every quality, from the richest meadow and arable to the wildest mountain pasture. There are no mines nor minerals in the Preston district, with the exception of some quarries of good building stone at Longridge But there is a very easy and cheap communication from Preston, both by canal and railway, to the adjoining coal-fields of South Lancashire; and the manufacturers of Preston are able to supply themselves with fuel, and to work their mills by steam-power, almost as well as if they were on the coal-field itself

The rural districts of the Preston division are rather thinly peopled. In the Broughton subdivision, near to the hills, there is not more than one person to every four acres of land, which is about one-half the average population of England and Wales The subdivision of Alston, which contains much good land, and the site of the Roman position of Ribchester, has about one inhabitant to every three acres. The district of Longton contains one person to every two acres, and the fertile district of

Walton-le-Dale, extending over the richest part of the valley of the Ribble, contains about one person to every single acre

The census division of Preston contains nearly four times as many inhabitants as it possessed at the beginning of the present century. At the census of 1801 this district contained only 29,899 inhabitants. During the first fifty years the population of the district increased to 96,545 persons Between 1851 and 1861 there was a further increase of 13,943 persons, and the Preston district at the census of 1861 contained a population of 110,488 persons.

The Borough of Preston—The town of Preston, although one of the most ancient parliamentary and municipal boroughs in Lancashire, with charters which date from the reign of Henry II., contained only 12,174 inhabitants at the commencement of the present century About that time the population began to increase rapidly, under the influence of the inventions of their celebrated townsman Sir Richard Arkwright, and of the canals constructed by Brindley through the coal-fields of South Lancashire These together brought the cotton manufacture into the town, and at the census of 1851 the population of Preston had increased to 69,542 persons Between the census of 1851 and that of 1861 there was a further increase of 13,419 persons, raising the population of the borough of Preston, in 1861, to 82,961 persons. According to an estimate laid before Parliament in 1866, the population of the borough of Preston in that year was supposed to be 90,652 persons*

The yearly value of property and income in the hundred of Amounderness, which includes the three districts of Garstang, Fylde, and Preston, amounted in the year ended 5th April, 1860, to the sum of £1,198,179 The rent of the land in the whole hundred was valued at £215,488; farming profits at the same, messuages or buildings, including those of the town of Preston, at £269,211, quarries at £472, there being no mines within the district; the salmon fisheries of the Ribble at £100, railway property at £87,294; gas-works at £10,147; other property and profits at £13,154, and the profits of trade at £386,768. More than one-half in value of the property of Amounderness hundred was within the borough of Preston The total yearly value of the property returned in that borough was £634,567. This consisted of the

* Electoral Returns, Boroughs and Counties, 1865–66.

following items:—Farming land £2652, farming profits the same, messuages or buildings £202,950; tithes £57, quarries £150, fisheries £50; railway property £87,294, gas-works £9500, other property and profits £11,737, and profits of trade £317,525

The Hundred of Blackburn —The hundred of Blackburn includes the divisions of Clitheroe, Burnley, Blackburn, and Haslingden.

The Clitheroe District.—The extensive census district of Clitheroe, covering an area of 114,697 acres, is a region of grassy hills seldom rising to a greater height than from 600 to 800 feet above the level of the sea, but with some lofty and rugged moors of twice that elevation, and with a few still loftier points, of which Pendle-hill, rising to the height of nearly 1800 feet, is the highest, and overlooks the whole dale of which it is the undoubted head The river Ribble flows through the green and beautiful valley of Ribblesdale, over a limestone bed, and receives the rivers Calder and Darwen from the south, and the river Hodder from the north, with many smaller streams The soil is very fertile in the valleys through which those rivers flow, and also on the limestone hills which rise on both sides of the Ribble and the Hodder But it is thin and barren on the loftier hills, most of which are formed of the millstone grit. The most valuable mineral in this district is the mountain limestone, which is very abundant. There is scarcely any coal in the Clitheroe district, but the great coal-field of Lancashire bounds it to the south; and now that railways have been extended into the higher part of the valley of the Ribble, coal will be obtained at a moderate cost. In addition to this, numerous rivers and streams supply water-power, and the purest water for bleaching and print works Thus, though the general character of the Clitheroe district is rural and pastoral, there are many manufactures carried on, especially such as are dependent on an abundant supply of pure water. Still, in comparison with other districts of Lancashire, the progress of the Clitheroe district has been slow during the present century, and in the last ten years there has been a small decrease of population The Clitheroe census district at the commencement of the present century contained a population of 15,143 persons, and in the first fifty years of the century the population increased to 22,368 persons Between 1851 and 1861 there was a decrease of 1892 persons, reducing the population in 1861 to 20,476.

The subdivisions of the Clitheroe district are Gisborn, Slaidburn, Chipping, Whalley, and Clitheroe. The first two of these districts are chiefly in Yorkshire, and do not call for any notice in this work, except as relates to the wild district of Bowland Forest in Slaidburn. This forest is chiefly situated in Lancashire, and contains 19,055 acres of mountain land, with a thinly scattered population of about 500 persons The greater part of Bowland Forest is in the parishes of Whalley and Slaidburn A very extensive range of lofty hills also exists in the subdivision of Chipping, in which district the population is not more than one person to about six acres of land. In the subdivision of Whalley there is some good land on the banks of the river Calder, and considerable manufactures, owing to the proximity of the coal-field The subdivision of Clitheroe contains much fine land along the banks of the Ribble, and several flourishing manufactories

The town of Clitheroe is an ancient parliamentary and municipal borough, with charters that date from the Henrys and Edwards Clitheroe contained 14,480 inhabitants in 1851, but between that year and the census of 1861, had declined to 10,864 persons.

The Burnley District.—The Burnley census district, covering an area of 54,126 acres, contains much good land along the banks of the river Calder, especially in the neighbourhood of Towneley Park, near Burnley, where there is very superior cultivation and some of the finest herds of cattle that are to be found in England. But a great portion of the land of the Burnley district is very high and moorish, and chiefly suitable for mountain sheep and young cattle. Innumerable streams flow down from the lofty hills that bound the county of Lancaster on the east, affording water-power in abundance The Burnley district also possesses much coal Hence it is thickly peopled, and rapidly increasing in population and wealth.

The Burnley district contained a population of 33,173 persons, at the commencement of the present century. This population was nearly doubled during the first fifty years, having advanced to 63,868 at the census of 1851 It increased still more rapidly between 1851 and 1861; the increase during that period having been 11,720 persons, swelling the population of the Burnley district to 75,588 persons at the census of 1861. The subdivision of Pendle is the most thinly peopled portion of this district, yet its population is nearly equal to the average of England and Wales, being about one person to two acres All the other subdivisions of the Burnley district are more thickly peopled The subdivision of Colne, including the town of Colne, contained a population of 21,764 persons in 1851, and of 21,203 in 1861 The subdivision and town of Padiham have also increased rapidly in population, the town containing 5675 persons. But the greatest increase has been in the subdivision of Burnley, which contained 31,853 inhabitants in 1851 and 42,702 in 1861.

The town of Burnley, including its suburb of Habergham Eaves, contained 28,700 persons in 1861.

The Blackburn District.—The census district of Blackburn extends over an area of 43,569 acres It is in general a hilly and even mountainous district, but with some good land along the banks of the river Darwen Numerous streams flow from the lofty hills, and great part of the district abounds in coal. These natural advantages have been improved with great energy Blackburn has also possessed the advantages of cheap water carriage, by the Leeds and Liverpool canal, for more than eighty years, and it is now well supplied with railway communication Hence this district is one of the most populous in England, and is every year increasing in numbers and wealth.

The Blackburn district at the commencement of the present century contained a population of 33,173 persons. This increased nearly three-fold during the first fifty years of the century, having advanced to 90,738 persons in the year 1851. The increase was still more rapid between 1851 and 1861, having been 29,199 persons in ten years, thus raising the population of the Blackburn district to 119,937 persons in 1861. The most thinly peopled of the subdivisions of the Blackburn district is Billington, on the banks of the river Ribble. This is a pastoral and agricultural district, not containing more than one person to every three acres of land. The subdivision of Harwood, though situated in a more hilly district, is well supplied with coal and water-power, and contains about one person to every acre. The population of Whitton and Mellor is about the same in proportion to the area. The subdivision of Oswaldtwistle is high up among the hills, but it is well supplied with coal and water-power, and contains three or four persons to every acre of land The population of the Darwen district is still better supplied with water-power and coal, and is equally numerous The subdivision of Blackburn is still more so.

The Town of Blackburn.—This town, made a parliamentary

and municipal borough under the parliamentary and municipal Acts of 1832 and 1835, contained 11,940 inhabitants at the commencement of the present century This number increased during the first fifty years of the century to 46,536. The increase was still more rapid between the the census of 1851 and that of 1861; the numbers having increased during that ten years by 16,985 and having amounted at the census of 1861 to 63,521 persons According to an estimate laid before Parliament, the population of the borough of Blackburn in 1866, was computed to be 73,522 persons*

The property and income of the town of Blackburn were valued in 1860 at £397,933, consisting of the following items —Rent of land £6446, profits of cultivation the same, messuages and buildings £143,757, quarries £1201, gas-works £6000; other property £13,299, and profits of trade £220,806.

The Haslingden District—The Haslingden census district extends over an area of 26,601 acres, and is altogether a region of lofty hills, divided from each other by narrow valleys, through which rapid streams descend flowing to the south Many of the hills rise to the height of 1200 to 1500 feet. The Haslingden district includes the ancient forest of Rossendale, which was for ages the wildest district in Lancashire Previous to the reign of Henry VII, it was a royal forest, in which there was nothing but deer or other wild and savage beasts It was disforested in the time of the Tudors, and gradually became occupied by herdsmen and cultivators of the soil, though the number of inhabitants at that time was only about eighty. In the reign of James I the forest lands were apportioned into nineteen vaccaries or cow-pastures, and let at the annual advanced rent of £122 13*s* 8*d*. On the spread of the woollen manufacture in the north of England, many of the inhabitants of the Rossendale district began to engage in that trade, being much aided by the abundant water-power supplied by the streams of the district, and by the wool of the Haslingden sheep that grazed on the forest hills About the beginning of the present century the cotton manufacture began to spread up these valleys, and it now extends through the whole of this district. The greater part of the hills are still uncultivated, and are too high and too much exposed for the growth of grain But the valleys, though narrow and winding, are carefully cultivated, and are kept green both in winter and summer by constant irriga-

* Electoral Returns, Boroughs and Counties

tion. Coal abounds throughout the whole district, and coal mines are sunk even in the highest hills Both steam and water power have been applied with the greatest care and industry in the Haslingden district, and from being a mere forest with eighty inhabitants, it has become one of the most flourishing manufacturing districts in England, with a population of nearly 70,000

The subdivision of Newchurch in Rossendale is the most populous part of the district, and includes the town of Bacup and the upper part of the valley of the Irwell. In 1861 the population of Bacup was 10,935 The subdivision of Rossendale is also very populous. That of Edenfield, though containing a greater quantity of good land, is somewhat less so The subdivisions of Haslingden and Accrington are also very thickly peopled. The town of Haslingden contained 6154 inhabitants at the census of 1851, and 6929 at the census of 1861 It is the loftiest town in England, being situated at an elevation of nearly 1000 feet above the level of the sea In 1851 the population of Accrington, New and Old, was 7481, and in 1861 it was 13,872.

The yearly value of the property and income of the principal places in the Haslingden district in 1861, was — Haslingden £59,576, Bacup £73,350, and Accrington, New and Old, £124,492.

The value of property in the Blackburn hundred, as estimated for the property and income tax, amounted in 1860 to £1,924,973. The rent of the land in the Blackburn hundred was £212,966, the farming profits were estimated at the same; the messuages and buildings were valued at £540,866, the tithes at £437, the fines at £80; the mines at £80,430, the quarries at £10,101, the fisheries at £72, the gas-works at £14,158, other property and profits at £24,138, and the profits of trade at £791,654

The Leyland Hundred and the Chorley District—The Chorley district extends over the greater part of the hundred of Leyland It covers an area of 52,213 acres. On the east it consists chiefly of wild mountain land, rising in the Rivington district to the height of 1500 feet. On the west side it contains a considerable quantity of good arable and pasture ground at a small elevation Coal is very abundant in the neighbourhood of the town of Chorley, and water-power and water available for bleaching and print works are found along the course of the Douglas, the Yarrow, and many smaller streams that rise among the hills to the north and east of the town of Chorley. In the subdivision of Brindle there is a considerable quantity of good land; there are several manufactories, and the population is more than one person to two acres The land is still better, and the population more numerous, in the subdivision of Leyland. In the Rivington district the soil is excessively wild and the country mountainous, rising at the highest point in the Rivington hills to 1545 feet, and at several points to from 1000 to 1200 feet In this district are the reservoirs of the Liverpool water-works, already described But this elevated district has great advantages for industry, in its numerous streams of water and its abundant supplies of coal. The Croston district is a level tract of rich meadow, pasture, and arable land, well-drained in many parts, though exposed to floods after heavy rains among the mountains The Chorley district, being rich in minerals and possessing numerous manufactories, contains about two inhabitants to every acre of land Coal is found and worked in the Chorley district, in the townships of Chorley, Coppull, Duxbury, Heath Charnock, and Charnock Richard

The hundred of Leyland, which includes the greater part of the census district of Chorley, in 1860 contained property and income valued at £489,613 a year This included the items of rent of land £137,160, profits of cultivation the same, messuages and buildings £85,113; quarries £1393, mines £18,094; fisheries £30, railways £330, gas-works £1220, other profits £977; and profits of trade £107,620 The property and income of the town of Chorley were valued in 1860 at £94,022.

The Salford Hundred—We come now to the great manufacturing hundred of Salford, containing the census districts of Bolton, Bury, Rochdale, Oldham, part of Ashton-under-Lyne, Manchester, Salford and Chorlton-on-Medlock, Barton-on-Irwell and Leigh, districts containing upwards of 1,000,000 of inhabitants, and yielding an income of upwards of £12,000,000 sterling per annum

The Bolton District—The census district of Bolton, or Bolton in the Moors, as it used to be called, extends over 43,806 acres of land. It is naturally one of the wildest districts in Lancashire; but industry and skill have rendered it one of the richest and most populous The land in the northern part of the Bolton district rises to the height of 1000 to 1500 feet, and much of it is still uninclosed, and overgrown with heath The valleys are narrow and winding, and there is little either of arable or of level ground, though much of the grass land is rich and verdant. But there is no part of Lancashire that is more abundantly supplied with running streams, and with water and water-power. The rivers Croal, Tonge, and Eagle, with numerous large brooks, flow down from the Turton, Horwich, and Halliwell hills, all ultimately discharging their waters into the river Irwell. Coal also is very abundant. The town of Great Bolton stands on the northern edge of the middle or main coal-field of Lancashire, and the town of Little Bolton on the southern edge of the lower coal-field. Coal is also found in the adjoining townships of West Houghton, Blackrod, Ainsworth, Tottington, Little and Middle Hulton, Little, Great, and Darcy Lever, Brightmede, Halliwell, Farnworth, Harwood, Horwich, Tonge, Kersley, Quarleton, and Turton

The district of Bolton contained 40,763 inhabitants in the year 1801, and during the first fifty years of the present century that number increased threefold, or to 114,712 persons at the census of 1851. Between the census of 1851 and that of 1861 there was a further increase of 15,558 persons, raising the population of the Bolton district to 130,270 in 1861.

The subdivision of Turton lies amongst lofty hills, in the wildest part of the Bolton district. It contains very little arable land, and much of the ground is still covered with heath and moss Yet from its great manufacturing resources, and the industry of its inhabitants, it is more populous than many of the richest districts of England, containing about one inhabitant to every acre of land, which is about twice the average rate of population throughout the whole of England. The Horwich subdivision is equally wild, but it contains numerous fine springs of water (which have caused bleachworks to be established on the banks of some of the purest streams), and also much coal During the last few years immense reservoirs have been formed in this and the neighbouring townships for the supply of Liverpool and Bolton, and of the numerous mills in the valleys. The subdivision of Edgeworth is also lofty and barren, but abounds in water-power and coal, and is inhabited by an industrious population, fully as numerous in proportion to the extent of the district as that of England generally In the subdivision of Halliwell, which is also situated amongst the hills, the population is twice as numerous in proportion to the area as the average population of England; whilst the population of Tonge with Haulgh is four times as numerous The subdivisions of Farnworth, Hulton, West Houghton, and Lever, are still more densely peopled; and in the subdivisions of Sharples, Little Bolton, and Bolton Eastern and Bolton Western, a population of 70,000 persons is collected on a few thousand acres of land

The Town of Bolton—The town of Bolton obtained a charter from King Henry III, in the year 1252, authorizing the inhabitants to hold a market and a fair. The manor of Bolton at that time belonged to William de Ferrers, earl of Derby, to whom the charter was granted by the king A few years previous to the granting of this charter, Ranulf, earl of Chester, from whom William de Ferrers inherited the manor of Bolton, had purchased the manors and townships of Bolton and Little Bolton, Hilton, Brightmede, Redcliffe, Urmston, Sharples, Haigh, Adlington, Darwen, Eccleshill, and Heaton, from Roger de Mersheya, for the sum of 200 marks of silver, to which forty marks were afterwards added on the completion of the purchase, the two sums being equal to about £2400 of modern money*

Between the reigns of Henry III., and Henry VIII., Bolton had so much advanced, that Leyland described it in his "Itinerary of England," drawn up for the information of the king, as having "a market which stood mostly by cottons" (really woollens) "and coarse yarn," and adds, that "divers villages in the moors about Bolton did make cottons" He further adds, "that they burn at Bolton some cannal, but more sea coal, of the which the pits be not far off" From that time to the commencement of the present century Bolton continued to advance steadily in industry and prosperity, but since that time it has advanced with constantly increasing rapidity In 1801 Bolton contained 17,977 inhabitants, which number had increased in 1851 to 61,171. Between the census of 1851 and that of 1861 there was a still further increase of upwards of 9000, and in 1861 the population of Bolton was 70,396 persons: according to a return recently laid before Parliament, the population of the borough of Bolton in 1866 was computed to be 75,516 persons †

The yearly amount of the property and income of the town of Bolton in 1860 was £586,363 Of this amount £215,947 was derived from messuages and buildings; £3600 from cultivation of land, and £366,812 from profits of trade.

The Bury District.—The census district of Bury lies to the east of Bolton. The river Irwell runs through it. The land extends

* Duchy Office, Cartæ Regum, No 79 † Electoral Returns, Boroughs and Counties, 1865–66, p 96

over an area of 32,990 acres. In the valley of the Irwell the land is very rich, especially in the meadows along the stream There is also some good land on the sides of the hills, and the tops of the hills are in many places planted with larches, firs, and other mountain trees The river Irwell and several smaller streams supply abundant water-power to the whole district. The middle or principal coal-field of Lancashire extends to the town of Bury on the south, and the lower coal-field joins it on the north and east. In and around Bury there are coal mines, at Bury, Ratcliffe, Ratcliffe bridge, Prestwich, Elton, Shuttleworth, Halcombe Hill, and Walmersley.

The Bury district is increasing rapidly in population. In 1801 it contained only 31,853 inhabitants. During the next fifty years that number had increased to 88,515, and during the next ten years there was a further increase of 12,627 persons, raising the population in 1861 to 101,142 persons

The Town of Bury.—The town of Bury is of great antiquity. In the time of Leyland, that is, in the reign of Henry VIII, iron was made in the neighbourhood of Bury, but at that time the art of smelting iron ore with coal was not known, and as Leyland says, "from lack of wood the blow-shops (furnaces) decayed there"

At the beginning of the present century the town of Bury contained 9152 inhabitants. In fifty years this increased to 31,262, and between the census of 1851 and that of 1861 the population of Bury increased to 37,564 persons According to a recent return laid before Parliament, the population of Bury in 1866 was computed to amount to 41,175 persons.* In 1860 the property and income of the town of Bury were returned at £356,875. Of this amount £206,284 was derived from buildings and land, and £145,660 from profits of trade All the subdivisions of the Bury district are densely peopled, and abound in industry and wealth. The subdivisions of the Bury district are Halcombe, Tottington, Walmersley, Birtle, Heywood, Elton, Radcliffe, and Pilkington.

The Rochdale District.—The census district of Rochdale, covering an area of 40,340 acres, lies chiefly among lofty hills that rise into rugged heath-covered mountains in the ridges which divide Lancashire from Yorkshire. There is a range of rich meadow land along the banks of the Roch, and of several of the smaller streams, and also a fair quantity of arable and good pasture land on the west

* Electoral Returns, Boroughs and Counties, 1865–66, p 95

side of the district. The rivers and streams are numerous, and the water-power is abundant The lower coal-field of Lancashire extends over the greater part of the district.

The Rochdale district contained only 26,577 inhabitants at the census of 1801. This number had increased to 72,514 in 1851. The increase was still greater, in proportion, between 1851 and 1861, having amounted to 19,243 persons, raising the population of the Rochdale district in 1861 to 91,757 persons All the subdivisions of the Rochdale district are thickly peopled: they are, Blachinworth, which extends up the sides of Blackstone Edge, above Littleborough, and along the banks of the river Roch, which flows down from those heights, and turns many mills in its course towards Rochdale, Wuerdale, on the banks of the same stream, Whitworth, in a hilly region towards the north, Spotland, Wardleworth, and Butterworth, with the subdivisions of Castleton Within and Castleton Without, containing the greater part of the town of Rochdale.

The Town of Rochdale—Rochdale is a very old town, being mentioned in the Domesday Survey under the name of Recedham. The woollen manufacture has flourished in that neighbourhood since the reign of Edward III, when some of the Flemish weavers, who came over to England in that reign, are said to have settled there. In 1801 Rochdale contained 8542 inhabitants, and in the first fifty years of the present century its population had increased to 29,198. In 1861 it had still further increased to 38,184 persons, and, according to a return laid before Parliament in 1866, the population of the borough of Rochdale was computed to amount to 43,668 persons * The value of the property and income of Rochdale in 1860 was £328,620. Of this amount £146,030 was derived from buildings and land, and £145,741 from profits of trade

The Oldham District—The Oldham census division extends over the range of hills known as Stennage, which divides Lancashire from Yorkshire, and over a portion of the plain that lies at their feet. The division rises on the east into lofty and barren mountains, from which the waters of the river Medlock and of several smaller streams rush down to the plain There is very good grass land along the banks of these streams, and still more on the level ground. But the great wealth of the Oldham district is in its rich veins of coal, belonging to the middle coal-field of Lancashire, which extend over nearly the whole district.

* Electoral Returns, Boroughs and Counties, 1865-66, p 202

The area of the Oldham district is 16,872 acres. The subdivisions of Royton and Crompton, though rising into lofty hills, are very thickly peopled; and those of Chadderton and Middleton, that lie nearer to the plain, are much more so

At the commencement of the present century, the Oldham census district contained 26,646 inhabitants During the first fifty years of the century that number had increased to 86,788 The rate of increase during the ten years between 1851 and 1861 has been still more rapid, having amounted to 24,479, thus raising the population of the Oldham district in 1861 to 111,267 persons.

The Town of Oldham—The town of Oldham has increased with great rapidity. In 1801 it contained 21,677 inhabitants, and in 1851, 72,357. The increase was still greater between 1851 and 1861, Oldham having contained a population of 94,344 inhabitants at the census of 1861 According to a return laid before Parliament, the borough of Oldham was computed to contain 107,729 persons in the year 1866*

The yearly value of the property and income of the town of Oldham in 1860 was £433,459. Of this sum £188,858 was derived from buildings and land, and £196,173 from profits of trade

The District of Ashton-under-Lyne—The extensive district of Ashton-under-Lyne, which covers an area of 38,657 acres, lies chiefly among mountains and hills, and extends up the Longdendale valley to the summit of the mountains that divide Lancashire and Cheshire from Yorkshire The division consists chiefly of wild moors and mountain pastures on the eastern side, with some good grass land and rich meadows towards the plain Numerous streams flow from the mountains, the most considerable of which are the Etherow and the Tame Coal is found in great abundance, not only in the lower parts of the district, but nearly to the tops of the mountains.

The district of Ashton-under-Lyne contained only 27,361 persons at the beginning of the present century In 1851 it contained no less than 119,199 persons The increase was also very rapid between 1851 and 1861, having amounted to 15,562 persons during those ten years, thus raising the population of the census district of Ashton-under-Lyne, in 1866, to 134,761 persons.

The Town of Ashton-under-Lyne—The town of Ashton-under-Lyne has increased very rapidly during the present century. In

* Electoral Returns, Boroughs and Counties, 1865–66, p. 187

1801 it contained only 6391 inhabitants. The number had increased to 30,676 persons in 1851, and to 34,886 in 1861 According to the estimate of a recent parliamentary return, the population of the borough of Ashton-under-Lyne in 1866 was 36,190.* The yearly value of the property and income of Ashton-under-Lyne, in 1860, amounted to £216,635. Of this sum £107,621 was derived from buildings and land, and £100,665 from profits of trade.

The City and District of Manchester.—Manchester, the capital of the manufacturing district of Lancashire, now really extends over the census divisions of Manchester and Chorlton, and is closely connected with that of Salford, from which it is only separated by a narrow river

The census district of Manchester covers an area of 12,628 acres. It is very thickly built over in many parts, and the population is overflowing in vast numbers into the districts of Chorlton and Salford

It has required a period of 1500 to 1600 years, if not longer, to raise Manchester to what it now is, although nearly three-fourths of its growth has taken place during the present century.

The great natural advantage of Manchester, in former times, was the fertile range of country that extends up the river Irwell to Bury, and down the same river to Warrington, together with the abundance of water and water-power supplied by the confluence of the three rivers—Irwell, Irk, and Medlock—within its limits. In modern times the greatest natural advantage of Manchester has been its position in the immediate neighbourhood of two of the Lancashire coal-fields. The upper or Manchester coal-field comes close upon the city, and even within it on the east, while the great middle coal-field of Lancashire approaches as near as to Pendleton on the west It thus possesses, and has for ages possessed, every advantage as a manufacturing city, that Nature could supply, and these have been improved by intelligence, skill, and the most persevering industry.

The original recommendations of the site of Manchester to the Romans, who either founded or greatly improved the city (which was known in ancient times as Mamucium, or Mancunium), were the fertility of the soil, the healthiness of the position, and the neighbourhood of rivers, which they used for the purpose of defence as well as that of communication These natural advantages

* Electoral Returns, Boroughs and Counties, 1865–66 p 73

maintained Manchester in existence during the whole of the Saxon period, with the rank of a burgh or town, which it held in the time of Alfred the Great and his son Edward the Elder, even after it had been almost ruined in the wars between the Danes of Northumberland and the Saxon kings. At the time of the Domesday Survey Manchester was the most considerable place in South Lancashire, though at that time much decayed, from the desperate wars that had been waged for so many hundred years in the north of England. In the year 1222 King Henry III granted the right to hold a weekly market and a yearly fair at Manchester, and in the year 1301 Thomas de Gresley, baron of Manchester, granted a charter to the burgesses of Manchester, with the usual privileges of local government and of trade

Between this period and the accession of the Tudor princes, Manchester became a considerable manufacturing town. When Leland visited it, in the reign of Henry VIII, he states that "Manchester was the fairest, best builded, quickest, and most populous town of all Lancashire, with divers fair mills on the river Irk, and with two market places," and speaks of the manufacturers of Manchester "as buying much Irish yarn at Liverpool" A few years later, in the reign of Queen Elizabeth, Camden speaks of Manchester "as excelling all the neighbouring towns in ornament, populousness, in its woollen manufacture, its court-house, church, and college" and speaks of the superiority of its woollen cloths, then known by the name of "Manchester cottons" These manufactures were known in the Brazils in the year 1573. In the reign of James I. cotton wool began to be imported into Manchester from the Levant; and, in the reign of Charles II, Andrew Yarranton, one of the principal writers on trade of that age, spoke of Manchester as being "the great master in all things that it trades in" About the year 1730 Manchester obtained the great advantage of cheap water-carriage to Liverpool, by the improvement of the Irwell and Mersey About the year 1760 it obtained the advantage of canal navigation with the Worsley coal-field, and about fifteen years afterwards, of canal navigation with Liverpool by the Bridgewater canal. Cotton machinery was introduced at Manchester soon after it was invented, and the steam-engine was applied to the working of that machinery during the last fifteen years of the last century. During that period Manchester was connected by canal navigation with the adjoining towns of Bolton, Bury, Rochdale,

Oldham, Ashton, and Stockport, besides being connected by the Rochdale and Huddersfield canal and the High Peak canal with the West Riding of Yorkshire, the coal-field of Cheshire, and the limestone district of Derbyshire. At the beginning of the eighteenth century the population of Manchester amounted to 10,000 to 20,000 inhabitants, at the accession of George III. in 1760 it was from 30,000 to 40,000, at the close of the century it was very nearly 100,000, in 1851 the population of Manchester had increased to 316,213 inhabitants. It 1861 it had further increased to 357,604 inhabitants, and according to a return recently laid before Parliament, the population of the city of Manchester in the year 1866 was computed to be 380,887 persons In a subsequent part of this work we shall trace the rise of this great city more fully, through successive ages, from the time of its origin to the age in which we live

The wealth of Manchester is enormous. According to the returns of the Property and Income Tax in the year 1860, the yearly value of property and income in Manchester was £5,775,453. Of this immense sum £2,060,181 was derived from buildings, land, and public works, and £3,715,272 from profits of trade. According to the same return the valuation of property and income in the division of Manchester was £7,212,054. Of this £1,637,570 was derived from messuages and buildings, and £4,239,416 from profits of trade

The Chorlton District—The rapid increase in the population of the Chorlton district, which adjoins on Manchester, arises chiefly from the overflow of the population and the spread of the wealth of Manchester into the adjoining townships The Chorlton district covers an area of 11,549 acres At the census of 1841 it contained 9342 inhabitants, and fifty years after, at the census of 1851, it contained a population of 123,841 persons, its population having increased more than twelvefold in that period. Between 1851 and 1861 the Chorlton district still further increased by no less than 45,738 persons, making its population in 1861, 169,579

The District and Borough of Salford—The census district and borough of Salford cover an area of 4830 acres Salford has had a separate jurisdiction from Manchester for many hundred years, and probably gave its own name to the hundred of Salford previous to the Norman Conquest The sources of its prosperity are, however, the same as those of Manchester, being derived from the same river which flows between the two places, conferring equal advantages on each, and from the proximity of the same coal-fields. In early times the coal-field was first worked in the upper field, which lies nearer to Manchester than it does to Salford, but at present valuable coal-fields are also worked on the Salford or western side of the Irwell.

Salford contained only 18,525 inhabitants at the commencement of the present century. Fifty years later the number had increased to 87,523 persons. Between 1851 and 1861 the population of Salford increased to 105,335. According to an estimate recently laid before Parliament, the population of Salford in 1866 was computed at 112,403 persons The yearly value of property and income in Salford in 1860 was £546,329 Of this amount £258,761 is derived from messuages and buildings, and £255,236 from profits of trade.

District of Barton-on-Irwell.—Following the course of the rivers Irwell and Mersey towards the sea, we come next to the census district of Barton-on-Irwell, covering an area of 23,279 acres This district contains much good land on its eastern and southern sides, but on the west and north it extends over the wide range of Chat Moss, formerly the largest of the peat mosses of South Lancashire, but now much reduced in extent by cultivation. The new red sandstone is the prevailing formation of this district, but coal has recently been found by sinking to a great depth through that formation into the coal measures that lie below it The first canal formed by Francis duke of Bridgewater runs through this district, furnishing a cheap and easy communication from the Worsley coal mines to the city of Manchester The navigable river Irwell also flows through it, and both the high road and the railway from Liverpool to Manchester pass through the district, and cross the canal at Patricroft, which is rapidly growing up into a considerable manufacturing town. The subdivision of Worsley, in this district, is rich in coal, and contains the great coal mines of the Worsley estate, to facilitate the working of which the duke of Bridgewater commenced his schemes of inland navigation. These works were commenced in the year 1759, and when the first earl of Ellesmere wrote an account of them, about twenty years ago, the total length of the tunnels which had been opened in seeking for a working coal was forty-two miles and one furlong, of which, however, somewhat less than two-thirds were in disuse, and had been rendered inaccessible.* These works have now supplied Manchester with large

* Quarterly Review, No. 146 Article, Aqueducts and Canals.

quantities of coal for more than a hundred years The adjoining subdivision of Barton-on-Irwell is chiefly agricultural; but of late years very valuable coal mines, and a rich vein of the iron ore, known as the blackband, have been discovered at Patricroft in this district. The subdivision of Stretford, lying between the river Irwell and the river Mersey, is a rich district, consisting chiefly of meadows, market gardens, and villas, into which the city of Manchester is rapidly extending Trafford Park, the ancient seat of the old Lancashire family of that name and place, lies immediately south of the river Irwell, and Davy Hulme Park, the seat of one of the branches of the ancient family of Norris, is situated at a little distance lower down the stream. The subdivision of Stretford is one of the richest and most carefully cultivated districts of Lancashire or Cheshire.

The Leigh District.—The census district of Leigh, covering 23,610 acres, is chiefly an agricultural and pastoral district on the southern side, and a mining and manufacturing district on the north It contains much good and rather strong land, very suitable for dairy purposes, and produces cheese of very superior quality. Several large streams flow from the hills on the north side of the district, and unite in the larger stream of Glazebrook, which flows down by the side of Bury Lane into the river Mersey Great part of the district lies on the middle or principal coal-field of Lancashire, and magnesian limestone of great value for forming cement or mortar, which retains its hardness under water, is found on the edge of the coal formation. The Atherton collieries in this district are among the largest and most productive in Lancashire, and furnish large quantities of steam coal for purposes of navigation.

The census district of Leigh contained 17,577 inhabitants in 1801 In the middle of the century, at the census of 1851, it contained 32,734, and at the census of 1861, 37,700. The town of Leigh in 1861 contained 10,621

The yearly value of the property and income of the hundred of Salford was returned in the year 1860 at the enormous sum of £12,339,410. This amount was divided amongst the four collecting districts of the hundred as follows:—Manchester, £7,212,054; Salford, £1,206,090; Bolton, £2,007,423, Middleton, £1,913,843

The Hundred of West Derby—The hundred of West Derby extends over the census districts of Warrington, Wigan, Ormskirk, Prescot, West Derby, and Liverpool, and contains nearly a million of inhabitants

The Warrington District.—The census district of Warrington extends over 36,164 acres, including land both on the Cheshire and Lancashire side of the Mersey, which flows through it. The soil of the district is in general very good, resting on the new red-sandstone formation on the uplands, and on deep beds of alluvium on the banks of the rivers Coal is found in the northern part of this district, and manufactures of various kinds are carried on both in the town of Warrington and in the neighbourhood of Newton, and of Ashton in Makerfield The subdivision of Newton contains much very good land, besides beds of coal at considerable depth. The subdivisions of Winwick and Sankey, on the banks of Sankey Brook, are almost entirely agricultural. That is also the case with the subdivision of Rixton, in which there is much good land, but also some extensive peat mosses. The land is excellent in the subdivision of Warwick, and in that of Latchford, on the Cheshire side of the Mersey.

The Town of Warrington.—The town of Warrington stands on the river Mersey, at the point where the old Roman road, running north and south, crossed that river, and for many ages Warrington bridge has been the chief means of communication between Lancashire and Cheshire. At the time of the Domesday Survey, Warrington was the chief place of the hundred of Warrington, which, like the hundred of Newton, has been incorporated with the hundred of West Derby The town of Warrington has increased considerably during the present century. In 1801 it contained 11,321 inhabitants; in 1851, 22,894; and in 1861, 26,431. According to a return laid before Parliament the population of Warrington was computed to amount to 28,940 persons in 1866.

The Wigan District—The Wigan census district covers an area of 47,018 acres. A considerable part of the land towards the north is hilly, almost mountainous, but there is some very good land along the banks of the river Douglas Numerous streams flow from the hills, most of which discharge themselves into the river Douglas The whole district abounds in coal, and there is scarcely any part of England in which coal is produced in larger quantities, or in forms applicable to a greater variety of purposes. The subdivision of Standish contains a considerable quantity of good land, and also much coal. The Aspull district is wild and hilly, but also rich in coal. The Hindley and Pemberton districts abound in coal, and the former has very extensive manufactures. The district of Upholland rises into lofty hills, containing coal and building stone of superior quality.

Ashton in Makerfield has much good land and many mines of coal. The Wigan census district in 1801 contained 42,565 inhabitants. In the next fifty years the population of the district increased to 77,539 persons. Between the census of 1851 and that of 1861, there was a further increase of 17,022 persons, raising the population of the Wigan district in 1861 to 94,561

The Town of Wigan—The town of Wigan is a very ancient place, standing on the line of the principal Roman road through Lancashire, and dates from the time of the Anglo-Saxons. It had charters in the year 1329. In 1343 the commissioners for collecting the tax of one-ninth on moveable goods voted by Parliament to Edward III., reported that the true value of the ninth part of the moveable goods of the men dwelling in the borough of Wigan was £5. 9*s.* 4*d.**

In the reign of Henry VIII, when Leland visited Wigan, he reported of it that it was as big as Warrington and better built, with a parish church in the midst of the town, and a population, some of whom were merchants, some artificers, and some farmers. He further stated that "Mr. Bradshaw had a place at Haigh, a mile or two from Wigan, where he had found much cannel, like sea-coal, in his ground, which was very profitable to him" Leland further states that cannel and coal pits were worked in divers parts of West Derbyshire, but that the great mine of cannel was at Haigh, two miles from Wigan.

In the civil war Wigan was fortified and held for King Charles, but was taken by the Parliament, and was the scene of a fierce battle between James, earl of Derby, and the Cromwellian general, Lilburne. Early in the eighteenth century, about the year 1725, the river Douglas was made navigable from Wigan to the mouth of the Ribble But the great cause of the progress of Wigan was the forming of the Leeds and Liverpool canal, which runs through Wigan, and gives it communication with Liverpool and the Mersey in one direction, with Preston and North Lancashire in another, and with Chorley, Blackburn, Accrington, Burnley, Colne, as well as the West Riding of Yorkshire, in a third

At the beginning of the present century the town of Wigan contained 10,989 inhabitants In the first fifty years of the century this number increased to 31,941. In 1861 it had further increased to 37,658. According to a return laid before Parliament the population of the borough of Wigan, in 1866, was computed at 40,889 persons

* Nonarum Inquisitiones. Lancashire.

The Ormskirk District.—The Ormskirk census district lies between the Wigan district and the sea It is very extensive, covering an area of 111,968 acres, and is the most purely agricultural district of South Lancashire. It extends from the foot of the hills to the sea-coast over a wide fertile plain, the eastern part of which rests on the new red-sandstone formation, and the south on the great alluvial beds Nearly the whole of the land in the Ormskirk district is suitable for the plough, and much of it is very skilfully cultivated It is furnished with every kind of tillage by the Leeds and Liverpool canal, which winds through it with a most serpentine course, from Liverpool to Burscough, in the neighbourhood of the river Douglas. The crops grown consist chiefly of grass, clover, potatoes, turnips, oats, and wheat; and large quantities of garden produce, as well as milk and butter, are raised for the Liverpool market. The streams of the district are not numerous, and have very little fall owing to the flatness of the country, there is no coal except a little in the neighbourhood of the town of Ormskirk.

The Ormskirk district is sub-divided into the sub-districts of Bickerstaffe, Aughton, Halsall, Formby, North Meols, Tarleton, and Scarisbrick. The occupations of the people in all these are almost entirely agricultural, and the only towns are Ormskirk and Southport, the latter a rapidly increasing watering-place on the sea-coast.

At the census of 1801 the district of Ormskirk contained 21,585 persons Fifty years later, at the census of 1851, the population had increased to 38,307. Between 1851 and 1861 there was a further increase of 7945 persons, raising the population of the Ormskirk district in 1861 to 46,252 The population of the town of Ormskirk in 1861 amounted to 6426.

The Prescot and St Helen's District.—The Prescot and St. Helen's district extends over an area of 56,859 acres. On the east of this district are the coal-fields of St. Helen's, which are amongst the richest in Lancashire, to the south is Widness on the river Mersey, which is rapidly becoming a manufacturing town, to the west are Huyton and Woolton, studded with villas, with the rich plain, known as the Broad green of South Lancashire, lying below them, and to the north are Prescot, Rainford, and Knowsley, with its extensive woods, undulating park, and ancient mansion, for ages the seat of the earls of Derby. The resources of this district are great and varied. Much of the soil is of excellent quality, resting on the new red-sandstone rock, but the coal-measures cover the whole eastern side of the district, running down southward to Whiston, and westward under Knowsley and Croxteth parks to within five miles of the sea

The census district of Prescot in 1801 contained 20,703 inhabitants, and fifty years afterwards the population had increased to 56,074 persons. Between the census of 1851 and that of 1861 the population of the district received a further increase of 17,053 persons, raising it to 73,127 in 1861 The town of St. Helen's contained, in 1851, 14,866, and in 1861, 18,396 inhabitants. The town of Prescot in 1861 contained 6066 inhabitants.

The West Derby District.—The district of West Derby extends over an area of 50,567 acres It includes the whole of the country around the town and port of Liverpool, and a large portion of the densely peopled district that now forms the suburbs of Liverpool. It is in general a fertile and pleasant country, resting on the new sandstone formation, which rises in this part of Lancashire to a height of from 250 to 300 feet above the level of the sea The West Derby district does not contain either coal or any other minerals, with the exception of brick-clay and building stone; but out of these materials the town of Liverpool and the surrounding villages have been built The general character of the district is suburban, villas and villages being scattered over nearly the whole Towards the north, in the direction of Bootle and Litherland, there is a quantity of level ground resting on the southern part of the alluvial plain of Lancashire This is of a particularly fertile though somewhat light soil It is carefully cultivated, and, like the rest of the neighbourhood, is covered with villas

At the commencement of the present century the West Derby district contained only 11,994 persons, but in the first fifty years of the century the population had increased to 153,279 persons. Between 1851 and 1861 the increase of the population of the district was even more extraordinary, having amounted to 72,566 persons, raising the whole population of the West Derby district to 225,845 persons in the year 1861

The Port and Borough of Liverpool.—Liverpool is now the greatest seaport of the world according to the extent of its trade It owes its existence and its capacity for commercial greatness to a wide, deep, and safe harbour, capable of receiving at one time thousands of the largest ships that traverse the ocean.

It is now between 600 and 700 years since the first impulse was given to the commerce of Liverpool by a charter of King John, who granted to all persons, who might take the king's burgages at Liverpool, all the rights that were at that time enjoyed by any other borough on the sea in the king's dominions. These rights were fully confirmed in the year 1227 by a second charter granted by Henry III, in which he gave to the burgesses of Liverpool all the rights of local government that were usually granted to boroughs in those times, together with freedom from the ancient customs paid to the crown, and the right to form a "Hanse," or mercantile trading body, to govern and direct the trade of the port, and to protect its rights. In the year 1298 Liverpool obtained the right of sending members to the first Parliament assembled by King Edward I, in which both the knights and burgesses of the kingdom were represented. In 1345 the commissioners appointed to collect the ninths of the moveable goods payable to the king, under a grant of Parliament, reported that the true value of the ninth part of the moveable goods of the burgesses of Liverpool was £6 16*s.* 7*d.*—a sum equal to about £100 in the money of the present time In the reign of Henry VIII, Leland, on his journey through England, found Liverpool to be a paved town, with a chapel, a castelet, belonging to the king, and a stone house—the tower—belonging to the earl of Derby. Hither "Irish merchants then resorted much, as to a good haven where there was small custom paid" These two circumstances caused the resort of merchants, "who brought good merchandise to Liverpool, including much Irish yarn that Manchester men did buy" In the reign of Queen Elizabeth, Camden speaks of Liverpool "as the most frequented passage to Ireland, and as a place more noted for its elegance and its populousness than for its antiquity." A hundred years later, in the reign of Charles II, Blome, in his "Britannia," describes it as a place "in which there were divers eminent merchants and tradesmen, whose trade and traffic, especially to the West Indies, have made it famous" He further added that the situation "afforded in greater plenty, and at more reasonable rates than most places in England, imported commodities from the West Indies, as likewise a quick return for such commodities, by reason of the sugar bakers and great manufacturers of cotton in the adjacent parts, and the rather that it is found to be the most convenient passage to Ireland, and divers considerable counties of England with which they have intercourse of traffic." In 1699 it was stated in a public petition from Liverpool that it was formerly a small fishing town, but many people coming from London in the time of the sickness (the plague of London), and after the fire, caused them to trade to the American plantations and other places This caused sundry other tradesmen to come and settle there, which had so enlarged their trade, that from scarcely paying the salary of the officers of the customs it is now the third port of trade in England, and pays upwards of £50,000 a year to the king. In 1708, in the reign of Queen Anne, powers were obtained to form the first dock at Liverpool; the second was formed in the reign of George II., and a third soon after the accession of George III Two others were formed between the first American war and the breaking out of the French Revolution. Another dock was formed about the year 1810, and soon after the close of the great French war docks began to be formed in rapid succession. This has continued to the present time, when the docks of Liverpool extend six miles in length, give accommodation to about 4,000,000 tons of shipping, and afford the means of carrying on an export trade of the value of £73,000,000 yearly in British goods and produce, and an import trade in foreign and colonial produce of not much smaller magnitude

The growth of the population of Liverpool during the last hundred years has been extremely rapid. In the year 1700 the population was not more than from 8000 to 10,000 persons At the accession of George III. it was from 25,000 to 30,000 Previous to the breaking out of the great French war about the year 1792 it was 60,000 At the census of 1801 Liverpool contained 83,653 inhabitants, or, including the whole of the present limits of the borough, 89,250. At the end of fifty years, at the census of 1851, the number of inhabitants in the borough of Liverpool was 375,955, and in 1861 the number had increased to 443,874, making Liverpool the most populous town in the United Kingdom, after the metropolis. According to a return recently laid before Parliament, the population of Liverpool in the year 1866 was computed at 482,409 persons.

If the suburbs of Manchester and of Liverpool, over as wide an area as those of London, were included within the population of the two places, so as to comprise within them an area of 78,000 acres, which is the area of the metropolitan district, both Liverpool and

Manchester would be found to contain from three-quarters to a million of persons. The population at present returned as belonging to Manchester is confined to an area of 12,000 acres, and that included in Liverpool is contained within an area of 4000 acres.

The inhabitants of the borough and port of Liverpool possessed in 1860 a yearly income, under the heads of property and income, amounting to £6,575,455. Of this immense sum £1,425,965 was derived from buildings, land, and public works, and £5,149,490 from profits of trade.

The yearly value of the property and income of the West Derby Hundred in the year 1860, was £9,916,841 This was derived from six collecting districts, in the following proportions —Liverpool, £6,575,455; Prescot first, £981,201; Prescot second, £634,567, Warrington, £976,132, Ormskirk, £482,924, and Wigan, £266,562.

The County of Chester.—Passing on to the county of Chester, we find a similar connection between the natural resources of each of the districts into which it is divided, and its population and wealth. Cheshire is divided into the hundreds of Macclesfield, Nantwich, Northwich, Bucklow, Eddisbury, Broxton, and Wirral. It is subdivided into eleven census divisions Three of these may be regarded as manufacturing and mining districts—viz, Stockport, Macclesfield, and Congleton. One of them is at once an agricultural and a mining district—namely, Northwich, the seat of the salt trade; two are purely agricultural—Nantwich and Altringham three unite agriculture with commerce—namely, Runcorn, Boughton, or Chester, and Wirral, and Birkenhead, which has recently been formed into a separate district, depends entirely on trade, commerce, and shipping

The Stockport District.—The district of Stockport covers an area of 3709 acres, and is the most thickly-peopled portion of Cheshire The greater part of the land is hilly and almost mountainous, but the whole of it abounds in streams, and much of it possesses rich beds of coal The subdivision of Marple in this district consists chiefly of lofty moors, through which the river Goyt descends to join the river Etherow, and thus to form the river Mersey Coal is found on the sides and even on the summits of these hills, at an elevation of 1500 to 1800 feet; and this abundant supply of fuel, with the water-power furnished by numerous streams, has filled the valleys and covered the hill-sides with population and industry The district of Hyde is still richer in minerals and manufactures, and Hyde itself has rapidly grown up into a large town of 13,722 inhabitants The districts of Cheadle and Hazlegrove possess a good soil and culture, and are within easy reach of the Poynton coal-field, from which Stockport also draws its chief supplies of coal This is a continuation of the richest part of the coal-field of Lancashire.

The population of the Stockport division in 1801 amounted to 32,772, in 1851 to 90,208; and in 1861 to 94,360 persons.

The Town of Stockport.—The town of Stockport is an ancient place, and has charters several hundred years old, but it contained only 14,850 inhabitants at the commencement of the present century In 1851 the number had increased to 53,835, and in 1861 to 54,681. The yearly value of the property and income of the borough of Stockport in 1860 was £271,582 Of this amount £149,741 was derived from buildings, &c, and £121,821 from profits of trade

The Macclesfield District—The district of Macclesfield, covering an area of 80,560 acres, is in general wild and mountainous, rising on the east side to the height of 1500 to 1800 feet. In former times it was known as the forest of Macclesfield. On the higher grounds there is little good ground, but the western side of the district, close to the Cheshire plain, is very fertile. Coal is found even to the tops of the highest ranges of hills, and this, with the numerous streams, of which the river Bollin is the largest, has created the prosperity of Macclesfield, where the silk and the cotton trades have been long established The subdivision of Rainow, rising to the tops of the lofty hills that separate Cheshire from Derbyshire, is very thinly peopled. It consists almost entirely of mountain land, and owes whatever population exists to the coal mines and slate quarries that are found amongst the hills The district of Prestbury is somewhat less lofty, and also contains mines of coal. The district of Bollington, in the neighbourhood of Macclesfield, has numerous streams and many mills, which is also the case with the extensive district of Sutton. Gawsworth, approaching and extending over the plain, is chiefly an agricultural and grazing district. That is also the case with the district of Alderley, although a copper mine has been discovered there, and although the beauty of the scenery on Alderley Edge has caused numerous villas to be erected along its sides, which command extensive views of the Cheshire plain and the distant hills The census district of Macclesfield contained 24,215 inhabitants in the year 1801. From that time to the year 1851 the progress of population was rapid, the numbers having increased to 63,327 at the census of that year During the ten years between 1851 and 1861 there was a slight decrease in the population of the Macclesfield district, which in the latter year amounted to 61,543 persons

The Town of Macclesfield—The town of Macclesfield in the year 1801 contained 10,613 inhabitants; in 1851 it contained 39,048, and in 1861, 36,095 The yearly value of property and income of the borough of Macclesfield in 1860 was £171,977 Of this amount £10,927 was derived from buildings, &c., and £91,050 from profits of trade

The Congleton District—The census district of Congleton, covering a wide area of 52,889 acres, is the third and last of the manufacturing districts of Cheshire. This district rises to the tops of the hills, and to an elevation of nearly 2000 feet on the eastern side, but stretches far into the plain on the west. The river Dane, with numerous smaller streams, flows from the highest hills, and, passing through the town and neighbourhood of Congleton, does much to create and sustain the manufacturing prosperity of the place. With the exception of the town and neighbourhood of Congleton, the whole district consists of agricultural or grazing land But extensive salt-works exist on the banks of the Wheelock river in the district of Sandbach The Congleton district contained 14,803 inhabitants in 1801, 30,512 in 1851, and 34,328 in 1861.

The Town of Congleton—The town of Congleton had 10,520 inhabitants in 1851, and 12,334 in 1861

The Nantwich District—The Nantwich district, covering an area of 111,126 acres of land, forms the upper part of the fertile valley of the Weaver It is at present a purely agricultural district, containing no minerals that are worked, although salt is very abundant in the neighbourhood of the town of Nantwich, and was extensively worked in former times. When Leland was in this neighbourhood in the reign of Henry VIII., he found that there were 300 salters, or manufacturers of salt, in the town of Nantwich, and that the brine from which the salt was made was conveyed by a canal to the different furnaces where it was evaporated At that time there were large quantities of firewood on the hills, but there is no coal within a considerable distance, and when the firewood was consumed the manufacture of salt died out

The Town of Crewe.—But a large town is rising in the Nantwich district, at the Crewe railway junction, where all the trains passing along the London and North-western railway from and to Lancashire and Cheshire, and places still further north, as well as those passing between London, Wales, and Ireland, now stop to re-arrange the carriages. There, also, immense manufactures of railway machinery are now carried on In ancient times the great system of Roman roads met at a place a few miles north of the present Crewe station, named Condate, which is supposed to have been Middlewich, or its suburb, Kinderton, on the banks of the river Dane

The Nantwich census district contained 24,163 inhabitants in 1801, 35,941 in 1851, and 40,954 in 1861.

The Northwich District—Descending the valley of the Weaver, we come to the Northwich district, containing 65,445 acres of land This is a rich agricultural and grazing country, and it also contains the most valuable and extensive salt mines and brine springs that exist in Great Britain The subdivision of Middlewich contains the town of the same name, with several salt-works The district of Over is also the seat of flourishing salt-works, in the neighbourhood of Winsford, on the Weaver. Northwich, on the same river, is the principal seat of the salt manufacture, and the capital of the district Weaverham is a beautiful grazing district, on the banks of the river from which it takes its name

The Northwich census district contained 17,253 inhabitants in 1801, 31,202 in 1851, and 33,338 in 1861.

The Altringham District—The Altringham census district extends over 73,665 acres of land, and lies along the southern bank of the river Mersey It is chiefly a grazing and agricultural district, and is one of the richest and most beautiful districts of Cheshire, containing many extensive parks, as Dunham Massey, and great numbers of handsome villas, in the neighbourhood of Bowden, and in other townships within a moderate distance of Manchester. The Bridgewater canal and several railways pass through this district

The Altringham district contained 21,681 inhabitants at the census of 1801, 34,086 in 1851, and 40,517 in 1861.

The remaining census districts of Cheshire are Great Boughton, or Chester Runcorn, Wirral, and Birkenhead. These all communicate with the sea, and three of them unite trade and commerce with great agricultural resources

The Chester District—The Chester or Great Boughton district includes a large portion of the plain of Chester, and reaches to the hills of Hawarden on the west, and to those of Delamere Forest on the east. It possesses a great range of the finest pasture and meadow land, together with the ancient and most interesting city of Chester, for ages the capital of the north-western division of England

The most inland and upland part of the Great Boughton district is that of Tattenhall, including the upper part of the hundred of Broxton. This district consists almost entirely of rich grass land, with hills rising at some points to the height of 500 to 600 feet, and commanding magnificent views of the plains of Chester and the mountains of Wales. The district of Hawarden runs up the valley of the Dee to above Eccleston, and then extends over the hills to the borders of Flintshire

The City of Chester—The city of Chester is the oldest, and was for many ages the greatest and most celebrated city, in the north-west of England Its history extends over a period of nearly 1800 years, and will be fully traced in another part of this work. It owed its origin chiefly to military considerations, and long maintained its position as a fortress on the borders of Wales, which was then a hostile country. In more modern times the fertility of its soil, and the advantages of its position on the river Dee, together with the residence of the bishop and the clergy of the cathedral, of numerous families connected with the country, and an extensive trade with North Wales and the interior of Cheshire, have maintained its position It has also a considerable trade at its port of Saltney, in coal, salt, iron ore, potter's clay, and other articles, and it is the centre of a rapidly increasing railway communication, not only with North Wales, but with the Irish capital and all parts of Ireland

The city of Chester has more than doubled its population in the present century In 1801 it contained 15,052 inhabitants This number had increased at the census of 1851 to 27,766, and in 1861 to 31,110. According to a return laid before Parliament, the population of Chester was computed to amount to 32,950 in the year 1866. The yearly income of the city of Chester in 1860 was £465,831, of which £314,453 was derived from buildings, land, and public works, and £151,378 from profits of trade.

The Runcorn District.—The Runcorn district covers an area of 45,776 acres, and lies on the southern bank of the estuary of the Mersey, near the point where the river Weaver flows into that stream The land is extremely rich, both on the banks of the

Mersey and up the valley of the Weaver, but it rises into very lofty hills behind Frodsham in Delamere Forest. The subdivision of Budworth in this district consists chiefly of pasture land, much of it of the best quality The subdivision of Daresbury is more hilly than that of Budworth. The district of Frodsham is very fertile, especially in the neighbourhood of the town, where the soil is deep and rich, and much of it laid out in market gardens Delamere Forest is a wild, recently reclaimed, and only partially cultivated district, rising to the height of 600 to 700 feet, and chiefly consisting of pasture land, with very extensive plantations of oak and other kinds of timber, belonging to the crown

The census district of Runcorn contained 11,408 inhabitants in 1801 This had increased to 25,797 in 1851, and to 26,792 in 1861.

The Town of Runcorn.—The town of Runcorn is a place of extreme antiquity, but owes its present prosperity to the improvement of the Mersey and Irwell navigation, effected about the year 1730, and to the forming of the Duke of Bridgewater's canal from Manchester to the river Mersey at Runcorn, which was completed about the year 1776 Its prosperity was still further increased by the forming of the Grand Trunk canal, from the river Mersey to the river Trent. By the formation of these several lines of water-carriage, Runcorn became the port for a very extensive inland communication It is now about to become an important railway position, the London and North Western Railway Company having constructed a magnificent bridge across the river Mersey at Runcorn, which will turn the passenger traffic between Liverpool and London through this place Runcorn has also very considerable manufacturing advantages, being situated within a moderate distance both of the coal-field of Lancashire and the salt-field of Cheshire, and with cheap and easy communication with Liverpool, Manchester, and Birmingham, and all the populous districts around those great centres of trade, commerce, and industry The population of Runcorn at the census of 1861 was 10,434.

The Wirral District—The Wirral district, extending over an area of 112,110 acres, was an exclusively agricultural and grazing district until about forty years ago, when the introduction of steam navigation, and the establishment of steam ferries between Liverpool and the Cheshire side of the Mersey, began to cause a large population to pour into Wirral, and to establish itself at Birkenhead, and at all the ferries from Eastham down to New Brighton. The interior of Wirral still consists almost entirely of an arable and grazing district, occupied by a rural population, but with many handsome villas, chiefly belonging to the merchants of Liverpool, springing up at numerous points In former times there was sufficient depth of water in the river Dee to enable the communication with Ireland to be carried on from Neston and Parkgate in this district; but that has long ceased to be the case Some attempts have also been made to work coal mines in the neighbourhood of Neston, but the works have not hitherto been very successful, although it is certain that the coal measures of North Wales do extend under the river Dee, and crop up in Wirral near Neston. The Eastham district is an agricultural country, in which cultivation has been greatly improved during the last twenty years, chiefly from the influence of capitalists from Liverpool, who have made extensive purchases of land in that neighbourhood The district of Woodchurch, forming the highest part of the hundred of Wirral, is still comparatively thinly peopled, but that of Wallasey, which was at one time considered the wildest part of Wirral, is now overflowing with population, and covered with beautiful villages and villas.

New Brighton has risen within the last thirty years to the position of a populous and attractive watering place, with a resident population of 2404 inhabitants

The Town and Port of Birkenhead.—By far the greatest increase both in population and wealth, in this district, is in the newly created parliamentary borough of Birkenhead. So recently as the census of 1811, the township of Birkenhead did not contain more than 110 inhabitants. At the census of 1851 it contained 34,000 inhabitants, at that of 1861, 51,649, and in 1866 Birkenhead was computed to contain 60,504 The introduction of steam navigation, and the establishment of steam communication between Liverpool and Birkenhead gave the first impulse to the progress of Birkenhead. Within the last twenty years most extensive docks have also been formed in the arm of the sea, formerly known as Wallasey Pool. These are now among the most extensive and perfect works of the kind in England. They are united with the docks of Liverpool, under the government of the Mersey docks and harbour board, and cannot fail to give a great and rapid extension to the prosperity of Birkenhead, and to afford greatly increased facilities to the extensive and ever increasing commerce of the Mersey. These works will be fully described in a succeeding chapter of this work

The yearly value of property and income in the parliamentary borough of Birkenhead in the year 1860 was £429,218; namely, in Birkenhead £364,797, in Tranmere £50,051; and in Claughton £14,370

The total amount of the property and income of Lancashire and Cheshire, together forming the north-western district, amounted in the year 1860 to £32,376,246, forming about the tenth part of the property and income of the United Kingdom for the same year To this, however, ought to be added the sum of £12,000,000 paid yearly as wages in the cotton manufacture, and a large but uncertain sum, either paid in wages in other occupations, or derived from incomes of other kinds of less than £100 a year Altogether the property and income of the two counties cannot be less than about £50,000,000 a year The population of the two counties amounted, at the census of 1861, to very nearly 3,000,000 of persons, and at the present time amounts to somewhat more than that number. In extent, they form about the fortieth part of the territory of the United Kingdom, whilst both in population and wealth they form about the tenth part

Such are the natural resources, and such the population and wealth, at the present time, of the north-western district of England, composed of the counties of Lancashire and Cheshire. We now proceed to trace the rise and progress of society, invention and industry, from the earliest ages to the times in which we live.

CHAPTER II.

LANCASHIRE AND CHESHIRE FROM THE EARLIEST AGES TO THE NORMAN CONQUEST.

IN commencing the history of a portion of Great Britain, in which trade and commerce have been carried to so great an extent in modern times, it is not uninteresting to remark, that it was the enterprise of a commercial and trading people that first discovered, and brought to the knowledge of the more civilized nations of ancient times, that there existed in the Atlantic Ocean, far beyond the Pillars of Hercules and the passage from the Mediterranean, two large and several smaller islands, yielding many valuable products, and inhabited by a people willing to trade with foreign nations. The merchants and navigators of Tyre, Carthage, and Cadiz—all of the Phœnician race—were amongst the earliest traders to, if not the first discoverers of, the British Islands, and it was from them that the Greeks, and the Greek colonists settled along the shores of the Mediterranean, obtained the knowledge which induced them to open a trade with these islands, at a somewhat later period. According to the statement attributed to Hamilco, the Carthaginian navigator, which claims to be the oldest notice that we possess of the British Islands, the earliest traders with the British Islands were the Tartessians, the ancient inhabitants of Andalusia, in the south of Spain, subjects of Tyre and Carthage, and residing in the neighbourhood of Cadiz or Gadira, where the Phœnicians had formed a colony, as early as from 1000 to 1100 years before the birth of Christ. This trade, having once originated, was carried on from Cadiz by the Phœnicians for many hundred years. The voyage from that port to the Æstrymnian or Scilly Islands, off the coast of Cornwall, at that time occupied about four months. The principal trading stations were in the small group of islands above named, which were stated to be close to the isle of Albion, and two days' sail from the sacred island of the Hibernians—a position answering closely enough to that of the Scilly Islands. The inhabitants of these islands were reported by Hamilco to be numerous, ingenious, and proud. They were fond of trade and commerce, but understood nothing of shipbuilding or navigation, and had no vessels except small canoes formed of skins and hides. The principal article which they supplied to the traders frequenting their coasts was tin—a metal that is still found, though in decreasing quantities, on the coasts of Cornwall, and which is scarcely found in any other part of Europe. The metal tin was known to the Greeks by the name of *kassiteros* as early as the time of Homer, and was no doubt purchased by them from the Phœnicians, who were the great merchants and navigators of ancient times, and whose voyages extended to the Indian Ocean in one direction, and to the west and north of Europe in another. It is not at all certain whether the earliest supplies of that valuable metal were obtained from the Indian or the British mines According to the illustrious Humboldt, the Greek name for the metal tin is derived from the Sanscrit name for the same metal, which, as he informs us, was *kastira* It is possible, and not improbable, that the Phœnicians of Tyre and Sidon, who made long voyages in the Indian Ocean at least a thousand years before the Christian era, may have found that metal in Banca or other islands of the Indian Archipelago, where it is still met with in large quantities, or in the great commercial *entrepôt* of Ceylon or Taprobane, where they traded with the merchants of the furthest East They may have brought the name as well as the metal into Europe from the East, even previous to the discovery of the tin mines of Cornwall. But wherever the name was first used, it was applied from a very early period to the British Islands, which were known as the Cassiterides, or tin-producing islands, long before they were known as the Islands of Britain *

It was also the enterprise of a commercial people that first brought the merchants and traders of the Greek colony of Massilia —the present Marseilles—who had settled on the southern coast of Gaul, upwards of 600 years before the Christian era, to the British Islands at a very early period These enterprizing traders carried on a large commerce with the interior of Gaul, and with the shores of the Atlantic Ocean, which they reached by ascending the river Rhone, and then descending the river Loire to the ocean They also used the Garonne and the Seine for the same purpose, and

* Heeren's Researches the African Nations, i 170 Heeren's Researches the Asiatic Nations, i. 318, 340. Humboldt's Cosmos, ii., note 128

after the conquest of Gaul by the Romans those rivers became the established mode of communication, from the shores of the Mediterranean to those of the Atlantic Ocean One of the earliest accounts that we possess of Britain is that given by Pytheas, a navigator of Massilia, who professed not only to have visited and travelled through Britain, but even to have carried his explorations as far as the northern island of Thule, which was probably one of the islands either of the Orkney or the Shetland group. According to the account of Pytheas, the Cassiterides, or Tin Islands—the Scilly Islands—were ten in number, and were all inhabited except one. The inhabitants traded with the Phœnicians of Cadiz, supplying them with tin, lead, and hides, and in return purchasing earthenware, vessels of brass, and salt. They subsisted chiefly on milk, and on the flesh of their cattle, and led wandering lives They wore long beards, and dressed in dark robes, fastened with leathern belts The geographer Strabo, who has preserved the account left by Pytheas, states that for many ages the Phœnicians of Cadiz had the whole trade with Britain in their own hands. They were so anxious to conceal it from other nations, that the captain of a Phœnician vessel, on its way to Britain, having been followed by a Roman galley for the purpose of observing his course, ran his own ship on shore, to avoid the danger of giving any information as to the best mode of reaching the British Islands, and afterwards received the value of his ship and cargo from the senate of Cadiz, as a well-deserving citizen who had sacrificed his property for the good of the state. But after the destruction of Tyre by Alexander the Great, the ruin of Carthage, and the conquest of Cadiz and all the Carthaginian possessions in Spain by the Romans, the trade with Britain seems to have fallen chiefly into the hands of the Greek colonists of Massilia, who were friends and allies of the Romans, and possessed the advantage of their protection and support.*

Expedition of Julius Cæsar to Britain.—About fifty years before the commencement of the Christian era, the conquest of the whole of Gaul by Julius Cæsar extended the frontiers of the Roman empire to the southern shore of the British Channel, and brought the Romans into immediate contact with the people of Britain. But the Roman armies did not reach the north-western districts of England until nearly 100 years after Julius Cæsar's expeditions into

* Strabonis Geographia, lib iii

Britain. In Cæsar's first expedition, B.C. 55, he remained in the island little more than three weeks—that is, from the 26th of August, according to the present computation, to the 20th of September, and at that time advanced only a few miles beyond the limits of his own encampment on the coast of Kent. In his second expedition, in the following year, Cæsar landed in the month of May, and remained about three months in Britain. During that period he marched through the part of Britain that now forms the counties of Kent and Surrey, led his army across the river Thames, and overran considerable part of the present counties of Middlesex, Hertford, and perhaps Essex. In this second expedition Cæsar captured the chief town in the dominions of Cassivelaunus, the most powerful prince in the southern part of the island, to whom the other British chiefs had committed the management of the war against the Roman invaders. After the capture of this city, which is supposed to have been the place afterwards known to the Romans as Verulamium, now known as St. Alban's, the British chiefs in the valley of the Thames, and to the south of that river, submitted to the Roman authority, and agreed to pay tribute to Cæsar.*

After the departure of Julius Cæsar from Britain, and the commencement of the civil wars of Cæsar and Pompey, and their successors, the influence of the Romans in Britain declined and became merely nominal. Some years after the accession of the Emperor Augustus, in the year 35 B.C., a demonstration was made against Britain. This was renewed ten years later, when the Britons, hearing of the intention of the emperor to invade Britain, sent an embassy to him, offering to acknowledge the Roman authority, and to pay the accustomed tribute. This was all that the emperor required, and, owing to his influence and prudence, Britain remained free from attack, not only during the reign of Augustus, but also during that of two of his successors.†

Strabo's Account of Britain.—It was during the peaceful reign of Augustus that Strabo—"that noble old geographer," as Humboldt calls him—visited Rome, and collected the valuable information that he has left us as to the productions of the British Islands, the commerce of the people with the Romans, the appearance and manners of the people, and the policy of Augustus towards Britain. He states that the greater part of the island is level, with much

* Dion Cassius, lib. xlix. and lii., sec. 38 and 22. C. C. Taciti de Vita Agricolæ, c. xiii.

† C. Julii Cæsaris, lib. v.

wood, but that there are several ranges of hills. It produces corn, cattle, gold, silver, iron, tin, and lead; and those articles, with slaves and dogs of matchless sagacity, form the principal exports. The imports, he says, are articles of small value, consisting of ivory, bits for horses, collars, amber, glass vessels, and personal ornaments The Britons, Strabo says, are taller than the Gauls, but their limbs are not so well knit. He states that, whilst at Rome, he saw several young Britons, who were half a foot taller than the tallest men there, but who were weak and not well formed. These were probably overgrown youths, taken to Rome to be shown. Yellow hair, he says, was not so common among the Britons as among the Gauls. In disposition the Britons resembled the Gauls. In manners they were ruder and simpler, some tribes not even knowing how to make cheese from the milk of their cattle, or to cultivate gardens, or to perform the more difficult operations of husbandry. With regard to their political relations with the Romans, Strabo says, that Julius Cæsar had twice passed over into Britain, but returned without effecting anything of much importance, or proceeding far into the island, on account of commotions amongst his own soldiers, the resistance of the barbarians, and the loss of many of his ships by the high tides of the ocean. Still, he defeated the Britons in two or three battles, and brought away hostages, slaves, and great booty. In the succeeding age several of the chiefs of Britain had joined themselves to the fortunes of Augustus, and had offered gifts in the Capitol; so that nearly the whole island had been rendered familiar to the Romans The Britons, Strabo adds, paid duties readily on articles imported into Britain from Gaul, and on articles exported from Britain into Gaul Hence it was not thought necessary to maintain garrisons in the island to collect other taxes. To do that would have required at least one legion, and some cavalry, and if an attempt should be made to collect a direct tribute of the inhabitants, the amount raised would scarcely defray the expenses of the garrison, and the existing duties would be diminished and their payment endangered by the commotions to which an attempt to enforce a direct tribute would give rise.*

The policy of the two next emperors, Tiberius and Caligula, did not differ materially from that of Augustus. Like him, they were satisfied with nominal submission. In the reign of Caligula, dissensions in the family of Cynobellinus (a British prince, more familiar

* Strabonis Geographia, lib iv

by Shakspeare's name of Cymbeline) induced Adminius, one of the sons of Cynobellinus, to pass over into Gaul with a small body of troops, and to throw himself on the protection of the emperor Caligula, who was at that time in Gaul, affected to consider this as a second conquest of Britain, and sent laurelled letters to Rome announcing the glorious event. These letters were ordered to be delivered to the consuls themselves, in the temple of Mars, in the presence of a full assembly of the senate.*

It was not until the reign of Caius Claudius, the fifth of the Cæsars, that the great military operations were commenced, which, after a long and desperate contest, brought the Roman armies to the banks of the Dee and the Mersey, the Ribble and the Lune, and established the power of Rome in the north-western district of England.

In the forty-third year of the Christian era, and nearly 100 years after Julius Cæsar's first expedition to Britain, the Emperor Claudius, having determined to make his name memorable by the conquest of Britain, commanded Aulus Plautius, a distinguished senator and general, to lead an army into Britain. This army consisted of four legions—the second, ninth, fourteenth, and twentieth. The last of these was afterwards established at Chester, where it has left innumerable marks of its presence. The pretext for this expedition was an appeal to the emperor by a British chief, named Bericus. He had been driven from his dominions by an insurrection of his own subjects, aided by Caractacus, or Cataracticus, and Tagodumnus, two of the sons of Cynobellinus.† Britain was at that time divided amongst upwards of thirty tribes,‡ who were generally at war with each other, and were only too ready to call in the Romans to assist them against their domestic enemies.

So little was known of Britain at that time, and so great a fear existed of passing into what was considered a new and unknown world, that the soldiers of Aulus Plautius rose in open mutiny when they were ordered to proceed into Britain. But at length they were induced to embark, and to pass over into the island.§

On the landing of the Roman army, the Britons, commanded by Caractacus and Tagodumnus, the sons of Cynobellinus, fell back behind a deep and wide river, probably the Medway, on the opposite bank of which they encamped, and prepared for battle.

* C. Suetonii de Vita Caligulæ, lib. iv. sec. 44. † Dion Cassius, lib. vi. sec. 10.
‡ C. Claudii Ptolomæi Geographiæ, lib. iv. § Dion Cassius, lib. vi. sec. 19 and 20.

The Romans immediately sent a body of Gaulish troops, trained to swim across wide rivers, to attack the Britons; but the Gauls were themselves attacked so fiercely by Caractacus that they were driven back almost into the river. Seeing the peril of the auxiliaries, Flavius Vespasian, afterwards the Roman emperor, and his son, Titus, afterwards the conqueror of Jerusalem, passed the river, and with difficulty held the position till nightfall In the course of the night the Roman army crossed the river, and on the following day it gained a victory over the Britons * The British army then retired across the Thames, and the Gauls, pursuing it hastily, were cut to pieces The Roman soldiers followed more deliberately, and Aulus Plautius, seeing that everything was ready for a great victory, sent to the emperor, to reap the laurels which it might have been too dangerous for a subject to gather for his own brow. Claudius immediately passed over into Britain, put himself at the head of the Roman army, and obtained another victory, which was followed by the capture of Camalodonum, the present Colchester After an absence of six months from Rome, Claudius returned there in triumph,† but the war in Britain continued to rage with undiminished fury. Aulus Plautius retained his command to A.D. 50. He succeeded at length in conquering the districts lying to the south of the river Thames, and some territory on the north bank, but did not advance beyond the valley of the Thames In the course of the obstinate conflicts in this part of Britain, Vespasian and Titus, his lieutenants, are said to have gained thirty battles and to have stormed twenty cities. But the spirit of Caractacus and the Britons was unbroken, and when Aulus Plautius left the island, that great chief was still in arms in South Wales and Herefordshire, the country of the Silures ‡

Aulus Plautius was recalled in the midst of an obstinate struggle, and was succeeded by Ostorius Scapula, another Roman general of great skill. Under his command the Romans pushed their conquests as far as the rivers Avon and Nene. To render their position more secure, Ostorius Scapula determined to form a line of forts or castles across the island, from the Avon to the Nene, as was afterwards done by other Roman commanders, from the Solway to the Tyne, and from the Forth to the Clyde. The attempt to carry out this plan produced an insurrection amongst the Iceni, who resided on the banks of the Nene and the Ouse, in the present counties of Norfolk

* Dion Cassius, lib vi. sec 19-23 † Dion Cassius, lib lx c 23. ‡ Dion Cassius, lib. lx. c 23

and Cambridge, and who saw themselves in danger of being inclosed by the proposed fortifications within the Roman lines, and of being thus cut off from communication with the other British tribes which were still resisting the Roman dominion They rose in great strength, and fortified themselves in a very strong position But the fortune of Rome prevailed · their position was stormed successfully, and they were compelled to receive the Roman yoke, although a native chief was left amongst them, with a shadow of authority.*

This great victory, joined to the earlier victories of Aulus Plautius, seems to have given the Romans influence beyond the limits of their immediate conquests. Amongst those who sought their friendship and support was Cartismandua, queen of the Brigantes—the people of ancient Lancashire and Yorkshire—a weak, selfish, and profligate woman, who seems to have been in everything the tool of the Romans. She apparently reigned in her own right, but scarcely ruled; for her husband, a chief named Venusius, was a resolute opponent of the Romans After various conflicts, he succeeded in expelling her from the Brigantine throne, though not until she had betrayed Caractacus, and done irreparable mischief to the independence of Britain.

Caractacus, having been driven back from the level country, had taken a position in the country of the Ordovices, the people of North Wales, who, like the Silures of South Wales, had made a determined resistance to the Roman armies The Roman commander, having secured his own rear by the slaughter of the Iceni, and having brought over Cartismandua and, as he supposed, her subjects to the Roman interest, advanced towards the position of Caractacus, through the country of the Cangi (probably a people of North Wales) He had laid waste the Cangian territory, and plundered the whole country, compelling the inhabitants to flee to the forests and mountains, and marching westward, "had almost reached the sea that lies opposite to Ireland," when he received the unwelcome news that the British party, in the country of the Brigantes, had risen against the adherents of Rome. This intelligence induced him to fall back, it being his policy not to push his conquests until he had secured his rear Such of the Brigantes as resisted him were cut to pieces; but a free pardon was granted to the rest. Ostorius Scapula then marched back to the borders of

* C C Taciti Annalium, lib xii. sec. 31. According to a note of Brotier, the learned editor of Tacitus, the line extended from Gloucester to Northampton See note, sec. 31, lib xii of Annalia

North Wales, to the country of the Ordovices, where Caractacus was defeated and compelled to flee to the country of the Brigantes There he was seized by Cartismandua, and delivered up to the Romans, who put him in chains, and sent him captive to Rome, where his noble demeanour excited admiration even amongst his enemies *

But the capture of Caractacus did not put an end to the resistance of the Britons A camp had been formed in the country of the Silures, and a chain of forts was about to be erected, when the Silures rose, and in a sudden attack killed the præfect of the camp, eight centurions, and the bravest of the soldiers Ostorius Scapula immediately hastened to their support with the light-armed cohorts, but was repulsed by the Silures. He then brought up the legionary soldiers, and after an obstinate battle repulsed the Britons, though with considerable loss. From that time the Britons kept him in constant alarm Repeated battles or skirmishes took place between detached parties roving in search of plunder. "They met," says Tacitus, "in sudden encounters, as chance directed or valour prompted, in the fens, in the forests, or in the narrow defiles, the men on some occasions led by their chiefs, and frequently without their knowledge, as resentment or the love of plunder incited their fury. Of all the Britons the Silures were the most determined They fought not merely with obstinacy, but with inveterate hatred. It seems the Roman general had declared that the very name of the Silures should be exterminated, like that of the Sigambri, formerly driven out of Germany and transplanted into Gaul. This threat reached the ears of the Silures, and roused their fiercest passions. Two auxiliary cohorts, whom the avarice of their officers had sent out in search of plunder, were surrounded by this daring people and made prisoners By a distribution of the spoils and captives the neighbouring states were drawn into the confederacy Ostorius Scapula at this time was worn out with anxiety He sank under fatigue, and died, to the great joy of the Britons, who saw a great and able commander, not indeed slain in battle, but overcome by the war." †

The death of Ostorius Scapula was followed by a general insurrection, headed by Venusius, the Brigantine, "who, since the loss of Caractacus, was the first in fame and military skill." In the course of this insurrection one of the legions, commanded by

* C C Taciti Annalium, lib. xii. sec. 32, 33, 37 † C C. Taciti Annalium, lib xii sec. 39

Manlius Valens, risked a battle, and suffered a defeat in the country of the Silures In the Brigantine territory, Cartismandua seized by stratagem the brother of Venusius and the rest of his kindred. The Brigantes were roused by this outrage, and "scorning to submit to a female government," with the flower of their youth attacked Cartismandua in the heart of her territories. But this attack was foreseen, and a detachment from the Roman army was sent to her assistance. After an engagement, in which the result was at first doubtful, victory inclined to the Romans. By this victory, and the success of the legion commanded by Cesius Nasica, the Romans barely held their ground in Britain during the administration of Didius Gallus and Veranius *

Caius Suetonius Paulinus, an officer of much greater talent but of a fierce and tyrannical character, was appointed the successor of Veranius. When he obtained the command the Romans had just sustained a severe defeat from the Silures, and the country of the Brigantes was again in the utmost confusion. In the hope of striking a great and decisive blow at the nationality as well as the religion of the Britons, the Roman general determined to attack the Druids, the priests and leaders of the British people, in their sacred and hitherto inaccessible island of Mona, the present Anglesea With this view he led the Roman armies across the plains of the Cornavii of Cheshire, forced the mountain passes of the Ordovices of North Wales, and suddenly appeared on the banks of the Menai Strait. Here the Druids received him with shouts of defiance, and kindled fires to consume the Roman prisoners. Suetonius Paulinus, however, found the means of crossing the strait, attacked the Druids, cut down the sacred groves, and consumed the Druids in their own fires †

At the time when Suetonius Paulinus appeared to be marching to the conquest of the whole of Britain, a great national insurrection broke out in the southern and eastern provinces, which the Romans had supposed to be effectually conquered. This insurrection was raised by Boadicea the queen of the Iceni, a people whom we have already spoken of, as the inhabitants of the present counties of Norfolk and Cambridge, in revenge for intolerable wrongs inflicted on herself, her daughters, and her people by the Romans The husband of Boadicea had been allowed to retain a show of power and some property after the insurrection of the Iceni, in the time

* C C Taciti Annalium, lib xii

† C C Taciti Annalium, lib xiv, c 20

of Ostorius Scapula. Dying about this time, he left his property equally between his two daughters and the Emperor Nero, hoping thus to secure friends for his family amongst the Romans. This disposition of his property did not, however, save it from plunder by the Romans, and the attempts to resist their violence brought the last cruelties and indignities on his wife and daughters. The queen, rendered desperate by these atrocious wrongs, called on the people to rise against the Romans, and was answered by a general insurrection throughout the whole of the southern and midland districts. Upwards of 120,000 men are said to have crowded round her standard. With this vast host she destroyed the Roman colony of Camalodunum or Colchester, routed the ninth Roman legion, under the command of Petilius Cerealis, seized upon London, which was already a great and flourishing city; and compelled Suetonius Paulinus to abandon all his conquests, and hastily to concentrate the whole of his troops, and to fight a great battle for existence. Unfortunately for the Britons, they had no general worthy of the name in command of their vast army, whilst the Romans, in Suetonius Paulinus, possessed a general of consummate skill. After drawing the Britons into a narrow position, in which their great numbers only rendered any successful movement impossible, the Roman commander suddenly attacked them and put them to the rout, slaughtering not less than 80,000 of their number. Boadicea died soon after, from grief, disease, or poison. From that disastrous day the whole of Britain south of the river Trent and east of the Severn, bowed without resistance to the Roman yoke. But although the insurrection of Boadicea was subdued, yet it had the effect of introducing a milder spirit into the administration of the southern part of Britain. It was felt at Rome that the insurrection had been caused by the cruelty of Suetonius Paulinus and his lieutenants. He was soon after recalled, and was succeeded by a governor of a milder spirit. Under his rule the southern province was tranquillized. This system, however, was not agreeable to the commanders of the Roman legions, especially to the commander of the most formidable of all—the Twentieth Legion. In consequence of these proceedings they raised an insurrection, and drove the governor out of the island.*

About the year 60 of the Christian era, the Britons, encouraged by the dissensions amongst the Roman commanders in Britain, and

* C. C. Taciti Annalium, lib. xiv., c. 31. Dion Cassius, lxii.

by the civil war which then distracted the empire, again rose in arms against them This insurrection was headed by Venusius the Brigantine, the husband of Cartismandua the queen of the Brigantes Of Venusius and Cartismandua the great historian Tacitus says —"To his own natural fierceness he added a rooted hatred of the Roman name He was besides the sworn enemy of Cartismandua the queen of the Brigantes, a woman of high descent, and flourishing in wealth and power In the reign of Claudius she had treacherously delivered up Caractacus to swell the pomp of the emperor's triumph From that time wealth had flowed in upon her with its usual consequences—luxury and dissipation She had banished Venusius, her husband, and taken Vellocatus, his armour-bearer, to her throne and bed. By this shameful act she lost her authority Convulsions shook her kingdom The discarded husband had the people on his side, whilst his rival had nothing but the passions and the cruelty of the queen Venusius was in a short time at the head of a powerful army. The subjects of the queen flocked to his standard, and a body of British auxiliaries joined him Cartismandua was reduced to the last extremities. She invoked the protection of the Romans, who sent some cohorts and squadrons of cavalry to her relief. Several battles ensued with various success. The queen was rescued from peril, but she lost her kingdom. Venusius wrested the sceptre from her hands, and the Romans were again involved in war."*

On the accession of the Emperor Vespasian to the imperial purple, Petilius Cerealis, who had been so signally defeated in the insurrection of Boadicea, but who had subsequently distinguished himself in the civil war which placed Vespasian on the throne, was appointed to succeed Vettius Bolanus as proprætor, and Julius Agricola was appointed to the command of the Twentieth Legion in Britain During his command Petilius Cerealis attacked the Brigantes, and though he did not subdue them, yet, according to the expression of Tacitus, "he fought many battles, and those not bloodless, and involved in war or acquired by victory great part of the country of the Brigantes"

On the recall of Petilius Cerealis, Julius Frontinus was appointed as his successor He directed the Roman arms against the Silures of South Wales, and claimed the honour of having conquered a tribe which had successfully resisted the Romans for thirty years.

* C. C. Taciti Historiarum, lib III, c. 45

Yet his victory was only partial: and when he was recalled the Ordovices, the people of North Wales, were in arms, and had recently destroyed a body of Roman cavalry stationed amongst them. At this time every thing threatened a general insurrection against the Romans in the northern and western districts of Britain.*

It was towards the close of the summer of the year 78, of the Christian era, that Julius Agricola was appointed to the government of Britain. He was a man worthy of a better age, uniting a great capacity for war, and for administration, with a generous temper and an enlightened intellect It was his singular good fortune to possess in his son-in-law, Cornelius Tacitus, an historian able to do justice to his character and his actions †

When Julius Agricola was appointed to the command of Britain, the southern and eastern parts of the island were completely subdued; but the Ordovices of North Wales were in arms against the Romans, the Brigantes were in commotion, and the countries now forming the highlands and lowlands of Scotland were untouched by the Roman arms

Agricola commenced his operations in the north-west district of Britain, probably the present counties of Cheshire and Lancashire, and perhaps at Deva or Chester, which was so long the head-quarters of his own legion From the valley of the Dee he advanced into the country of the Ordovices, forming the present counties of Denbigh, Carnarvon, and Flint. Here he defeated the native tribes in a great battle, and advancing rapidly to the Menai Straits, crossed them without ships, and again subdued the island, which Tacitus names Mona, and which is the Anglesea of modern times.‡ In his second campaign Julius Agricola advanced northward into the country of the Brigantes, that is, into the present counties of Lancaster and York. The force under his command is supposed to have consisted of about 30,000 infantry and 6000 cavalry Before involving himself in a country of mountains and forests, and amongst the changing waters and rushing tides of the estuaries, which so deeply indent the western side of the island, Agricola examined the country in person, especially the estuaries, of which his historian has left us a striking description "Nowhere," says Tacitus, "is the wonderful power of the ocean to be seen to a greater extent than here, driving back the waters of the rivers or forcibly carrying

* C C Taciti de Vita Agricolæ, c. 17

† C C Taciti de Vita Agricolæ, c 18

‡ C C. Taciti de Vita Agricolæ, c 18.

them away with its own Neither are its flowings and ebbings confined to the usual limit of land and shore, but it works and winds itself far into the land, and even forms bays in rocks and mountains, as if the same were its natural bed" After carefully exploring this unknown region in person, and forming camps in the strongest positions of the country, Agricola advanced, offering the inhabitants their choice of war or peace, keeping them in constant alarm by sudden attacks, but at the same time tendering them his own friendship and the clemency of the emperor. By this union of mildness and force he strengthened the Roman party, and gradually broke down the resistance of the Brigantes Thence many cities and states, which had hitherto refused to acknowledge the authority of Rome, were induced to lay aside their hostility, and to allow their cities to be surrounded with fortifications, and occupied by garrisons Amongst these were probably, not only Chester, but Manchester, Ribchester, and Lancaster, whose names proclaim that they were great Roman encampments Not satisfied with a mere military occupation, Agricola, like a statesman and a man of generous and enlightened mind, spent the succeeding winter in introducing the refinements of civilized life amongst the people whom he had subdued, urging them, both in public and private, to assume the Roman dress and manners, to educate their children in the Roman language and literature; to adorn their cities with temples, forums, and well-constructed houses, and even to cultivate the pleasures of the bath, of the portico, and other refinements of civilized life. Although the fixed idea of Roman policy, which was that of bending the whole world to submit to the authority of imperial Rome, had its full share in this advice, yet it was in the circumstances generous as well as wise It was also successful, the toga, the badge of the race, whom one of their greatest poets has described as—' rerum dominos, gentemque togatam"—began to be worn and honoured, the Brigantine and Cornavian youth aspired to speak the language of Cicero, not only for the purpose of conversation, but also for that of oratory; and the cities built on the banks of the Dee, the Irwell, the Mersey, the Ribble, and the Lune, were gradually adorned with all the requisites of civilized life Numerous memorials of these have been discovered in modern times, and are still discovered daily. It is not only as the conqueror, but as the civilizer of this district, the advocate and promoter of a policy of mildness and justice, and the generous eulogist of the temper and understandings of its earliest inhabitants, that the name of Julius Agricola is entitled to the respect of all succeeding generations *

In the following campaigns of Agricola he completed the conquest of the Brigantes, and carried the Roman arms to the foot of the Grampians Much of what Agricola conquered was afterwards lost, but the country of the Brigantes, and that of the Cornavii, including the whole of the present counties of Lancaster and Chester, remained a part of the Roman empire. About forty years after the retirement of Agricola from Britain the Emperor Hadrian formed a mound eighty miles long, extending from the mouth of the Solway to that of the Tyne A stone wall was afterwards built along the same line, which continued to be the boundary of the Roman empire, almost as long as the Romans remained in Britain

The result of the victories of Agricola and of his successors was to reduce the southern part of Britain to submission to the Roman dominion, and establish the Roman authority permanently, but less securely, in the northern districts of England and along the borders of Wales. But the countries north of Hadrian's wall, though sometimes overrun, were never conquered There is also reason to believe, from the fact that the Romans stationed and kept two of the three legions which formed the garrison of Britain on the frontiers of Wales, that the resistance to their authority continued in that mountainous region long after the age of Agricola York and the Roman wall in the north, and Chester and Caerleon in the west, were the four great military positions of the Romans in Britain during three hundred years, and we may very safely conclude that those were the points longest threatened by the unsubdued resistance of the Britons

The avowed objects of Roman policy were to conquer the world, and to hold it in submission. Hence the Roman government was altogether military, and more especially so in recently conquered countries in which the spirit of resistance was only partially subdued The task of governing the Roman provinces in Britain, and of resisting the inroads of the daring tribes which still held the unconquered parts of the island, was committed, as we have said, to three legions The Second Legion was stationed in South Wales, at Isca Silurum, afterwards Caerleon, on the river Usk, the Sixth was stationed at Eboracum or York,, and the Twentieth was stationed

* C C. Taciti de Vita Agricolæ, c 20

at Deva or Chester The Twentieth Legion, whose head-quarters were fixed at Chester for upwards of three hundred years, ruled the north-western district of Britain, occasionally assisted by the Sixth Legion, which seems at times to have furnished garrisons for Manchester and Ribchester The Twentieth Legion took part in constructing nearly all the great works that were formed by the Romans in Britain, and seems itself to have constructed nearly everything that was formed by the Romans in the present counties of Chester and Lancaster

Ptolemy's account of the Cornavii and the Brigantes—The earliest detailed account that has come down to us of that part of Britain which lies between Morecambe Bay on the north, and the river Dee on the south, and of the British tribes by whom it was inhabited, is contained in the Geography of Claudius Ptolemy, of Alexandria, which contains a brief account of the different regions of the ancient world, from India and the islands of the Indian Sea to Britain This work is supposed to have been written in the reign of the Roman Emperor Hadrian, and that part of it which relates to Britain is believed to have been composed after the year 130, in which year that emperor came over to Britain. He brought with him the Sixth Legion, and established it at Eboracum, or York, which from that time became the Roman military capital of Britain. Ptolemy mentions Eboracum, or York, as the head-quarters of the Sixth Legion, but he is silent as to the existence of the *vallum*, or mound of earth and turf, which Hadrian erected across the island, from the present Wallsend, near the mouth of the Tyne, to the mouth of the river Eden, near Carlisle Hence it has been conjectured that Ptolemy's information with regard to Britain was collected soon after the arrival of Hadrian in Britain, but before he had constructed the most celebrated work formed by him in the island At that time the greater part of the southern portion of Britain had been nominally subject to the Romans, from the time of Agricola's campaigns, which ended A D 80. But the northern parts even of the present kingdom of England had been very partially conquered, and Caledonia, the present Scotland, not at all. Many years after the death of Hadrian the struggle between the Romans and the Brigantes and other northern tribes of Britain was renewed with very doubtful results

At the time when the work of Ptolemy was composed the southern part of Britain was a Roman province, but the native inhabitants still formed upwards of thirty different tribes or clans, and the greater part of the territory was known by their names. The banks of the river Dee, now forming the county of Chester, were at that time inhabited by a British tribe named the Cornavii, whose territory extended northward to the river Mersey, and ended at the present Runcorn, the promontory of the Cornavii. The territory of the Brigantes had for its southern boundary the river Mersey on the western side of the island, and the Ouse and Humber on the eastern

In the most flourishing period of the Cornavian tribe its territory is supposed to have extended from the river Dee to the mouth of the river Severn, and to have included the greater part of the counties of Cheshire, Shropshire, Stafford, and Worcester. Deva, or the city of the Dee, the present Chester, is mentioned by Ptolemy as the chief town of the Cornavian tribe, and the head-quarters of the Twentieth Roman Legion The territory of this ancient British tribe formed one of the richest portions of Britain. The grassy plains lying between the Mersey, the Dee, the Trent, and the Severn, afforded pasture for the herds of cattle which formed the chief wealth of the ancient Britons, the virgin soil yielded grain in abundance, with slight cultivation, the woods and forests abounded with game, the streams and rivers, and the adjoining seas, supplied all the most valuable kinds of fresh and salt water fish, numerous springs of brine furnished inexhaustible supplies of salt for home use and for commerce, and iron, copper, lead, and silver, were found in the hills and mountains of the Cangi, a subdivision of the Cornavian tribe. But their territory was almost everywhere level, and easily accessible to the Roman soldiers, and the Romans, having once established the head-quarters of the Twentieth Legion at Chester, or, as it was then called, Deva or Devana, seem to have held that position for upwards of 300 years.

But even these, which are amongst the more level parts of Britain, do not appear to have been conquered without a most determined resistance on the part of the inhabitants After so many hundred years we can still trace some of the camps of the ancient Britons, on the most commanding points of the Cornavian territory. One of the strongest of these camps stands on the brow of a hill about 500 feet high, in the range of the Peckforton hills, a chain of heights that extends from Beeston castle to the river

Dee. The hill on which this fortress was erected now bears the name of Bickerton Hill, and the fortress is called the Maiden castle. One front faces the plain of Chester, and is protected on that side by precipitous rocks, more than 100 feet high The rear and sides of the camp are defended by a double line of earthworks of a semicircular form, which are still very strongly marked, though overgrown by heath and gorse. The breadth of the camp from north to south is about 140 yards, the thickness of the rampart is eight yards; the width of the ditch that separates the inner from an outer line of defence is fifteen yards; and the only entrance into the camp is through a narrow passage near to the precipice, guarded by strong earthworks The view from the Maiden castle extends over a large part of the territory of the ancient Cornavii Northward it reaches to the estuaries of the Mersey and the Dee, and to the hills of Lancashire beyond the former; eastward it extends to the hills that divide Cheshire from Derbyshire, westward it reaches to the most distant ranges of the Denbighshire mountains, southward it includes Shropshire and the highest points of Worcestershire and Herefordshire Similar fortifications of greater extent existed on the summits of the Wrekin and the Clee hills of Shropshire, both of which are very conspicuous from the ramparts of the Maiden castle There are also several other British camps on different parts of the Cheshire hills There is one 300 yards in breadth, and covering nine acres of ground, in Delamere Forest, a little to the south of the village of Kelsall. Near this camp, and further within the forest, are seven ancient mounds, known as the "Seven Lows," or hills, which are supposed to indicate the tombs of British warriors. There are five other tumuli at Twemlow, in the same neighbourhood. The remains of a third camp are found at the northern extremity of Delamere Forest, at the point where the steep rocks of Helsby hill rise above the river Mersey This may have served as a place of refuge against the pirates who in early times infested the neighbouring seas, or against the attacks of the hostile tribes that then inhabited the northern bank of the Mersey. The promontory on which this camp at Helsby stands commands an extensive and beautiful view of the shores and the entrance to the Mersey, and of the plains and the distant hills of Lancashire One of the strongest of these ancient entrenchments, now known by the name of Buckton castle, is situated amongst the wild ravines at the north-eastern extremity of Cheshire, between Staleybridge and Saddleworth It is protected on one side by a precipice, on the others by ditches and ramparts of earth, and it commands a magnificent view, extending on one side far over the Cheshire plain, and on the other to the summits of the Yorkshire and the Lancashire hills

The mountains of Lancashire, and the valleys which they divide, were inhabited at the time of the Roman conquest by a most powerful British tribe, named the Brigantes, of whom we have already had occasion to speak Their territory extended across the island, and included the whole of the north of England from the Mersey and the Humber to the Tweed and the Solway, and perhaps even further, as an image dedicated to the goddess Brigantia has been found as far north as Annandale, in Scotland The Brigantes are more frequently mentioned by Greek and Roman writers than any other British tribe, and they seem to have maintained a long and desperate struggle with the Romans Seneca, in one of his poems, claims for the Emperor Claudius (who never approached to within 200 miles of their territory) the honour of having conquered the azure-armed Brigantes Juvenal proposes to a needy centurion to make his fortune by plundering the castles of the Brigantes Tacitus speaks of them as the most numerous of the tribes of Britain, and describes the intrigues of their queen, Cartismandua, with the Romans, and the wars of their great chief, Venusius Ptolemy, in his Geography, mentions that their territory extended from sea to sea, and gives the names of ten of their principal towns, of which Eboracum, or York, and Ribodunum, or Ribchester, appear to have been the most important After being partially subdued by the Romans, they appear to have risen again; and in the time of the Emperor Antoninus Pius they not only expelled the Romans from their territory for a time, but overran great part of the adjacent territories, where the Romans were more firmly established

The country inhabited by the Brigantes was naturally much wilder and more mountainous than that inhabited by the Cornavii, and gave greater facilities for resisting the attacks of an invading army. A chain of hills and mountains, rising to the height of from 1500 to 2500 feet, intersected the Brigantine territory from north to south, sending out numerous branches to the east and west At the base of these hills there were great forests and extensive swamps, stretching nearly to the German Ocean on one side, and to the Irish Sea on the other. The principal approaches into the

Brigantine territory on the east were by way of Danum, the present Doncaster, and by Warrington and Mamucium or Mancunium, the present Manchester, on the western side of the hills These are the points at which the Romans formed their great roads from the southern parts of Britain to the *vallum*, or fortification, extending across the island from the Tyne to the Solway.

The only Brigantine town situated within the limits of the present county of Lancaster that is mentioned by Ptolemy, in his account of the Brigantine territory, is Rigodunum, or more properly Ribodunum, the fortress on the Ribble, the memory of which is preserved by the Roman station of Ribchester. This ancient British town seems to have been one of the most flourishing places in this district. It stood on the banks of a fine river, in a fertile country, and on the main line of communication across the northern part of the island, from the port of the Setantii on the Irish Sea, and the estuaries of the Ribble and the Wyre, to the German Ocean and the estuary of the Humber. Either the Ribble, the Wyre, or the Lune is spoken of by Ptolemy as the Setantian port; and the same geographer gives a sufficiently clear description of the bays and harbours along the coasts of Lancashire and Cheshire, from Morecambe Bay to the entrance of the Dee, to show that the coast was tolerably well known He describes the river Ribble and its estuary by the name of the Belisama, from which it would appear as if he supposed that there was some connection between the name of the stream and that of Baal or Belisama, who were amongst the fancied deities of the Phœnicians, the earliest visitors to Britain. It has been thought that other traces of that great people are found in the names of some of the promontories, especially that of Belinus, now the Land's End of Cornwall. A number of traditions connected with the worship of the sun, known to the Syrians as Baal, also exist amongst the Celtic population of Great Britain and Ireland

The result of recent researches into the ancient languages of Britain, has induced some of the ablest linguists of modern times to conclude that the early inhabitants of these islands belonged to what is now called the great Indo-European family of nations. This argument is fully traced in Dr Prichard's work on the eastern origin of the Celtic nations, as proved by comparisons of their dialects with the Sanscrit, Greek, Latin, and Teutonic languages, and in other works of great authority Although the descendants of the people who spoke that ancient language in Britain have either been driven back into the mountains, after centuries of determined resistance, or have been so completely blended with the Angles, Saxons, and Danes, as to render it impossible to trace the extent of their influence, this at least is certain, that most of the mountains, the rivers, the bays, and the wastes of Lancashire and Cheshire still bear their original Celtic appellations The names of our most ancient cities and towns, such as Lancaster, Ribchester, and Manchester, are also partly Celtic and partly Roman. There are also mingled with the language of ordinary life numerous words of Celtic origin, which still bear testimony to the influence which the Celtic race has had, in forming both the language and the character of the English inhabitants of this island.

The Romans, having at length obtained possession of the northern districts of what we now call England, proceeded to render their dominion firm and lasting, by constructing military roads, by means of which the territories of the Brigantes and the Cornavii, as well as those of the other tribes of Britain, were united with the rest of the Roman empire. The remains of these roads are still to be traced in Lancashire and Cheshire, and many of them are so clear that they are laid down on the Ordnance maps of the two counties, from surveys made only a few years ago

Roman Roads in Lancashire and Cheshire.—In order to give the legions stationed at York, Chester, and along the Roman wall, security in their position at the extremity of the empire, amidst a disaffected population, and in the face of an active enemy, it was necessary that they should have a secure line of communication with each other, and with the Roman troops in other parts of Britain, as well as with the Roman legions in Gaul, and with Rome, the capital of the empire. The most important military positions in Britain in the eyes of the Romans were—first, the ports of Rutupium (Sandwich), and Dubris (Dover), on the coast of Kent, by means of which they communicated with Gaul and Rome, second, London, where they crossed the Thames, and where all the principal military roads in Britain united, third, the head-quarters of the three Roman legions in Britain, namely, those of the Second Legion at Isca Silurum, or Caerleon, on the river Usk, in Monmouthshire, a few miles above the present town of Newport, those of the Twentieth Legion at Chester, and those of the Sixth Legion at York, and fourth, the line of the vallum, or military wall, from the mouth of the Solway to the Tyne, which formed the northern boundary of the empire In addition to these four points, from which the whole military system of Britain was directed, there were also numerous fortified camps, which were of importance in carrying out the system of defence. Amongst these were nearly all the towns and cities that still bear the name of "caster" or "chester" in connection with some prefix of British origin, as Lancaster, Ribchester, Manchester, and Chester, as well as some places which have no such mark, as Exeter, Norwich, Lincoln, and York. All these were connected with each other, with London, and with the ports of Rutupium and Dubris, by means of military roads, constructed with great skill, and maintained with constant labour, either of the Roman soldiers or of the British people

The great line of Roman road, nearly 500 miles in length, which is described in the Itinerary of Antoninus,* in the second Iter, was the road by which the north-western division of England was connected with London and Gaul, in the south, with the head-quarters of the Sixth Legion at York, on the east; and with the line of the Roman wall near Carlisle, and at Wallsend, near Newcastle, on the north The general course of this road may still be pretty well traced through the counties of Middlesex, Hertford, Bedford, Northampton, Warwick, and Stafford, into Cheshire. It followed a line not very different from the present line of the London and North Western railway, and like that railway, sent out a branch line into Shropshire to Uriconium at the foot of the Wrekin, which branch was continued into the valley of the Severn in one direction, and into that of the Dee in another The line thus described reached Deva, or Chester, by way of Mediolanum and of Bovium. From Deva it ran eastward across the present county of Chester by way of Condate—a station twenty miles from Chester and eighteen from Mamucium or Mancunium—to Mamucium, the present Manchester Leaving that city it crossed the hills into what we now call Yorkshire, and ran by way of Cambodunum, a station in the neighbourhood of Huddersfield and Halifax, and by Calcaria, the present Tadcaster, to York, then the head-quarters of the Sixth Legion, and the military capital of Britain. From York the line of road described in the second Iter ran due north to Cataractonium, a place supposed to be the present Catterick bridge, near Richmond, in Swaledale. Thence it turned west by north, and so continued its course through the deep valleys and over the lofty mountains of York-

* Monumenta Historica Britannica, xxi

shire, Westmoreland, Cumberland, and Durham, until it reached the Roman wall, near the present city of Carlisle, and also the mouth of the Tyne

On comparing the lines of road described in the other Iters of Antoninus, with the great line of communication described in the second Iter, it will be found that several of them joined in with it at different points Thus the road described in the tenth Iter joined that described in the second at Mediolanum, and ran by Condate and Mamucium northward through Lancashire and Westmoreland to Galava, probably the present Keswick, where it again came within a short distance of the line described in the second Iter. The line described in the eleventh Iter joined that described in the second at Chester, and ran through North Wales to the Menai Strait, crossing the vale of Clwyd at Vara, now Bodvari, and the vale of Conway at Conovium On connecting these and the other Iters with the great line laid down in the second, it will be found, that the ancient inhabitants of Lancashire and Cheshire had pretty nearly as good means of communication with all parts of Britain, by the roads constructed by the Romans, as they had by the modern high roads, previous to the introduction of railways

In addition to the lines of road which are described in the Itinerary of Antoninus, other lines have been traced in the counties of Chester and Lancaster The following are the principal lines in the two counties, including as well those mentioned in Antoninus, as those discovered by modern research

At least five lines of road ran from Chester in various directions Amongst them were the following:—A Roman road ran from Chester up the valley of the Dee This road has been traced in a direct line across the river Dee, below the Old bridge, past Edgar's Cave, along the Eaton road, across the ford at Aldford in a direct line to Stocklach, beyond which place it reached Bangor, afterwards celebrated in the history of the early British church.* From Bangor this road was continued into the valley of the Severn, probably at Uriconium, and joined the roads which ran along the borders of Wales, as well as the main road from Rutupium, in Kent, to the vallum or wall on the Caledonian border. Another Roman road, part of which is still marked on the Ordnance Map, connected the city of Chester, by a shorter route, with the great

* Journal of Architectural, Archæological, and Historic Society of Chester, &c., p 189 Observations by the Rev. W H Massie, on the Site of Bangor Monachorum.

line of road from the north to the south of Britain. This road crossed the fertile plain of Chester, ran through the pass at Beeston, where it has been recently traced under the rocks on which the castle stands, and joined the great road from north to south, either at Kinderton, near Middlewich, or at some point not very distant from that great centre of communication. A third road ran from Chester across the range of hills, afterwards and still known as Delamere Forest, to the valley of the Weaver near Northwich, where it fell in with the main road from north to south. From Chester, to the rise at the pass of Kelsall, the modern road is carried either along the line of this road or close to it. Near Tarven the Roman road is still used as the existing highway, for a distance of four miles, running into it from the direction of Street farm. It rises into the forest west of Kelsall.* Thence it runs towards Eddisbury Hill, a magnificent military position fortified at a later period by Ethelfleda, the daughter of Alfred the Great. Here the road has the appearance of two rather high embankments, from between which the gravel way has been removed. In one part, sixty or seventy yards long, where the new red sandstone crops out, there are two deep ruts, with the horse track between them, whilst the soft rock has been cut down on each side, so as clearly to define the breadth of the road. Beyond Eddisbury Hill the road is nine or ten yards wide, with a well-marked crown, and shallow ditches on each side, and traces of mounds or cops beyond them. Gravel is spread over the surface, and it is said by the foresters, that there is a strong bed of solid gravel eighteen inches deep below. The road descends to the corner of the forest inclosures, where it is planted over, and runs in a right line towards Northwich, near which place it falls in with the great Roman road that ran through Cheshire and Lancashire from north to south. Another road, marked in the Ordnance Map through the greater part of its course, ran directly from Chester to the present town of Warrington, along the line of hills which overlooks the river Mersey. Here it fell in with the western branch of the two great roads, which intersected Cheshire and Lancashire from the valley of the Weaver to the banks of the Lune.

By means of these numerous branch roads, the Roman garrison of Chester communicated easily, rapidly, and in every direction

* Transactions of the Lancashire and Cheshire Historic Society. Paper "On the Cheshire Watling Street, and Traces of Roman Occupation in Lancashire and Cheshire," by John Robson, Esq., vol. iii., p. 70.

with the great north-western road, and had the shortest possible lines of communication with York, and with the north-eastern districts of Britain and the Roman wall.

Another road, following an opposite direction, ran from Deva or Chester through the midst of North Wales to the Menai Straits This is the road described in the eleventh Iter of Antoninus The stations beyond Chester were Vara, the present Bodvari, in the valley of the Clwyd, and Conovium, supposed to be the present Caer-Hen, on the banks of the Conway By means of this road, and the road up the valley of the Dee, the Twentieth Legion ruled the country of the Ordovices. It had also a strong position at, and no doubt a good line of communication with Caerguerle, in the rocky pass which connects the vale of Gresford with the valley of the Alyn and the ancient Roman fortress at Mold

Kinderton, near Middlewich, was another great centre of communication in the present county of Chester From this point roads have been traced in six different directions, running north, south, east, and west. One line ran to Chester, another towards Derbyshire, and one if not two towards Shropshire; whilst a line of road, the most important of all, entered Kinderton from the direction of Chesterton near Newcastle-under-Lyne, in Staffordshire, and ran almost due north through the counties of Chester and Lancaster, and so onward to the Roman wall.

The learned historian of Cheshire, Dr. Ormerod, states, in a communication to the Historic Society of Lancashire and Cheshire, that the line of the Roman road from Chesterton to Kinderton, which had not been examined at the time when he published his great work, has since been fully investigated. The gravel bank of the road was found in a course of excavations at Brindley Moor farm, within the estate of Dr Latham, to the east of Bradwall Hall farm, and about four miles south of Kinderton. Upwards of 600 Roman denarii were also discovered near the edge of Bradwall township.*

The position of Kinderton was carefully examined in the year 1849, by the venerable archdeacon Wood, and other members of the Archæological Society of Chester. Amongst other things they found there a great plateau or roadway fifty yards wide, with six

* Transactions of the Historic Society of Lancashire and Cheshire Communication by Dr G Ormerod, vol ii p 218.

roads branching from it in different directions.* The road running northward from this point towards Northwich is named King or Kind Street. When Camden visited this part of England in the reign of Queen Elizabeth this road was extremely conspicuous, on account of its elevation and the nature of its materials, which were different from any found in that part of Cheshire.† In the year 1762 the whole line of road from Kinderton to Manchester was carefully examined by Mr. Thomas Percival, who published an interesting account of it in the first volume of the Archæologia. The line runs northward by Ravenscroft bridge, where it crosses the Dane, to Broken Cross, near Northwich.

Near Northwich this road divides into two branches, one of which runs to Manchester, by way of Dunham Massey, and then northward to the valley of the Lune, by way of Bury, Blackburn, and Ribchester; the other also runs northward, but by way of Stretton, Warrington, Wigan, and Preston, to Lancaster.

The line of the Roman road from near Northwich to Manchester, is the same as that of the present highway, with the exception of a divergence at the Saxon borough of Altringham. It crosses the Mersey at Stretford, and proceeds to the ancient Castle-field at Manchester, near the point where the river Medlock falls into the Irwell.

From Manchester to the northern limits of the county of Lancaster, this ancient highway of the Romans was examined with extraordinary care, at the time of the Ordnance survey, by the late John Just, of the grammar-school, Bury. The result of his labours is seen in the Ordnance Map of that part of England, and will be found described in three learned and interesting papers, two of them contained in the Memoirs of the Manchester Philosophical and Literary Society, and the third in the Papers and Proceedings of the Historic Society of Lancashire and Cheshire.‡ In the following sketch of this road we take that learned and sagacious antiquary as our guide.

* Journal of the Architectural, Archæological, and Historic Society of Cheshire, Chester, and the neighbourhood, p. 45. Paper "On the probability that Kinderton, near Middlewich, is the Condate of the Roman Itineraries," by the Venerable Isaac Wood, Archdeacon of Chester. Read at the Meeting of the Society, May 6, 1850.

† Camden's Britannia, p. 486.

‡ Memoirs of the Manchester Philosophical Society, Second Series, vol. vi. p. 409. Paper entitled "An Essay on the Roman Road in the vicinity of Bury, Lancashire," by Mr. John Just, corresponding member; a second paper, in the Memoirs of the Manchester Philosophical Society, entitled "On the Roman Military Road between Manchester and Ribchester," by John Just, Esq., corresponding member of the Society; and a third paper, in the Transactions of the Historic Society of Lancashire and Cheshire, entitled "On the Roman Roads in Lancashire, with a particular account of the Tenth Iter of Antoninus," by the same author.

This road, as we have already stated, enters Lancashire at the old ford over the Mersey at Stretford, or the ford of the stratum or street. This was the boundary of the Roman provinces of Flavia Cæsariensis and Maxima Cæsariensis, afterwards of the Saxon kingdoms of Mercia and Northumberland, as it is now the boundary of the counties of Lancaster and Chester. The present road through Stretford lies on the site of the old Roman road. In constructing the modern city of Manchester, with its thousands of streets and hundreds of thousands of inhabitants, all traces of the ancient road have been swept away on the surface of the ground; but the gravel of the road was found, six feet below the present level, in digging a drain, so recently as the year 1821.

This road left the Castle-field, Manchester, either upon or parallel to the road to Strangways (a name which is derived from the road), and followed the new line of road thence to Bury. There the line of the Roman road again corresponds with that of the modern road at Prestwich. Hence it ran on, passing the Dales, and crossing the river Irwell. The remains of the road are frequent and conspicuous in the parish of Radcliffe, it rises at Offyside, passes through Edgeworth, and again rises to the heights at Black-snape, where it falls into the same line as the public road between Bury and Blackburn. Near Blackburn, as near almost all large and populous towns, the traces of the road are lost amidst buildings, streets, and gardens. They are soon found again towards Rivedge, and may there be traced to the high grounds at Ramsgreave. From Ramsgreave the road may be seen stretching down to the Ribble, near Ribchester, and beyond that river to the limits of the horizon on the top of Longridge Fell. A line of fences marks its course to the Ribble, and a road, and the green lane on Longridge, its direction beyond the river. Between Ramsgreave and the Ribble there are places where the road is "nearly as perfect as when the last Roman soldier marched homeward from the spot." Close to the Ribble the road makes an angle to the ford below the bridge, which leads from Walton-le-Dale to Ribchester. "Ribchester," says Mr Just, "an undoubted and extensive Roman station—a mine of antiquities—is more than half a mile lower down the stream than where the Romans crossed it."

Crossing the Ribble the road re-appears at Stony Gate, and fine remains of it are found to the summit of Longridge Fell. From the top of Longridge Fell, the valley of the Hodder is seen in front

"Perhaps," says Mr. Just, "at this point, as extensive a bird's-eye view of a Roman road may be seen as the north of England contains. Backward it may be seen to Ramsgreave, four or five miles distant; forward to Browsholme heights, an equal or greater distance So true were the Romans in their method of laying out their lines of military road, that, with the exception of a very slight angle indeed on the summit of Blacksnape, even the accuracy of the Ordnance survey could not detect a deviation from a perfectly straight line, between this place and Manchester, a distance approaching thirty miles. Amongst the mountains seen hence in the distance, the top of Penygent stands most prominent, with the eye fixed upon its summit, the whole line of Roman road seems to stretch directly towards it, as if it had been the object aimed at They appear hence to have had some striking object in the distance to direct them On Browsholme height Penygent disappears from the horizon, and Ingleborough starts up Again an angle is made on the top of the hill, and the line of the road proceeds straight from it towards Ingleborough, on the horizon Beyond the Hodder to the foot of Croasdale a continuous ridge marks the course of the road It ascends the height of Croasdale, care being taken that it shall no where approach the steep part of the mountain, from which troops on the march could be assailed with stones rolled upon them, or with missiles From Croasdale the road is continued above Whitingdale, until it passes the heights of Botton Head Fell, the present road from Slaidburn to Hornby occupying the site the whole way.

Towards the foot of Botton Fell the road is again very conspicuous, and is known as "the Roman road" to the inhabitants. On the high ground on the Hill estate at Tatham some parts of the road are still almost perfect. Here it deviated from the usual straight line, on account of the steep banks of the river Wenning On the highest point of the Hill estate an angle is formed, to gain the ford at Bentham bridge Beyond the Wenning the road is still known as the Roman road The line is less clear between the Wenning and the Greta, but north of the Greta the road is most conspicuous Here the road turns northward, "and forming, across the flat grounds at Collingholme, as fine a specimen of remains as can be found in the whole Iter, it passes into an old road leading to Overtown, leaving the Roman station at Overborough, nearly a mile to the west" After passing Leck Brook it joins the long level of the high road from Kirkby-Lonsdale, to Ingleton; and having there crossed the boundary between Lancashire and Westmoreland, stretches along Wandale's lane in Casterton, straight up the vale of the Lune.

The line of road formed by the Romans from the valley of the Weaver, near Northwich, to the valley of the Lune at Lancaster, passed by Stretton, Warrington, Winwick, Newton in Makerfield, Haydock, Wigan, Preston, Garstang, and Ashton It has been traced at numerous points, by very careful and competent observers, and in the neighbourhood of Lancaster two of the Roman milestones have been found, still bearing the names of the emperors in whose reign it was either formed or reconstructed

Between Northwich and Warrington this line of road is best seen at Stretton, a place whose name is evidently taken from the circumstance that a Roman road—one of the *strata viarum* of Lucretius—ran in that direction In the neighbourhood of Stretton and Appleton the course and construction of the road have been very carefully traced by Mr. Lyon, of Appleton Hall, and the Rev. Mr Greenall, of Stretton The road is eighteen feet wide at this point, as is stated in an inscription by the roadside, at the point where the modern road runs close to the road made by the Romans. It is here composed chiefly of gravel * The course of the road from Stretton to the banks of the Mersey was traced from field to field in the year 1849 by Dr. Hume, of Liverpool, Mr Lyon, of Appleton, Mr Robson, Mr. Beamont, and Dr Kendrick, of Warrington, and other members of the Historical Society of Lancashire and Cheshire †

In the grounds adjoining Appleton Hall, where a section of the road had been laid open, it was found to be nineteen and a half feet in breadth. A little further north it is seen at the top of a stone quarry, showing itself in the face of a deep cutting in the rock Proceeding towards Warrington, two sections of the road were laid bare, one twenty and the other fifteen feet wide. At the Townfield, where the road had been carefully examined so early as the year 1831, by Mr Beamont and Mr. Robson, of Warrington, the road was twelve or fourteen yards wide; and in a field, named the Stony Lunt, another road was discovered branching off from the main line, and running westward, nearly parallel with the present highway to

* Communication by J Robson, Esq, in Transactions of the Historic Society of Lancashire and Cheshire, vol ii p. 77

† Notes on a Roman Road near Warrington, by the Rev A Hume, LL.D, F S A, in Transactions of the Historic Society of Lancashire and Cheshire, vol. ii p 27

Chester This is no doubt the point of junction of the line of road from Chester to Warrington, already described, and the course of which, across the hills that skirt the southern bank of the Mersey, is laid down in the Ordnance Map* At Wilderspool, opposite to Warrington, the road is composed of a broad foundation of ashlar stones, with a bed of gravel on the top From this point it runs straight towards the Mersey, which it passed by a ford.

After crossing the river Mersey, the road is again found at the top of the Orford avenue, running northward.† Its course was traced from Warrington to Wigan by the late Rev. Edmund Sibson, of Ashton in Makerfield,‡ and the part of it near Warrington has been traced with great care by Mr Robson, of Warrington

Little remains of the road between Wigan and the valley of the Ribble—a circumstance easily accounted for by the scarcity of road-making materials in this part of Lancashire; a fact which has no doubt caused the stone and gravel of the Roman road to be applied to the constructing or repairing of the modern roads of the district.

When Sir William Dugdale, and, a few years later, when Dr. Kuerden, the earliest of Lancashire antiquaries, visited the neighbourhood of Preston, in the reign of Charles II, the line of the Roman road from the Ribble to the Lune was easily traceable across Fulwood Moor, in the direction of Broughton and Garstang The "rampire," or raised line of the road, was at that time "conspicuous to the observations of many learned men, as well as vulgar people"—to adopt the language of Dr Kuerden This road has been recently traced by Mr Hardwick, of Preston, and is described by him in an interesting paper in the Transactions of the Historic Society of Lancashire and Cheshire.§ He states that he found a large fragment of the ancient road, now used as a private road, to the south of the Ribble This is described in the Ordnance Map as Mainway Gate On the north side of the river, opposite the ford where the road is supposed to have crossed, a zigzag indentation on the face of the bank may still be seen. From this point Mr. Hardwick supposes that the road passed in a straight line over the end of Church Street to Preston Moor. A small portion of the

* See Ordnance Map of Cheshire

† Historical and Antiquarian Notes on Warrington and its Neighbourhood, by John Robson, Esq, in Transactions of Historic Society of Lancashire and Cheshire, vol iv p. 203

‡ Baines' History of Lancashire, vol iii. p 574

§ On the Roman Remains recently Discovered at Walton-le-Dale, Preston, by Charles Hardwick, Esq, in Transactions of Historic Society of Lancashire and Cheshire, vol viii p 127 agger may still be seen on the moor, where the land slopes towards the brook. This road, running from south to north, was here intersected by another road running from west to east, and hence ran northward, by way of Broughton and Garstang, to Lancaster.

Striking memorials of this road have been found in the neighbourhood of Lancaster, in the form of two "milliaria," or milestones, which formerly directed travellers in their course upon the road Both these milliaria bear the name of the Emperor Philip, in whose reign they were doubtless erected * One of them was turned up by the plough in the township of Ashton, near Lancaster, the other was found at Borough, south of that place, in cutting the bed of the canal. As the Emperor Philip murdered his predecessor, Gordian the younger, in the year 244, and was himself murdered in the year 249, we may fix the date at which the western branch of the Roman road through Lancashire and Cheshire was either formed or extensively repaired, at that time. We are also able to fix a date to the eastern branch of the road, so ably described by Mr. Just Another Roman milestone, of a much earlier date, was found some years ago at Caton, near Lancaster † It had been washed down the brook called Artlebeck, no doubt, from the Roman road which ran along the higher grounds. This milestone bears the much more illustrious name of the Emperor Hadrian. As his reign commenced in the year 117, and ended in the year 138, we may fix the date of this first and greatest of the works formed by the Romans in Lancashire and Cheshire at that time, and may assign the honour of it to this emperor, who claimed, on one of his coins, to be the restorer of the Roman dominion in Britain, and who certainly did much to preserve it, by the magnificent works which he caused to be constructed

It is worthy of notice, that the older and more perfect line of road formed by Hadrian was in the course of time superseded, as the main line of communication from north to south, by the line of road formed or improved in the time of the Emperor Philip This was the natural result of a transition from war to peace The north of Britain was not tranquillized, and scarcely conquered, in the time of Hadrian, for in a subsequent reign, that of Antoninus Pius, between the years 138 and 161, the Brigantes, the original

* Whitaker's History of Richmondshire, vol. ii pp. 211–213

† Whitaker's History of Richmondshire, vol ii p 215, and the History and Antiquities of Lancaster, by the Rev Robert Simpson, M A., p 119

inhabitants of what we call the North of England, were not only in insurrection, but had overrun a considerable portion of the Roman province lying to the south of the Mersey and the Humber In this state of things the roads were constructed for purely military purposes, and were carried through the mountainous districts, where the means of resistance were the most formidable, with a view of keeping the people in subjection In the interval of 100 years, between the death of Hadrian and the accession of Philip, the Roman dominion had become firmly established, and the wants of peaceful industry had superseded the stern requirements of war. Hence the easiest and shortest line of communication was chosen, and thus the line from Lancaster, by way of Preston, Wigan, and Warrington, became, what it has long been and still is, the chief line of communication from north to south The railway from Lancaster to Warrington now follows this line, with very trifling deviations.

In addition to the lines of road intersecting the present county of Lancaster from north to south, was a line of road which crossed that county from west to east, running from the river Wyre, near the present town of Poulton in the Fylde, to the eastern border of Lancashire at Chadburn, from which point it was continued to Olicana or Ilkley in Yorkshire, to Eboracum or York, and ultimately to the Humber, thus forming a line of road from the Irish sea to the German Ocean

At the time of the Ordnance survey this line of road was very carefully examined by Mr Just, of Bury, and the Rev. Mr Thornber, of Blackpool, both of whom published accounts of it, to which some particulars were added by Mr T. Langton Birley.* The following is the substance of these accounts —

The line of this road is first traced about a mile from Poulton in the Fylde. On the cultivated land the indications of the road are only slight, but on the turfy ground, where it had been piled up in an immense agger, it still serves, as it has done for ages, as a gravel bank, for supplying materials to repair the common roads of the neighbourhood Across the mossy flats in the neighbourhood the line of the road is very clear, and many sections of it are presented where wide ditches have been dug in place of fences. At Weeton

* The Roman Roads of Lancashire, Part ii, On the Seventh Iter of Richard of Cirencester, Transactions of Historic Society of Lancashire and Cheshire, vol. iii p. 3, by John Just, Esq, Evidences of Roman Occupation in the Fylde District, by the Rev William Thornber, B A., ibid iii. p. 57, and Additional Notes on the Seventh Iter, by T Langton Birley, ibid iii. p 55

Moss it is seen in the form of an immense embankment of several yards in height, its base standing in water, which cannot be got off owing to the nature of the levels. On the higher and dryer ground a substratum of gravel is all that remains, but at Weeton Moss there is an excellent specimen "Here," says Mr. Just, "modern plunder is fast despoiling the laborious workmanship of the Romans, the lack of gravel in the district leading the inhabitants to the road of the Romans. The gravel here seems to have been brought from the debris of some river." About midway in the town of Kirkham the line of the Roman road falls in with the main street, and continues to the windmill at the top of the town Nearly the whole length of the long street at Kirkham is either upon the Roman road, or in close proximity to it "In the Fylde country the Roman road has crossed the swampy low grounds between hill and hill, and made angles or slight curves on the summits in threading its course through the morasses This seems highly probable, for, by bringing the lines to bear on the Ordnance Map, every deviation from an intersection with the line it diverges from is on the very apex of the hill intervening" The road all along this part of its course is known as the Danes' pad or path, but the Danes were no roadmakers in the age when Earl Agmund and his fierce companions in arms ruled, and gave their leader's name to this part of Lancashire

From the top of Loxham Hill there is no difficulty in tracing the agger to Preston Moor. At Newton, Mr Hornby cut through it in sinking a marl pit Numerous and continuous remains mark the line of the road near Clifton, frequently bold and prominent on the headlands of the fields, and close to the fences. From Clifton church the road passes through Lea towards Fulwood Moor. Across several fields together a bold ridge shows its course before the investigator Approaching Fulwood Moor, it appears again in the road leading to Preston, and there for a couple of miles it shoots past that town, under the ancient familiar name of Watling Street. Beyond this point its remains are still quite evident, until the line of the Preston and Longridge railway is passed From Pedder hall it inclines northward, running directly towards Pendlehill At Nook the road is suddenly lost, at the high point of ground which brings Ribchester in sight.

In Ribchester the road has been met with in draining below the present level of the ground, near the parsonage, and a complete section of it is exhibited on the banks of a rill which there runs down from the high grounds. Then the line falls in with the road leading up to the parsonage, and again shows its bold agger, till, crossing the footpath to Anchors Hill, it falls in with the midway point of the side of the rectangle of the station, where would be the Decuman gate, and where a causeway under the soil in the gardens of Ribchester shows the buried remains of the "via principalis," within the area of the station

It is not until we have got over Ribchester bridge, and gained the rising ground to the south of Samlesbury hall, that we again find the track of the Romans. Ascending the elevated ground, we discern the Roman remains again close to the modern road to the hall Having gained the crest of the hill, the road makes a curve, and then directs its course along the ridge towards Pendlehill, in the distance Fine continuous remains here mark the course of the road. Advancing about three miles, the road approaches the river Calder, but no trace can be seen at any of the crossings At Pendleton Brook there is a remarkable specimen of the road "The agger," says Mr. Just, "has been levelled near the brook, and a specimen made, worthy of inspection. The gravel has been spread on the surface of the ground, and a thin charred line marks out the sward covered over by the road-makers. Upon this stratum of gravel a course of flags has been laid, nicely fitting one with another, though not apparently of any definable shape or size The flags form a nice, rounded, compact surface, now covered with eight or ten inches of soil, and of the exact width of twenty-one feet This is the most complete patch of the Roman road to be met with in Lancashire along this Iter' The brook being crossed, no difficulty exists in tracing the line It runs about a mile to the south-east of Clitheroe, and beyond that town it falls in, as is frequently the case, with a long continuous fence, which has been set up upon it for convenience At length the line begins to ascend the higher ground towards Chatburn Between Chatburn and Downham the line again becomes obvious, and forms a perceptible ridge along the rich limestone pastures of this fertile district. Having passed Pendlehill, the ridge directs itself straight towards Downham hall, passes in front of the same by the present public road, and ascends the high ground to the north of the village of Downham Along the crest of the hill it is very marked. At some distance beyond, considerably to the right hand, it keeps along the high ground, and a little further it passes Chatburn Brook, which is the boundary betwixt the counties of Lancaster and York, making its way to the city of York by Olicana (Ilkley) and Calcaria (Tadcaster) From York it was carried on to the Humber, and thus formed a complete line of communication across the island, and much the easiest that existed at that time

A Roman road has also been traced from Manchester to Wigan, but passing through a populous district of country, and through fields in a high state of cultivation, few traces of it now remain When Whitaker published his "History of Manchester" in the year 1773, it could be traced with great ease in the neighbourhood of Hope hall and Worsley Traces of it are still found in Worsley Park, on Moseley Common, near Cleworth hall, on Little Shakerley Common, and on Amberswood Common. It approached Wigan to the south of Ince hall *

In addition to these numerous roads, the Romans seem also to have formed a road across the district of Furness from Conishead Bank to the banks of the Duddon This road is said to have proceeded from the Thorn at Conishead Bank, west, through Street Gate, to a place where it passes the line of the present Ulverstone road, and thence by Lindale to Dalton Here it turned up what is now called Dale Lane, and slanting over the rocks by St Helen's, crossed Godwene, and bending a little took the direction of Roan Head, to Duddon sands †

The Cities, Towns, and Stations of the Romans in Lancashire and Cheshire—Such are the remains of the principal Roman roads of Lancashire and Cheshire after a lapse of fifteen to sixteen hundred years. They were the earliest, the greatest and the most useful works that were constructed in the two counties, and many of our most flourishing cities and towns owe both their origin and their continuance, through times of difficulty and depression, to the advantages afforded by these admirable lines of communication Amongst the cities and towns whose prosperity has been developed or sustained by these great works, we may confidently name the following places:—In Cheshire, Chester, Nantwich, Middlewich, Northwich, Stockport, and Altringham in Lancashire, Lancaster, Manchester, Ribchester, Preston, Kirkham, Wigan, Warrington, Newton in Makerfield, Clitheroe, Blackburn, and Bury All these

* An Account of the Roman Way from Manchester to Wigan, by the Rev Edmund Sibson, minister of Ashton in Makerfield Read before the Manchester Philosophical Society, April 15, 1845, vol vii p. 529 of Transactions

† West's Furness.

cities and towns are on, or in close proximity to, the ancient Roman roads, and for many hundred years had no other means of communication.

The object of the Romans in forming the roads above described was to unite the camps which they constructed in different parts of the two counties with each other, and to connect them with the general military system of the empire. Chester, Manchester, Ribchester, and Lancaster, the chief places in the valleys of the Dee, the Mersey and Irwell, the Ribble and the Lune, were the four great camps of the Romans in those counties, as their names clearly indicate, and as the numerous remains found at each place plainly prove: but marks of the residence of the Romans have also been found at Northwich, Kinderton near Middlewich, Stockport, and on the Cheshire side of the Mersey, opposite to Warrington, as well as at Wigan, Walton-le-Dale, Kirkham, and Overborough, in Lancashire, whilst indications of their occasional presence have been discovered in many other parts of the two counties.

In choosing the positions of their great permanent camps in Cheshire and Lancashire, the Romans were influenced by the general considerations which always guided them in making such a choice. The great recommendations of a position for a Roman camp were, that it should be in a position naturally strong and defensible, that it should not be commanded from any neighbouring height, that the situation should be healthy at all seasons of the year, and not liable to be flooded after heavy rains, and that the surrounding country should furnish wood, water, and forage, in as great abundance as possible. The Romans generally secured all these advantages by constructing their camps on slightly rising grounds, situated in the bends of rivers, as at Lancaster and Chester, or at the point of junction of two streams, as at Manchester and Ribchester, and by choosing the most fertile districts of the valleys through which these rivers ran, as the places for their encampments. This observation applies to all their encampments in the north-western counties. The advantages of those positions, in point of external resources, of strength in war, and of facilities of communication at all times, have caused most of them to become and remain the sites of flourishing cities and towns, in all states of society.*

The City of Deva, Devana, or Chester.—First in rank and importance of all the Roman stations in the north-west of England

* Vegetius, lib. i. c. 2

was Deva, or Chester. "An illustrious city" says Camden, "which Ptolemy names Devana, and Antonine, Deva, from the river Dee, which we name Chester and Westchester, which the Britons named Caerlegion (the camp of the legion), Caerleon Vaur (the camp of the great legion), Caerleon ar Dufyr Dwy (the camp of the legion on the Dee), to distinguish it from the camp of the Second Legion on the Usk, and caer, or the camp, par excellence, and which the Saxons named Legeacester (the camp of the legion), names all derived from the Twentieth Victorious Legion "Under the Romans," says the late Reverend Chancellor Raikes, "Chester became a colony, a military station, a centre of warlike operations whilst conquest was being pursued, a centre of civilization and commercial intercourse when the dominion of the empire was established." The position of Chester united all the advantages which the Romans sought in the positions of their camps, with the additional advantages of a safe and commodious port, and an easy communication both by land and water with a rich and fertile district. The river Dee, which is here so broad as to require one of the largest arches in the world to span it, protected the position on the side of the mountains, which was the one most liable to attack Within the inclosure formed by the winding of the Dee, and opposite to the point where the shallows of the river created a ford, a natural mound, easily increased by art, furnished the place for a citadel, which commanded the passage of the river, whilst a line of red sandstone rocks, and a bank rising steeply from the Dee, furnished a steep vantage-ground for a line of walls around the camp, and the city which grew out of it It is impossible to tell what British works, if any, the Romans found here, when they first encamped on the banks of the Dee, but whatever they may have been, they disregarded them, and constructed their fortifications according to their own well-devised principles of castrametation. The form of the works and walls of Chester is entirely Roman, and at all parts presents the figure which that great people preserved in their camps, when the nature of the ground rendered it possible It is, in fact, the most perfect outline of a Roman fortress that exists in the north of Europe *

A tower on the present castle mound bearing the name of Julius

* Camden's Britannia, 483 Inaugural Address of the late Rev Henry Raikes, Chancellor of the Diocese of Chester, delivered at the first meeting of the Architectural, Archæological, and Historic Society for the county, city, and neighbourhood of Chester · Journal of Proceedings, vol. i p 16 Pennant's Tours in Wales, vol., i p. 208

Cæsar, but more probably founded by Julius Agricola, formed the strongest point of the fortification, and, as we have said, commanded the ford across the river, leading into the country of the ancient Ordovices, as more recently it did the bridge leading into North Wales. From this commanding point the Romans ran the wall of the city along the brow of a steep hill, through which the rocks occasionally crop out on the western front of the camp or city, until it again reached the river Dee at the north-west angle of the works, near the outwork which now connects the water tower with the walls. In doing this they inclosed, between the western side of the wall and the bend of the river, that beautiful meadow now named the Roodee, containing nearly a hundred acres of land, and forming at once a fertile pasture, a healthful ground for exercise, and a delightful place of amusement, on which the officers and soldiers of the legion and the Roman colonists could indulge themselves in horse and chariot races, and in the athletic and gladiatorial games, which formed the delight of the Roman people and soldiery It was at once calculated to serve as a Campus Martius and an amphitheatre, the walls and the sloping banks on both sides of the river affording accommodation for a greater number of spectators, than were ever crowded within the walls of the great amphitheatre at Verona, or even into the mighty Colosseum itself One of the four principal gates—the present Watergate—was on this front of the walls, opening towards the Roodee and the river.

It is probable that the north-west angle of the Roman walls was originally washed by the waters of the Dee, and that thus the camp and fortress were thoroughly protected on the west side by the stream of the river. But in the course of ages the channel of the Dee declined from the wall, and rendered it necessary to construct a new outwork. This work, known as the Water tower, belongs to a much later age, and consists of a round tower of red sandstone, joining to the ancient walls by a long open gallery embattled on each side Beneath it was a wide arch, through which the waters of the tide ran, before the reclamation of land from the bed and stream of the river during the last century. This tower formerly ran out into the river, and there vessels lay, which fastened their cables to its sides by great iron rings fixed in the stone.

With the exception of the Water tower, the whole of the walls of Chester stand on the old Roman foundations From the north-west to the north-east angle of the walls the line of wall runs along the edge of an elevation, which at the highest point rises to the height of sixty-four feet. On this side the massy foundations of the Roman wall may still be seen, deeply imbedded in the rock, and on this front of the wall was the Northgate, a curious piece of antiquity, founded by the Romans, but strengthened or remodelled in later ages to suit the military necessities of the times. This gateway stood till the year 1808, when it was pulled down, to form a more commodious entrance into the city

The Phœnix tower stands at the north-east angle of the wall. The present erection (named from the crest of one of the city companies) was built in the year 1613, but in the time of the Romans the walls were strengthened with towers at this and in many parts, especially on the north and east sides, where they were most liable to be attacked. These towers were within bowshot of each other, in order that the archers and slingers might discharge a cross-fire on an enemy attempting an attack at any point between them. They were generally round, according to the recommendations of the Roman engineers, who considered that round towers were less liable to be crushed by the blows of the battering-ram than square ones. The thickness of the walls of Chester answers to the breadth prescribed by Vitruvius. Two persons can walk abreast upon them, and the great architect and engineer directs that the walls of fortified cities should be of such a breadth that two armed men may pass each other without any impediment *

From the Phœnix tower to the Eastgate, the wall was protected at intervals with towers The Eastgate was the chief entrance to the city—the "porta principalis"—the termination of the great road named Via Devana by the Romans, and Watling Street by the Saxons, which crossed the island from Dover to Chester. This gate was of Roman architecture, and consisted of two arches, much hid by a tower erected over it in modern days. The Eastgate was pulled down in the year 1769 to make a wider entrance to the city. "I remember," says Pennant, in his delightful "Tours in North Wales," "the demolition of the ancient structure, and on taking down the more modern case of Norman masonry, the Roman appeared full in view. It consisted of two arches, formed of vast stones, fronting the Eastgate Street and the Forest (or Foregate) Street, the pillar between them dividing the street exactly in two This species of double gate was not unfrequent. The Porta

* Vitruvius, lib 1 c. 3 & 5 Pennant's Tours in Wales, vol 1. pp. 209, 210

Esquilina and the Porta Portese at Rome were of this kind. I must conclude that the mode seems to have been derived from the Grecian architecture; for at Athens stood a dipylon, or double gate, now demolished The gate in question faced the great Watling Street Road, and near the place where the military ways united Through this was the greatest conflux of people, which rendered the use of the double portal more requisite." With regard to the ancient gates of Chester, Pennant, who had the advantage of seeing them all, states that from each side of the gates projected a propugnaculum, or bastion, in order to assail an enemy in flank who might attempt to enter Between them, in the entrance, was the cataracta, or portcullis, ready to be dropped in case the enemy forced the gates, so that part of them might be caught within the walls and the rest excluded To provide against the danger of the gates being set on fire, there were holes above, in order to pour down water to extinguish the flames *

From the Eastgate to the river outside the walls is a deep fosse, formed in the rock, which was probably cut by the Romans to strengthen the defences on this the most vulnerable part of the city. The line of this fosse continues the rectangular shape of the original Roman camp, out of which the city of Chester was formed

With regard to the south or Bridgegate entrance into the city, Pennant, writing in the year 1778, says —"I must now descend towards the bridge, in search of the few further relics of the ancient (Roman) colonists. After passing through the gate on the right is a sunk flight of steps, which leads to a large round arch, seemingly of Roman workmanship It is now filled up with more modern masonry, and a passage left through a small arch of very eccentric form. On the left of the gate, within the very passage, is the appearance of another round arch, now filled up. This postern is called the Shipgate, or Hole in the Wall. It seems originally to have been designed for the common passage over the Dee into the country of the Ordovices, either by means of a boat at high water, or by a ford at low, the river here being remarkably shallow. What reduces this to a certainty is, that the bank on the Handbridge—Welsh—side is cut down as if for the convenience of travellers, and immediately beyond, in the field called Edgar's, are the vestiges of a road pointing up the hill, which, we shall hereafter have occasion to say, was continued towards Bonium, the present Bangor." Other

* Pennant's Tours in Wales, vol i p. 209

branches of the same road extend to the Menai Strait, crossing the valleys of the Alyn, the Cluyd, and the Conway, winding round the mountains of the Snowdonian range, and giving an easy access to the whole of North Wales to the soldiers of the Twentieth Victorious Legion, encamped at the ancient Deva.*

The walls of Chester are nearly 2000 Roman paces, or two Roman miles, in circumference. As the Roman *passus*, or pace, contained five feet, this is not much less than two English miles, the exact circuit of the walls being one English mile, three-quarters, and one hundred and twenty-one yards. Although the superstructure of the walls has been more than once rebuilt, it has always been constructed on the Roman foundation. Hence the original form of the outline is retained, and thus the walls of Chester form the most perfect specimen of a Roman camp and Roman fortress that now exists in the north of Europe The views from the walls included a wide range of country, and brought within view of the Roman garrison all the most commanding points in the mountain ranges of Denbigh and Flint—the rock of Beeston, rising suddenly from the Cheshire plain, the line of the Peckforton and Forest hills, the rich plains of Chester, and the graceful windings of the Dee through the green meadows that adorn its banks †

The city of Deva, or Chester, which grew up within the line of the Roman encampment, was well supplied by the engineers of the Twentieth Legion, and the indefatigable soldiers of that energetic corps, with all the appliances of Roman civilization Four massive gates formed entrances to four principal streets, which crossed each other at right angles, and numbers of cross streets struck off, also at right angles, from the principal streets, so as to divide the city into many smaller parallelograms "The present form and arrangement of the city," says the late Chancellor Raikes, "is precisely that which was drawn out by the Roman general."

The spot where the four main streets intersected each other was the prætorium, the residence of the Roman governor, and the seat both of military and civil government. It occupied a considerable space of ground. Beside the apartments required for the accommodation of a man of the highest rank, it contained the quarters of his "contubernales"—the young Roman noblemen who were trained to war under his care—as well as the "augurale," where prayers, sacrifices, and all the other rites of religion were performed, and the

* Pennant's Tours in Wales, vol i p 154 † C S Plini, Hist Nat, lib. ii c. 21

tribunal where the governor decided on the lives and fortunes of the soldiers and subjects of Rome.*

No pains were spared in furnishing the city with other appliances of Roman civilization, and enough remains to the present time to show that it was one of the best constructed, as well as one of the most flourishing, cities of Britain. In ruder times, long after the departure of the Romans from this island, the remains of their works excited wonder and even fear amongst our ancestors, as great as the admiration which they excite at the present day. The massy foundations of their palaces, baths, and their deep and wide excavations, which probably existed in greater number at that time than they do now, were supposed to be the remains of the caverns and dungeons built by a monstrous giant, to whom they gave the name of Leon Vaur—a name derived from a confused tradition as to the great legion of the Romans. "In this city," says the old translator of Higden's "Polychronicon"—whose translation was the second work printed in the English language at the press of Caxton—"in this city been ways under earth, with vowtes (vaults) and stone work wonderly wrought, there been churches and vowtes, great stones egraved (engraved) with old men's names thereon. There is also Julius Cæsar's name wonderly in stones egrave, and other noblemen's names, with the writing about." The author of the "Polychronicon" says, in another place, "Looking at the foundations of stone, and the enormous ways, they seem rather to have been founded by the labour of giants or of the Romans than by the toil of the Britons." Several of the works which called forth these expressions of admiration still exist, and stones are frequently found inscribed with the names of the gods and men of imperial Rome, although much that excited the admiration of our ancestors has been destroyed, carried away, or again buried in the earth, probably to be again dug up or laid open at some future time.

Amongst the works which have been frequently laid open, and as often closed again, are the ancient pavements of the city. These, though covered with a vast mass of earth and ruins, have often been explored. So recently as the year 1849, two different lines of pavement, formed in very distant ages, were discovered in making an excavation near the Eastgate, the most frequented of all the entrances into the city. One of these was three feet, and the other no less than nine feet, below the present level of

* Pennant's Tours in Wales, vol. i. p. 226.

the streets. About the same time was discovered a wide excavation, thirteen feet in depth, and extending across Bridge Street and other streets of the city In addition to these works of utility, lines of Grecian pediments and richly-carved Corinthian capitals have recently been laid open, which are evidently the remains of buildings of much greater beauty and magnificence than any that have outlived the ravages of time and war.*

The ancient and famous rows of Chester, which are unique in northern Europe, also probably originated in the portico, the favourite lounging place of the Romans. On this subject the late Chancellor Raikes observes, "When Tacitus describes the process by which Roman manners diffused themselves through Britain, and gradually completed the subjugation of the country, he speaks of the natives of Britain as acquiring a taste for two of the features of Roman civilization—'porticus et balnea,' the portico in which they delighted to stroll and sun themselves, and the baths, which were the national luxury" The rows, or covered vestibules, which run along the principal streets of Chester are supposed to be almost as ancient in their origin as the walls, for had they been the work of a more modern age, or a different race, there is no reason why they should have been exclusively confined to the Roman city of Chester From the description given by Plautus of the "vestibula" and the "ambulacra" of Rome, they appear to have been used for precisely the same purposes as the rows at Chester If there be any difference, it is in the fact that in the latter city the promenade is on the level of the first, instead of that of the ground, floor of the houses. This circumstance renders the rows of Chester both drier and pleasanter as places of exercise and amusement; and it may probably have given considerable advantage to the soldiers and colonists of the city, in defending the houses and streets of this frontier garrison, in case of insurrection within the walls, or an irruption of an enemy from without The depth to which some of the streets are cut in the rock, would also tend to make the streets more defensible from the houses and rows

The hypocausts or heating apparatuses which have been discovered at Chester, seem to have belonged to mansions of the highest class, and to have been used for many purposes besides that of heating baths The hypocaust in Bridge Street, commonly

* Paper by William Ayrton Esq, in Transactions of Historic Society of Lancashire and Cheshire, vol i p 82

known as the Roman Bath, has recently been fully exposed to view, by pulling down, for the purpose of reconstructing, the buildings by which it had been covered. During the excavations, several huge pillars and beams of oak were found in their original positions, as well as a low plinth of stone, which seemed to have run round the interior of a hall of the same date The workmen found long rows of hollow tiles, or bricks, in form almost of a honeycomb, and acting as flues or cells for heating air, but in after times filled up with grout and rubbish; also many stone pillars which had supported the ancient floor; and from underneath the foundations of the adjoining houses some portions of the original floor was dug up, as far back from the street as forty feet at least. It was composed in the usual way, of a mass of mortar, broken bricks, and hardened grout, about a foot in thickness, wherein were embedded little tesseræ, white and black, one inch square, forming the corner of an angular interlacing pattern A great quantity of Roman coins, pottery, and tiles of the ordinary kind, were also found in the course of the excavations. It has been the custom to call this the Roman Bath, but the hypocaust was only an extensive system of hot-air flues and chambers, underneath some large apartment, and the few pillars and openings still left formed but one corner of the once extensive apparatus.*

In digging the foundation of a new house in Watergate Street in January, 1779, another hypocaust was discovered, larger than that in Bridge Street. It contained two sudatories, one having ten pillars, and a vacant place in the middle. Adjacent to it was a small apartment with the walls plastered, which probably was the room where the slave stood, who supplied the apparatus with fuel Before this was a large chamber with a tesselated pavement of black, white, and red tiles, each about an inch square. Adjoining was a sudatory, and beyond that a small tiled apartment.†

Part of a third mosaic pavement, but without any heating apparatus, was discovered in the year 1803, in digging a cellar in what was then known as the Nuns' Garden, near the castle. It was five feet square, and was found about six feet below the present surface of the ground A fourth tesselated pavement was discovered in the year 1814, near the gateway of the castle, part of which was destroyed in making excavations, and the other part closed up‡

* Observations of the late Rev W H Massie, in Journal of Archæological Society of Chester, vol i. p 356

† Pennent's Tours in Wales, vol i p. 154 ‡ The Chester Guide, p 26

In addition to structures which are still so perfect that their plan and object can be understood, there have been found various remains of ancient buildings, whose object is not so evident, and immense quantities of fragments of buildings, broken up and scattered about in all parts of the city. In 1847 several courses of masonry, belonging to the original foundation of the old Eastgate, were laid bare, just outside the present gate They lay about four feet from the surface, and extended sixty feet beyond the gate From the care with which they are pointed and finished it is probable that they were more than mere foundations, and most likely served for guard-rooms or dungeons In 1813 the remains of an extra-mural cemetery were discovered, in sinking the foundation of a cellar at Netherleigh house, a short distance from Chester It contained a considerable number of large vases of red clay, regularly arranged in vaults, each vault containing four or six vases. Several of these were filled with calcined bones. One of the vases was perfect, but the rest were fractured by the workmen who broke open the vault A half-length figure, dressed in a priestly costume, was discovered at the same time. In Weaver Street, in excavating for a sewer, a regularly formed road of marble blocks, set in sand, has been discovered, with four feet above it a layer of charcoal, and at a depth of ten or eleven feet a quantity of Roman tiles In Common Hall Street a row of foundations was discovered formed of concrete, composed of broken marble stones, in hard mortar, about nine feet apart, at a depth of ten feet, and presenting the appearance of having supported columns, a large square block of stone four feet two inches square, and sixteen inches deep, resting on a bed of concrete, a portion of a column of a very debased classical form, about two feet in diameter, fixed in concrete at the depth of ten feet, together with mouldings, broken tiles and pottery, coins of Antoninus Pius and Tetricus, a quantity of bones of various animals, including a stag's head with the horns sawn off, and a wild boar's tusk. In an adjoining street was also discovered a moulded block from a cornice, with a rude inscription, and a pig of lead embedded in a thick wall, also the capital of a pillar The tiles are of various forms, some overlapping each other, some with a kind of pattern or letters, others with marks of animals' feet. In 1840 several tiles, marked Leg. XXVV., were dug up in Water Street; and about the same time the capital of a Corinthian column was discovered at Handbridge, and near it a coin of Trajan. A quantity of remains of

Roman origin have also been found on the site of St. John's Hospital.*

In addition to walls, streets, and buildings, many remains have been found at Chester connected with occupations, public amusements, and with the arts of private life. Amongst these was the figure of a Roman soldier, over the old Roman Eastgate, in dress and arms greatly resembling a Scottish highlander; a figure of a gladiator, of the kind called "retiarius," furnished with a net to entangle his adversary (who was armed with a trident), and a dagger to dispatch him; a figure of a shepherd with a Phrygian cap, found in a house in the White Friars; Roman fibulæ for fastening robes; vases of earthenware and slate; innumerable specimens of Roman earthenware of all kinds, from the finest Samian ware to the rudest pottery, and often inscribed with the maker's name; spear heads, portions of many articles for kitchen purposes; a gold ring with an onyx stone; pigs of lead with Roman inscriptions; and a gold torque weighing thirteen dwts., recently found in St. Werburg.

Amongst the most curious and interesting remains of the Romans found at Chester, are the numerous altars raised by them to the gods and goddesses of the Pantheon.

First in dignity amongst these is an altar devoted to Jupiter Tanarus, "Greatest and Best," by Titus Elupius Galerus, the prefect of the Twentieth Legion. According to Selden, who quotes Lucan in support of his theory, the name of Tanarus, which follows that of Jupiter in the above inscription, ought to be Taranus. That, it seems, was the name of a Gaulish, and therefore of a British deity, whom the author of this inscription attempted to identify with the classic Jupiter, according to the politic custom of the Romans, who taught the nations whom they wished to hold in subjection, that their own gods and the gods of Rome were the same divinities, under different names. The date of this inscription is fixed, by the names of the consuls, Commodus and Lateranus, as the year 154. A figure, supposed to be that of Minerva armed, with her altar and bird of wisdom,† was formerly very visible, sculptured on a rock on the Welsh side of the old bridge. This memorial of the daughter of Jove, whom Horace places second in rank to Jupiter, is now nearly

* Paper by William Ayrton, Esq., in Transactions of Historic Society of Lancashire and Cheshire, vol. i. p. 79. First Report of Chester Archæological Society.

† Pennant's Tours in Scotland, vol. i. p. 4.

worn out by time. An altar without an inscription, but accompanied by a medal struck in honour of Neptune, who is represented with a ship and trident, and of Hercules and Pallas, was found in the year 1828 A statue, supposed to be that of Cupid, executed in a better style of art than any other found at Chester, has been recently discovered. The winged, fiery boy was joined in worship with Venus, who was supposed to be the peculiar patroness of the Julian race It was in the name of Venus the Victorious that the army of Julius Cæsar fought in the battle of Pharsalia, when, as before and since, Venus proved more than a match for Hercules, who was invoked by the soldiers of Pompey. A small votive altar was recently discovered at Boughton, by Mr. William Ayrton, dedicated by Julius Quintilianus to the Genius of Avernus, that is, to the ruler of the infernal regions, another entrance of which was supposed to be found at the lake of Avernus. A beautiful altar, dedicated to Fortune, Esculapius, and Safety, by the freedmen and family of a distinguished Roman, no doubt in memory of his having been restored to health. The inscription on this altar is much defaced, but emblems of the deities invoked, and various sacrificial instruments are cut on the stone. Fortune was worshipped as a goddess in all parts of the Roman empire, and Pliny complains that the belief in this inconstant being had destroyed all belief in any higher god "All over the world, in all places and at all times, Fortune is the only deity whom any one invokes She alone is spoken of, she alone is praised and blamed. To her are referred all our losses and all our gains; and in casting up the accounts of mortals, she alone balances the page. We are so much in the power of chance, that chance is regarded as a god, and hence the existence of God himself becomes doubtful"* About the beginning of the last century a statue was found at Chester, which, from its form and position, was supposed to be that of one of the attendants, in a group representing Mithras, or the sun; who was worshipped as a god, first amongst the eastern nations and afterwards amongst the Romans. The statue found at Chester was represented with a Phrygian cap, with a little mantle across its shoulders, and a short jacket on its body. It was placed standing, with a torch in its hands, declining This is supposed to have been an emblem of the decline of the sun at midwinter. At that season of the

*C S Plin, Hist Nat., lib. ii c 5

year, horse races and chariot races were celebrated in honour of the sun, and these, to annoy the Christians, were chiefly fixed on the day on which they celebrated the birth of Christ

A beautiful altar has also been discovered at Chester, raised to the Genius of the Emperors by Flavius Longus, a tribune of the Twentieth Legion, and Longinus his son, natives of Samosata, on the Euphrates, but then serving on the banks of the Dee. The emperors whose genius is invoked are supposed to have been Diocletian and Maximian The altar was found in digging the foundations of a cellar in Eastgate, on the ancient pavement, which consisted of square stones. Around it were found the marks of sacrifice, consisting of the heads, horns, and bones of the ox, the roe, and the buck. And with these remains were two coins, one of Vespasian, and the other of Constantius, the father of Constantine the Great. On the latter, on one side, is the head of Constantius, with the inscription "Fl Val Constantius Nob C," and on the other a figure of a genius, holding in one hand a sacrificing bowl, and in the other a cornucopia. On the reverse of the coin are the words, "Genio Populi Romani" It has been suppose that this coin was deposited at the time when the altar to the Genius of the Emperors was erected, and that, together, they were intended to serve as a memorial of the restoration of the power of the Roman emperors in Britain by Constantius, after the overthrow of Carausius and Allectus, who for a time usurped supreme authority in Britain, and separated the island from the rest of the Roman empire. An altar has also been discovered at Chester dedicated to the Genius of Avernus, another altar, dedicated to the nymphs and fountains, by the soldiers of the Twentieth Legion, a third dedicated to the genius of the place-"Genio Loci," and a fourth dedicated to the deity of Augustus—"Numini Augusti" So recently as 1850, an altar was discovered at Chester dedicated, by Hermogenes the physician, to the preserving deities The inscription on this altar is in the Greek language Translated, it reads, "I, Hermogenes the Physician, set up this Altar to the Preserving and Almighty Deities."* It is probable that the altar was erected by the physician of the Emperor Hadrian, in memory of some escape that he had experienced, whilst following the perilous fortunes of his master in Britain Hermogenes is spoken of as the physician of Hadrian by Dion Cassius, who relates that the emperor, in his last illness,

* Journal of the Chester Archæological Society, p 200

directed his freedman to stab him in a spot, under the breast, which Hermogenes had pointed out to him as painlessly fatal. The freedman fled in terror, on which the emperor refused to take food, and died of starvation, exclaiming in his last moment, "It takes many doctors to kill an emperor" In addition to numerous inscriptions discovered at Chester in honour of the gods of Rome and Greece, an inscription has also been discovered in honour of the nymphs of the Brigantes. This inscription is mentioned by Selden and by Gale, and is probably genuine, for the worship of the ancient divinities of Britain continued for many years after the Roman conquest. A statue of a goddess named Brigantia has been discovered in Annandale, which appears to have been erected by order of the Emperor Julian the Apostate, at the time when he was attempting to restore the worship of the heathen deities Coins have also been discovered at Chester which bear evidence to the prevalence of Christianity in Britain and Gaul about 350 years after the death of Christ. These coins are marked with the head and name of Magnentius, an emperor or usurper who headed a great military insurrection in those provinces about that time It appears from these coins that Magnentius bore on his standard, or "labarum," the cross—the emblem of the Christian faith—the Alpha and the Omega, with the initials of the Saviour's name As this money was circulated in Gaul and Britain, it creates a presumption that Christianity was at that time the religion of a large portion of the British people, though it may be that paganism still lingered in the wilder parts of the island

Chester is also rich in Roman coins These commence with the arrival of the Romans, and continue to the time of their departure from the island. Amongst the earliest is a coin of the Emperor Nero, A D. 54 to 68, among the latest, one of Valentinianus, A D. 367 to 375. These coins thus extend over a period of more than three hundred years, beginning probably with the time of the advance of the Roman legions through Chester, to storm the sacred island of the Druids; and extending very nearly to the time when the Twentieth Legion was withdrawn from Britain, to assist in defending Italy and the walls of Rome from the attacks of Alaric the Goth

It will be seen from the above details that quite enough still remains at Chester—after the lapse of eighteen hundred years—to show that it was a flourishing city under the Romans. The great sources of wealth in all ages and countries are agriculture, mining, manufactures, and commerce, and it is a subject of interest to inquire what was the foundation of the ancient as well as of the modern prosperity of Chester, and of the other cities and towns of the north-western district of Britain

There is no reason to doubt that the statement of Strabo as to the rudeness of the agriculture of Britain previous to the arrival of the Romans, is correct. He states that the Britons understood none of the finer processes of cultivation, and did not even know how to make cheese from the milk of their cattle If so, we may perhaps attribute the first manufacture of the famous Cestrian cheese to these ancient masters of the world However this may be, it certainly was during the dominion of the Romans in Britain that agriculture, horticulture, and pasturage rose to importance, and that the soil of Britain was so well cultivated as to be capable of furnishing large quantities of grain for foreign consumption The Rhenish provinces of Gaul were fed with grain from Britain, in the time of the Emperor Julian, during a terrible famine produced by a desolating irruption of the Germans The Romans delighted in agriculture and horticulture, and in the rearing and improving of cattle, and practised these arts in every part of the empire "Almost all the flowers, the herbs, and the fruits that grow in our gardens," says Gibbon, "are of foreign extraction, which, in many cases, is betrayed even by the names The apple was a native of Italy, and when the Romans had tasted the richer flavour of the apricot, the peach, the pomegranate, the citron, and the orange, they contented themselves with applying to all these new fruits the common denomination of apple, discriminating them from each other by the additional epithet of their country. In the time of Homer the vine grew wild in the island of Sicily, and most probably on the adjacent continent but it was not improved by the skill, nor did it afford a liquor grateful to the taste, of the savage inhabitants. A thousand years afterwards, Italy could boast that, of the four-score most generous and celebrated wines, more than two-thirds were produced from her soil. The blessing was soon communicated to the Narbonnese province of Gaul, but so intense was the cold to the north of the Cevennes, that, in the time of Strabo, it was thought impossible to ripen the grapes in those parts of Gaul. This difficulty, however, was gradually vanquished, and there is some reason to believe that the vineyards of Burgundy are as old as the age of the Antonines. The olive in the western world followed the progress of peace, of which it was considered to be the emblem. At length it was carried into the heart of Spain and Gaul. The cultivation of flax was transported from Egypt to Gaul. The use of artificial grasses became familiar to the farmers both of Italy and the provinces, particularly lucerne, which derived its Latin name and its origin from Media."* The result of this improvement of cultivation was that the famines, which were so frequent in the early ages of Rome, were unknown when the empire had reached its full extent The accidental scarcity of any single province was immediately relieved by the plenty of its more fortunate neighbours Thus, as already mentioned, Britain supplied the occasional deficiencies of Gaul "Six hundred vessels," says Gibbon, "formed in the forest of Ardennes, made several voyages to the coast of Britain, and returning from thence laden with corn, sailed up the Rhine, and distributed their cargoes to the several towns and fortresses along the banks of that river"†

Amongst the plants which the Romans succeeded in naturalizing in Britain, were flax, lucerne, and all the more valuable kinds of fruit trees. They even introduced the vine, which continued to be cultivated in the southern districts of Britain till after the Norman conquest. As a product of luxury, the vine was grown in the open air long after the retreat of the Romans So late as the reign of Henry VIII, there was a vineyard attached to one of the monastic houses of Chester, and, if we are to believe Strabo, the county of Chester owes the art which gives value to its rich pastures to the Romans. On this subject Pennant says, "I must not omit the most valuable memorial which the Romans left in a particular manner to this county—the art of cheese-making; for we are expressly told that the Britons were ignorant of it till the arrival of the Romans The Cestrians have improved so highly in this article, as to excel all countries, not excepting Italy, the land of their ancient masters"‡

The question as to whether the Romans established a colony at Chester, the head-quarters of the Twentieth Legion, as they undoubtedly did at York and Caerleon, the head-quarters of the Sixth and Second Legion, is now chiefly interesting in reference to the tenure and cultivation of the adjoining lands When the Romans established a colony, the colonists were generally the soldiers of a favourite army or legion, who began by turning out

* Gibbon, vol. i c 2 † Gibbon, vol ii c 19 ‡ Gibbon, vol i c 2

the original proprietors of the soil. Thus, when Augustus established a colony at Cremona, the poet Virgil and all his neighbours were expelled from their farms in the adjoining district of Mantua, and the former only recovered his land by the special favour of the emperor. We ought perhaps to hope, in the interests of the original possessors of the soil around Chester, that it was not a colony, or, at least, that it did not become so, until that title was assumed as an honorary distinction, without any previous acts of confiscation This was the case, according to Gibbon, in the time of the Emperor Septimius Severus —"During the latter part of his reign, the calm of peace and prosperity was once more experienced in the provinces; and many cities, restored by the munificence of Severus, assumed the title of his colonies, and attested by public monuments their gratitude and felicity." It was the boast of Severus to have restored peace and order even in Britain, and it is very probable that his son Geta, who possessed some of his great qualities, may have been the restorer of the prosperity of Chester He and his brother assumed the purple at York, and were not likely to be sparing in honours to the legions of Britain, which first saluted them as emperors The coin on which Chester is spoken of as a colony, is one of the short reign of Geta, and bears the inscription Col Devana., Leg. XX. Victrix

The principal commerce of Britain in the time of the Romans consisted in the metals, and those were and are found in great abundance on the banks of the Dee, and in the adjoining district of North Wales Agricola, in animating his soldiers to fight valiantly against Galgacus exclaimed "Britain produces gold, silver, and the other metals, the reward of victory," and Galgacus, in exhorting his soldiers to resist the invaders, reminded them of the misery of toiling in the mines to supply tribute to the Romans Gold was formerly found in Britain, if not abundantly, yet to such an extent as to render it worth collecting Silver is still extracted in considerable quantities from the silver-lead ores of North Wales, and other mining districts of Britain Iron, lead, copper, and tin are amongst the most valuable products of the island. The workings of the Romans can still be traced amongst the lead mines in the hills which overlook the estuary of the Dee, and pigs of lead bearing Latin inscriptions have been recently dug up amongst the Romans ruins of Chester Even in modern times, lead, silver, and other metals of the value of a million and a half sterling, were extracted from the Halkin mountain, a small portion of this district, in the course of a few years; and in the time of the Romans the lead mines of Britain were so productive, that the emperors, who received tribute in that and other metals, forbad the producing of more than a certain quantity of lead each year, for the purpose of keeping up the price of the metal. Immense iron pick-axes, resembling those used by the Romans in mining operations, have been found in the Flintshire hills, with wedges, fibulæ, and many other relics of the Roman miners The scoriæ of Roman iron-works have been met with in the parish of Hope, and a great mass of copper, with a Latin inscription, has been discovered on the banks of the Conway. All these metals are found in abundance on the west bank of the Dee, along with coal, and must have furnished the materials for an extensive commerce "These pigs of lead, the produce of Roman industry," says Chancellor Raikes, "first mentioned in Camden's 'Britannia' as being found in the neighbourhood of Chester, and two of which have been recently discovered, are memorials of the early period at which the mineral wealth of this district was known, and of the commerce to which it gave rise"

We have no information as to the extent to which the river Dee was used for purposes of internal communication in the time of the Romans, but that eminently practical people never lost an opportunity of turning natural advantages to the best account In Italy they made the Tiber navigable by damming up the waters of the Tinia and the Glanis, and discharging them at stated intervals into that river, and in Gaul they established lines of water communication from the mouth of the Rhone to the mouths of the Garonne, the Loire, and the Seine We know from Gildas that the Thames and the Severn were both used for purposes of navigation after the departure of the Romans from Britain, and no doubt they were so used during the Roman occupation. The Dee, though a wild mountain stream in the first part of its course, becomes a fine navigable river when it reaches Bangor At that point it approaches near enough to the tributaries of the Severn, to have aided in forming a line of water communication from Chester to Gloucester, and thence down the valley of the Thames to London

When the Romans first landed in Britain, the seas between Britain and Ireland had a bad reputation Solinus says that the sea between Britain and Ireland is stormy and restless, so that it is only navigable during a few days in each year. But the Romans afterwards became more familiar with the western seas. Even in Pliny's time the whole of the coasts of the Western Ocean were navigated, from Cadiz and the Straits, round Spain and Gaul, to Britain. The greater part of the Northern Ocean was also navigated, the fleets of Augustus having coasted round Germany and the present Denmark, as far as the promontory of the Cimbri, from which point they saw a great sea "which extends to the country of the Scythians"* Cadiz, or Gades, was the resting-place of the Romans, as it had previously been of the Carthaginians, in their voyages to Gaul and Britain. The products of those countries were taken to Cadiz, and thence to Rome, and from Rome the lead and tin of Britain were sent across the Mediterranean, and down the Red Sea, to India and the East, to be exchanged for silk, spices, and other oriental luxuries †

At the time when Chester was the head-quarters of the Twentieth Legion, the Romans had outposts in several places in the valley of the Dee, or of its tributaries. The most important of these outposts were at Flint, at the bridge or ford of the Dee between Holt and Farndon, and at Caerguerle, in the pass leading towards Mold. They probably also had a position at Bangor or Bonium, and a very curious memorial of their presence has been found near Malpas.

Many Roman remains have been found in the neighbourhood of Flint castle. Amongst these are a button of twisted gold-wire, studded with small globular pieces of solid gold, part of a necklace with golden links, a fragment of a glass ornament of a rich blue colour, part of a vase, a small brazen seal, a stylus or pen, a spoon for a lachrymatory, a brazen bodkin, a fibula or brooch gilt and enamelled with deep blue in front, a forceps, a bulla or Roman amulet, a locket, a key and ring, a ring of brass, and another of silver ‡ Pennant thought that he could trace remains of a Roman fortification, on the ground on which the town and castle of Flint now stand.

The castle of Holt, which is spoken of in an old document as the castle of the Lion or Legion, was probably an outwork of the Romans, constructed to secure the course and passage of the river. Coins of Antoninus, Galienus, and Constantinus, have been

* C. S. Plini, lib ii c 27 † Gibbon, c. ii p 72 ‡ Pennant's Tours in Wales, vol i p 99

found here, and there are the remains of ancient slopes on the banks of the river, which have very much the appearance of Roman workmanship *

At Caerguerle on the banks of the Alyn, at the entrance of Molesdale, are also remains of a Roman station, at the foot of the rock on which the ruins of the castle still stand The works seem to have been rectangular, one side forming a slope along the banks of the river In Camden's time a hypocaust was discovered near this place The floor was of brick, set in mortar, the roof supported by brick pillars, and consisting of polished perforated tiles On some of the tiles were the words "Legio XX.," which points out their founders † Large beds of iron cinders have been discovered at Caer-Estyn, in this parish, the supposed refuse of Roman furnaces ‡

An interesting memorial of the presence of the Romans in the north-western district of Britain was discovered in the year 1812, at Bickley, near Malpas, in Cheshire It consisted of a tablet of copper, inscribed with a decree of the Roman senate and of the Emperor Trajan, by which the veterans of eleven alæ, and four cohorts of auxiliary troops, then serving in Britain, were presented with the freedom of Rome Amongst the troops mentioned in the inscription as serving in Britain were men of numerous races, including Thracians, Pannonians, Gauls, Spaniards, and mountaineers from the Alps The Romans thus kept in subjection one race by means of another, for whilst troops from all parts of the Roman empire were serving in Britain, British troops were serving in the most remote provinces of the empire In the "Notitia" it is mentioned that the fourth ala of Britons was serving in Egypt, the twenty-sixth cohort of Britons in Armenia, the "invincible young Britons' in Spain, and the veteran Britons in Illyricum §

Such are the traces of the Romans in the lower part of the valley of the Dee, and ascending its wild and beautiful banks into the recesses of the Welsh mountains, the remains of that great people may be traced to the point at which it rushes from the lake of Bala. They may also be found in the beautiful valleys of the Clwyd and the Conway, and along the shores of the Menai Straits In the Roman times, Deva or Chester was the military capital of the whole of this district, and there are few parts of it in which

* Pennant's Tours in Wales, vol i p 274.

† Camden's Britannia, vol ii p. 828.

‡ Pennant's Tours in Wales, vol ii p 47.

§ Mr Roach Smith's Collectanea Antiqua, vol. ii p 134

the marks of their power and greatness cannot be traced to the present day.

Roman Stations at Northwich and Kinderton—Leaving the plain of Chester and the valley of the Dee, and crossing the Forest hills, we find numerous remains of the Romans in the valley of the Weaver, and of its tributaries the Dane and the Wheelock.

Castle Northwich, standing on a lofty and almost precipitous height which overhangs the present town of Northwich, was one of the positions which the Romans occupied in the valley of the Weaver, and by means of which the Twentieth Legion, stationed at Chester, kept up its communications with the garrison at Manchester, and with the Sixth Legion at York. The Roman road, as we have shown, can be clearly traced from Chester to the neighbourhood of Northwich, and from Northwich to Manchester and York. It is difficult to trace it in the immediate vicinity of Northwich, owing to the obliterating effects of cultivation, of building, of floods in the valley, and of the sinking of the ground caused by the working of brine-pits and salt-mines Owing to the last of these causes, the modern road has sunk six feet, and much of the neighbouring land still more.

Castle Northwich possesses all the advantages which the Romans sought in a military position The ground is lofty, commanding, and almost encircled by the windings of the river Weaver. The situation is healthy at all seasons, and the fertile banks of the river furnish forage and supplies of every kind sufficient for the wants of a numerous garrison. The river Dane, descending from the borders of the Derbyshire hills, flows into the Weaver, opposite to the heights on which the Romans formed their camp, and hence from this point the garrison, which could at any time be easily reinforced from Deva, commanded not only the upper and lower parts of the valley of the Weaver, but also the valleys of the Dane and the Wheelock. "Northwich," says Archdeacon Wood, in a communication to the Archæological Society of Chester, "is a Roman station, and judging from its position, and from the large remains of foundations of buildings which have been dug up, and the antiquities which have come to light, it must have been a station of commanding strength, and of very great importance" Urns containing calcined bones, large quantities of Roman pottery, and a mortarium, inscribed "Marius fecit," have been recently found at Castle Northwich, within the position occupied by the Romans in ancient times.

A salt-pit of very great antiquity, and which probably yielded tribute to the Romans, still exists in the town of Northwich. At Hartford, near to the present railway station, three Roman funereal urns have been recently found.*

A Roman road, still clearly marked, and which was almost perfect when Camden visited this part of Cheshire, in the reign of Queen Elizabeth, formed an easy connection between the Roman position at Northwich and an equally well-marked position of the same people at Kinderton, now a suburb of Middlewich, situated on a point where the river Dane is joined by a smaller stream, named the Croco. The outline of the Roman camp is still perfectly distinct, in a field called the Harbour field. This name, Harbour, which occurs continually on the line of the old Roman roads, is supposed to be either a corruption of the old Saxon words heer-burh, the army's hill or camp, or of hea-burh, the chief town or camp.† The camp at Kinderton is not a perfect parallelogram, although approaching as nearly to it as the formation of the land and the course of the streams will allow. The sides are not exactly facing the cardinal points, but sufficiently so to be designated by them. The camp is bounded on the north by the river Dane, and on the west by the river Croco, their confluence being at the north-west angle. The fosse is plainly discernible on two sides of the parallelogram, though it has been greatly defaced by being levelled a few years ago. Several coins and other small articles have been found in levelling and ploughing the field, and in July, 1849, when the ground was opened at several places, to ascertain how far the gravel of the road extended, in each place opened small fragments of Roman pottery, some of Samian ware, were thrown out, sufficient to show the place to have been an ancient encampment of the Romans. Its position at the confluence of two rivers, in a healthy situation, and in the midst of a fertile district, together with the form of the earthworks, and the numerous Roman roads which radiate from it in various directions, prove this not less clearly. This position, as already mentioned, seems to have been a great centre of communication in ancient times; for lines of Roman road can be traced, running in the following directions.—Towards Chesterton, near Newcastle-under-Lyne, which was the high road to London, Gaul, and Rome,

* Transactions of the Historical Society of Lancashire and Cheshire, vol. ii. p. 138.

† In the ancient Anglo-Saxon poem of "Beowulf," the Freslanders are described as returning to their "hamas and hea-burh," their homes and chief town or fortress.—*Kemble's* "Beowulf."

following very much the direction of the London and North-western railway as far as London, towards Nantwich, Wem, and the valley of the Severn, towards Holme's Chapel, by way of Saltersford, and so on to the Derbyshire hills, to Manchester and Warrington, and finally, towards Deva or Chester. This position seems to have been to the Roman roads much what the Crewe station, which lies only a few miles south of it, is to the modern system of railways.

The Roman Mamucium, or Mancunium, now Manchester.—Passing eastward from the valley of the Weaver to that of the Mersey and Irwell, we find another great Roman station at Mamucium or Mancunium, the present Manchester. This city has been from the most remote times the chief place of the valley of the Mersey and the Irwell, and of the hilly district from which those rivers flow. It was in the time of the Romans the military position from which they governed the district, and kept up the communications between the soldiers of the Twentieth Legion at Chester and those of the Sixth Legion at York, through the narrow and difficult passes in the mountains which separate the western from the eastern side of the island. Few positions were of greater consequence, it being of vital importance to the Romans to have the power of throwing their whole military strength at will, either on the east or west side of that range. Mamucium, on the west side of the mountains, and Cambodunum, on the east, were the two fortified positions by means of which this was effected. Mamucium was not only the fortress by which the communication was kept open through the mountains, but also the position from which the swampy forests forming the Caet Maes, or woody plain of Lancashire and Cheshire—of which Chat Moss, Carrington Moss, and other great swamps on both sides of the Mersey now form the remains—were kept in subjection. The roots of thousands of large trees, the remains of ancient forests, probably destroyed in warlike operations, are still found in these swamps. It is uncertain whether the trees of which they are the remains were destroyed by the axe or by fire, but it is evident that many of them did not perish from natural decay, the wood being still quite sound. In the corresponding marshes on the opposite side of the hills, as Hatfield Chace and Thorne Waste, excavations appear at the roots and on the stems of numerous oak trees, some apparently cut down with axes and wedges, others burnt down, and Roman coins have been found with them.* In some of

* De La Prime, Philosophical Transactions, 1701. Phillips' Yorkshire, p. 104.

the Lancashire mosses, that of Chat Moss especially, the trunks of the trees seem to have been overthrown in a similar manner, to have fallen across the natural water-courses by means of which the country was drained, and thus to have enlarged the great peat mosses which extend for so many miles down the valley of the Mersey The Romans do not seem at any time to have formed roads through the centre of this wild district, though it is encircled by Roman roads running along the high grounds of Cheshire and Lancashire, from which it still presents the appearance of an immense woody plain All these roads communicate with the old Roman station of Mamucium.

Mamucium or Mancunium is first mentioned in the "Antonine Itinerary," and is twice spoken of there as a Roman position—in the second and in the tenth Iters—in the former of which it is called Mamucium, and in the latter Mancunium Both Mamucium and Mancunium are said to be eighteen miles distant from Condate, and Mamucium is said to be twenty miles distant from Cambodunum, on the direct road from Deva, or Chester, to Eboracum, or York There is, therefore, no reason to doubt that both those names apply to the same place, and to the city of Manchester Opinions are divided as to the origin of the name Camden and Horsley both derive it from Maen, the ancient British name for a rock, and justify the application of the name on the ground that the Roman fortress at Mamucium or Mancunium was built on the red sandstone rock which forms the steep bank of the river Irwell Whitaker, the historian of Manchester, derives the name from Maencunion, which, he says, means "the city of tents," it having been the site of an ancient British encampment This seems a less probable derivation than that of Camden and Horsley, yet, as it has been recently shown by Mr. Harland, that Mamucium, and afterwards Mamcestre, were the names of the present Manchester, for many ages, neither of these derivations can be considered as altogether decisive of the question

"There can be no doubt that the point where the Medlock falls into the Irwell, near what is still called the Castle-field, would be a favourite spot for the Romans on which to raise their chief castrum, while the junction of the Irk with the Irwell, at the other extremity of the Deansgate, being a like situation, it is probable that they there placed one of their "castra æstiva," or summer camps No evidence exists of any British encampment having previously existed on the spot"* This position possessed all the advantages, in point of strength and healthfulness, which the Romans sought in their camps, and the surrounding valleys of the Mersey, the Irwell, the Medlock, and the Irk, furnished supplies for the wants of the garrison and the population which collected round it The lines of the Roman camp, and the remains of a castle of stone, were very perceptible at Manchester until the middle of the last century, when the prodigious increase of the city swept them away Camden, writing in the reign of Queen Elizabeth, in 1590, in speaking of Manchester as the ancient Mamucium or Mancunium, says that it rises on the left side of the Irwell, at the point where it is joined by the Irk, and scarcely three miles from the Mersey. "In an adjoining park of the earl of Derby's," he adds, "I saw the foundations of an ancient square castle, called Mancastle, at the point where the Medlock falls into the Irwell I do not say that this is the ancient Mancunium," he observes, "but either some Roman station, or perhaps the work which Edward the Elder constructed, when, in the words of Marianus, 'In this year he sent an army of Mercians into Northumberland, and restored and garrisoned Manchester'"† Subsequent investigations have clearly proved that this was at least a part of the Roman camp at Mamucium Stukeley, who visited Manchester early in the last century, in 1724, says that the Roman camp "is on the west side, going to Manchester from Chester by way of Stretford, and on the north bank of the Medlock, a quarter of a mile from the present town of Manchester" Horsley, who visited the same place a few years later, says, "When I was at Manchester, I examined with care the Roman station west from it The field in which it stands is called Castle-field The river runs near it, on the east side The ramparts are still very conspicuous" The remains of the Romans are much more fully described by Whitaker, in his "History of Manchester," a work of extraordinary learning and ingenuity, though rather a history and dissertation on the ancient Britons, and on the Roman and Saxon dominion in Britain, than an account of the city of Manchester

In addition to the ancient ramparts and the Roman road around Manchester, many Roman remains have been found there, especially

* Mamecestre being Chapters from the Early Recorded History of the Barony, the Lordship or Manor the Vill, Borough, or Town of Manchester Edited by John Harland, F S A 3 vols 1861 Being vols liii lvi and lviii of the Chetham Society's Remains, Historical and Literary, connected with the Palatine Counties of Lancaster and Chester

† Camden's Britannia, p 618

in the Castle-field. A stone with an inscription was found there in the year 1793, from which it appears that the Roman garrison of Manchester included the first cohort of Frisian troops—about 700 men—and that that cohort, amongst other public works, had constructed a length of twenty-four miles of the roads about Mancunium. This inscription, according to Dr Holmes' reading, is as follows —"Cohors prima Friseanorum quæ viam munivit millia passuum XXIIII." The remains of an altar found at Manchester, in the year 1829, show that a corps of Norican troops, from the passes of the Alps, also formed part of the garrison of the ancient Mamucium, and in addition to these auxiliary troops, we find marks of the presence of an officer of one of the prætorian legions, and of detachments of the Twentieth and the Sixth Legions, in that garrison.

But the opinion that the garrison of Mamucium was composed chiefly of Frieslanders is supported by other inscriptions discovered at Manchester, some of them as early as the time of Camden, and is curious, taken in connection with other facts, from the light which it throws on the military system of the Romans There were three principal garrisons in the present county of Lancaster, each of which had its outposts; and in order that these garrisons might be as little likely as possible to combine against the Romans, they were taken from different nations. The garrison of Mamucium were Frieslanders and Noricans, the garrison of Ribchester were Sarmatians, raised on the edge of the great plains on which the emperor of Russia now raises the Cossacks of the Ukraine, and Asti from the mountains of Thrace; and the garrison of Alaunc, or Lancaster, were Gauls or Germans, raised on the banks of the river Sambre With regard to one of the tribes from which the garrison of Mamucium was taken—namely, the Frisiabones or Frisavones, now known as Frieslanders—they are mentioned twice by Pliny, first, as the inhabitants of an island situated at the mouth of the Rhine, between the river Meuse and the Zuyder Zee, and second, as a nation of Belgic Gauls, who claimed a close affinity with the neighbouring Batavian and German tribes The following inscriptions have been found on funeral stones erected in honour of officers of this corps who died at Mamucium, after serving, the one twenty-three years, the other twenty —"Cohors prima Frisingensium, Centurioni Marco Savonio, Stipendiorum Viginti trium," and "Centurionis Candidi Fidesii, annorum Viginti, mensium Quatuor"

In the year 1612 an altar was found under the root of an old oak tree, on the banks of the Medlock, dedicated to Fortune the Preserver, by a centurion of the Sixth Legion. According to Horsley, the reading of this inscription is—"Fortunæ Conservatrici, Marcius, Centurio Legionis Sextæ Victricis" This inscription renders it probable that the garrison of Manchester included a detachment of the Sixth Legion, whose head-quarters were at York, and whose name and emblem—a capricorn or sea-goat—is found on so many inscriptions in Yorkshire An oblong brick or tile found at Manchester a few years since, with the inscription, "F CXXVV Fecit Cohors Vicesima Victrix Veleriana," is perhaps the mark of the occasional presence of a detachment of the Twentieth Victorious Legion A still more interesting object was found about the same time, namely, an altar erected by a retired standard-bearer of one of the prætorian legions to one of the emperors All that is legible are the following words, or parts of words —"Neris Imperatori olim signifer Legionis Vexillationis Prætoriæ et Noricor Votum solvit libens merito" A specimen of pottery, probably the handle of an amphora, has also been found in the Castle-field, at Manchester, marked with the name of the first cohort of Frisians

Many other articles connected with the Roman times have been dug up or discovered on or near to the same site Amongst these were a number of Roman urns, of earthen vessels, with several coins, and a lachrymatory of blue glass, found on the edge of the camp, in the year 1765. A Roman bulla of gold, one of the personal ornaments of Romans of good family, was found about the same time in deepening the Duke's canal, close to the second lock on the Irwell. In 1777, a number of Roman coins were found on the banks of the Medlock, and in the year 1808 a number of Roman dishes, made of pewter, were discovered, and sent to the British Museum * According to an analysis made by Dr. Woolaston, they were composed of three parts tin, and one part lead.

In the year 1821, some workmen who were digging a drain in the township of Hulme, near Manchester, came on the line of the Roman road from Mamucium to Deva, six feet below the present level of the ground At the same time three large stones were discovered, embedded in the earth. On one was the figure of a man standing upright, on another a carved representation of a human head, with the hair turned backwards, and on the third the

* Lyson's Reliquiæ Britannico-Romanæ, vol i part iv plate 5

representation of a man dressed in a flowing robe, and with his hands crossed over his breast, and locked together Subsequent to this, a great variety of articles were discovered near the old Castle-field, by the workmen employed by the Bridgewater trust. These are deposited at Worsley hall, the seat of the earl of Ellesmere. Amongst them were a small leaden bust of a female, probably a household divinity, four inches high, a lion's face, in pottery, a fragment of a bowl, representing a deer chase, fragments of another bowl, of red pottery, with figures representing a man standing, another sitting, and a Cupid within a circle, two iron heads of spears or javelins, the head of an iron axe, a stylus of iron, a bronze and a copper bulla, a circular metallic brooch, inlaid with seven stones, a votive altar, erected by a standard-bearer to one of the emperors, a Cupid inclosed within a coating of red earthenware, and numerous fragments of pottery of very beautiful workmanship A very deep well has been found in Castle-field, which is supposed to have been that of the garrison.

The Roman coins found at Manchester are very numerous Amongst them are coins of Otho, Vitellius, Vespasian, Domitian, Nerva, Trajan, Hadrian, Antoninus Pius, Constantius, and Tetricus.

Many remains of the Romans have been discovered at different places in the valleys of the Mersey, the Irwell, and the smaller streams that flow into them, or amongst the wild hills from which those rivers descend The arm of a silver statue of Victory, probably belonging to one of the Roman legions, was discovered some years ago on Blackstone cage, near Littleborough It was probably lost in a conflict with the tribes of the neighbouring hills Ascending the pass in the hills through what is now called Mottram-in-Longendale, there was a Roman camp, supposed to have been called Melandra castle, just beyond the present limits of Lancashire. It is also believed that the Roman garrison at Mancunium held an out-post at Stockport The head of a spear, supposed to be Roman, has been found in the neighbourhood of Leigh, and a beautiful bronze strainer or colander in Chat Moss.

Descending the Mersey to Warrington, remains of the Romans are found on both sides of the river There are the outlines of a camp at Wilderspool, on the Cheshire side of the Mersey Large quantities of pottery, and the remains of furnaces, supposed to have been used in the manufacturing of earthenware, and still containing ashes, were found in the same neighbourhood. Numerous specimens of red and black pottery, and many coins, have been found, including one of the Emperor Marcus. In a field near the camp were found vases, fibulæ, coins, and fireplaces, with ashes still in them. At Appleton, urns full of calcined bones and other remains of mortality have also been discovered, close by the line of the public road This seems to have been here, as everywhere else, the favourite burial-place of the Romans—the place where the "Siste! Viator," engraved on the monuments of the dead, continually met the traveller's eye

Lower down the Mersey, on the shore of the estuary near Runcorn, a very interesting memorial of the Roman dominion in Britain was found, in the time of Camden, in the form of twenty masses of lead, inscribed with the name of the Emperor Domitian, the tyrant who recalled Julius Agricola from his command in Britain. These pieces of lead are also marked with the name of the people in whose territory, and by whose labour, they were produced. The Cangi appear to have been the people who produced them, as the Brigantes were the people who produced similar masses of lead found in Yorkshire Some difference of opinion exists as to the position of the country of the Cangi, but it seems to have been a country abounding in lead mines, for pigs of lead stamped with that name have not only been found on the banks of the Mersey, but also at Hints Moor, Staffordshire,* and even as far south as Hampshire.† It may have been Derbyshire, but the probabilities are rather in favour of North Wales, for Tacitus speaks of the country of the Cangi as being almost within sight of the Irish sea, and Ptolemy mentions a promontory of the Concangi, which was on the coast of Wales

Very few remains of the Romans have been found in the south-western part of Lancashire, near the sea-coast, but in the year 1838 an earthen vessel was dug up at Spink farm, in the township of Tarbock, containing thirty-three silver, and forty-seven copper coins, of the Roman period. Amongst them were coins of the Emperors Nerva, Trajan, Hadrian, Antoninus Pius, and Aurelian, and one struck in honour of Julia, the daughter of the Emperor Titus, and of Venus, the august queen—R Venus Augusta,‡ or, as Horace has it, "Venus, Regina Cnidi, Paphique"

* Pennant's Tours in Wales, vol v

† The Celt, the Roman, and the Saxon, by Thomas Wright, Esq., p 233

‡ Transactions of Historic Society of Lancashire and Cheshire, vol iv p. 11

Roman Stations on the Douglas and the Ribble—Proceeding northward we come to the valley of the Douglas, closed on the north and north-east by the Rivington hills, and separated from the valley of the Mersey by the high lands which our Anglo-Saxon ancestors named the Billenghaugh, of which the Billinge-hill is the highest point. A Roman road runs through this valley, leaving Wigan on the right, and another line of road, also of Roman origin, has been traced from the neighbourhood of Wigan to Manchester. The other principal remains of the Romans found on the banks of the Douglas, consist of a number of Roman urns discovered at Wigan and a gold coin of Vitellius found at the same place.*

The Roman and British Station of Ribodunum or Ribchester—Ribchester on the river Ribble was a Roman station, and a flourishing city. It is mentioned as Rigodunum in Ptolemy's account of the cities of the Brigantes, and is the only town or city within the limits of the present county of Lancaster that is named by him. The evidences of Roman occupation found at Ribchester are more striking than those found at any other place in the north-western district of England, with the single exception of Chester.

Ribchester, or the camp on the Ribble, stands on the north bank of that river, which is there a wide and impetuous stream, and between two small brooks, which flow into it from Longridge Fell and the adjoining heights. Its position is strong, and easily defensible against the modes of attack in use in the time of the Romans, and from its easy communication with the estuaries of the Ribble and the Wyre on one side, and with the Yorkshire valleys on the other, as well as from the natural fertility of the surrounding country, it possessed sources of great prosperity. The ruins, which remain to the present day, prove that it was a flourishing place, although its wealth and prosperity have been transferred in modern times to Preston, which Camden describes as the "succedanea proles" of Ribchester.†

It appears from the inscriptions found at Ribchester, that the garrison of that place was composed of a detachment of the Twentieth Legion, and of an ala or wing of Sarmatian horsemen, probably raised either on the banks of the Dniester or at the mouth of the Danube. The name of the latter occurs so frequently as to create the belief that they formed the ordinary garrison of Ribchester,

* Transactions of Historic Society of Lancashire and Cheshire, vol. ?, p. 41

† Camden's Britannia, p. 618

though other inscriptions induce us to believe that they were occasionally aided by legionary soldiers of the Sixth and Twentieth Legions, from Eboracum and Deva. Ribchester commanded the passage of the Ribble, which has been at all times the most important military position in Lancashire; and from its vicinity to the estuaries of the Ribble and the Wyre, and its close communication with the interior, it must have been a position of great value, in furnishing supplies and reinforcements to the Roman fleets in the western seas. We know from the life of Agricola that he was assisted in his operations against the Caledonians by a powerful fleet, and there is no reason to doubt that his successors availed themselves of the same means of attack and defence.

A circumstance which has served to bring to light the ancient wonders of Ribchester is, that the current of the river Ribble is continually wearing away its banks, and exposing to view the foundations of ancient buildings, and other objects long buried under ground. When Dr Stukeley visited Ribchester in the year 1725, he remarked, "The river Ribble is very broad in this place, rapid, and sonorous, running over the pebbles, and, what is much to be lamented, over innumerable Roman antiquities, for in the long tract of time it has eaten away a third part of the city." In the account of "Roman Ribchester," drawn up by the late Mr. Just and Mr Harland, in the year 1850, for the information of the members of the British Archæological Association, they state that "the river Ribble has encroached vastly upon the area of the station. Taking the extent of the fosse on the western side as a complete side of the station, and from the angle close to the river at the southern extremity, making a straight line perpendicular to this side, we find that the other angle to complete the rectangle would be on the other side of the river, just over the fence of the field, and directly opposite to the brook which forms the boundary of the station on the east. At an estimate by the eye, there may have been one-fourth of the area of the station washed away by the river, burying within its sandy bed Roman treasures and relics, probably for ever. In a line with this, or nearly so, the fishermen state that the Roman wall of the rampart extends into the river, and that at low water they can stand about middle deep on the sunken remains; when off the remains, on either side, the water is beyond their depth." They add, "So active are the encroachments of the stream during floods, that houses have disappeared from the bank in our recollection, and many more in that of the oldest inhabitants. Unless man more successfully opposes the action of such floods, in a few generations the station at Ribchester will disappear, not swallowed up by an earthquake, as tradition affirms of its pristine glory, but by the stream which, serpent-like, now insidiously winds past it. Most of the relics discovered have been washed up by the encroachments of the river"*

Although the walls of the ramparts around the station have totally disappeared above ground, their foundations still exist, and were laid bare in the year 1850, by means of excavations, with a view of obtaining information for the congress of the British Archæological Association, which that year assembled at Manchester They were found to consist of loose stonework without mortar, or the cement coating common to such foundations. The rectangle inclosed within the fortification was 300 yards in length on its longest side, and from 130 to 140 on its shortest Except to the west, no line of military way can now be traced up to the station. This enters it midway in the rampart on the northern side, where stood the Decuman gate The Prætorium was opposite this, and hence stood where the Ribble now flows.

The ancient city of Ribchester was adorned with a temple, supposed to have been dedicated to Minerva Belisama, and with a greater number of altars, dedicated to the gods of Rome, Greece, and Syria, than almost any other city in Britain.

In the year 1811 some workmen employed in endeavouring to stop the encroachments of the Ribble, nearly opposite the church, met with the foundations of two parallel walls, nearly north and south, strongly cemented, and about twenty-four yards distant from each other Within the wall was a ragged floor, and near the south end the remains of a large flat stone with a Latin inscription The commencement of the inscription is destroyed, but it appears from the latter part of it, that it records the restoration of a temple which formerly stood on the spot, and its dedication "to a most powerful divinity and queen," whom Dr Whitaker, who investigated the subject with admirable learning and sagacity, supposes to have been the goddess Minerva. Further search was made in the summer of 1813, and subsequently, for the remains of this interesting ruin, the result of which was that a column and a square moulded corner of the temple, still upright and in their original positions, were

* Paper on Roman Ribchester, by John Just and John Harland, Esqs. Journal of British Archæological Association, vol vi p 229

found, which, with other remains, showed that a temple of the length of about 112 feet, with sixteen columns, had stood on the spot. Within the walls of this temple were found a stratum of charcoal, supposed to have been produced by the burning of the roof and windows, several skeletons of men scattered about, who are supposed to have perished when the temple was destroyed, and many beautiful remnants of amphoræ and pateræ of red Samian ware.*

The inscription found in this temple was so much fractured and worn, that the first portion is in a great measure conjectural. What is quite clear is, that it records the restoration from the ground and the dedication of the temple to a powerful goddess and queen The title of regina or queen is rarely applied in inscriptions to any of the goddesses except Juno, of whom it is the almost invariable title, but Dr. Whitaker thinks that in this case it is applied to Minerva, on the ground that a helmet belonging to a statue of that goddess was found close to this temple, and that the term regina is applied by the poets to other goddesses besides Juno, as, for instance, by Horace to Diana, and, he might have added, to Venus What, perhaps, is even a stronger reason is, that the temple stood on the banks of a river dedicated to Belisama, whose worship was closely connected with that of Minerva

In the year 1815 the removal of a very fine sculptured stone, which lay imbedded in the stonework of Salesbury Hall, near Ribchester, led to the discovery of an inscription to Apollo "On the front of the stone," says Dr Whitaker, "is a basso-relievo of Apollo reposing on his lyre, better designed than any work of a Roman-British artist which I have ever seen. On the second are the figures of two priests in long robes, holding the head of some horned animal between them, on the third is the inscription in question; the fourth is rough, having been originally attached to the wall' A copy of the inscription on this stone was published by Camden in his "Britannia," in the year 1590, but with his usual frankness he confessed that he could make nothing of it Dr Whitaker induced Lord Bulkeley to detach the stone from the wall of Salesbury hall, in the year 1815, and then the whole inscription appeared. It is not without its difficulties even now, but Dr. Whitaker reads it thus —"Pio sancto Apollini Apono, ob salutem Domini nostri, Ala equitum Sarmatum Bieneten, sub Dionio Antonio, centurione Legionis Sextæ Victricis"—(To the sacred Apollo Aponus,

* Whitaker's History of Richmondshire.

for the safety of our lord, the wing of Sarmatian horse of the Brenetenni, under Dionius Antonius, a centurion of the Sixth Victorious Legion). "It now turns out," says Dr Whitaker, "to be a dedication to Apollo Aponus, or the indolent Apollo, the god of medicine, who restores health by relaxation or repose, on behalf of an emperor, who unfortunately is not mentioned" He adds that there were certain mineral springs at Aponi, near Padua, long frequented by the Romans under the name of Fontes Aponi It appears from the above inscription, if it be correctly read, that the Sarmatian horse were under the orders of a centurion of the Sixth Legion. A corner-stone has also been found at Ribchester, inscribed ' Leg. XXVV fecit," showing that a portion of the Twentieth Legion was also stationed at that place, and assisted in erecting some of the buildings there Many other inscriptions in honour of the gods of the Pantheon have been found at Ribchester.

An altar, dedicated to Mars and Victory, "Deo Marti et Victoriæ," is mentioned by Camden, in his account of his first visit to Ribchester, and when he was there a second time, in 1603, he met with the largest and finest altar that he had ever seen, dedicated to the "Deis Matribus"—certain mysterious beings, worshipped as the Mothers of the Gods, the Mothers, and the Mothers of the Gods of Syria Horsley reads the inscription on this altar, "Deis Matribus, Marcus Ingenninus, Decurio alæ Astorum, susceptum solvit libentissime merito"* Inscriptions to the Mothers of the Gods have been found in many parts of Britain, and of the Roman empire They are generally figured as three females, especially in an inscription found at Cologne, where the figures are quite perfect The wing of Asti mentioned in the above inscription was another body of troops, of the Thracian race, stationed at Ribchester Camden, in his account of what he saw at Ribchester, adds, "I likewise saw a little altar there, turned out among rubbish, with this inscription, 'Pacifero Marti Elcg Aui Ba. posuit ex voto' This was so small that it seemed to have been some poor man's portable altar, and used only for incense and salt flour cakes, whereas the other was much larger, and fit for offering the greater sacrifices of animals Here, also, was dug up a stone, on which was carved a naked figure on horseback, without saddle or bridle, brandishing a spear with both hands, and insulting over a naked man on the ground, holding in his hand something square, probably a shield.

* Britannia, Roman, p 303

Between the horse and the prostrate figure were the letters D. M. (Dis Manibus), under the figure, Gal (or perhaps Al) Sarmata—Alæ Sarmatarum. "The rest of the many letters," he says, "are so decayed as not to be read, nor can I form any conjecture about them"

In addition to dedications to the gods, a funeral inscription has been found at Ribchester, in which Julius Maximus, an officer of the Sarmatian horse, consigns to the earth the remains, and commends the virtues, of "his incomparable wife, his dutiful son, and his mother-in-law, of dearest memory."

Amongst the objects of a miscellaneous nature found at Ribchester are—a splendid helmet, a handsome drinking cup; Roman pateræ, with figures of wolves and flowers upon them, from the workshop of Probus, a floor composed of Roman tiles, a ruby ring, with a figure of Mars, the finger of a copper statue, urns, the base of a pillar, and a most noble shaft, seven feet long and handsomely turned, which was taken out of the river, a Roman partition wall, the joists and boards of a floor of ash, found four feet under the present surface, the top of a great two-handed amphora or wine jar, a gold finger of a statue, and another brass finger, as large as a man's, two intaglios of Mercury, with wings on the feet, a well-balanced steel-yard, and coins of numerous emperors One of the most interesting discoveries of Roman antiquities is that made at Ribchester in the year 1796, the particulars of which were detailed by the late Charles Townley, Esq, in the "Vetusta Monumenta," published by the Society of Antiquaries.* The remains are chiefly of bronze, and were found in a hollow that had been made in some waste land near to the church, and at the bend of the river The principal article was a helmet, of beautiful workmanship It consists of two pieces one of these, the skull part, is ornamented with the figures of eleven combatants on foot, and six on horseback, the other is the mask or visor to cover the face, which has very effeminate features, and joins exactly to the skull part, to which it is fastened by rings and studs, some of which still remain. The helmet appears to be too slight for defence, and the mask is of very superior workmanship to the head-piece The articles found along with it consisted of pateræ of various dimensions; a bust of Minerva, three inches in diameter, with the remains of nails and cramps by which it was fastened to a circular disk; four circular plates with

* Vol iv pp 1-12

mouldings; a colon or colander; two portions of a candelabrum, and various other articles.

In the year 1833 an altar was dug up in the churchyard at Ribchester, with an inscription, from which it appears that it was erected as an offering for the safety of Caracalla, the worthless son of the Emperor Septimius Severus, who died at Eboracum, or York, in the year 211. The latter part of the inscription is illegible, but the following portion of it is tolerably clear —"Pro Salute et Victoria Invicti Imperatoris Marci Aurelii Severi Antonini Pii, et Juliæ Augustæ matris Domini, et Castrorum suorum" . . —(For the Safety and Victory of the unconquered emperor, Marcus Aurelius Severus Antoninus Pius, and of Julia Augusta, mother of our Lord, and of his camps)

Numerous coins have been found at Ribchester, beginning even before the date of the arrival of the Romans in the north-western part of Britain, and extending to the time of Constantine and his successors. Amongst them are coins of Augustus, B C. 29 to 14, of Titus Vespasian, A D 79 to 81, of Nerva, A.D. 96 to 98; of Trajan, A D. 98 to 117, of Hadrian, A D 117 to 138; of Commodus, A D. 180 to 192, of Septimius Severus, A D. 193 to 211; of Caracalla, A D. 211 to 217, of Diocletian, the persecutor of the Christians, A.D. 284 to 305; and one of a Christian emperor, bearing the cross and the motto of Constantine, "In hoc signo vinces"

Many memorials of the Roman occupation of Britain have been discovered between the Ribble and the Lune Kirkham appears to have been a Roman station. In that neighbourhood have been discovered the umbo of a Roman shield, an urn filled with bones, a battle-axe, and numerous coins * A collection of upwards of 400 Roman denarii, beginning in the reign of Vespasian and extending to that of Caracalla, was found by some brickmakers in the year 1820, near Rossal point, at the mouth of the Wyre † An urn, and another collection of Roman coins, were discovered in the reign of Charles II in Myerscough park, in the valley of the Wyre. ‡ A fibula, a spear head, a wine-strainer, a drinking-cup, and a battle-axe, have been dug out of Pilling Moss.§ An ancient anvil, a pair of scissors, and a number of plates of brass, were found at Stalmine ||

The Roman Alauna or Longovico, now Lancaster—Lancaster,

* Transactions of Historic Society of Lancashire and Cheshire, vol iii. p. 69 † Ibid vol iii p 66
‡ Ibid vol viii. p. 134 § Ibid vol iii p. 114 || Ibid vol. iii. p 120.

or the camp on the river Lune (apparently named Alauna or Aluana, after the river or after a god or goddess named Alaune, Alauna, or Ialone), though by some writers supposed to be the Longovico mentioned in the "Notitiæ," is the third and last of the Roman camps in Lancashire, which preserves the memory of the Roman dominion. There also, as at Manchester, Ribchester, and Chester, numerous evidences of the power and greatness of the Romans have been discovered. The position of Lancaster, standing on a steep hill, on the bend of a wide river, is at once commanding, beautiful, and healthy, and, like Chester, it united to these advantages the further recommendation of possessing a port, equal to all the requirements of Roman navigation, and admirably suited to give shelter and furnish supplies to the fleets employed in resisting attacks from the northern side of the wall of Hadrian There is evidence that one of the Roman roads, which ran up the valley of the Lune, was formed by that emperor, who also formed the first earthwork from the Solway to the Tyne, to protect the northern frontier of the Roman province, and there is also evidence that a basilica or court of justice, and set of public baths, were erected at Lancaster, at a very early period of the Roman occupation These are indications of a position of the first order, and one that was probably formed for naval as well as for military purposes; for it was near Lancaster that the road formed by Hadrian approached nearest to the sea, before turning into the interior and ascending the hills of the Cumbrian range, through which it was carried over steep and almost inaccessible heights to the vallum, the frontier of the empire in Britain From this circumstance, and from the fertility of the neighbouring country, it is probable that Lancaster was one of the principal ports of the Romans on the north-west coast of Britain for warlike purposes Some writers are of opinion that Lancaster was the "Portus Setantiorum" mentioned by Ptolemy.

The Roman camp, from which Lancaster takes its name, stood on the bold hill on which the castle and church now stand, and is supposed to have occupied the site of the present castle Portions of the castle still standing, or which were standing within a few years of the present time, are believed to have been of Roman origin This was the case with regard to the foundations of Hadrian's and the Dungeon towers The general figure of the Roman camp at Lancaster was an ellipsis. The walls were protected by several towers, and the work was defended by a double wall and a moat. A wall so ancient as to be named "the old wall," in deeds executed about the time of the Norman conquest, encircled the Castle hill, and portions of this wall continued in existence until modern times When Stukeley visited Lancaster, about the year 1724, he found "a great piece of the wall, on the north-east end of the hill, still standing." He says that it was built of white stone, held together by very hard mortar, that it reached to the Bridge lane, and hung over the street, at the head of the precipice, in a dreadful manner. 'I suppose," says Stukeley, "it originally inclosed the whole top of the hill, where the church and castle stand, which is steep on all sides, and half inclosed by the river Lune, so that it is an excellent guard to this part of the sea-coast, and commands a very great prospect both by sea and land. There was a spring of water inside the walls, under the tower. All the space of ground north of the church is full of foundations of stone buildings, Roman, I believe, and much stone has been taken up there"

The inscriptions discovered at Lancaster throw much light on the history of the place in Roman times.

Amongst the most curious of these inscriptions is the following, in which the horsemen of an ala of Belgian cavalry, raised on the banks of the river Sambre, and then in garrison at Lancaster, dedicated to one of the Roman emperors, supposed to be Caracalla, a basilica or court-house, and baths, which they had rebuilt from the ground, after the original building had been destroyed by age Dr. Whitaker, who expended extraordinary learning and ingenuity in examining and restoring this inscription, read it as follows "Imperatore Marco Aurelio Antonino Augusto, Balneum refectum, et Basilicam vetustate conlabsum, a solo restitutum, equites alæ Sebussianæ Antoninianæ, sub Octavio Sabino, viro Consulari, Præside nostro, curante Flavio Ammansio, Prefecto equitum dictorum, undecimo kalendas Septembrio, Censore secundum et Lepidum secundum Consul"—(To the emperor Marcus Aurelius Antoninus Augustus, these Baths restored, and this Basilica, decayed by age, rebuilt from the ground by the Antonine wing of Sebussian horsemen, Octavius Sabinus, of consular dignity, being President, Flavius Ammansius, Prefect of the said horsemen, superintending, the 11th of the Kalends of September, Censor and Lepidus, a second time, Consuls)

The following facts appear to be established by the above inscription:—

The Sebussian horsemen raised on the banks of the river Sabis, now the Sambre, formed a portion at least of the Roman garrison of Lancaster. These horsemen are mentioned more than once in ancient inscriptions found in Britain—amongst other places, on an altar discovered in the county of Durham. This altar is dedicated to Silvanus, the god of forests and field sports, by Caius Tetitius Viturius Micianus, prefect of the Sebussian horse, in memory of his having slain an enormous wild boar, which had set at defiance all hunters before him. Thus we have men from the banks of the Sambre serving in Lancashire during the Roman dominion, in addition to the Frisians, Noricans, Sarmatians, and Thracians, already mentioned.

Another fact which appears from this inscription is, that the Roman position at Lancaster was provided with a basilica, and with public baths. These must have been erected at a very early period of the Roman dominion, for when restored by the Sebussian horsemen, they had fallen into decay from time. The existence of a basilica at Lancaster renders it probable that it was the centre of the legal and judicial business of the district, as early as the time of the Romans.

Another inscription has been discovered near Lancaster, which is also very curious, especially if we interpret it as Dr. Whitaker does. The inscription is "Deo Mart. Sabino, P. et milit. N. Barc. S. Eiios P. O."

The altar containing this inscription was discovered at Halton, near Lancaster. Dr. Whitaker, speaking of this inscription says, "This is no less curious and valuable than the last; indeed, both as to the motive assigned and the expression, it is unique. Milite in barca: the last is a semi-barbarous Latin word, which is exactly translated by the modern bark, and it is evident that the altar now before us was a votive offering raised when the body of soldiers who made the offering were embarking on some military expedition. Among all the formulæ of Roman inscriptions, I have never seen anything resembling this." It ought to be stated, however, that this reading is by no means certain. N. Barc. may possibly be a contraction of In barca; but Mr. Just was disposed to consider it a contraction of "Numerus Barcariorum," the company of the Barcarii; and his view is supported by the fact, that a body of troops described by the title of Numerus Barcariorum is mentioned, in the 'Notitia Imperii," as serving in Britain, at the time when that work was drawn up. If we take Mr Just's reading, we may infer that that corps was serving at Lancaster, and dedicated the above altar to the god of war; if Dr Whitaker's, it would appear that a corps of soldiers, name unknown, but commanded by Sabinus, embarked there on service in the northern seas of Britain.

Another very curious inscription found at Lancaster is the following, in which the divinity, who was believed to preside over the Lune, is supposed to be invoked "Deo Ialono Contre Sancissimo, Julius Januarius Ex Decurione." The God Ialone thus invoked by Julius Januarius, was not one of the gods of Greece or Rome, but some British divinity, and probably the god who was supposed to preside over the river Lune An altar, dedicated to the goddess Elauna, was discovered on the banks of the Greta in the year 1702, which is also supposed to have been dedicated to a nymph, who was believed to preside over the same beautiful stream* Another altar has been discovered at Lancaster, dedicated to Mars Cocidius The inscription is, "Deo Sancto Marti Cocidio, Vibinius Lucius, Beneficiarius Consulis, Votum Solvit Lubens Merito"—(To the sacred Mars Cocidius, Vibinius Lucius, a consular beneficiary, willingly and dutifully discharged his vow) The Mars Cocidius of Lancaster is even a greater mystery than the Jupiter Tanarus of Chester The title of Cocidius is probably given to Mars from the circumstance of his having been more especially worshipped at some place, or in some district in Britain, or elsewhere, bearing that name. A somewhat similar case is that of an altar discovered at Caerleon, the ancient Isca, in Monmouthshire, dedicated to Jupiter Dolichenus, this name, thus applied to Jupiter, is derived, according to Mr Roach Smith, from Doliche, a place in Macedonia, famous for its iron mines. A similar inscription on an altar to Jupiter Dolichenus has been found at Rome, and there Dolichenus is spoken of as a place where iron is found—"Ubi ferrum nascitur" The Cocidius applied to Mars in the Lancaster inscription is probably derived in a somewhat similar manner. Dr. Whitaker supposes that the Cocidius of this inscription is the same as the Cocis mentioned in an inscription described by Horsley, in his "Britannia Romana," as having been discovered in the north of Britain, this, however, throws no light upon the subject, unless we are to conclude that Cocis or

* Phillips' Yorkshire, p 48

Cocidius was the British name of the god of war, or that he was worshipped with peculiar honours at Coccium, on the banks of the Ribble, or some other place of similar name

Quite as interesting as the above inscriptions, and much more intelligible, are the milliary stones or Roman milestones found at Caton, Borough, and Ashton, near Lancaster The inscriptions on these stones throw light on the origin of the two great lines of road which the Romans formed through the present county of Lancaster. The first of them seems to have been formed by the Emperor Hadrian, between the years 117 and 138, at the time when he was constructing the great works which established the power of the Romans in the north of Britain The second was formed by the Emperor Philip, a successful Arabian soldier, who obtained possession of supreme power in the year 244, by murdering his predecessor Gordianus, and who was himself murdered in the year 249 The inscription on the milliary stone erected on the line of road formed by the Emperor Hadrian reads as follows:—"Imp Caes Tr Hadrianus Aug, Pont. Max, Trib Pot, Cos III, Pat Patriæ. Centuria Secunda, Mill Pass Quinque"—(To the Emperor Cæsar Trajan Hadrianus Augustus, high priest, possessed of tribunitian power, in his third consulship, the father of his country the second century or centuria, the fifth mile). It would be curious to ascertain what was the starting-point from which this fifth mile was computed. On a milliary stone found in Leicestershire the distance is stated to be three miles from Ratis, which is the old Roman name for what we call Leicester, and the probability seems to be that the stone above described, which was found at Caton, near Lancaster, was erected at a distance of five miles from Lancaster. Both the milliary stone found at Caton, and that found near Leicester, bear the name of the Emperor Hadrian, and seem to have been erected in the same year, that is, in the year of his third consulship, from which we may infer that the main line of road through Britain was formed by that very able and energetic emperor The inscription on the mile-stone erected in the time of the Emperor Philip is as follows —"Imp. C M Julio Philippo Pio Fel Aug"—(To the Emperor C M Julius Philippus, Pious, Fortunate, and August). A monumental inscription was also found in digging in the older part of the town in the year 1772, in this inscription the remains of Lucius Julius Apollinaris, a native of Treves, are devoted to the gods of the shades.

In addition to the monuments with inscriptions, many other

Roman memorials have been discovered at Lancaster. Amongst them is a headless figure of the goddess Ceres, who was much worshipped among the Romans One of the epithets applied to Ceres—that is, "Mater Divum," Mother of the Gods—is found on an inscription at Ribchester, already mentioned; and many other inscriptions to the mothers of the gods, in some of which they are described as the Syrian goddesses, have been found, both in Britain and on the continent The above inscription is curious, as showing the origin of the worship of Ceres to have sprung out of the superstitions of Syria.

In addition to the figure of Ceres, a figure of Apollo playing on a lyre has also been discovered at Lancaster. A large hewn stone, about three tons in weight, was found some years ago, about six feet below the surface of the ground, which is supposed to have been a corner-stone of some large building In addition to this, there have been discovered four sculptured heads, two lions cut in freestone, a Roman sepulchre containing half-burnt fragments of wood, bones, and ashes, with broken pateræ, urns, Roman bricks, coins, horns of animals, a sepulchral lamp, a human skull, and two fragments of a thick wall, about five yards distant from each other

The coins found at Lancaster are extremely numerous, and extend over the whole period of the Roman occupation, from the reign of Otho, in the year 69, to that of Magnus Maximus, in the year 387* Amongst the emperors, or members of the imperial families, whose coins have been discovered at Lancaster, are the following:—Otho, Vespasian, Domitian, Hadrian, Antoninus Pius, Marcus Aurelius, Commodus, Probus, Diocletian, Constantius Chlorus, Licinius, Constantine the Great, and Magnus Maximus

The Romans had another station on the banks of the Lune, at the point where the stream known as Leck Beck falls into the river As usually happens in Roman stations, it was placed at the angle formed by the confluence of the two streams The modern name of this station is Overburrow, from the Saxon, Overburgh—the higher fortress—and it was probably so named to distinguish it from Lancaster, situated lower down the stream of the Lune. Overburrow is supposed to be the site of the Bremetonacæ of the Romans, which was situated twenty miles north of Coccium, on the Ribble. Leland speaks of Burrow or Overburrow as the site of "a notable town," from the remains of antiquity found there, and

* Simpson's Antiquities of Lancaster, p 121

since his time many additional remains have been found, especially an altar dedicated to a Sabine deity—Deo Sango—by Naulus Trebius Atta, and also a golden bulla.

It will be seen from the above details that the ancient governors of the world have left marks of their presence, and memorials of their power, in every part of the north-western district of Britain. The cities which the Romans built became the residences, first of British chiefs, and then of Saxon kings, after the departure of the Romans from this island. The most celebrated of those cities—Chester, Manchester, and Lancaster—have been places of note from the time of the Romans to the present day. It is a proof of the influence of the Romans in developing the resources of Britain, that they left behind upwards of 200 towns and cities when they retired from Britain, according to a list given in the work of Anonymus of Ravenna—having only found sixty towns and cities in Britain when they arrived in the island, according to the list given in Ptolemy's Geography.

The dominion of the Romans was never so firmly established in Britain as in Gaul and in Spain. In Britain itself there was always a part of the island in which the inhabitants defied the Roman arms, and the Romans do not appear ever to have established themselves either in Ireland or in the western islands. Tacitus informs us that it was the intention of Agricola to have passed over into Ireland with his army, in order that, by the conquest of that country, he might have removed the dangerous spectacle of national independence from the sight of the Britons. But he was withdrawn from his command before he could make the attempt, and his successors soon found the difficulties of conquering Britain itself too great, to leave either time or means to attempt the conquest of another country. Hence the Britons never altogether lost the animating example of independence in a neighbouring nation.

As early as the age of the Emperor Hadrian, the Romans, after having spent more than half a century in conquering the more accessible and fertile parts of Britain, adopted a defensive attitude towards the inhabitants of the wilder and more mountainous districts of the north. That emperor, in running a line of fortifications across the island, from the mouth of the Solway to that of the Tyne, may probably have intended to use it as the basis of further conquests, and it was employed for that purpose in the succeeding reign of Antoninus Pius, when the Roman frontier was for a while pushed forward to the banks of the Clyde and the Forth. But the ground thus gained was soon lost; and when next we hear of the Roman frontier in Britain, it had again been forced back to the Solway and the Tyne. Not only so, but the British tribes dwelling to the north of the Roman wall, the Mætæ, who dwelt near the wall, and the Caledonians, who dwelt further north, had either forced their way across the wall, or had turned it, by an attack from the sea, and were pressing forward into the Roman provinces of Britain. This happened in the reign of the Emperor Commodus, about the year 180 of the Christian era, and this attack was beaten back with great difficulty.

About twenty years later, the position of Roman affairs in Britain had become so alarming, that the Emperor Septimius Severus proceeded thither with his two sons, Caracalla and Geta, and with a large army He established his head-quarters at York, and from that city advanced not only beyond the wall, but to the furthest limits of Britain, after fighting many and desperate battles In this campaign the emperor lost 50,000 men, partly by the sword, partly by the hardships of a desperate contest amongst mountains, swamps, and forests The presence of the emperor and of so vast a force produced a moment of tranquillity; but no sooner had the legions been withdrawn to the south of the wall, than the whole people rose again in arms The news was brought to the emperor as he was lying on his deathbed at York, and he died there, breathing out vain threats of extermination against the race which had so bravely resisted the masters of the world After the death of Severus, his sons patched up a peace as hastily as possible with the British tribes dwelling north of the wall, and returned to Rome, there to intrigue and conspire against each other, until the younger brother was murdered by the assassins of the elder, in the arms of his mother.

When next we obtain any clear light as to the condition of Britain, we find the whole island in open insurrection against the Roman emperors, Maximian and Diocletian. The leader of this revolt was Carausius, a Batavian or Manapian sea-captain, who had been appointed by the emperors to the command of a fleet, which they had formed in the British seas, to resist the incursions of the Saxons, Franks, and other German pirates, who had made an attack on Britain, in the reign of the Emperor Probus, in 287. This fleet was manned by Batavian and other seamen from the neighbouring coasts, and placed under the command of a daring and able chief of the same race, named Carausius, who soon became so formidable that the emperors were induced to buy his submission, by raising him to the rank of Cæsar. Even this did not secure his submission, for he at length rose in open revolt, and, having obtained the command both of Britain and the British seas, for thirteen years defied all the strength of the emperors In the thirteenth year of his reign, he was murdered by contrivance of his minister, Allectus, who assumed a similar power His rule was very short, for his fleet was taken by Constantius, the father of Constantine the Great, and he was himself defeated and killed in battle. By his defeat and death the Roman power was re-established in Britain

It would appear that by this time the southern and central districts of Britain had become in a great degree Romanized, especially in the cities and towns, where the Romans had formed colonies, and kept up garrisons At the same time, it is clear that a large portion of the island was still in the hands of the native inhabitants. In the reign of the Emperor Valentinian, the Picts and Scots—which latter name included the people of Hibernia—had overrun the greater part of Britain. They captured London, and defeated the Romans in a great battle, killing Fallofaudes, the Roman dux or commander in Britain, and Nectarinus, the commander of the maritime coasts The genius of Theodosius, the general of Valentinian, averted the threatened catastrophe for a few years. He even defeated the Britons, and drove them back as far as the Roman wall, if not further, but this was merely a temporary success, for the energies of the empire were exhausted, and a few years later the Roman legions were withdrawn from Britain, to defend Italy and Rome from the northern barbarians.

The first large body of troops withdrawn from Britain by the Romans was the Twentieth Legion, whose head-quarters had been at Chester for upwards of 300 years. This legion was withdrawn to enable Stilicho, the general of the Emperor Honorius, to hold his ground in Italy, and to defend Rome itself, from Alaric and his army of Goths. In Claudian's account of the army which assembled for that final struggle, he mentions a legion which came from the extremity of Britain, where it had bridled the fierce Scot, and noted the figures burned with hot iron on the body of the lifeless Pict. This was no doubt the Twentieth Legion, for the Second and Sixth Legions are mentioned in the "Notitia," or muster roll of the Roman army, in the time of Honorius, as remaining in Britain after the Twentieth Legion had left the island. The other legions left Britain about the year 449, and their departure was the signal for the appearance of a new race of conquerors, whose descendants still possess the land.

THE ANGLES AND SAXONS IN LANCASHIRE AND CHESHIRE.

Before the Romans retired from Britain, the Saxons had made themselves known and feared along the eastern and southern coasts of the island, and soon after the departure of the Romans, the Angles, from whom England is named, poured into the northern and central parts of South Britain, from Germany. As early as the reign of the Emperor Valentinian, about the year 370 of the Christian era, and long before the time of Hengst and Horsa, the Saxons are mentioned, as having for many years wasted the shores of Britain with continual ravages.* The Saxons were then so well known, and so much dreaded, that one of the armies which the Romans maintained in Britain was especially appointed to guard the coasts most exposed to their attacks † Those coasts were named the Saxon shore in Britain—"littus Saxonicum per Britannias'—as the coasts on the opposite side of the channel were named, for the same reason, the Saxon shores of Gaul and Belgium The Saxon shore in Britain was under the command of a military officer, named the Comes or Count of the Saxon shore This officer had under his orders a force of about 3000 infantry and 600 cavalry, with which he garrisoned nine fortified positions. The first and most northern of these positions was at Branodunum or Brancaster, on the coast of Norfolk, garrisoned by a squadron of Dalmatian cavalry. Another body of horsemen guarded Garriannonum, now Burghcastle, between Norwich and Yarmouth A third position, named Othonæ, which cannot be identified with certainty, was garrisoned by a company of Fortensian infantry. On the south side of the estuary of the Thames, the first com-

* Ammianus Marcellinus, vol I p 28 Gibbon, c. xxvi

† Notitia Utriusque Imperii, Monumenta Historica Britannica, p 23

pany of Vetasii were in garrison at Regulbium, now Reculver, on the Kentish coast Further south, the commander of the Second Augustan Legion held Ritupæ, or Richborough, near the present Sandwich. Ritupæ was the port by which the Romans usually communicated with Gaul, and was of so much importance, and in so much peril, in the reigns of Arcadius and Honorius, when the Roman power was falling into ruin, as to be made the head-quarters of the Second Legion, which for upwards of 300 years had been stationed at Caerleon in South Wales. The next was the well-known position of Dubris or Dover, garrisoned by a body of Tungrians. After Dubris came Portus Lemanis, or Lymne, also on the coast of Kent Further west, and on the coast of Sussex, the commander of the Saxon shore had two garrisons. The first was at Anderida, near Pevensey, a place so named from the great primeval forest, afterwards called Andradswald by the Saxons, which extended in length 120 miles, in breadth thirty miles, and covered the wealds of Kent and Sussex, down to the time of Queen Elizabeth, when it was the chief seat of the English iron manufacture.* Further west was the Portus Adurni, situated at the mouth of the river Adur, which enters the sea near the present New Shoreham and Bognor From the positions of these places, it appears that the earliest attacks of the Saxons on Britain were directed against the districts comprised in the present counties of Norfolk, Suffolk, Essex, Kent, and Sussex, being the parts of the coast most accessible from the continent. If the term Saxon shore means the shore peopled, not wasted, by the Saxons, as is believed by writers of eminence,† we must carry back the date of the first settlement of the Saxons in Britain to a period 100 years before the landing of Hengst and Horsa, 150 years previous to the great conflict between King Arthur and the Saxons on the banks of the river Douglas in Lancashire; 200 years previous to the advance of the army of the Northumbrian Angles, under King Ethelfrith to the walls of Chester, and nearly 400 years before the final conquest of Chester by Offa, king of the Mercians

The Saxons or Anglo-Saxons, whose descendants are now found in every quarter of the globe, are spoken of by Ptolemy the geo-

* Camden's Britannia Sussex

† J M Kemble's Saxons in England, vol i p 14 Lappenburg's History of England, vol i p 46 Palgrave, vol i p 384

grapher, about the year 140 of the Christian era, as a German tribe, occupying three islands near the mouth of the river Elbe* Ammianus Marcellinus, speaking of the events of the year 364, says —"At this time the Picts, the Saxons, and the Attacoths (the Scots, the original natives of Ireland), vexed Britain with continual woes" A few years later, Orosius described the Saxons as a people dwelling in the pathless swamps on the shores of the ocean † Egesippus, speaking of the terror produced by the arms of Rome, says, that "Saxony, inaccessible in its marshes, trembled." Claudian claims for his hero, Stilicho, that he moistened with Saxon blood the shores of the Orkneys. Sidonius describes the Saxons as a race of pirates, the terror of the ocean He says of them that they are of all enemies the most terrible, attacking suddenly, escaping craftily, overwhelming those who resist, dispersing those whom they surprise. He says that shipwrecks only exercise their courage, do not affright them, for they are not only acquainted but familiar with the perils of the sea, and make their attacks in storm and tempest, as being then least expected. Zosimus says of the Saxons of his age, that from their greatness of mind, their strength of body, and their power of enduring fatigue, they were regarded as the bravest of the Germans

Though the Saxons are spoken of, in the first instance, as the inhabitants of a few small islands off the coast of Germany, they possessed, at the time when they undertook the conquest of Britain, the extensive districts of Germany which are now known as Hanover, Westphalia, and Holstein, but which were then known as the country of the Westphali, the Eastphali, and the Angles ‡ Their territory was bounded by Friesland on the south, and Denmark on the north Many of the Frieslanders accompanied the Saxons and Angles to Britain, for they were well acquainted with the country, garrisons of Frieslanders having been stationed at Manchester and other places during the Roman dominion in Britain The Angli or Angles, from whom the conquerors of Britain obtained the name of Anglo-Saxons, and from whom the southern part of Britain took the familiar name of England, were a powerful tribe of the Saxon race. They were no doubt the Angli spoken of by Ptolemy and Procopius,§ and probably the Angli and Angri varii of Tacitus ‖ A very ancient German poet speaks of the Angli as

* Ptol Geog, vol ii p 2 † Orosius, vol vii p 32 ‡ R G Latham on the English Language vol i p 51
§ Procopius, lib iv ‖ C. C Taciti Germania. R G Latham on the English Language, vol i p 76

the third people of Saxony, and gives the names of the Eastphali and the Westphali as the other two. The venerable Bede states that the Angles peopled all the country on the north side of the river Humber, that is, the counties of York, Lancaster, Durham, and Northumberland, and also the districts of the East Angles, the Middle Angles, and the Mercians;* whilst the Saxons peopled the south and western districts of England, and the Jutes the kingdom of Kent and the Isle of Wight. A law of the reign of Edward the Confessor states, that "Yorkshire (which then included great part of the present county of Lancaster), Lincolnshire, Nottinghamshire, Leicestershire, Northamptonshire, and as far as Watling Street, and seven miles beyond it, were under the laws of the Angles." It also says that the division of counties, which in all other parts of England was called a Hundred, was in these counties called a Wapentake.†

Although the first expeditions of the Saxons to Britain, and probably the first settlements on the Saxon shore, were made many years previous to the time of Hengst and Horsa, who are said to have landed on the coast of Kent in the year 449,‡ yet there is historical evidence, independent of the traditions collected by Bede, that the attacks of the Saxons on Britain became much more formidable at that time than they had been previously; and also that the Saxons then began to aspire to the conquest of the whole island. Prosper of Aquitaine, in describing the events of the year 441, says, "Britain, long torn by slaughter and revolutions, at this time fell under the hands of the Saxons."§ This is very nearly the time which Bede fixes for the landing of Hengst and Horsa, and the conquest of Kent by the Saxons.‖

The invasion of Britain by the Saxons, though hastened and facilitated by the confusion which then existed in the island, was not an isolated movement of a single tribe, but part of that great irruption of the Germanic race, into the provinces of the Roman empire, which took place in the earlier part of the fifth century, and received a fresh impulse, near the middle of that century, from the irruption of innumerable swarms of Huns, from the plains of Scythia, into Germany. So early as the year 396, the Goths, a Germanic race, whose original home is supposed to have been in the forests of Thuringia, but who had long been settled near the mouth of the

* Beda, lib. i. c. 15. † Ancient Laws and Institutes of England, folio edition, p. 196.
‡ Beda, lib. i. c. 15. Saxon Chronicle, a. 439. § Prosper Tyro, a. 441. ‖ Beda, lib. i. c. 51.

Danube,* overran the eastern provinces of the Roman empire, under the command of their famous leader, Alaric, and advanced to the gates of Constantinople.† In the year 400 the same Goths, under the same commander, overran the greater part of Italy, but were repulsed by the great Roman general, Stilicho. Six years later another swarm of Germans, under the command of a chief named Radagius, laid waste great part of Italy, and threatened Rome, but were again repulsed by him. In the year 410, after the murder of Stilicho by his worthless master, the Emperor Honorius, Alaric again advanced into Italy, and took and plundered imperial Rome itself. Two years after the capture of Rome, Adolphus, king of the Visigoths or Western Goths, led the Goths into Gaul; and between the years 414 and 418 the Goths, aided by the Alani, Suevi, Vandali, and other German tribes, crossed the Pyrenees, conquered Spain, and established a Gothic dynasty in the Peninsula. About the same time the Goths firmly established themselves in the province of Aquitaine, in the south of France. The Burgundians also established themselves in the same kingdom; and between the years 420 and 450 the Franks, also of the German race, overran and conquered the other provinces of Gaul, and ultimately gave to the whole country the name of France.

In the latter part of this period, from the year 440 to the year 452, the great German migration was urged forward with redoubled violence, by the irruption of innumerable hosts of Huns, and other Scythian tribes, into Germany, under the command of the terrible Attila, named "the Scourge of God." The Huns were a Finnish or Uralian tribe, who were driven forward into Europe, about the year 400, by the irruption into their territory of the Hiongnæ, a tribe of herdsmen of Turkish origin, who dwelt in tents on the great plains of Central Asia, and who were themselves driven from their original homes and grazing grounds by the revolutions of the Chinese empire.‡ The tribes thus expelled from their pastures traversed the vast plains of Central Asia for a distance of more than 3000 miles, urging forward into Sarmatia—the present Poland and Germany—the Huns and other tribes, from the sources of the Ural river. The resistance of the Germans, who were themselves pressing forward into the richest provinces of the Roman empire, was for a while comparatively feeble; and hence the Huns, in the language of

* R. G. Latham on the English Language.

† Gibbon, c. xxx.

‡ Humboldt, Ansichten der Natur, vol. i.

Jornandes, ruled Scythia and Germany, never before united under one sovereign It was at the time when the power of Attila and the Huns was greatest, between the years 440 and 452, that the Saxon and other tribes of Germany began to pour into Britain, in increased numbers, in search of new homes, and thus a grand migration of races and nations, originally dwelling on the frontiers of China, gave a fresh impulse to the peopling of Britain by the Germanic race. Three years after the date which Bede fixes for the landing of Hengst and Horsa in Britain, Attila was defeated in a great battle, at Chalons on the Marne, by the united armies of the Roman empire and the Germanic invaders of that empire. But the Huns maintained their ground in Germany for a considerable time, and it was during this period that the Saxons, Angles, and Frisians, impelled, some by hope, others by fear, crossed the channel under various leaders, and either began or gave a new impulse to the conquest of Britain.

At the time when the Saxons commenced the conquest of Britain, they found the island divided between two hostile races, engaged in mortal strife with each other At that time the Romanized Britons held the eastern and southern districts of the island, whilst those tribes of Britons which had from the first resisted the Romans, and had been the first to throw off their yoke, held the west and the north The Roman wall continued to be the northern line of demarcation, probably until the time when the Romans retired from the island. But in the west, Deva or Chester was abandoned by the Romans before the year 408, and Caerleon shortly after No doubt those positions, and many others, fell into the hands of the Britons, and for 100 or 200 years after the landing of the Saxons were still held by them

As far as the vague records of that age enable us to judge, the western and northern parts of Britain were at this time divided into several small British states The first was Damnonia, the kingdom of Arthur, which bore also the name of West Wales, and comprised the present counties of Devon, Cornwall, Somerset, and Dorset* Next was Cambria, the land of the Midland Britons, including the whole of the present principality of Wales, and the greater part of the present counties of Chester, Shropshire, and Hereford Then came Cumbria, comprising the present counties of Cumberland and Westmoreland, and at least the northern part of Lancashire. Deira

* Lappenburg's History of England, vol i p 120

followed, including the rest of the country from the Humber and the Mersey to the Tyne; and Bernicia, comprising the country from the Tyne to the Forth Further to the north-west were the states of Reged and Strath Clyde, forming the eastern part of the Lowlands of Scotland, and last, the country of the Scots and Picts, north of the Forth and the Clyde.

The two most illustrious British names connected with this contest, that have come down to modern times, are those of Arthur and Cadwalla. The latter is strictly historical; but with regard to King Arthur, it is difficult to tell where fiction ends and history begins, in the accounts which have reached us of his life and exploits

Nothing is more probable than that the great struggle between the Britons and the Saxons, which continued for so many ages, produced both heroes and generals "Then it was," according to Nennius, "that the magnanimous Arthur, with all the kings and military force of Britain, fought against the Saxons, and though there were many more noble than himself, yet he was twelve times chosen their commander, and was as often conqueror" That the Britons fought well, and were ably led, is proved by the long duration of the conflict Arthur was probably the ablest and most illustrious of these leaders According to the account of his exploits given by Nennius, he fought and won four battles on the banks of the river Douglas, which is in the present county of Lancaster, and one at Chester, the city of the legion. The district on the banks of the Douglas is described by another early writer as the country of the Linen. This name seems to be partially retained in the name of Ince, near Wigan, whilst the memory of a great battle, fought in the times of the pagan Saxons, appears to be preserved in the name of Wigan—the Saxon god of war—for Wig and Hilda were the Mars and Bellona of the Saxon mythology If this account is correct, the Saxons made their way into Lancashire as early as the year 516, but were then defeated, and driven back across the hills which separate Lancashire from Yorkshire. We hear nothing more of their progress in the north-western district of England until the year 607, when Ethelfrid, king of Northumberland, having conquered the whole country to the north of the Mersey, led his army to Chester.

The Saxon or Anglian kingdom of Northumberland, which extended southward to the banks of the Humber and the Mersey, and included the present counties of Lancaster, York, Durham, and Northumberland, is stated by Bede and the Saxon Chronicle to have been founded by Ida, an Anglian chief, who arrived on the coast of Northumberland in the year 547 with an army of adventurers, carried in forty to fifty ships It is stated, on the same authority, that he built a fortress on the coast of Northumberland, which he named Bebbenburh, from the name of Bebba, his queen. The original fortress at Bebbenburh, or Bamboro', consisted of a stockade of timber; the Saxons and Angles of that age knowing little, if anything, of the art of building with stone or brick. But in a later age a strong castle of stone was built on the rock on which Ida's fortress stood, and on which the ruins of Bamboro' castle still stand After reigning twelve years, Ida was killed in a battle with Urien, king of Cumbria and Reged. His successors not only held their ground, but conquered the kingdoms of Bernicea and Deira, which Ethelfrid joined to form the kingdom of Northumberland, about the year 600, in some cases reducing the Britons to subjection, in others driving them out altogether, and setting Angles and Saxons in their place Both Walley on the river Calder, and Manchester on the river Irwell, are mentioned as places situated in the kingdom of Northumbria, and it is stated by Dr. Latham, in his recent work on the English Language, that "an examination of the provincial dialects still spoken in Lancashire, Yorkshire, and the other northern counties, shows that everything north of a line drawn from Warrington, on the river Mersey, to Chesterfield in Derbyshire, belongs to the ancient Saxon or Anglian kingdom of Northumberland"* This includes the whole of the present county of Lancaster, and a small portion of Cheshire. But the greater part of the latter county belonged to the Saxon kingdom of Mercia, which rose into importance as Northumberland declined, and ultimately comprised the seventeen counties lying between the Humber, the Mersey, the Thames, and the Severn, including the three great cities and ports of London, Gloucester, and Chester.

The Angles and Saxons, like all the Germanic tribes, were dwellers in the forest and the field. They had no towns of their own in those early times, but dwelt, scattered and divided, according to the expression of Tacitus, "as a fountain of pure water, a fertile field, or a sheltering grove attracted them." During their long wars with the Britons, which continued for several hundred years, they formed

* R G Latham, vol i.

themselves into numerous clans or companies, taking the names of their leaders. Each of these tribes undertook to conquer and defend the portion of territory that allured its taste The names of more than 600 of these tribes have been traced, of whom twenty-six settled in Lancashire and twenty-five in Cheshire They named the lands which they conquered after the names of their tribes Thus Warrington was the town of the Varini; Altringham, the home of the Altringi, Bellingham, the home of the Belini, Adlington, the town of the Athelings or Princes. Most of the English names ending in "ing" are supposed to be those of ancient Anglian or Saxon tribes The land thus conquered belonged to the whole tribe, was named the Mark, and was included within marks or bounds, generally cut on the trees of the forest, to guard it against the intrusion of other tribes. Each tribe thus dwelt within its own mark, and in time of war the bravest chief was chosen to lead the warriors of the different marks to battle. They had at first no kings, as Tacitus informs us, speaking of their German ancestors, but only chiefs chosen to lead them in war

The movement of the Anglo-Saxons into the north-western district of England appears to have received a great impulse, about the year 600, from the military genius of Ethelfrid, king of Northumbria. Of this chief and warrior the venerable Bede says, in his account of his reign—"At this time Ethelfrid, a most worthy king, and ambitious of glory, governed the kingdom of the Northumbrians, and ravaged the Britons more than all the great men of the English, insomuch that he might be compared to Saul, once king of the Israelites, excepting only in this, that he was ignorant of the true religion. For he conquered more territories from the Britons, either making them tributary, or driving the inhabitants clean out and planting English in their places, than any other king or tribune. To him might justly be applied the saying of the patriarch blessing his son—'Benjamin shall ravin as a wolf; in the morning he shall devour the prey, and at night he shall divide the spoil'"* In the year 603 Ethelfrid freed his dominions from the perils of invasion, by repulsing and destroying the army of Ædan, king of the Scots, at a place called Degsaston, and in the year 607 he turned his arms against the Britons of Cheshire and North Wales "Having raised a mighty army," says Bede, "he made a very great slaughter of that perfidious nation, at the city of Legions, which by the

* Beda, lib ii c 34

English is called Legacestir, but by the Britons, more rightly, Caerlegion" On this occasion he caused to be slain upwards of 1100 priests of the British monastery of Bangor, who had accompanied the Britons to the battle-field, to aid and encourage them with their presence and their prayers "Thus," adds Bede, "was fulfilled the prediction of the holy Bishop Augustine (though he himself had been long before taken up into the heavenly kingdom), that those perfidious men should feel the vengeance of temporal death also, because they had despised the offer of eternal salvation."† The sole crime of the Britons on this occasion consisted in defending their homes and national independence against the swords of the Saxons, and their religious independence against the claims of Augustine and the bishop of Rome This the historian of the English church thinks proper to speak of in the above passage as an act of perfidy; but he has left us ample particulars in other parts of the same work, which enable us to judge how little any such term was justly applicable to the bishops and priests of the ancient church of Britain

At the time when the Saxon armies first appeared on the banks of the Dee under King Ethelfrid, the ancient British form of Christianity was prevalent there, and Bangor, on the banks of that beautiful stream, was the principal school of British learning and religion. In the monastery of Bangor there were so great a number of monks, all living by the labour of their own hands, that the monastery, being divided into seven parts, with a chief over each, no one of these divisions consisted of less than 300 men—giving a total of upwards of 2100 persons, all devoted to purposes of religion From ten to twelve years before that time Augustine the monk had been despatched to Britain by Pope Gregory I, to teach the Christian religion amongst the Saxon Pagans He landed in Kent, in the train of the Christian Princess Bertha, daughter of the king of the Franks, who came over as the bride of Ethelbert king of Kent, a powerful Anglo-Saxon prince, whose dominions included the greater part of the south of England, and whose influence was felt as far north as the river Humber. The teaching of Augustine and the influence of a young wife moved the heart of Ethelbert, who adopted the Christian faith himself, and used his influence with great success in spreading it amongst his subjects In a few years the knowledge of the Christian religion, as taught by Augustine and his companions, was widely spread in the southern districts

† Beda, lib ii c. 2

of England, but unfortunately, during the same period, an angry feeling had sprung up between Augustine and his followers on one side, and the bishops and teachers of the ancient British church on the other, which gave additional malignity to the final struggle between Christianity and paganism in Britain, and long delayed the establishment of the Christian religion in the northern and midland districts of England

The real ground of difference between Augustine and the British bishops seems to have been that Augustine claimed an authority over the British church, which it firmly refused to admit. The professed ground of difference was, that the British bishops would not consent, on the demand of Augustine, to give up a mode of computing the time at which the feast of Easter should be held, which they had long employed In the mode of calculating the time for keeping Easter, the British, Scottish, and Irish churches adhered to the traditions of the Eastern church, in opposition to those of the Church of Rome.

From the account which Bede has left us of the conference which took place between Augustine and several bishops of the British church at a place called Augustine's Dale, on the borders of the West Saxons and the Wiccii (people of Warwick), and of a subsequent conference, at some spot to which he does not give a name, it appears that the British bishops were willing to act with Augustine as equals, but refused to submit to him as a superior.

Seven bishops of the Britons, and many most learned men, "particularly," says Bede, "from the most noble monastery which, in the English tongue, is called Bancornbury" (Bangor), over which Abbot Dinooth is said to have presided at that time, were present at the second synod. Before attending that synod they consulted "a certain holy and discreet man," who led the life of a hermit, as to whether they ought, at the preaching of Augustine, to forsake the traditions of their own church. He advised them to do so, if Augustine appeared to be a man of God "How shall we know that?" said they He replied, "Our Lord said, 'Take my yoke upon you, and learn of me, for I am meek and lowly of heart,' if, therefore, Augustine is meek and lowly of heart, it is to be believed that he has taken upon him the yoke of Christ, and offers the same to you to take upon you But if he is stern and haughty, it appears that he is not of God, nor are we to regard his words" They demanded again, "And how shall we discern even this?"

"Do you contrive," said the anchorite, "that he may first arrive with his company at the place where the synod is to be held, and if at your approach he shall rise to you, hear him submissively, being assured that he is the servant of Christ, but if he shall despise you, whereas you are more in number, let him also be despised by you." Unfortunately, Augustine did not receive the British bishops with the courtesy of an equal, but with the assumption of a superior. He was seated when they entered, and remained seated, on which they became angry, charged him with pride, and, according to Bede, contradicted all he said The final demands of Augustine were, that the British Christians should keep Easter at the due time—that is, as the Church of Rome kept it, that they should administer baptism according to the custom of the "Holy Roman Apostolical Church," and that they should jointly, with Augustine and his companions, preach the gospel to the English nation. "On these conditions," said Augustine, "we will tolerate all the other things you do, though contrary to our customs" They answered they would do none of these things, nor receive him as their archbishop, "for they alleged amongst themselves," says Bede, "that if he would now not rise up to us, how much more will he contemn us, as of no worth, when we shall begin to be under his subjection." "To whom the man of God," continues Bede, "is said in a threatening manner to have foretold that, in case they would not join in unity with their brethren, they would be warred upon by their enemies, and if they would not preach the way of life to the English nation, they should, at their hands, undergo the vengeance of death All which, through the dispensation of the divine judgment, fell out as he had predicted.

The venerable Bede, as already stated, speaks of the miserable slaughter of the priests of the British church, by Ethelfrid's army at the battle of Chester, as a fulfilment of the warning or prophecy of Augustine The conduct of Augustine has been variously interpreted. Some, especially in former times, have thought, as Bede evidently did, that Augustine spoke as a prophet, by the inspiration of God, and that the slaughter of the British priests was a just punishment for their refusal to listen to the teaching of Augustine, and the authority of Rome; others have thought that it was nothing better than a malignant wish, which being bruited abroad led to its own fulfilment; whilst others, neither raising Augustine so high as the former of these suppositions, nor sinking him as low so the latter, have concluded that it was only a sagacious warning, as to what must be the fate of the Christian Britons if they did not make common cause with the Christian Saxons Such a warning or prediction would have been well founded, both as relates to the Christian Britons and to the Christian Saxons, for discord certainly brought great evils on both A union of the Christians of Wales and Kent might have averted the massacre of the Britons at Chester And such a union between the Christians of Wales and Northumberland would have saved the latter kingdom from conquest and desolation A few years after the slaughter of the Britons at Chester, Cadwalla, king of the Britons, formed a close alliance with Penda, the pagan king of Mercia, and while together, they defeated and killed Edwin, the first Christian king of Northumberland, and all his sons, ravaged his dominions with fire and sword, and compelled Paulinus, the most celebrated of the followers of Augustine, to save himself by a hasty flight into the kingdom of Kent.

The conversion of Edwin, king of Northumbria, to Christianity, ultimately cost him both his throne and his life, yet it was for a while followed by a great increase of power and influence. Edwin was the first king of Northumbria who held the rank of Bretwalda, or paramount sovereign of Britain He not only ruled the Northumbrians, that is, all those who lived north of the river Humber, but with great power commanded all the nations, as well, of the English and the Britons who inhabit Britain, except only the people of Wales. He was also powerful by sea, as well as by land, and conquered the Mevanian islands of the Britons—Anglesey and Man—lying between Ireland and Britain, at that time Anglesey contained 960, and Man 300 families. Within his own dominions all was for a while peaceful and tranquil. "It is reported," says Bede, "that there was such perfect peace in Britain, wherever the dominion of King Edwin extended, that, as is still proverbially said, a woman with her new-born babe might walk throughout the island from sea to sea, without receiving any harm That king took so much care for the good of this nation, that in several places where he had seen clear springs near the highways, he caused stones to be fixed, with brass dishes hanging at them, for the convenience of travellers; nor durst any man touch them, for any other purpose than that for which they were designed, either through the dread they had of the king, or from the affection which they bore to him."

Unfortunately, not only the honours but the life of Edwin were rapidly hastening to a close. The superstitions which his ancestors had inherited from a remote antiquity were not to be extinguished without a struggle, and the conversion of Edwin and the Northumbrians was followed by the forming of the new and powerful pagan state of Mercia, which rapidly extended to all the central districts of England, from the Humber and the Mersey, to the Thames and the Severn A chief was found in the person of Penda, the first king of Mercia, possessed of courage and talents which enabled him to wage a bloody, and for many years a successful war, against the Christian kingdoms of Northumbria and Kent.

The divisions of the Saxon and British Christians, which had proved so fatal to the Britons at the battle of Chester, now proved equally so to the Saxons of Northumbria. No sooner had Penda become formidable in Mercia, than he found a powerful ally in Cadwalla, a king of the Britons of Wales, who joined him eagerly in an attack on Edwin and the kingdom of Northumbria.

In the year 633, the seventeenth year of the reign of King Edwin, and the sixth after his conversion to the Christian faith, Penda and Cadwalla, having united their armies, made a combined attack on the dominions of Edwin, who hastened to the frontier of his kingdom to meet them The armies met on the plain still known as Hatfield Heath, on the southern border of Yorkshire. Here a great battle was fought on the 12th October, in the year 633, in which Edwin was slain, and his army destroyed or dispersed. In the same year, but before Edwin fell, Osfrid, one of his sons, a warlike youth, was slain, and Eanfrid, another of his sons, driven by necessity, went alone to Penda, by whom he was afterwards murdered The victory of Penda and Cadwalla was followed by a great slaughter of the Northumbrian nation and church Penda and all the nation of the Mercians, as worshippers of Woden, Thor, and Frea, detested the Northumbrians, as apostates from their own religion, whilst Cadwalla, though a Christian in religion, fiercely revenged the wrongs of his race and church, refusing to pay any respect to the faith and religion of the English, or to correspond with them, more than with pagans The affairs of the Northumbrians being thus in confusion, and death threatening on every side, Paulinus, taking with him Queen Ethelberga, whom he had brought to Northumbria, returned into Kent by sea, and was honourably received by the king, Eadbald, and Archbishop Honorius, at whose request he took the office of bishop of Rochester, which office he held until the day of his death.

During ten long and ruinous years Northumbria groaned under the tyranny of Penda and Cadwalla. Bede, who relates with exultation the triumphs of Ethelfrid, shudders at the victory of Cadwalla Of him he says, that though he bore the name and professed himself a Christian, he was so barbarous in his disposition and behaviour that he neither spared the female sex nor the innocent age of children, but with savage cruelty put them to tormenting deaths, ravaging all the country far and wide, and resolved to cut off all the race of the English within the borders of Britain.

The first attempt of the Northumbrians to re-establish their independence only brought upon them greater calamities. Osric, of the royal family of Deira, and Eanfrid, the son of Ethelfrid, of the royal race of Bernicia, obtained the rule of their respective provinces of Northumbria, and endeavoured to keep them, by apostatizing from the Christian faith, but they were both slain by Cadwalla, the one in battle, the other when he came, with only a handful of soldiers, to sue for peace After that Cadwalla reigned over the provinces of the Northumbrians, "not like a victorious king, but like a rapacious and bloody tyrant" "To this day," says Bede, "that year is looked upon as unhappy and hateful to all good men, as well on account of the apostasy of the English kings, who had renounced the faith, as of the outrageous tyranny of the British king Hence, it has been agreed by all who have written about the reign of the kings, to abolish the memory of those perfidious monarchs, and to assign that year to the reign of the following king, Oswald, a man beloved of God"

Oswald, son of Ethelfrid, the restorer of the independence of Northumbria and of the profession of Christianity in that kingdom, had taken refuge amongst the Scots after the defeat of his father, and had amongst them been instructed in the Christian faith, probably in the celebrated monastery of Iona On the death of his elder brother, Eanfrid, he advanced into Northumbria with a small but valiant army, and defeated and killed Cadwalla, although the latter had more numerous forces, and boasted that nothing could resist them. Oswald raised his standard of the cross at a place called Heavenfield, near the Roman wall, and not far from the present town of Hexham The cross being made in haste, and the hole dug in which it was to be fixed, the king himself, full of faith, laid hold of it, and held it with both his hands till it was made firm by throwing in the earth. This done, he raised his voice, crying to his army, "Let us kneel, and jointly beseech the true and living God Almighty, in his mercy, to defend us from the haughty and fierce enemy; for He knows that we have undertaken a just war for the safety of our nation." All did as he had commanded, and advancing towards the enemy at dawn of day, they attacked him at a place named Denisburn, and gained a victory which freed Northumbria from its invaders, and placed Oswald on the throne of his ancestors.

King Oswald, having restored the independence of his country, immediately set to work to restore the knowledge and practice of Christianity, which had gone to decay since the death of King Edwin and the retirement of Paulinus to the more peaceful region of Kent. With this view he sent to the elders of the Scots, amongst whom himself and his followers when in banishment had received the sacrament of baptism, requesting them to send him a bishop, by whose instruction the Northumbrians might be taught the advantages and receive the sacraments of the Christian faith In compliance with this request they sent him Bishop Aidan, "a man of singular piety and moderation" The king appointed Aidan to the episcopal see in the isle of Lindisferne, or Holy Island, from which many of the churches between the Tyne and the Tweed had their beginning, as those from the Tyne to the Humber and the Mersey had from York The king himself in all cases gave ear to his admonitions, and industriously applied himself to build and extend the church of Christ in his kingdom:—"Wherein when the bishop, who was not skilful in the English tongue, preached the gospel, it was most delightful," says the venerable Bede, "to see the king himself interpreting the word of God to his commanders and ministers, for he had perfectly learned the language of the Scots during his long banishment. From that time many of the Scots came into Britain, and preached the word in those provinces of the English over which King Oswald reigned. Churches were built in many places, and the people joyfully flocked together to hear the word of truth."

During a period of nine years King Oswald ruled the kingdom of Northumbria, and besides assisting to restore the Christian faith amongst his own subjects, did much to establish it amongst the East Saxons in the valley of the Thames, and to the south of that river He also greatly extended the dominions of his ancestors, and through his good management the provinces of Deira and Bernicia, till then at variance, were united and formed into one people. Unfortunately the terrible Penda, the destroyer of Edwin, still survived, and proved himself to be the evil genius of the second, as well as of the first Christian king of Northumbria.

In the year 642 Oswald was killed in a great battle, with the pagan king and nation of the Mercians, at Maserfield or Makerfield, near Winwick and Warrington, on the frontiers of the kingdoms of Northumbria and Mercia. Makerfield is the ancient Saxon name of the district, through which the great Roman road that intersected both Mercia and Northumbria passed, on its entrance into the latter kingdom, and as it is the only place which bears that name, there is every reason to believe, both from the name and the position, that it is the place where Oswald fell, uttering the exclamation, "The Lord have mercy on the souls of my poor soldiers!"—who were dying to save him.

"Oswald being translated to the heavenly kingdom," his brother Oswy, an abler soldier, though not so good a man, succeeded to the throne of Northumbria, and held it for twenty-eight years with much trouble, being harassed by the pagan King Penda, and by the pagan nation of the Mercians, who had slain his brother, as also by his son Alfred, and by his cousin-german Ethelwald, the son of his brother who reigned before him The rule of succession to the throne was very loose amongst the Northumbrians, as amongst all the Anglo-Saxon nations, and though this occasionally placed a man of talent on the throne, out of his turn, as in the cases of Oswy, Offa, Alfred the Great, and Athelstane, yet it caused deadly family feuds, and involved the whole of the Saxon kingdoms in almost incessant wars of succession.

From the year 642 to the year 655 the kingdom of Northumbria was tributary to Penda, though Oswy was allowed to retain a shadow of authority, but at the end of that time the tyranny of the Mercians and of their king became intolerable, and King Oswy headed an insurrection of his people. In the course of this insurrection a great battle was fought between him and Penda, at a place named Winweyde, in which the army of Penda was totally defeated, and Penda himself was slain, with thirty of the chiefs who had followed him to battle. In Bede's account of this battle, it is stated that the greater part of the army of Penda was swallowed up by the river Winweyde, the waters of which were at that time much swollen by heavy rains. There is not at present any stream in England that bears the name of Winweyde, but the stream that flows through the meadows below Winwick, and which is now known as the Sankey brook, is as much liable to be suddenly flooded as any English stream It ought, however, to be stated that Bede, in his account of this battle, states that it was fought in the district of Leodis, which is generally supposed to be the district of Leeds, in the West Riding of Yorkshire

Wherever the battle of Winweyde was fought, it put an end to the profession of the pagan religion amongst the kings of the Anglo-Saxon race The successors of Penda very shortly adopted the profession of the Christian religion, and the seat of a bishopric was established at Lichfield, on the banks of the river Trent, which for a time almost rivalled Canterbury and York in the extent of its authority When the kingdom of Mercia was at the height of its greatness, Lichfield obtained for a short time the rank of an archbishopric The whole of the county of Chester, and that portion of Lancashire that lies between the Mersey and the Ribble, were for many ages included in this diocese

But though the defeat and death of Perda was followed by the spread of Christianity throughout the kingdom of Mercia, it was not followed by the permanent subjection of the kingdom of Mercia to the kings of Northumbria On the contrary, the dynasty which Penda had founded continued to reign for more than 100 years, and gradually extended its dominions until they stretched from the Mersey and the Humber on the north, to the Thames on the south, and from the Trent and the Ouse on the east, to the Mersey and the Severn on the west. When the kingdom of Mercia attained its greatest extent, under King Offa, it included seventeen of the present counties of England, of which the present county of Chester was the most northerly It was in the time of King Offa that the great line of defence known as Offa's Dyke was formed, from the banks of the river Dee, near Holywell, to the banks of the Severn, near the point where it receives the waters of the Wye In length this dyke was about 130 miles, and it was formed for the purpose of serving both as a line of demarcation between England and Wales, and a line of defence against the attacks of the Welsh mountaineers In the early part of his reign, King Offa repulsed the Welsh from Hereford, and afterwards overran the small British kingdoms, of which Shrewsbury and Chester were the capitals.

After the Angles had firmly established themselves in the present counties of Lancaster, York, and the northern and eastern districts of the kingdom, and after a mixed race of Angles and Saxons, differing only in name, had formed the kingdom of Mercia, of which Cheshire was the most northern shire, they both began to cultivate the arts of peace. Christianity was everywhere introduced, the church of St. John's, outside the walls of Chester, was built as early as the reign of Wolfhere, the grandson of the pagan king Penda, and the fame of St. Werberga, the daughter of the above king, spread to the county of Chester, of which she became the patron saint There her bones were deposited in the monastery of St Werberg, and at her shrine the most stupendous miracles were supposed to be worked The whole of the county of Chester, and much the greater part of the present county of Lancaster, were included within the diocese of Litchfield, whilst the northern parts of the county of Lancaster, as far south as the river Ribble, were included in the diocese of York At an early but uncertain period, the whole of the territories of what form now the two counties of Lancaster and Chester, were divided into hundreds or wapentakes, and these were again subdivided into townships, or probably tenships, that is, into communities of ten members, each of the ten being held responsible in case of offences committed by any of the rest Parishes were also formed in an early age, each of them comprising several townships These were generally, if not always, supplied with a parish church, many of which existed at the time of the Domesday Survey.

The cultivation of the soil, and the keeping of cattle, sheep, and swine, were the chief occupations of the Angles and Saxons, who delighted in rural life, and spread themselves over the whole country, forming in the first instance "marks," in which the whole community held the land in common, and afterwards separate villages. At the time of the Domseday Survey there were from 200 to 300 small vills or villages scattered over the two counties, most of which appear from their names to have been formed by the Angles and Saxons, those only along the sea-coast having been founded by the Danes. Ancient cities erected by the Romans were occupied by the Saxon and Anglian chiefs, and became their seats of government; but they do not appear to have built any other places, deserving of the name of towns and cities. Chester, Manchester, Ribchester, and Lancaster continued to be the principal places in the north-western district, during the Anglian period, though we have few particulars relating to them, beyond the facts that Chester continued to be a fortified city, and that Manchester was a Saxon or Anglian burg, which was the name given by both Angles and Saxons to their principal towns.

THE DANES AND NORTHMEN IN LANCASHIRE AND CHESHIRE.

THE boundaries of the kingdoms of Northumbria and Mercia, formed by the Mersey and the Humber, remained without any material change until the invasion of the kingdom by the Danes or Northmen, by whom both those kingdoms, as well as the kingdom of East Anglia, were conquered and peopled, so extensively as to produce a complete blending together of the Saxon and Danish races in all the northern and eastern districts of England. Innumerable traces of the presence and alternate ascendancy of these two powerful races are still found in Lancashire, Yorkshire, Lincolnshire, and indeed in all the counties in the northern and eastern parts of England. The Danes and Northmen, though originally, like the first Saxons, mere pirates, soon became the founders of extensive settlements in the northern and eastern districts, and at the present time many hundred places exist which, from the terminations of their names, are supposed to have been of Danish origin. This is believed to be the case with nearly all places ending with the letters *by*, that being the Danish or northern name of a town or place, just as burgh or borough is the Saxon termination. It is only, however, in the northern and eastern parts of England that this Danish termination is found Thus, while there are in Yorkshire 150, in Lincolnshire 195, in Cumberland forty-two, in Lancashire thirteen, and in Cheshire nine places still existing, whose names bear the Danish or Norwegian termination *by*—"a town"—there is scarcely a place with that termination, in the counties of Bedford, Berks, Buckingham, Devon, Dorset, Hereford, Hertford, Middlesex, Oxford, Salop, Somerset, Surrey, Sussex, or Wilts.

In the counties of Lancaster and Chester the traces of the residence of the Danes or Norwegians are very numerous along the sea-coast, from the northern bank of the river Dee to the northern boundary of the county of Lancaster, but they are nowhere found in the interior. It would therefore appear that though the Danes and Norwegians not merely overran, but peopled the coasts of the two counties, they did not succeed in establishing themselves firmly in the inland districts of either, though they probably may for a time have succeeded in reducing even those districts to nominal subjection There is historical evidence that both Chester and Manchester were ruined in the wars between the Saxons and Danes, but there is also evidence that the Danes did not succeed in establishing themselves permanently at either of those places or in the adjoining districts. All, or nearly all, the names of places in those districts are of Saxon, and not of Danish origin. On the other hand, the names are almost entirely Danish or Norwegian along the sea-coast, and both on the Lancashire and Cheshire coast we find the names still preserved of the ancient courts held by the Danes, and known by the name of "Thingwalli," or Thingwalls

In Cheshire also the Danish names are found on the coast, at Frankby, Pensby, Irby, Kirkby, Helsby, Childer, Thornton, Thingwall, and other places, but they are not found in the interior, the Danes having never established themselves to the east of the fortress of Chester

The Danish districts in Lancashire appear to have included the whole of the sea-coast from the Duddon to the Mersey Furness was named and peopled by the Danes or Northmen, and most of the older places in that district still bear Danish names Amongst these are Ulverstone, Ulpha, Donnerdale, Walney, Kirkby, Satterthwaite, and Conishead The hundred of Lonsdale was also named by the Danes The name of Lancaster is Danish, "caster" being the Danish way of spelling the word derived from "castrum," as "chester," found in Manchester, Ribchester, and Chester itself, is the Saxon mode of spelling the same termination An ancient Runic inscription has been found at Lancaster. Amounderness, the name of the next hundred, is purely Scandinavian, and is derived from the name of the Danish earl Agmund, and the Danish termination "ness," a promontory. Garstang, like Garston, is derived from the name of another Danish chief, and the names Kirkham, Fylde, and Blackpool, are also northern. Leyland the name of the next hundred on the sea-coast is probably Danish. The Derby hundred was certainly named by the Danes, as we learn that the town and county of Derby also were. Most of the other towns and villages in the West Derby hundred were also named by them, including Formby, Crosby, Kirkby, Roby, Ormskirk, Thingwall, Garston, and Widness In the interior, on the other hand, there are few Danish names. The hundred of Blackburn was probably named by the Angles, the termination "burn" being Anglian Anglezark, or Arx, the citadel of the Angles, also preserves the name of the same people Salford, and the ancient hundreds of Newton and Warrington, seem to have been named by the Saxons, there being scarcely any Danish names in those hundreds.

Until about the year 870 the river Mersey was the boundary between the Anglo-Saxon kingdoms of Northumbria and Mercia, but about that time it became the boundary between the territory of the Danes and that of the Saxons. The Scandinavian sea rovers, known in England as Danes, in France as Normans, and in Ireland as Eastmen, first landed in England about the year 787 From that time to the year 840, according to the Saxon Chronicle, bands of these adventurers landed on the shores of England almost every year. At first they appeared only in the summer months, and having plundered the country, returned before the winter set in, to their haunts on the coasts of Norway, Sweden, and Denmark, carrying off their captives and other booty. But in the year 840 they first remained in England during the winter months; and, becoming bolder with success, formed plans of conquest and permanent occupation These they ultimately carried into effect, conquering the whole of England north of the Mersey and the Humber, and the central counties as far as the river Thames There they came in contact with the kingdom of the West Saxons, and with that race of heroic kings, of whom Alfred the Great was the first and the noblest By them the course of the Danes was arrested; the central districts of England were gradually rescued from their grasp, and the Danish chiefs of Northumbria, though never permanently subdued, were reduced to a nominal subjection to the Saxon kings.

The kingdom of Northumbria was one of the first of the conquests made by the Danes in England The invading army which made this conquest was commanded by a chief named Heafdean. This army landed on the eastern side of the island, in the autumn of the year 866, and after wintering there, marched forward in the spring of the following year to York, the capital of Northumbria The invaders found that kingdom divided and weakened by civil war, the king having been deposed, and a rival having seized the throne. A desperate contest was still raging between them, but on the approach of the Danes the two claimants of the crown joined their forces to resist them It was, however, too late for resistance; and in a great battle fought at York, in the year 867, both the Saxon claimants of the throne of Northumbria were killed, and their armies were defeated by the Danish invaders Thus ended the Saxon kingdom of Northumbria, which the Danes divided among themselves, reducing the Saxons to subjection, and establishing themselves in all the more fertile districts of the northern counties There innumerable traces of their presence are still found, both on the eastern and the western sides of the kingdom, but they are not nearly so numerous in the hilly and mountainous districts of the interior, where the Saxons long held out against them.

The conquest of Northumbria only roused the eagerness of fresh swarms of Danes, and other adventurers from the northern seas, to overrun and conquer the whole kingdom. Having subdued Northumbria, they poured into the central districts of England, forming the kingdom of Mercia, in vast numbers, and after a succession of campaigns, they succeeded in overrunning the whole country as far as the river Thames, and in subverting the kingdom of Mercia, as they had previously subdued the kingdom of Northumbria

More than two-thirds of England having been thus conquered, the invaders directed their attacks against the kingdom of the West Saxons, which at that time included the counties of England lying to the south of the river Thames Their first attacks were successful, but in the end the valour, constancy, and military talents of the great Alfred gave the victory to the West Saxons The Danes, after being defeated in numerous battles, were driven out of every part of the kingdom of the West Saxons, and were glad to make peace, on condition of surrendering to King Alfred all those parts of the kingdom of Mercia lying to the south and west of the old Roman road, known to the Saxons by the name of Watling Street, which ran across the kingdom from London to Chester, dividing England into two tolerably equal parts In this division the Danes obtained the whole of East Anglia, the whole of the kingdom of Northumbria, and a large portion of Mercia. There they built numerous towns and villages, and became to a considerable extent blended with the Saxon inhabitants, though they still retained their Danish spirit of conquest and adventure.

The Danish king or chief with whom King Alfred concluded this treaty, and whose name has come down to us as Gotherm or Guthorm, consented to abandon paganism and to receive Christianity, and he was accordingly baptized, Alfred acting as his sponsor: and during the life of this chief, the boundaries agreed upon in the treaty between Alfred and the Danes were faithfully kept, and the kingdom had an interval of rest. But after the death of Guthorm, an enormous host of Danes and Northmen poured into the kingdom, under the command of Hasten, a Danish chief, who appears to have rivalled Rollo, the conqueror of Normandy, and even Canute, the conqueror of England, in the greatness of his military talents, and who would probably have rivalled them in success, if he had not had to contend against the still greater military genius and constancy of Alfred the Great.

The army of Hasten, which had previously laid waste the northern provinces of France, embarked for England, at Boulogne, in 251 vessels, in the spring of the year 893, and passed over to Limnemouth in Kent, a place where a Roman fortification existed, traces of which are still found. It there landed at the east end of the great forest called Andrad's Wald, which then extended across the wealds of Kent, Sussex, and Hampshire, for a distance of 120 miles. The Danes formed an intrenched camp at Appledore, near Limnemouth, in which camp they left their booty and the women and children who accompanied the army. Hasten himself sailed up the river Thames, and landed at Milton, on the southern bank of that river, where he formed another camp. He then led over the mass of his army to the north bank of the Thames, and formed a third camp at Banfleet in Essex. From this point he marched through the Danish provinces of Mercia, East Anglia, and Northumbria, everywhere calling the Danish settlers in those provinces to arms. He thus collected a large army, multitudes thronging to his standard, and with his troops thus reinforced, he commenced an attack on the kingdom of the West Saxons, and that part of Mercia which was then subject to Alfred. The contest between these two great leaders of the Saxon and the Danish race was long and arduous; and it was not until Alfred had defeated Hasten in three campaigns, in the course of which the seat of war changed rapidly from the banks of the Thames to those of the Severn, and from the Severn to the Mersey and the Dee, that he finally vanquished the invaders, and compelled them to retire from England

The first great battle between Alfred and the Danish army under the command of Hasten was fought at Farnham in Surrey, where the king gained a great victory. Scarcely was it gained when he learned that the Northumbrian Danes, the inhabitants of Lancashire and Yorkshire, had sailed round the island in their ships, had landed in Devonshire, and were laying siege to the city of Exeter. Alfred immediately marched into Devonshire, and defeated the Northumbrians, in a battle near Exeter Meanwhile the citizens of London, which was already a great city, had collected an army, with which they attacked the Danes, and laid siege to the camp that Hasten had formed at Banfleet, on the river Thames. This camp the citizens of London took, and they found in it, amongst other prisoners, the wife and sons of Hasten, the invading chief These Alfred, with his usual generosity, gave up in all honour to Hasten

After the loss of their camp the Danes marched rapidly along Watling Street, across the whole kingdom of England, to the borders of Wales, where they took and fortified a position on the banks of the river Severn, at Buttington bridge, above Shrewsbury. This position was convenient for communicating with the Welsh, who were the hereditary enemies of the Saxons. To this point, however, the Danes were quickly followed by a powerful army, under the command of Alfred's lieutenants, which blockaded them in their camp at Buttington, and reduced them to the utmost straits for food. The Danes, after eating their horses, being rendered desperate by hunger, made a furious assault on the besieging army, and though many of them were killed, the greater part succeeded in cutting their way through the Saxon lines, and retreated rapidly across the kingdom to the coast of Essex, where they found their ships waiting for them

"When they came to Essex," says the Saxon Chronicle, "to their forces and their ships, the survivors gathered together a great army from the East Anglians and the Northumbrians, before winter, and committing their wives, and their ships, and their wealth to the East Angles, they went or marched at one stretch, day and night, until they arrived at a western city in Wirral, which is called Legacester (Chester, the city of the Legion) Then were the forces" of King Alfred "unable to come up with them before they were in the fortress; nevertheless, they beset the fortress about for some days, took all the cattle that were without, slew the men whom they were able to take without the fortress, and burnt all the corn, or with their horses ate it every morning" The invaders, thus pressed and straitened, abandoned Chester and retired into North Wales, but they were unable to remain there, having been deprived of the cattle which they had taken in their march through England, and with them of all means of subsistence. After plundering the Welsh border as far south as Brecknock, they returned into North Wales, and crossed the Dee and the Mersey into Northumbria, that is to say, into Lancashire, which was at that time a part of the Danish Kingdom of Northumbria. "They marched over Northumbria in such wise," says the Saxon Chronicle, "that the forces of King Alfred could not overtake them before they came to the eastern parts of the land of Essex, to an island in the sea, near the mouth of the Thames, named Mersea." There they remained in safety during the winter, the Saxons having no fleet, and no means of annoying them in such a position

In the following year several desperate battles were fought between the armies of King Alfred and the invaders, on the banks of the Thames and the Severn; but in this campaign Hasten did not succeed in reaching the banks of the Mersey and the Dee All these battles ended so unfavourably to the invaders, that the entire army of Hasten broke up in despair, in the spring of the year 897. Some of the men returned to East Anglia, others to Northumbria; whilst others, with Hasten, crossed the sea, to plunder the fertile banks of the river Seine, along which they advanced, nearly to the walls of Paris

But even after the flight of Hasten and his host, the Danes settled in the northern counties of England, forming the kingdom or earldom of Northumbria, continued to be formidable to the Saxons They plundered the adjoining districts of Mercia with their armies, and they also sailed round the coasts of the kingdom, on plundering expeditions, in vessels of a peculiar kind, called Esks. "Then the king" (Alfred) "commanded long ships to be built, to oppose the Esks They are full twice as long as the others Some had sixty oars, and some had more. They were built swifter, and slenderer, and also higher than the others, they were shaped neither like the Frisian nor the Danish, but, as it seemed to him, that they would be more powerful." These vessels were the commencement of the navy of England. They were greatly increased in number during the reigns of his successors, Edward the Elder, Athelstane, and especially of Edgar, whose fleets commanded the British seas, but they were neglected, betrayed, or destroyed in the reign of Ethelred the Unready, and the kingdom was thus again thrown open, first to the Danes, under the great kings Sweyne and Canute, and afterwards to William the Norman

After the formation of a fleet by Alfred the Great, the yearly incursions of the Danes ceased for a long time It does not appear, however, that he succeeded in establishing his own direct authority in the Northumbrian provinces, though the Northumbrian Danes paid him an occasional and partial homage

After the death of Alfred the Great, and on the accession of his son, Edward the Elder, the war recommenced between the Northumbrian Danes and the Saxon kings and chiefs In this conflict, Ethelfleda, the daughter of King Alfred, who was married to Ethelred, whom Alfred had appointed Earl of Mercia, proved herself to be as able a leader as her father, her brother, or any other member of her heroic race

The Northumbrian Danes began the war in the year 911. According to the Saxon Chronicle, 'they despised the peace which King Edward and his 'witan' (or parliament) offered to them, and overran the land of Mercia" After plundering the province of Mercia, and collecting a great booty, they began to march towards Northumbria, but on their return they were overtaken by the West Saxon forces of Edward, and the Mercian army of Ethelfleda, who defeated them in a great battle Amongst the earls slain was Agmund, "the governor," from whom the Lancashire hundred of Agmunderness, now written Amounderness, was probably named. The great Danish earls, Agmund, Orme, and Gair, have all left memorials of their existence, if not of their exploits, in the names of the hundreds, towns, and villages of Lancashire, and traces of a road, named "the Danes Path," can still be seen in that part of North Lancashire which is named Amounderness

After the defeat of Agmund and his followers, Ethelfleda and Edward, to guard against future attacks from the same quarter, began to erect fortresses in all parts of Mercia, and along the borders of Northumbria In the year 913, Ethelfleda built fortresses at Stafford and Tamworth, to defend the approach into her dominions along the valley of the Trent, but the principal line of defence fortified by Ethelfleda and King Edward her brother, was that of the rivers Mersey and Dee.

The Roman fortifications of Chester and Manchester, destroyed by the Danes, were restored by Edward and Ethelfleda, and in addition to these two main points, both commanding great roads from north to south, they also constructed a line of forts along the south bank of the river Mersey. The first of these forts was built at Runcorn, where an ancient ferry exists between Lancashire and Cheshire, or, as they were called in the Saxon times, between Northumbria and Mercia This fort stood on a low rock, which runs into the Mersey on the Cheshire side The outline of the fortress can still be traced, on what is called the Castle rock, and when perfect and well garrisoned it must have commanded the passage of the river. This fort of Runcorn was built by Ethelfleda, in the year 915 A fort of less certain origin existed at Latchford, opposite to Warrington, and commanded the ford and passage of the Mersey at that point. A few miles higher up the stream of the Mersey there was another fort at Thelwall, which was restored and strengthened by King Edward the Elder, in the same year in which he rebuilt the works at Manchester The Saxon Chronicle, in describing Edward's campaign in the year 923, says —' He proceeded with his army late in the harvest to Thelwall, and ordered the borough to be repaired and inhabited and manned And he also ordered another army from the people of Mercia, while he sat there, to go to Manchester, in Northumbria, to repair and to man it" This passage shows clearly that the boundary of Northumbria was south of Manchester A third fort was constructed on the banks of the Mersey, at Warburton in Cheshire, opposite to what is now known as Hollins ferry. In the rear of all the forts built on the banks of the Mersey, Ethelfleda constructed a much stronger fort on Eddisbury Hill, one of the highest points of Delamere Forest, which there rises nearly 600 feet above the level of the sea. This fort commands the Roman road from Chester to Manchester, which runs within a bowshot of its base, and is within easy reach of the vale of Chester on the west, and the Vale Royal on the east It has a distant view of the estuary of the Mersey, and is the finest military position in the county of Chester, commanding all the approaches to the south, both from the Dee and the Mersey.

Including Chester and Manchester, this gives a line of seven Saxon fortresses, erected or restored by the son and daughter of Alfred the Great, along the line of the Dee and the Mersey, a distance of not more than thirty miles in length. The erection of these fortresses clearly shows that Edward the Elder and Ethelfleda, though successful in driving the Danes from the kingdom of Mercia, which extended as far north as the river Mersey, were not able to subdue the Danes of the Northumbrian province. This is further proved by a Saxon deed of the reign of King Athelstane, the son and successor of Edward, which deed is dated in the fifth year of his reign over the Anglo-Saxons, and the third year of his reign over the Northumbrians and Cumbrians. It would appear, therefore, that Athelstane did not succeed to the rule of Northumbria, but conquered that country, in the second or third year of his reign over the West Saxons and Mercians.

It was not, however, without another and much more desperate struggle, that Athelstane succeeded in firmly establishing his authority, in the provinces lying to the north of the Mersey and the Humber. In the tenth year of his reign the whole of the Danish and Norwegian chiefs who had established themselves in the north of England, as well as those who had settled on the east coast of Ireland, and in the numerous islands of the Western seas, from the Shetland islands to the Isle of Man, and from the Isle of Man as far south as the Channel Islands, united to invade the kingdom of Athelstane, and succeeded in landing an army, which was estimated by writers of the succeeding age at 30,000 men, on the shores of England This army was commanded by Anlaf, a Danish or Norwegian chief who had established a small kingdom at Dublin, and in the neighbouring districts of Ireland, and who is described in the writings of that age as "the arch pirate," being the leader of the sea-kings who then infested the western seas. Anlaf is said to have been joined in this expedition by Constantine, king of the Scots; by the king of Cumbria, and numerous other chiefs, British and Danish. At the head of this host Anlaf and his allies landed in the kingdom of Mercia They were there encountered by Athelstane and his brother Edmund Atheling, at the head of the whole force of the West Saxon and the Mercian kingdoms. A battle took place, which is described as the greatest and most desperate that was ever fought between the Danes and the Saxons, in which the

Danes were totally defeated This battle was fought at a place named Brunenburh, or "the town of the springs,' which was probably Bromborough, on the banks of the river Mersey, at the western extremity of the line of fortresses, formed by Edmund and Ethelfleda to protect the north-western entrance into the kingdom of Mercia

It appears from the accounts of this great battle, that the fleet which brought the invading host consisted of 615 ships The accounts of the battle are somewhat various, much the finest of them being a noble poem in honour of the victory, which is preserved in the Saxon Chronicle The prose accounts are rather meagre One of them, under the date 937, is as follows —"This year Athelstane and Edmund his brother led a force to Brunenburh, and there fought against Anlaf, and, Christ helping, had the victory, and slew five kings and seven earls" Another account is somewhat fuller Under the same date, 937, it says —"Therefore, after thirteen years, a fierce battle was fought against the barbarians at Burnandune, and that fight is called 'great,' even to the present day There the barbarian tribes are defeated, and domineer no longer They are driven beyond the sea The lands of Britain are consolidated together, on all sides is peace and plenty, nor ever did a fleet come again to the land except in friendship"

It is stated by Sharon Turner, in his "History of the Anglo-Saxons," that great uncertainty prevails as to where this battle was fought, but he mentions Bromborough in Cheshire, on the banks of the river Mersey, as one of the places where it is likely to have occurred It should be mentioned, however, that Henry of Huntingdon, writing about 200 years after the battle, speaks of it as having occurred on the banks of the river Humber The Saxon accounts, however, do not confirm this statement, nor is there any place named Brunenburh on the banks of that river

Wherever the battle of Brunenburh was fought, it was followed by the establishment of the authority of the Saxon kings in Northumbria, and more especially in that part of the ancient province of Northumbria which lies between the Mersey and the Ribble, and which is described in the Domesday Survey as the district "inter Ripam et Mersham" In a subsequent part of his reign Athelstane granted the lands about the present town of Preston to the monks of the abbey of Ripon, in the kingdom of Northumbria, and we find that the country south of the river Ribble was from this time united to the earldom of Mercia and to the great bishopric of Lichfield, which at that time extended over the whole of the central districts of England.

The actual government of the county of Chester, and of that part of Lancashire which lies between the Mersey and the Ribble, appears to have fallen at this time into the hands of the earls of Mercia, several of whom are known in history by the title of the Saxon earls of Chester They were the descendants of the ancient kings of Mercia, and inherited much of their power and pride But they were nominally subject to the West Saxon kings of the race of Alfred, who had liberated the country from the Danish yoke, and whom they acknowledged as their supreme lords, though reluctantly, and not without frequent struggles for independence These struggles between the West Saxons and the Mercians again laid open England to the Danes, who on one occasion landed near Chester, and forced their way as far south as Tamworth, which was the earliest residence of the kings and earls of Mercia, and on another occasion advanced from the south, under their great King Canute, as far as the banks of the Dee and the Mersey, overrunning the whole country, and receiving the submission of Uctred, the great thane of South Lancashire, as well as that of the principal thanes of Cheshire. The names of the most powerful of the Saxon earls of Chester or Mercia were Wolfric, Alfric, Edric, Leofric (who repaired the abbey of St Werberg at Chester), Algar, and Morcar, the two last of whom were the representatives of that ancient and powerful race at the time of the Norman conquest, in which they and all their fortunes perished.

The country between the Mersey and the Ribble also seems to have belonged to the Saxon earls of Mercia or Chester at the time when it is first mentioned This was in the year 1004, when Earl Wolfric made a will, by which he left his estates between the Ribble and the Mersey to his sons Elfhelme and Wulfarge, subject to a payment by each of them of 3000 sceattas—a coin then in use—to the abbey of Burton-on-Trent, of which he was the founder *

But the country to the north of the river Ribble still continued to be connected with the great Danish earldom of Northumbria, and was ruled by the earls of Northumberland, until Harold, the last of the Saxon kings, granted that earldom to his brother Tosti. He did not retain it long, being expelled by the people In his

* Dugdale's Monasticon, vol iii p. 28 Palgrave's Rise of the Commonwealth, p. 292

desperate efforts to recover the earldom, he joined the king of Norway, invaded England, and was killed in a battle fought with his brother, King Harold, at Stamford bridge, near York. The whole of North Lancashire is full of memorials of the Danes. The termination of the name of Lancaster—"caster," as distinguished from "chester"—is Danish; and so also are the names of Lonsdale, Amounderness, and Furness, the ancient divisions of that district. In recent times the treasure of one of the Danish sea-kings, containing coins of every nation, from England to Constantinople, has been dug up at Cuerdale, near Preston. A Runic stone, supposed however, to have been of Saxon origin, has been discovered at Lancaster, inscribed with the words—"Gebiddeth fo Cynibold Cuthburut" —(Pray for Cynibold, the son of Cuthbert.)*

From the time of the battle of Brunenburh to the Norman conquest the Saxon kings maintained their authority in the north-western district, though not without occasional struggles with the Danes. King Athelstane established a mint at Chester, many of the coins of which are still in existence; and one of the most remarkable events in the life of King Edgar, whose power both by land and sea was greater than that of any other Saxon king, was his visit to Chester. In that city he is said to have received the homage of all the kings of the western seas, who, in sign of their submission, rowed Edgar in his royal barge, from his palace to the ancient church of St John the Baptist, outside the walls of Chester. This story is very likely to be true, for Edgar shares with Alfred the honour of having founded the British navy, which during his reign had attained sufficient strength to overawe all the piratical chiefs of the neighbouring seas.

Unfortunately for the English people, the death of Edgar was followed by a long period of misgovernment and confusion, in the course of which the navy, constructed with so much care, was either disbanded or betrayed to the Danish chiefs, who again began to pour into the kingdom at the head of formidable armies. The great leaders of the Danes were Sweyne and Canute, kings of Denmark, the latter of whom succeeded in rendering himself king of England as well as of Denmark, and ruled the kingdom much more wisely and ably than most of his predecessors. After his death the kingdom fell into the hands of one or two kings of the Saxon line, men

* Transactions of Historic Society of Lancashire and Cheshire, vol i p 126. Paper on Reading of Lancaster Runic Inscription, by John Just, Esq, John Harland, Esq, and J M Kemble, Esq

alike destitute of energy and ability On the death of Edward the Confessor, the last of the royal line of the Saxons, the crown was claimed by Harold and by William the Norman, the latter of whom established his claim by the battle of Hastings, in which Harold was slain, and the Saxons were compelled to yield to the superior energy and military discipline of the Norman race.

At the time when the Saxons were vanquished by the Normans, the territory included in the present counties of Lancaster and Chester was divided into three parts The first of these was the county of Chester, which was held by the Saxon earls of Chester, or, as they were generally called in the Saxon times, the earls of Mercia. The second was the county included in the present Lancashire hundreds of West Derby, Salford, Blackburn, and Leland, known as the country between the Ribble and the Mersey—"inter Ripam et Mersham" This was held by King Edward the Confessor at the time of his death The third division consisted of that part of North Lancashire which lies between the river Ribble, the borders of Yorkshire on the east, and Westmoreland and Cumberland on the north This district was at this time, and for a considerable time afterwards, regarded as part of the ancient Danish earldom of Northumberland, and was returned under the head of "Yorkshire," or as it was then called "Euroicshire," York or Eboracum being the capital of the earldom of Northumberland At the death of Edward the Confessor, that part of the present county of Lancaster was held by Tosti, earl of Northumberland, the brother of Harold, who afterwards became the last Saxon king of England In the year in which the battle of Hastings was fought Earl Tosti joined the Danes in an attack on his brother Harold, and was defeated and slain in a great battle fought at Stamford Bridge, near York This occurred about twenty days before the battle of Hastings, in which Harold himself was defeated and slain by the Normans

CHAPTER III.

LANCASHIRE AND CHESHIRE FROM THE NORMAN CONQUEST TO THE REVOLUTION OF 1688.

THE progress of society in Lancashire and Cheshire from the Norman conquest to the downfall of the Stuart dynasty, that is, from the commencement of the reign of William I, in the year 1066, to the expulsion of James II, in the year 1688, was even slower than in the kingdom in general During that period the increase of population, the improvement of industry, the augmentation of wealth, were all checked in those counties by the frequent recurrence of internal strife, and by incessant wars with the Welsh, Scotch, and Irish nations, which fell with more than ordinary severity on the people of the northern and north-western districts of England, whose numbers were drained by incessant levies Yet even in those turbulent times progress was made for the kingdom was secure, by its perfect military organization, against the attacks of the foreign invaders who had so long wasted its shores, the barons joined with the people in extorting the great charter of their rights from the Crown, parliaments elected by the landowners of the counties and the burgesses of the towns were established, with an acknowledged right to control the public purse, numerous charters secured the right of self-government for local purposes, and many of the cities and towns, both of Lancashire and Cheshire, came into existence, and made the first steps in their progress towards population and wealth

Lancashire and Cheshire under the Norman and Plantagenet Kings. —Immediately after the Norman conquest, the counties of Chester and Lancaster were formed into earldoms or honours (as several of the earldoms of the kingdom were then called) under great military chiefs It was at that time that the Norman earldom of Chester, which still exists, and is held by the heir-apparent to the throne, was created, with the same style and titles which continue to the present day At that time also the honour of Lancaster was created, which soon received the more familiar name of the earldom of Lancaster, and later rose to the still higher dignity of the dukedom of Lancaster, a dignity which the sovereigns of England also continue to hold to the present time. The first of these dignities, the earldom of Chester, existed as an independent power for a period of nearly 170 years, that is, from the year 1070, when it was created by William the Conqueror, to 1238, when it was united to the crown, and made an appanage of the heir to the throne, by Henry III. The honour, earldom, and duchy of Lancaster were more or less independent of the crown from the year 1068 (when the whole county of Lancaster was granted, with other extensive estates, to Earl Roger de Montgomery, known as Roger de Poictou or Roger Pictavensis), to the year 1399, when Henry of Bolingbroke, duke of Lancaster, seized upon the throne of England, and made himself king, by the style and title of Henry the Fourth

In the earlier part of the above periods, the earldom of Chester was the more powerful of these two great feudal dignities, and it will therefore be well first to trace its history, and afterwards that of the honour, earldom, and dukedom of Lancaster, to the time when they were both united to the crown.

The Earldom of Chester.—The first Norman earl of Chester was named Gherbod, and was a Fleming by nation. He was appointed by William the Conqueror to the earldom of Chester, two or three years after the battle of Hastings But he never succeeded in establishing his authority, either in the county of Chester, or in that district of North Wales over which both the Saxon and the Norman earls of Chester claimed authority. According to Ordericus Vitalis—a monkish historian of that age, who was born in the neighbourhood of Shrewsbury, and who was well acquainted with English affairs, especially with the wars carried on on the borders of Wales—Earl Gherbod met with great difficulties, both from the English and the Welsh; and without having effected anything, returned to Flanders, where he had large hereditary possessions There he had the misfortune to be taken prisoner by a neighbouring chief, by whom he was kept in imprisonment for many years *

After the expulsion of Gherbod the Fleming, the united forces of the Saxons and the Welsh advanced from Cheshire into Shropshire, and laid siege to the town of Shrewsbury, which had been

* Ordericus, p 522

made the seat of another powerful earldom, under Robert de Belesme or Robert de Montgomery, the elder brother of Roger Pictavensis, and the founder of the castle and town of Montgomery, which still bear his name. On hearing of the insurrection of the Cheshire men and the Welsh, the Conqueror advanced to meet them, compelled them to retire from before Shrewsbury, and himself marched with his army to the city of Chester, which he besieged and took. He strengthened the works by building a Norman castle, to command the city; and appointed his nephew Hugh Lupus, or Hugh the Wolf, as he was called from his ferocity, and Hugh d'Avranches, from his place of birth in Normandy, to be the governor and earl of Chester.*

Hugh Lupus is supposed to have been appointed earl of Chester about the year 1070 As he had both to hold in subjection a hostile Saxon population, and to resist the incessant attacks of the Welsh, whose spirit was unbroken after centuries of conflict, the Conqueror determined to render the city and the county of Chester the seat of a great military power, always ready to resist insurrection within or invasion from without, and prepared to spread the authority of the English crown, over as much of North Wales as could be brought into subjection to it For this purpose he gave to his nephew, Hugh Lupus, the city of Chester, and the whole counties of Chester and Flint, with the exception only of the lands which were held by the bishop In addition to these vast possessions in Cheshire and Flintshire, William also gave his nephew extensive estates in twenty others of the counties of England, thus creating a principality rather than a mere earldom Moreover, the king gave to Hugh Lupus the right to hold the earldom of Chester by the sword, as freely as the king himself held the kingdom of England by the crown. He thus rendered Cheshire a county palatine, within which the earl was legally entitled to exercise an authority very little, if at all, inferior to that of the king himself, in his dominions at large

Hugh Lupus and his successors were not slow to avail themselves of the all but regal powers thus given to them They surrounded themselves with the most warlike barons and knights of that warlike age, to whom they gave lands, and whom they established in castles erected in the strongest positions in Cheshire and Flintshire. These barons the earls of Chester called together

* Ordericus, p 522

at their pleasure, in parliaments held in the city of Chester, which were framed on the model of the early English parliaments, composed of the great barons and great ecclesiastics of the whole kingdom, held by the kings of England at Westminster They also made war and peace at their pleasure, against the people and princes of North Wales; against the king's enemies, when they were on good terms with the crown, and against the king himself, whenever they quarreled with the reigning sovereign.

Few if any particulars have been preserved of the wars which Hugh Lupus carried on against the Welsh; but we are informed by the annalists of that time, that Hugh Lupus, with his lieutenants, Robert de Rodalent, or Robert of Rhudlann, and Robert de Malo-Passu, or Robert of Malpas, with others of his fierce barons, shed much Welsh blood * We also find from well authenticated records, that they built several fortresses or castles within the county of Chester, and that they organized a system of military defence against the incursions of the Welsh chieftains, whom, however, they never completely subdued

The most celebrated of the retainers of Hugh Lupus were the following —Robert Fitz Hugh, baron of Malpas and seneschal or steward of Cheshire, who is supposed to have been a natural son of the earl himself, and whose name is preserved in the town of Malpas; Robert de Rodalent, a baron who took his name from the ancient castle, built by the Saxons previous to the Norman conquest, at Rhudlann, at the foot of the beautiful vale of Clwyd, William Fitz Nigel, baron of Halton, the founder of the great family of de Lacy, who were for many generations constables of Chester, or commanders in chief of the armies of the earls of Chester, and who, after the union of the earldom of Chester with the crown, received the title of earls of Lincoln, retaining the dignity and power of constables of Chester, William Maldebeng, baron of Nantwich, Hugh de Mara or Delamere, Fitz Norman, baron of Montalt, who was lord of the great castle at Mold in Flintshire, and of the valley of Molesdale, through which the river Alyn flows down to the Dee; Hugh Fitz Osborne, lord of Pulford, Hamo de Masci, baron of Dunham Massey, Bigot, lord of Alford, Gislebert de Venables, baron of Kinderton, Richard de Vernon, baron of Stockport, Richard de Rulos, and Ranulf Venator, the founder of the family of Grosvenor

* Ordericus, p 522

"Under Hugh, the first earl of Chester," says the late Chancellor Raikes in his inaugural address, "and his immediate successors, we may suppose that most of the castles were built which form objects of antiquarian research in the neighbourhood of Chester, but which are melancholy evidences of the state of society at the time, since they were evidently built to protect the frontiers from the continued invasions of the Welsh. Some of these still remain, and from their extent and magnificence, appear to have been the residences of the earls themselves. Many more have perished, and can only be traced by the banks which form the outline of their plan. They were probably of an inferior description, and are rather to be considered as guard-houses, for the protection of some particular posts, than as regular fortresses. It shows us, however, the fearful insecurity under which men lived at that time, when we see that every ford where a passage might be found for men or cattle, through the morasses with which the surface of the country was overspread, was occupied in this manner by a stronghold. There are traces of this kind at Dodleston, at Alford, at Pulford, at Holt, at Shotwick, besides the larger and more distinguished holds at Beeston, Halton, Chester, and Hawarden; and probably few years passed but that some inroad of the Welsh carried fire and slaughter to the very gates of Chester, and swept the cattle and produce from the field. The Welsh name of the suburb of Hand-bridge or Beyond-bridge, which is still denominated the Burnt City, bears record of the insecurity of those times. During all this period Chester must have been a scene of never-failing excitement and continued interest. It was the entrance to the northern part of the principality; and within its walls must have been collected the armies which gradually effected the subjugation of Wales, and annexed it to the crown of England."*

Besides forming a local aristocracy and a line of military defence in Cheshire, and along the borders of North Wales, Hugh Lupus, the first earl of Chester, reorganized and endowed on the most lavish scale the abbey of St. Werberg, which stood on the site on which the cathedral of Chester now stands. This abbey had already, before the Norman conquest, been liberally endowed by the Saxon

* Inaugural address by the Rev H Raikes, A M, chancellor of Chester and historian to the society, delivered at the first quarterly meeting of the Chester Architectural, Archæological, and Historic Society, on Easter Monday, April 1, 1850

earls of Mercia, but in the latter years of Hugh Lupus, that nobleman determined to atone for his many sins, and to secure, as he imagined, eternal happiness for himself and his wife, by making grants to the monks of the abbey of St. Werburg the Virgin, "who should assiduously pray God for the soul of King William (Rufus), and of his mother, Queen Matilda, and of his brothers and sisters, and for the soul of King Edward (the Confessor), as well as for the salvation of their own souls, and for the souls of their fathers, and mothers, and predecessors, and heirs, and kinsmen, and their barons, and all Christians, whether living or dead." *

The date of the above charter of the abbey of St. Werburg is the year 1093, being the seventh year of the reign of William Rufus The earl continued to hold the earldom until the year 1101, the second year of King Henry I Thus, dating his accession to the earldom in the year 1070, he ruled over the counties of Chester and Flint for a period of thirty-one years. According to the authority of Ordericus, this earl was rapacious and profuse, more a lover of hunters and falconers than of tillers of the ground and ministers of religion. He was loose in his life and morals, gross in his habit, and though a formidable soldier in his youth and early manhood, he became unwieldy in his later years

On the death of Hugh Lupus, in the year 1101, he was succeeded in the earldom of Chester by his only son, Richard, the second earl, who was then a boy of ten or twelve years of age He only held the earldom until he reached his twenty-fifth year, when he was drowned, on his return from Normandy with his youthful bride, the daughter of Stephen, earl of Blois, together with Prince William, the eldest son of King Henry I, and with many other young men of the highest rank amongst the nobility of England and of Normandy. † The only acts recorded of Earl Richard are that he still further enriched the abbey of St. Werburg at Chester, by granting to it the land of Ulfric, outside the north gate of Chester, and three dwelling-houses, two in the city, and one outside the walls. At the same time further grants were made to the same church and abbey by his barons ‡

* Remarks on the charters of Hugh Lupus and Ranulf Second to the Abbey of St. Werburg, by the Rev W H Massie, with appendix, containing a translation of the Charter, in the Journal of the Architectural, Archæological, and Historic Society of Chester, part third, pp 270 to 297

† Ordericus, p 871 ‡ Charter of Hugh Lupus and Randle Gernons.

Randle or Ranulf the first, surnamed de Meschines, succeeded to the earldom of Chester, on the premature death of Earl Richard, in the year 1119. He was the eldest son of Margaret, the sister of Hugh Lupus, and of the Border earl of Cumberland. That earldom was surrendered by Earl Randle on his accession to the earldom of Chester. Earl Randle added greatly to the wealth of the earldom by his marriage with Lucy or Lucia, the daughter of Algar, the Saxon earl of Mercia, and widow of Roger Romare, one of the Norman favourites of the Conqueror The Countess Lucy was the sister of the two great Saxon chiefs, Edwin, earl of Mercia, and Morcar, earl of Northumberland, and was the inheritor of a great portion of their wealth By this Saxon lady Earl Randle had several children He appears to have been peaceful in his dispositions and domestic in his habits Few incidents of importance are recorded of his life, but according to the custom of his time, he was a liberal benefactor of the church, and of the abbey of St. Werburg

Ranulf or Randle, the second of three earls of Chester who bore that name, was the son of Earl Ranulf the first, and succeeded to the earldom on the death of his father, in the year 1128. Earl Ranulf the second, named de Gernons, and de Briscard, was an active intriguer, and made the best use of the troublous times in which he lived, to increase the wealth and power of his earldom, though in the end his intrigues were crowned with no great success

On the death of Henry I. in the year 1135, Stephen, earl de Blois, the nephew of William the Conqueror, seized the crown of England in defiance of Maude or Matilda, the daughter of the king, who had married, first, Henry V, emperor of Germany, and afterwards Geoffrey de Plantagenet, from whom the royal family of that name, which ruled this country for 300 years, sprang. The claim of Stephen was vehemently resisted by a large portion of the nobility, and nearly the whole of his reign was a continued civil war, in which sometimes the adherents of the king, and at others the supporters of the empress and of her son, Henry Plantagenet, duke of Normandy, afterwards King Henry II, were triumphant Early in this conflict the earl of Chester seized upon the castle and city of Lincoln, which were then among the most considerable in the kingdom; and King Stephen having brought up an army to recover them, was defeated and taken prisoner by the earl, in the year 1140.

In the course of the following year King Stephen escaped from prison, and having got together another army, was on this occasion successful in defeating the earl of Chester and his associates, but the earl being still formidable, a treaty was entered into between them, by which the king agreed to purchase the earl's support, by presenting him with numerous and extensive estates, in addition to those already possessed by him

It appears from a deed preserved in the office of the duchy of Lancaster, that King Stephen on this occasion conferred on Ranulf, earl of Chester, the castle and city of Lincoln; the castle of Belvedere; Grantham with the soke, the castle of Newcastle-under-Line, in Staffordshire Rolea, with Torksey, the towns of Derby and Mansfield, Stanley and Oswardbec, with all the land of Roger de Bulay, the whole honour of Blida, and all the land of Roger Pictavensis, from Northampton to Scotland, except the land of Roger de Montbegon in Lincolnshire. The king further gave to him and his heirs the honour of Lancaster, with its appurtenances, and all the land between the Ribble and the Mersey. He also gave him Grimsby and Horncastle in Lincolnshire With these and other grants, and with his hereditary estates, the earl of Chester is supposed to have held nearly the third part of the kingdom

But Earl Ranulf was not a man to be either subdued or won, and on the very earliest opportunity he was again found in arms against King Stephen. On this occasion he was on the winning side Having joined his forces to those of Henry Plantagenet, the son of the Empress Maude, they pressed King Stephen so closely that he was at last compelled to come to terms with the Plantagenet party. The conditions agreed upon were, that Stephen should retain the throne for the remainder of his life, but that on his death the crown of England should descend to Henry Plantagenet, whilst Stephen's private estates, including the great earldom of Morton and the honour of Lancaster, descended to his own son, William de Blois

But Earl Ranulf did not serve either Henry or Stephen without being well rewarded for his services, and one condition of his supporting Henry was, that he should confirm to him all that had been granted by Stephen, and something more In a deed dated 1152 (17 Stephen) we have an account of numerous grants made to Earl Ranulf of Chester by Henry, duke of Normandy, before he was raised to the throne of England In this deed are named all the estates granted in the previous deed of King Stephen to the same earl, and some others Amongst them Henry gave or confirmed to the eail of Chester the castle of Vere and other places in Normandy; the whole honour of Roger Pictavensis, wherever he possessed anything; the whole honour of Blida; the whole honour of Ely, as Robert Mallet and his ancestors held it; Stafford and the whole county of Stafford, except the lands of the bishop of Chester, those of Earl Robert de Ferrers, Hugh de Mortuomar, Gervase Paganes, and the forest of Cannock, which Henry retained in his own hands; the fee of Alan of Lincoln, the fee of Hugh de Scotiney; the fee of Robert de Chaly, the whole fee of Robert the son of Otho; the whole fee of Norman de Vere, the fee of Robert de Stafford; thirty pounds' worth of land in Grimsby; the town and castle of Nottingham, and whatever Henry had in Nottinghamshire, the whole fee of William Peveril, Derby, and Stanley, near Coventry, and to each of his six barons, one hundred pounds' worth of yearly rent from land There is no clear information as to the causes by which this powerful earl was induced to part with the estates in Lancashire granted to him both by Stephen and Henry II, but we find that, after the death of Stephen, they descended to his son, William de Blois, and not to the earl of Chester

A year or two previous to the death of King Stephen, Ranulf the second earl of Chester of that name died, and was succeeded by the second earl Hugh, known by the name of Hugh de Keveilioc, from the castle of Keveilioc.

Earl Hugh Keveilioc succeeded to the earldom of Chester about a couple of years before Henry Plantagenet, duke of Normandy, ascended the throne, with the title of Henry II When Earl Hugh succeeded to the earldom, the Welsh were in arms, had overrun the county of Flint, and approached even to the walls of Chester. In the year 1155 Earl Hugh de Keveilioc succeeded in defeating the army of the Welsh, commanded by the great Welsh chief, Owen Gwynedd, in a battle fought at Balderton bridge, within sight of the walls of Chester. The Welsh, though repulsed, were not discouraged; and they collected so large a force in the more mountainous parts of the county of Flint as to place the whole English frontier in great danger. To guard against invasion, King Henry II brought together a large army, which he united with the forces of the earl, and encamped at Saltney, near Chester Having little or no experience of mountain warfare, King Henry advanced incautiously into the wilder parts of Flintshire, which were at that time covered with thick forests. With his army in this position he was suddenly attacked by the Welsh, commanded by David and Conan, the sons of Owen Gwynedd, at Coleshill, when his army was totally defeated, and driven back into the castle of Basingwerk, near Holywell, and into the city of Chester. After this severe lesson, the king and the earl became much more cautious in their methods of attacking the Welsh They restored the fortifications of Basingwerk, in which they placed a garrison of Knights Templars, and they also restored and strengthened the castle of Rhuddlan, at the foot of the vale of Clwyd. These efforts, however, were only partially successful, for in the year 1165 the gallant Welsh prince, Owen Gwynedd, laid siege to Basingwerk castle, took it, and levelled it with the ground

In the latter years of his life Earl Hugh de Keveilioc joined the sons of Henry II, Henry, Richard, and John, in their unnatural rebellions against their father, and though defeated, succeeded in retaining his earldom He died peacefully in the year 1181, and was succeeded by his son, the third Ranulf, named de Blundeville

Earl Ranulf de Blundeville became earl of Chester in the year 1181, in the twenty-eighth year of the reign of Henry II, and held the earldom for no less than fifty-one years, during the reigns of Henry II., Richard I., John, and Henry III. He passed his life in the midst of great events, in the course of which the foundations of the English constitution were laid, by the granting of Magna Charta, and the great charter of the forest. In these, and in all the events of the troublous times in which he lived, he took an active part, and in all the great events of his life proved himself to be a lover of his country, and a true and upright man

At the time when Ranulf de Blundeville succeeded to the earldom of Chester he was still under age, and during his minority the earldom was administered, under the king, by Gibert Pipard as vice-comes or sheriff. It appears from the accounts which he rendered to the exchequer that the whole money value of the earldom at that time was only £252 12*s* 7*d* a year, a sum equal to about £3000 a year of our present money.

The first great public service rendered by Earl Ranulf was in joining with, other great lords, in resisting the rebellion of Prince John against his brother, Richard I. With their united forces they drove his supporters from the field, and captured all his castles, more especially that of Nottingham, which was then considered one of the strongest places in the kingdom.

After the accession of King John to the throne, Earl Ranulf de Blundeville directed his attention principally to the affairs of his own earldom He waged war against the Welsh, sometimes with great success, at other times merely holding his ground against their attacks. In one of his campaigns he was besieged by a large Welsh army in the castle of Rhudlann, where he was reduced to great straits, and was only saved by the rapid advance of the constable of Chester, at the head of a tumultuous army, hastily assembled at the fair of Chester

In the wars between King John and the barons, the earl of Chester endeavoured to act as a mediator between the contending parties, supporting both the rights of the crown and those of the people He was hence more than once denounced as a traitor by both parties, but he steadily maintained his position, and was able to render great services to the country

After the death of King John, the earl of Chester was one of the three earls to whom the administration of the kingdom was committed. At that time the dauphin of France was in England, with a strong military force, which had been sent for by the barons, to assist them in their conflict with King John The first object of Ranulf de Blundeville was to free the kingdom from the presence of the dauphin and his army Having failed to do this by peaceful means, he gave battle to the French in the neighbourhood of Lincoln, and inflicted on them so severe a defeat that they were glad to retire, and to leave the English parties to fight out their own battles After the retirement of the French, Henry III, then a boy of eleven years of age, was placed on the throne, under the guardianship of Hubert earl of Kent, and William Marshal earl of Pembroke, and Magna Charta, and all the charters granted by King John to the barons, were solemnly confirmed

After the settlement of the crown, Earl Ranulf returned to his hereditary possessions, where he made peace with Llewelyn king or prince of North Wales, and having thus secured peace at home he proceeded to the Holy Land, where he arrived in the year in which Damietta was taken by the Christians. He remained in Syria three years, performing the part of a gallant soldier of the cross, after which he returned to his own country, and again assumed the direction of the earldom

On the return of Earl Ranulf from the Holy Land, he built the castle of Beeston, the largest and strongest of the Norman castles, in

Cheshire He also built the castle of Chartley in Staffordshire, and founded the abbey of Delacrosse, near Leek, in the same county, removing to it the monks who had been previously established at Pulford, near Chester.

In the year 1227 the earls of Chester and de Ferrers took arms against King Henry III, who was pretty nearly as great a tyrant as his father King John, and compelled him again to re-enact and confirm Magna Charta and the charter of the forests.

In the year 1229 King Henry assembled all the nobles of his kingdom at Portsmouth, with the intention of leading a large army into France to recover the territories of the dukes of Normandy and counts of Anjou, which had been seized by the French, during the civil wars in the reign of King John. Whilst the nobles of the kingdom were assembled at Portsmouth, the king presented the earl of Chester with the honour of Lancaster, and with all the land which belonged to the crown between the Mersey and the Ribble

With a view of adding still more to the value of his estates in the honour of Lancaster, the earl of Chester, in the year 1230, purchased the estates of Roger de Merseia, a wealthy knight, who possessed large property in many parts of the kingdom Among the estates purchased by the earl from Roger de Merseia, were the manors of Bolton, Little Bolton, Tonge, Halgh, Brightmede, Radcliffe, Urmeston, West Leigh, Sharples, Halghe, Standish, Longtree, Swinton, Charnock, Heath Charnock, Duxbury, Adlington, Whithull, Hirlton, Scarisbrick, Heaton near Lancaster, Darwen, and Eccleshill These estates, now worth millions, were purchased by the earl of Chester for 240 marks of silver

In the year 1232 the king assembled a parliament in London, at which he demanded large supplies, for the purpose of carrying on the war in France As he had hitherto met with nothing but defeats, after incurring enormous expenses, the peers of his kingdom, headed by Earl Ranulf of Chester, refused to grant further supplies until the affairs of the kingdom were better administered

This was the last public act of Earl Ranulf, who died at his castle at Wallingford on the Thames, in the year 1233, after having held the earldom of Chester for fifty-one years

John the Scot, the nephew of Ranulf de Blundeville, the great earl of Chester, succeeded to the earldom on the death of Earl Ranulf, and was the last earl unconnected with the Royal Family who held that honour. He died in the year 1238, with some suspicion of poison, and on his death the king seized on the earldom of Chester and united it to the crown From that time to the present the earldom has been held by the heir-apparent to the crown, or by the reigning sovereign, when there was no heir-apparent.

At the time when the earldom of Chester was resumed by the crown, a considerable portion of the lands originally belonging to it had been alienated in various ways, and granted to different persons and public bodies, including the barons, the knights, and the religious houses of the country; but the earldom was still a very valuable possession This will be seen from the following summary of the revenues and expenditure of the earldom, taken from the yearly account of William de Melton, treasurer of Chester, in the thirty-first year of King Edward, the son of King Henry (Edward I., 1301) —

The mayor and citizens of Chester at that time paid to the earl a yearly rent of £100—fully equal to £1000 of our present money—for the fee farm of the city of Chester, including all the ordinary rights of the crown (Jura Regalia)

Master Richard, ingeniator (the engineer of the earldom of Chester), paid the sum of £200 for the rents of the mills, salmon fishery of the Dee, and the bridge of Chester, which he held at fee farm for his life

Ranulph de Merton paid 12*s* 4*d*., as tenant in the fee of the countess of Warwick

Diverse men of the city and county paid 62*s*. 11½*d* of chamberlain's rent, which amounted in full to 30 marks. Others paid 8*s* 4*d*, towards the same rent

Diverse villages, which owed a rent of seventeen head of swine, for having their swine in Delamere Forest, paid 60*s* in money.

Diverse villages paid £17 12*s* 4*d* for frithmote

Master John Burgoillon, bailiff of the manor of Macclesfield and Overton, paid £232 for the farms of these manors.

The abbot of Vale Royal paid £76 for the farm of the town of Northwich

Sir Hugh de Calveley and Matthew de Hulgrave paid £84 for the farm of the town of Middlewich.

Sir Robert de Brescy, sheriff of Chester, paid 210 marks for the farm of the sheriff.

Sir William de Spinstorne, tenant of the office of advocate of the earls of Chester, paid £48

Adam de Lawton, tenant of the passage or ferry of Lawton, paid 66*s* 8*d*. for the farm of the ferry—the full rent being 5 marks.

Traherne ap Howel (a poor Welsh prisoner) paid 2*s* for the fruit of the garden of the castle

Sir Reginald de Grey paid 8*s* 8*d*. for the rent of 13 acres of land in Handbridge, thus paying 8*d*. per acre, equal to about 12*s* per acre of present money.

The sum of £8 4*s* 5½*d* was paid from the returns of two parcels of land which belonged to Hugh de Thornton at Thornton, in Wyrall, and at Poulton, in Walleye; the whole rent being 30 marks

Master John Bourgoillon, escheator of Chester, paid £41 7*s*. 5½*d* from the rents of the manors of Trafford and Dunham, which belonged to the earl of Arundel, deceased, and were in the hands of the earl of Chester on account of the nonage of the heir.

Rad. de Hardeswell did not pay anything from the wardship of the manor of Wermington, which had been in his hands, because Warin de Maynwaring, the heir, had not attained his majority.

Ranulf de Praers, parson of Bertunleh, paid £6 for the wardship of the lands and heirs of Thomas de Crue (Crewe).

John de Legh paid £4 8*s* 10½*d* for the wardship of the lands of Ranulf de Ruter.

Thomas de Worth paid £4 8*s* 10*d* for the wardship of two portions of land which belonged to Hugh de Tyderington, deceased

Alda de Sannford, sister and heir of Sir Thomas de Sannford, paid £10 for the relief of her brother's estate

Diverse men on the borders of Delamere Forest paid 3*s* 7*d*, for sending swine into the forest, "although this year there were no acorns"

Diverse men in the neighbourhood of Delamere Forest paid £6 12*s* for the trespasses of themselves and their cattle on the forest

Four casks of wine from the prises of the earl of Chester, at Chester, produced £10, being sold at 50*s* each

The carcasses of 98 pigs sold for £6 2*s*. 4*d*.

A cask of wine, sold to Jordan de Bradeford, produced 50*s*

The carcasses of two oxen sold at the castle of Flint produced £9 8*s* 4*d*

William de Donecastre, David de Gignon, and other merchants, paid £19 1*s*. 8½*d*, for customs of wool and skins, shipped to foreign parts

The abbot of Chester paid 6*s*., being part of the arrears of a yearly sum of 1*s* charged under title of Chamberlain's rent

The amercements on the common pleas of the earl of Chester, before Sir William Trussell, justice of Chester, produced the sum of £27 16*s*. 10*d*.

The damages in the pleas of the crown produced £15 19*s* 11*d*

The defaults and amercements before the justice on his circuit produced £12 5*s*. 6*d*.

Various fines, felonies, and causes, produced £188 10*s* 6*d*.

The sum total of the receipts of the county of Chester was £1889 8*s* 1½*d*

The sum total of the receipts of the county of Flint, which were also payable to the earl of Chester, was £426 13*s*. 5*d*.

Total receipts of earldom in Cheshire and Flintshire, £2316 1*s*. 7½*d*, equal to at least £30,000 of present money

In the same year the payments from the revenues of the earldom were as follows:—

To the lord abbot of St. Wereburge of Chester, 10*s* of ancient alms, granted to him to find lights in the chapel of St. Mary of Hilldeburgheye (Hilbre Island).

To the same abbot, 100*s*, as tithe of the fishery at the bridge of Chester

To the same abbot, £4, for the tithes of Frodsham, which he resigned at the request of the king, to the abbey of Vale Royal, founded by Edward the First.

To the prioress and nuns of Chester, receiving yearly £16 from the king, in return for certain tithes at Over, given up to the abbot of Vale Royal—£4 16*s*

To the same, in recompense for four acres of land at Godesbache, which they surrendered to the king, for the service of the same abbot, and for the small tithes in the township of Bradeford, Littleowres, Sutton, and Merton, belonging to the parish of Over, which township was assigned by our lord the king to the abbot of Vale Royal—£26 12*s* 2*d*.

To the brothers preachers of Chester receiving yearly 13 marks, at the exchequer at Chester—£8 13*s*. 4*d*

To the master and brethren of the hospital of St. John, out of the north gate of Chester, £4 11*s*. of ancient alms.

To the Lepers of Boughton, 20*s*.

To the abbot of Whalley, 20*s*

To the abbot of Vale Royal, receiving yearly a cask of wine for celebrating mass in his abbey, 50*s*

To Sir William Trussell, justice of Chester, and keeper of the castles of Chester, Rhudllan, and Flint, £100

To William de Melton, chamberlain of Chester, £20

To Gilbert de Wyley, rider of Delamere Forest, 40*s*.

To Master Richard, ingeniator of Chester, daily 1*s*.—£18 4s

To Robert de Rosby, gardener of the castle of Chester, 3*d*. per day—£4 11*s*

To Walter de Mandlan, keeper of the forest of Wyrall, 6*d*. per day—£11 2*s*

To Richard de Ruges, forester of the forest of Wyrall, in the place of William de Stanlegh, removed for certain offences, 9*d*. per day—£30

To Richard de Sutton, and Isabella, his wife, for the sergeancy of the peace, giving them 1*s*. for every thief beheaded, namely, for Robb of Cristelton, 1*s*, for William de Wrennebury, 1*s*, and Ade le Signeleer, 1*s*—3*s*

To Walter de Friburgh, Conrad de Ribslayn, Hayne le Scheller, and Frie Froule, German miners, retained at wages in the service of the prince, by order of the chancellor and treasurer, to work in the mines of copper at le Dessard in Englefield (Flintshire), £6 10*s* Memorandum—That the said miners could not do anything with the mine, and after trial were dismissed

To Ade, son of Richard Suel, for carrying letters of the prince from Chester to Carnarvon, 1*s*

To Henry de Wakefield, for carrying letters to Newcastle-on-Tyne, 2*s*. 6*d*.

Repairs of Chester Castle, £15 16*s* 6d

Repairs of Talynt Castle, £12 12*s*. 10*d*, £15 17*s*. 2*d*, £14 10*s*. 3*d*.

To Peter Balistro (the engineer) for going from Chester to Flint to amend the balistas, 32*s*. 8*d*.

Repairs of Rhudllan Castle, £26 17*s*. 8*d*

To Master John Burgoillon, farmer of the manor of Macclesfield, 6*s*. 10*d*, for repairing certain defects in the houses, for repairing the fences of the parks, and for making a machine for taking the wolves, frequently coming into the park and destroying the game.

To Traherne ap Howel ap Res, and Lewellin ap Gronow ap Heilin, Welsh hostages in the castle at Chester, £6 1*s* 8*d*

Paid to Walter Reginald, treasurer of the prince, £1687 16*s*. 4*d*

Sum total of payments, £2048 11*s* 4*d.*

Owing to the chamberlain, £552 4*s* 5½*d.*

The Earldom and Duchy of Lancaster.—Having traced the history of the earldom of Chester from the Norman conquest to the time when it was united to the crown by Henry III, let us trace that of the honour, earldom, and duchy of Lancaster from the first-named period, to the time when the possessors of the dukedom of Lancaster became sufficiently powerful to seize upon the crown itself.

The honour of Lancaster, with nearly the whole of the lands of the present county of Lancaster, was granted by William the Conqueror to one of his great military followers, Roger of Poictou, soon after the battle of Hastings, fought in the year 1066. The date of the grant to Earl Roger was probably about the year 1068, for Matthew Paris and other authors inform us, that William returned from a visit to Normandy in the year 1068, and then proceeded to bestow the lands of the Saxon nobles and thanes on his own followers, with a lavish hand. Of the family of Roger of Poictou, the first possessor of the honour of Lancaster, we have the following particulars, from a manuscript discovered by Andrew Duchesne, and republished by Sir William Dugdale,* in his account of the Alien Priory of Lancaster.

Roger of Poictou was the third son of Roger viscount de Montgomery, and of Mabile, countess of Alençon, his wife. They were the founders of the abbey of St. Martin de Sees in Normandy, to which their son Roger of Poictou gave the church of Lancaster and other estates, after the conquest of England. The sons of Roger de Montgomery rendered William great assistance in effecting the conquest of the kingdom, and were afterwards most liberally rewarded out of the lands of England. Robert de Belesme, the eldest son, received the earldom of Shrewsbury, and the greater part of the lands of Shropshire, which earldom was held by Hugh, the second son, after the death of Robert. Roger, the third son, received the whole of the county of Lancaster, with nearly 200 manors in other parts of England, and Philip and Arnulf, younger sons, also received large estates in Pembrokeshire. The husbands of the daughters of Roger de Montgomery were not less splendidly rewarded. The earl of Morton, or Mortaine, the husband of Matilda, received the greater part of the lands of Cornwall and Devonshire, and Hugh de Novo Castello, married to Mabile, and Robert Fitz

* Dugdale's Monasticon, p. 999.

Hamon, married to Sybilla, were also splendidly provided for at the expense of the conquered.

But the immense possessions of the family of de Montgomery or de Belesme did not prosper with them. On the contrary, they rendered them so confident in their own strength, as to induce them to join in a conspiracy to dethrone the Conqueror, and again to divide England into three parts, corresponding with the Saxon division of the kingdoms of the West Saxons, Mercia, and Northumbria. The parties to this conspiracy were Adolfus, earl of Norfolk and Suffolk, Earl Waltheof of Northumberland, and Earl Roger of Poictou, each of whom was to have had a third of the kingdom This conspiracy, which was formed in the year 1074, was discovered and defeated by the Conqueror, who returned hastily from Normandy to crush it. This he did effectually, by beheading Earl Waltheof, and first imprisoning, and then driving from the kingdom, Roger of Poictou and his associates. Their estates were seized by the king, and at the time when the Domesday Survey was made, in the year 1086, everything that had belonged to Roger of Poictou was held by the king, in Lancashire and in all other parts of the kingdom. This continued to be the case to the death of William the Conqueror

In the interval between the granting of these estates to Earl Roger and their forfeiture, the earl granted portions of them to several Norman knights, some of whose descendants still hold the lands granted to their ancestors at the Conquest In the hundred of West Derby, Earl Roger granted lands to Norman knights named Goisfrid, Roger, William, Warren, a second Goisfrid, Tetbald, Robert, and Gislebert, in the Warrington hundred, he granted lands to other Normans named Roger, Tetbald, Warin, Radulf, William, Adelard, and Osmund. In the Blackburn hundred, Earl Roger granted lands to Roger de Busli and Albert Greslet, the founders of the old Lancashire families of De Boiseuil, lords of Penwortham, and of de Gresley, lords of Manchester In the Salford hundred, he granted lands to knights named Nigel, Warin, a second Warin, Goisfrid, and Gamel. In the hundred of Leyland, he granted lands to Girard, from whom the ancient Lancashire family of Gerard is descended, and to Robert, Radulph, Roger, and Walter. It does not appear, however, that the great mass of the tenants of the crown were dispossessed, either by the Conqueror or by Earl Roger, for Saxon and Danish thanes and drengs (which is the Danish equivalent for thane) were holding very nearly 200 manors, between the Ribble and the Mersey, twenty years after the Conquest, that is, in the year 1086, when the Domesday Survey was made.

But on the death of William the Conqueror, a war for the possession of the throne of England broke out between William Rufus, the second son of the Conqueror, and Robert, his elder brother, which ended (as is well known) in the triumph of William Rufus. In the course of this war Roger of Poictou, who had still great estates in France, succeeded in gaining the favour of William Rufus, by abandoning the cause of Robert, which he had at first adopted, and passing over to that of his younger and more successful rival. By this act of loyalty, or treason, Earl Roger regained the favour of the king, and was rewarded by the restoration of his estates in the honour of Lancaster and other parts of England

Whilst thus possessed of his estates in England for the second time, Roger of Poictou and his followers made numerous grants, from his property in the honour of Lancaster, to the abbey of Shrewsbury, founded by his brother Robert de Belesme, the first Norman earl of Shrewsbury, and to the abbey of St. Martin de Sees in Normandy, founded by his father and mother Thus, to the abbey of Shrewsbury Earl Roger gave the fisheries of Thelwall, Wolston, and Poulton, on the river Mersey, and Godfrey, his vice-comes or sheriff, gave to the same abbey the church of St Mary in Walton (Walton-on-the-Hill, which then included the chapelry of Liverpool), also the town or township which is named Gerstan (Garston, near Liverpool), and the church of Kirkham To the abbey of St. Martin de Sees, Earl Roger granted the priory of Lancaster, with many other possessions Thus, he granted to that monastery the church of Lancaster, the church and one-third of the town of Hesson (Heysham), the church and title and fishery of Preston, the churches of Kirkham and of Melling, and Bolton (Boelton), with the church and the tithes of Preesal In the southern division of the county he gave to the abbey of St Martin de Sees the tithes of Salford, Derby, Hale, Everton, Walton, Crosby, Meols, &c The witnesses of this grant are the earl himself and his daughter Sybilla, Godfrey, the vice-comes or sheriff, Albert Grelet, or Gresley, from whom the barons of Manchester descended, R FitzRobert, G Boiseul or Bussell (ancestors of the barons of Penwortham), Arnulfus (Earl Roger's younger brother), P de Vilares or Villiers (baron of Warrington),

Ociu the son of Chetel, and Ulf the son of Torolf. The two latter were probably Saxon or Danish landowners.

At the death of William Rufus, in the year 1180, from an arrow shot by Walter Tyrrell in the New Forest, Robert, the eldest son of the Conqueror, again claimed the crown of England, but was a second time defeated, his youngest brother Henry Beauclerc having succeeded in gaining it. On this occasion Duke Robert was supported by many of the Norman earls, including the whole house of Montgomery and their friends and allies. On his side were ranged Robert de Belesme, earl of Shrewsbury, Roger de Poictou, Arnulf Montgomery, lord of Pembrokeshire, and their brother-in-law, the earl of Morton. But Henry had the support of the English people, as well as that of many of the Norman lords, and after defeating the Montgomerys in the field, he besieged them and their supporters in the castles of Shrewsbury and Arundel. Robert de Belesme, finding his affairs desperate, acknowledged Henry as king and surrendered at discretion, submitting himself to Henry's mercy. His brothers submitted at the same time, and on surrendering Arundel and the rest of their castles, the king granted them their lives, and a safe-conduct into Normandy. Henry, however, confiscated the estates of all the Montgomerys, and of the earl of Morton, their brother-in-law. Matthew Paris states that this occurred in the year 1105. The confiscated estates of Roger of Poictou consisted of nearly 300 manors or townships in Lancashire, seventy-six in Yorkshire, three in Essex, fifty-nine in Suffolk, eleven in Nottinghamshire, seven in Derbyshire, ten in Norfolk, and forty-four in Lincolnshire. These immense possessions were long known as the honour of Roger Pictavensis. They were granted by Henry I, together with the still larger estates of the earl of Morton, to Stephen, earl of Blois and Champagne, the nephew of Henry I, and the grandson of the Conqueror by his daughter Adela, married to Earl Stephen's father.

Whilst Stephen held the earldom of Morton and also the honour of Lancaster, along with the other estates of Roger Pictavensis, he founded the magnificent abbey of Furness, in North Lancashire, whose ruins still excite the admiration of all beholders.

Simon Dunhelmis states, in his account of the events of the year 1123, that Stephen, earl of Morton and Boulogne, afterwards king of England, that year gave to the Abbot Geofridus Savinuncensis, the town and township of Tulketh, in the province which is called Agmunderness (Amounderness), on the banks of the river Ribble, that he might found an abbey there. But the site was afterwards changed for the secluded and beautiful valley of the Deadly Nightshade in Furness The abbey of St. Mary of Furness was founded in the year 1127, the twenty-fourth year of the reign of Henry I, by Stephen, earl of Morton and Boulogne, when the monks were removed from Tulketh, and was long the great religious foundation of North Lancashire

In the sheriff's account or pipe roll of the 31 Henry I (1122), which is the oldest sheriff's account now known to be in existence, we find a brief account of the land between the Ribble and the Mersey, then held by the men of Stephen, earl of Morton The particulars given are very few, but the title itself is sufficient to show that both South and North Lancashire then belonged to Earl Stephen He continued in great favour until the king's death, which occurred on the 2nd December, 1135; and evidence that he held his possessions in Lancashire until that time will be produced in the course of the present chapter

Some years before the death of King Henry I his only son William perished by shipwreck, along with the youthful earl of Chester, as already mentioned, while crossing from Normandy to England After the death of his son, King Henry, in the hope of securing the crown of England to his only remaining child, Maude or Matilda, compelled all the nobles of the kingdom to swear fealty to her. Matilda was the widow of Henry V, emperor of Germany, by whom, however, she had no issue She subsequently married Geoffrey, surnamed Plantagenet, son of Fulk, count of Anjou, by whom she had a son, Henry Plantagenet, who ultimately ascended the throne Stephen earl of Morton, the nephew of the king, was one of the great nobles who were thus compelled to swear allegiance to the Empress Maude, but no sooner was King Henry dead than he seized on the throne, and caused himself to be crowned, with the title of King Stephen, having the support of William the archbishop of Canterbury, who swore that King Henry, whilst he was *in extremis*, certain grounds of offence having sprung up between himself and the empress, had disinherited her, and appointed Earl Stephen, his nephew, to be his heir But not relying on this pretended title, Stephen proceeded to purchase friends amongst the more powerful nobles of the kingdom, and especially the most powerful of all, Ranulf I. earl of Chester. With a view to gain his support, Stephen granted to him, along with other territories, the lands between the Ribble and the Mersey, and all the lands belonging to the honour of Roger Pictavensis, from Northampton to the borders of Scotland

The general result of the war between King Stephen and Henry duke of Normandy was, that Stephen retained the crown for his life, but that he was succeeded in the throne by Henry, his own great estates, as earl of Morton, passing to his son William, who was at once earl of Morton, Surrey, de Warenne, and Boulogne.

That the honour of Lancaster was one of the estates held by this powerful earl, is proved by several grants made by him in that capacity Thus, he granted or confirmed to William de Walton, the office of bailiff of the hundred of West Derby and the district of Makerfield, and gave to him lands in Walton, Wavertree, and Newsham * He also made an additional grant to the abbey of Furness, founded by his father

On the death of William de Blois without issue, the honour of Lancaster, with the lands between the Mersey and the Ribble and the Ribble and the Duddon, together with the other estates of the earldom of Morton, reverted to the crown, and were held by King Henry II. during the greater part of his life Amongst his acts of ownership were the following —The king granted to Warin de Lancaster, baron of Kendal and governor of the castle of Lancaster, the manors of Raven Meols, Ainsdale, Up-Litherland, Liverpool, Lee Francais (near Preston), and 8*d* per annum of rent in the borough of Preston, which then belonged to the king, to defray the expenses of the castle of Lancaster. This appears from a deed of John, earl of Morton, afterwards King John, in which he confirms the above-named manors to Henry, the son of Warin de Lancaster, describing them as the lands "which Henry my father, gave to Warin his father" This grant of Henry II. is the earliest document in which the name of Liverpool is mentioned. It appears from another deed of John, earl of Morton, that his father King Henry II confirmed to Walter de Walton the lands in Walton, Wavertree, and Newsham, already mentioned, as granted to him by William de Blois, earl of Boulogne, Warenne, and Morton King Henry also imposed a tallage or tax on the tenants of all his lands in the honour of Lancaster, the particulars

* Rolls de Quo Warranto, 20 Edw I, p 382

of which are given in the sheriff's account, or as it is called the Great Roll of the Pipe, for the 23rd Henry II Amongst the manors and townships which paid this tallage were Hest, Oxcliffe, Preesal, Hambleton, and Stancil, in the northern parts of the county, and West Derby, Hale, Formby, Crosby, Wavertree, Walton, Thingwall, Litherland, and Salford, in the southern parts

The next possessor of the honour of Lancaster was John earl of Morton, afterwards King John, the ungrateful and rebellious son of Henry II., and brother of Richard the Lion-hearted John was created Earl of Morton in the year 1183, and on the accession of his brother Richard to the throne, in the year 1189, he was confirmed in the possession of the earldom of Morton, and many other vast estates Whilst holding the earldom of Morton, John confirmed a grant of Roger Pictavensis to the priory of Lancaster of the tithes of his demesne lands, that is, of all his parks and chaces in the honour of Roger Pictavensis Under this grant Toxteth Park, originally a deer park of King John, and many other parks and chaces, paid tithes to the priory of Lancaster, indeed, in a return made so late as the time of the great Civil War, certain commissioners stated that Toxteth Park was in the parish of Lancaster, though fifty-six miles distant from that place.

Richard I on his accession to the throne, to show his affection for his only surviving brother, John, confirmed him in the possession of the earldom of Morton, in Normandy and England, with the counties of Nottingham, Derby, and Lancaster He still added to his power and wealth by giving him the castles of the Peak (Pec) and Bolsover in Derbyshire, and the honours of Wallingford in Oxfordshire, and Tickhill in Yorkshire. He also gave to him in marriage Avise the daughter and heiress of the earl of Gloucester, with that earldom, which was then one of the richest in the kingdom "But," says Tyrrell, "he afterwards found cause enough to repent having made him too great for a subject" Shortly afterwards, however, Richard still further increased the power and wealth of John, by giving to him the earldoms of Devonshire, Dorset, and Cornwall.

On the 11th December, 1189, five months after his accession to the throne, Richard embarked for the Holy Land, according to a rash vow which he had made. He appointed the bishops of Durham and Ely justiciaries of England, and associated others with them to govern the kingdom in his absence Of course, everything fell into confusion, and his perfidious brother availed himself of his absence to contrive his destruction

Richard, after performing innumerable feats of valour in the Holy Land, was shipwrecked, on his return to England, at the head of the Adriatic, and cast on shore in the dominions of his mortal enemy, the duke of Austria. The duke, after keeping him prisoner for some time, delivered him into the custody of the Emperor Henry of Germany, who refused to set the gallant king at liberty until he paid a ransom of 100,000 marks, a sum equal to at least £1,000,000 of our present money This sum was ultimately paid. But John, in connection with the king of France, who had conspired together, the one to seize Richard's possessions in Normandy and Anjou, and the other to seize the crown of England, offered the emperor 80,000 marks if he would detain Richard in prison until the Michaelmas following, and £1000 per month for every month that he was afterwards detained He was in fact detained, on one pretence or another, upwards of fifteen months

The letters of John containing this perfidious offer were shown to Richard whilst still in prison,* and being seen and read, added unspeakably to the misery of the captive king Fortunately, however, other letters were discovered in England, which enabled the loyal subjects of Richard to defeat the plans of his ungrateful and treacherous brother Adam of St. Edmunds, one of John's clerks or secretaries, who had been sent over from Normandy, where John then was, with letters and directions to fortify his castles against the king his brother, was taken prisoner by the lord mayor of London, and all his letters were read. On this it was unanimously resolved by the king's council that Earl John should be deprived of all his lands, and that his castles should be besieged This was accordingly done. His lands were seized, the bishop of Durham, a warlike prelate, laid siege to the castle of Tickhill in Yorkshire, David, brother of the king of Scots, Ranulf, earl of Chester, and Ferrers, earl of Derby, besieged Nottingham, and the archbishop of Canterbury besieged and reduced the castle of Marlborough in Wiltshire. After that the castle of Lancaster, "which was held by Theobald, the brother of Walter, for Earl John," was surrendered, with that of St Michael's Mount in Cornwall, but the castles of Nottingham and Tickhill held out until the king's return to England.

* Hoveden, p 731

On the 30th of May, 1194, immediately after the return of King Richard, a great council was held at Nottingham, and on the second day he required judgment against his unworthy brother, Earl John, who contrary to his fealty had seized his castles and wasted his dominions, as well in England as beyond seas, and had confederated with his enemy the king of France Thereupon the council decided that John should be peremptorily cited, and if within forty days he appeared not, nor stood to the law, he should forfeit his right to return to the kingdom John not appearing within the time fixed, was adjudged to lose all his honours and estates—a sentence which was confirmed by a solemn resolution of the peers

In consequence of the above judgment, the honour of Lancaster and all the other estates of Earl John were seized; and several of his principal tenants in Lancashire were fined heavily, or as the sheriff's accounts, or pipe roll, of the 6, 7, and 8 Richard I express it, were compelled to purchase the favour of the king

The following is a translation of a part of the pipe roll of the 6 Richard I —

"Theobald Walter renders account of the fee of Lancaster, for the 6th year of King Richard, £100

"New pleas and new agreements made by the men of Earl John, in Lancaster, for having the favour of the king —

"Adam de Kelett, for the king's favour, 20 marks

"Henry de Rademan, for the same, 20 marks

"Benedict Gurnett, that he may hold his land in peace, and the forestership of which he is seized, and his inheritance, 20 marks

"Adam the son of Osbert, for having the favour of the king, 10 marks

"Gilbert de Croft, for the same, 10 marks

"Richard de Molinell (Molyneux), for the same, 100 shillings

"Henry Falconarius (owner of Liverpool), for the same, 15 marks.

"Robert, priest of Walton, for the same, 30 marks

"Walter de Parles, for the same, 100 shillings.

"William Pincerna (Butler), lord of Warrington, 30 marks.

"Roger de Middleton, that he may have seizin (possession) of his land, 5 marks

"Alurus the son of Outram, for the same, 8 marks.

"Robert Fitz-Henry, for having the pardon and the favour of the king, 20 marks

"Adam de Biri (Bury), for the same, 15 marks.

"William de Radclive (Radcliffe), for the same, 8 marks

"Richard de Urmeston (Urmston), for the same, 40 shillings.

"Robert de Prestwich, for the same, 4 marks

"Jordanus de Mamcastre (Manchester), for his services to Earl John, £20

"Hugo Boissel, for his relief, and because he crossed the sea with Earl John, 40 marks (Boiseuil, baron of Penwortham)"

In the same pipe roll there occurs (under the heading of "Concerning those who paid the whole," that is, the whole fine, which many did not do in the year in which it was imposed) as follows :—

"The same Theobald renders account of 20 marks for the fine of William of Kellet, for having the favour of the king, and of 10 marks from William Furneis, for the same, and of 4 from Daniel the clerk, for the same, and of 10 marks from William of Heste, for the same, and of 100 shillings from Galfrid of Gersingham, for the same, and —— from Robert the son of Gillcringhal, for the same, and of 40 shillings from Gilbert of Valeton (Walton), for the same, and of 20 shillings from Richard of Ditton, for the same, and of 40 shillings from Henry of Holland, for the same, and of 1 mark for Henry of Melling, for the same, and of 10 marks from Matthew Gurnett, because he was in the army of Kendal, with the men of Earl John, that he may again have possession (seizin) of his land, of which he was dispossessed (*disseisitus*); and of 3 shillings from Hugh of Haye (Haigh), for peace and the favour of the king, and 4 shillings from Adam of Chernock, for the same. Sum £72, 1 mark"

The following items are also added in this roll —

"Robert the son of Osbert owes 100 shillings for the favour of the king The abbot of Furness paid 1 mark for the confirming of his charters and liberties, and for having right between —— and Gilbert Fitz-Reinfred in the land of Newby and Moelton, and for having his goods"

In the sheriff's account, or pipe roll, of 7 Richard I, also occur the following entries respecting the same transaction —

'Theobald Walter accounts by Benedict Gurnett as follows —

"Richard the son of Roger owes 20 marks, because he was with Earl John.

"William the son of Sucin owes 100 shillings, for the same

"Giraldus de Claiton owes 5 marks for himself and his knights, for the same.

"Rad de St George pays 6 marks for having his lands of Wallington."

In the sheriff's roll of the 8 Richard I also occur the following entries —

"Concerning the fines of the men of the Earl John—

"William de Rademan paid £48 6s. 8*d* for having the favour of the king

"William the son of Sucin paid 100 shillings for the same.

"Giraldus de Claiton and his knights paid 5 marks for the same."

King Richard died on the 5th April, 1199, having, it is said, previously bequeathed his kingdom to his brother John, though in point of legal right it ought to have passed to his nephew Prince Arthur, whom John afterwards murdered, or caused to be murdered, in prison Along with the crown, John became possessed of the estates of the earldom of Morton, including the honour of Lancaster

In the first year of the reign of King John, he confirmed to the knights and thanes of Lancashire a charter which he had granted as earl of Morton, authorizing them to thin their own woods, and to kill several kinds of game in the forests of the honour. The price paid for this charter was £239 8s 11*d*—fully £3000 of present money, and ten chaseurs or goblets *

In the same year he confirmed to the church and priory of St Mary of Lancaster a grant of tithes in all his demesne lands, which grant was originally made by Roger Pictavensis shortly after the Norman conquest

In the same year King John also confirmed to Henry Fitz-Warin the lands between the Ribble and the Mersey, which Henry II had granted to Warin, who was at that time falconer to the king †

In the pipe rolls of the 3 and 4 John, the sheriff who accounts for the revenues of the honour of Lancaster is Richard de Vernon, but in the sixth year of his reign John conferred the keeping of the honour on Gilbert Fitz-Reinfrid He held that office until the seventeenth year of John's reign, when Gilbert Fitz-Reinfrid joined the king's enemies (that is, the insurgent barons), was fined 12,000 marks, as a traitor to the king, and was deprived of the keeping of the honour of Lancaster,‡ which keepership was afterwards conferred on Ranulf earl of Chester §

* Rot Pipæ, 4 John † Rot Chart m 5, n 35
‡ Rot Fin 17 John, m 6 § Rot. Pat 17 John m 3

But the most important act of John's reign, so far as the county of Lancaster is concerned, was the granting a charter to the borough and port of Liverpool, by which he conferred upon them all the liberties and free customs which any free borough on the sea in his dominions possessed. The particulars of this charter and of all the other charters granted to the boroughs and cities of Lancashire and Cheshire, will be given in a succeeding part of this work, in which the rise and progress of those cities and boroughs will be traced from the earliest times.

The reign of King John closed in confusion and civil war. After having been compelled by his barons to sign the Great Charter, and the Charter of the Forest, John seized the earliest opportunity to break his oath, and to renew the war with the barons. For this purpose he brought into the kingdom an army of foreign mercenaries, who were invited to take for their reward whatever they could seize and subdue. At the head of this host he spread destruction throughout the country, laying waste the lands and seizing on the persons of all who opposed him. The barons, driven to desperation, called in the aid of the French king, Philip, who sent to their aid a large army, commanded by the dauphin Louis, and a celebrated soldier, the Comte de Perche. In the midst of this murderous strife, King John died suddenly, on the 19th October, 1216.

The death of King John saved the monarchy of England, as well as the liberties of the people. A great number of the barons, headed by Ranulf earl of Chester, William de Ferrers earl of Derby, and other great nobles, at once declared for John's son, Henry III., then a boy only nine years of age, and against Louis the dauphin. The party of the youthful king, under the command of the earl of Chester (as already mentioned), summoned the dauphin to leave the kingdom, and that summons having been scornfully rejected, they gave battle to him in the month of May, 1217, near Lincoln, and defeated his army with great slaughter. This defeat was followed by the loss of a large fleet, bringing reinforcements from France, and Louis, finding his cause desperate, agreed to return to France, and to give up all claim to the kingdom of England.*

On the accession of Henry III., Ranulf earl of Chester received, in addition to his other honours and estates, the rich earldom of Lincoln, and was also made keeper of the honour of Lancaster.

The earl of Chester continued to hold the office of custodian of

* Knyghton, Col. 2429, anno 1217.

the honour of Lancaster on behalf of the king, until 10 Henry III, Jordanus the son of Roger acting as his deputy William de Ferrers earl of Derby, who was brother-in-law to the earl of Chester, acted as custos of the honour in the 10th and 11th Henry III, and Adam de Yoland in the 12th, 13th, and 14th*

In the year 1229 Henry, having reached the age of manhood, was seized with an ardent desire to recover the possessions of the English crown in France, which had been lost during the turbulent reign of his father For this purpose he summoned all the nobles and tenants of the crown to meet at Portsmouth, on Michaelmas day, 1229, for an expedition to France

Whilst at Portsmouth, with the other great peers of the kingdom, Ranulf earl of Chester received from King Henry a grant of extensive lands between the Ribble and the Mersey The following is a translation of this grant †--

"For the earl of Chester and Lincoln. The king grants and confirms to the earl of Chester and Lincoln all the land which he has between Ribble and Mersey in the county of Lancaster, that is to say, the town of West Derby with the wapentake and everything appertaining to it, the borough of Liverpool with its appurtenances, the town of Salforth (Salford) with the wapentake and all its appurtenances, and the wapentake of Leyland with all its appurtenances, to be had and held by him and his heirs, in demesnes, forests, and inclosures, homages, services, and all appurtenances, and with all liberties and free customs, to the aforesaid lands, borough, wapentakes, forests, and inclosures pertaining he paying to the king and his heirs yearly at the feast of St Michael, a falcon, or in place of it 40 shillings at the exchequer, for all service And that the said earl and his heirs have and hold all things mentioned above, with their appendages, well and in peace, freely, quietly, and undividedly, in demesnes, forests, inclosures, homages, services, woods and plains, meadows and pastures, ways and paths, meres and marshes, waters and mills, and in all their appurtenances, with all liberties and free customs to the aforesaid lands, homages, wapentakes, inclosures, and forests pertaining, by the aforesaid service of one falcon (asturca) or of 40 shillings, at the feast of St. Michael, for all service Witness. Thomas, bishop of Norwich, H. de Burgo, earl of Kent, R., earl of Cornwall, and others Given by my proper hand as above, at Portsmouth, on the 18th October, and 13th of my

* See Rolls of the Pipe for those years. † Rot Chart 13 Henry III m 3

reign."* This grant, whilst it passed the king's lands between the Ribble and the Mersey to the earl of Chester, did not grant the castle, town, or honour of Lancaster, those being still retained by the crown.

In the sheriff's roll of the following year (14 Henry III.) the earl of Chester's name is interleaved in each of the several manors, and the rents formerly received are accounted for as follows — "Nothing in the treasury. And to Ranulf earl of Chester £68 18*s* 4*d*, by the letter of the king, in which is contained, that the king has given to him the whole land that he had between the Ribble and the Mersey"

In the year 1230, being the year following that of the preceding grant, Ranulf earl of Chester acquired by purchase, from Roger de Merseia, a large addition to his lands between the Ribble and the Mersey The deed by which this purchase was made is as follows —

"To all present and future, inspecting this charter, Roger the son of Ranulph de Marresheya, greeting Know that I have sold, and perpetually from my heirs demised, to the Lord Ranulf, earl of Chester and Lincoln, the manor of Boulton, with all its appurtenances, and whatever I or my heirs may have in the said manor of Boulton, in little Boulton, in Tonge, and in Halgh, in Brethmet (Brightmede), in Radeclive (Radcliffe), in Ormeston, Applebey, in Sharpley (Sharples), in Hughe (Haigh), in Standishe, in Longtre, in Sevington (Shevington), in Chernoc, in Hedchernoc, in Dacbera, in Adelinton (Adlington), in Whitball, in Hirelton, in Scarisbreck, in Heton juxta Lancaster, in Meols, in Derwente (Darwen), in Eccleshill, and in all other places, to the said lands belonging, in homages, fees, customs, lordships, wardships, reliefs, rents, escheats, presentation of churches, and in all things which I or my heirs have or can have from the said lands, without reservation To be had and held from me and my heirs, by the said earl and his heirs, freely and quietly, peacefully and entirely, with hereditary right, in woods and plains, in meadows and pastures, and in all places to these manorial lands pertaining, rendering to me and my heirs one penny at Easter for all services, the said earl paying me 200 marks in silver, &c

"Witnesses The Lord Abbot of Chester, William, justiciary of Chester, Rudolf de Bray, Richard de Burney, Godfrey de Dalton, Godfrey de Appleby, John de Lexington; Gilbert de Uxton; and Roger de Derby, with many others."

* Close Rolls, 13 Henry III m 2

Ranulf earl of Chester, as already mentioned, died at his castle of Wallingford, on the 28th of October, 1232, after possessing the earldom for fifty-one years He left no issue, and was succeeded in the earldom by his nephew, John, surnamed the Scot, earl of Huntingdon, son of Earl David, brother to the king of the Scots, by Maude, sister of Ranulf III The other lands and territories of Earl Ranulf were divided amongst his four sisters and coheirs. Earl John enjoyed his title of earl of Chester only for a short time. He died in the year 1237, without issue, and in the year 1247, the 31st Henry III, the earldom of Chester was annexed by the king to the crown *

In the tenth year of the reign of Henry III (1225), the estates above mentioned being still in the hands of the king, a tallage or tax was laid on the several towns and townships held directly by him, as lord of the honour of Lancaster The following is an account of this taxation of each manor or township, from the sheriff's account, or pipe roll, of that year —

Lancaster tallage, by Master Alexander de Dorsete and Simon de Hal —

The town of Lancaster taxed in the sum of 14 marks 2 shillings Paid on account, £4 6*s*.

The town of Liverpool taxed in the sum of 11 marks 8 shillings and 8 pence Paid on account, £3 15*s*

The township of West Derby taxed in the sum of 8 marks 4 shillings and 4 pence Paid on account, £3

The township of Everton taxed in the sum of 5 marks 2 shillings Paid on account, 40*s*

The township of Great Crosby taxed at 8 marks 5 shillings Paid on account, £3 5*s*

The town of Saurford (Salford) and Barton, with Ordsal and Flixton, taxed at 8 marks 5 shillings and 4 pence Paid on account, 42*s*

The township of Singleton taxed at 4 marks 5 shillings and 4 pence Paid on account, 20*s*

The township of Brockton taxed at 4 marks 10 shillings and 8 pence Paid 40*s*

The town of Preston taxed at 15 marks and 6 pence Paid on account, £5 10*s*.

The township of Sline taxed at 30 shillings and 8 pence Paid on account, 30*s*.

* Rot Pat. 31 Henry III m 6

The township of Wray taxed at 5 shillings Paid on account, 4*s.*

The township of Riggebi (Rigby) taxed half a mark. Paid the whole

The township of Stanhull taxed 3 shillings. Paid the whole.

The township of Overton taxed 23 shillings. Paid the whole.

The township of Skerton taxed 15 shillings and 6 pence Paid the whole.

The tenants of the honour of Lancaster, holding in theinage, paid 10 marks that they might not be tallaged.

This would include the barons, knights, and thanes who held the other towns and townships of the county These compounded for the tallage by paying a gross sum; but according to the custom of that age, they reserved the right of imposing a tallage on their tenants, whenever the king imposed a tallage on the tenants of his own lands Thus there is no doubt that all the other towns and townships were tallaged, at the same time with the places mentioned above, but their tallages were paid to the lords and thanes, not to the crown, and hence they do not appear in the sheriff's accounts

On the death of Ranulf, earl of Chester, all his lands, with the exception of those in the county of Chester, were divided amongst his four sisters and their husbands. In this division, the lands between the Ribble and the Mersey were assigned to William de Ferrers, earl of Derby, and Agnes, who was one of the sisters of Earl Ranulf of Chester* The earl and countess of Derby paid to the king the sum of £50 for their relief or entrance to their estates In the following year the king issued this order respecting these lands —"W. de Ferrers, earl of Derby The king to the barons of his Exchequer, greeting Know that William de Ferrers, earl of Derby, and Agnes his wife, are bound to pay to us yearly, at our exchequer, one asturca (hawk) or 40*s*, for the land between the Ribble and the Mersey, that we gave to Ranulf, formerly earl of Chester, and which was assigned to the earl and Agnes, his wife, as a part of the portion which fell to her, of the lands that belonged to the said earl of Chester. And, therefore, we command you that you receive the said rent from them yearly, and give them acquittance for the same—Witness myself, at Westminster, the 21st day of October"

In the 26 Hen III. (1241-42), William, earl of Derby, paid a

* Rot. Claus 17 Henry III m 17

fine of £100 to the king, to have possession of the wapentake between the Ribble and Mersey, which the king had seized and taken into his own hands for some offence, real or pretended, on the part of the earl

In the year 1247 (32 Hen. III.) William de Ferrers died, and within a month his countess, Agnes, followed him to the grave Matthew Paris makes the following remark on their deaths.—"In the same year, about the feast of St Catherine, died William, earl de Ferrers, a man truly peaceful and just, well-stricken in years, and long afflicted with the gout In the same month also died the countess, Agnes de Ferrers, of the same age, repute, and goodness"

William de Ferrers, son and heir of William and Agnes de Ferrers, succeeded to his father's titles and estates, in the 31 Hen. III; and in the following year, on doing his homage, had livery of Chartley castle, Staffordshire, and of the lands and castles of his mother in Lancashire, as appears from the following extract from the fine rolls of that year —"For William de Ferrers—The king has taken homage of William de Ferrers, for all the lands and tenements which were formerly held by Agnes, countess of Derby; and it is commanded to Henry de Wengham, and to his escheator in the county of Stafford, that the said William have full seizin of the castle of Chartley, and of all the lands and tenements which were of the said Agnes, without delay

"Witness the king, at Windeshores (Windsor), the 10th day of December

"Also, it is commanded to Thomas de Stanford and Robert de Creppmg, escheators beyond the river Trent, that the said William have full seizin of the castles of West Derby and Liverpool, and of all lands and tenements which were formerly of the said Agnes, without delay

"Witness as above"

In the 34 Hen III, the king appointed Robert de Latham to keep the castle and county of Lancaster so long as the king thought fit; thus showing that the earl of Derby, although he had the lands between the Ribble and the Mersey, did not hold the honour of Lancaster.*

In the 36 Hen. III., the king granted permission to William, earl of Derby, to maintain between the Ribble and the Mersey a

* Regalia, 34 Hen III Rot 1

Lightning Source UK Ltd.
Milton Keynes UK
UKHW011316041019
351005UK00006B/572/P

9 781376 886726